THE RIGHT TO LEARN

Educational strategies for socially excluded youth in Europe

Edited by Ides Nicaise

With contributions from

Ides Nicaise, Mia Douterlungne and Ilse Vleugels
Hoger Instituut voor de Arbeid (Catholic University of Leuven)

Sheila Riddell, Alastair Wilson and Kay Tisdall
Strathclyde Centre for Disability Research and Centre for the Child and Society (University of Glasgow)

Neus Roca Cortés
Centre d'Iniciatives|Recerques Europees a la Mediterrània (Barcelona)

Emer Smyth and Breda McCabe
Economic and Social Research Institute (Dublin)

Joaquim Bernardo and Nelson Matias
Instituto de Estudos Sociais e Económicos (Lisboa)

Ben Hövels, Ton Eimers, Sjaak van den Berg, Kees Meijer and Renze Portengen
Instituut voor Toegepaste Sociale Wetenschappen (Catholic University of Nijmegen)

The POLICY
PP
PRESS

First published in Great Britain in November 2000 by

The Policy Press
University of Bristol
34 Tyndall's Park Road
Bristol BS8 1PY
UK
Tel no +44 (0)117 954 6800
Fax no +44 (0)117 973 7308
E-mail tpp@bristol.ac.uk
http://www.policypress.org.uk

ISBN 1 86134 288 8

Ides Nicaise is Research Manager at the Hoger Instituut voor de Arbeid (Catholic University of Leuven) and Chair of the Belgian Anti-poverty Unit.

This research has been carried out with the financial support of the European Commission DG Education and Culture, in the context of the Societies programme.

Hoger instituut voor de arbeid
Katholieke Universiteit Leuven
E. Van Evenstraat 2e
B-3000 Leuven
tel. +32 16 32 33 33
fax +32 16 32 33 44
e-mail hiva@kuleuven.ac.be
http://www.kuleuven.ac.be/hiva

Cover design by Qube Design Associates, Bristol.
Printed in Great Britain by Hobbs the Printers Ltd, Southampton.

Contents

List of tables and figures   iv

List of abbreviations   vi

Introduction   I

Part One: A status quaestionis

one   The educational situation of disadvantaged children   15

two   Strategies to reduce educational inequality:
a general framework   37

Part Two: Equal opportunity strategies

three   Learning duties and learning rights   53

four   Financial and material assistance for low-income pupils   75

five   Integrated services for disadvantaged young people   97

six   Early childhood education   123

Part Three: Equal treatment strategies

seven   Curricular reforms   147

eight   Social expectations, poverty and pedagogical innovations   163

nine   Teacher training   183

ten   Parent–school–community relationships   199

eleven   Provision, integration and inclusion for children with
special educational needs   221

Part Four: Equal outcomes strategies

twelve   Educational priority policies   249

thirteen   Learning support   273

fourteen   Alternative curricula, transition systems and
second-chance provisions   289

Conclusions and recommendations   313

Bibliography   327

Appendix: Background information about poverty and education
in the six countries covered by this study   371

Index   407

List of tables and figures

Tables

1.1   Poverty and education of household head in the six   32
study countries

2.1   Synopsis of relevant measures, programmes and projects   45-6
aimed at more equal opportunities

2.2   Synopsis of relevant measures, programmes and projects   47–8
aimed at more equal treatment

2.3   Synopsis of relevant measures, programmes and projects   49
aimed at more equal outcomes

3.1   Educational participation among 18–year–olds, 1995 (%)   61

4.1   Number of pupils in the state system who benefit from   81
socioeconomic assistance measures (state education
system – continental Portugal) in 1991/92

4.2   Coverage of the pupil population with school canteens   83
in Portugal (%)

4.3   Summary of financial and/or material support for pupils   90
in different countries

5.1   Partners to be involved in the provision of integrated   100
services

5.2   Content of the activities   100

5.3   Features of Integrated Approaches in six countries   108

5.4   Organisations mentioned as being involved in   116
integrated approaches

7.1   Curricular reforms and measures   149-50

12.1   Specific objectives of the Educational Priority   251-3
Policies, by country and type of measure

12.2   Overview of operational criteria relating to needs   256

12.3   Examples of types of actions in the different   264
intervention areas

14.1   Overview of measures in participating countries   295

A1   Selected indicators relating to social exclusion and   373
education in Belgium

A2   Selected indicators relating to social exclusion and   377
education in Ireland

A3 Selected indicators relating to social exclusion and   381
    education in the Netherlands
A4 Selected indicators relating to social exclusion and   389
    education in Portugal
A5 Selected indicators relating to social exclusion and   396
    education in Spain
A6 Selected indicators relating to social exclusion and   401
    education in the United Kingdom

Figures

1   Proportion with at least upper secondary education, 1998   8
2   Participation in education by age, 1998   8
3   Educational participation by type of curriculum, 1998   9
1.1   Unemployment by level of education, 1998   33
1.2   Adjusted odds of participation in adult education in   33
      four study countries
3.1   Length of compulsory education in the European   54
      Community
3.2   The proportion of children leaving secondary   66
      education with no qualifications
6.1   Educational participation among young children in the   127
      study countries
12.1 Operational scheme of the educational priority policies 260
14.1 Measures taken against early school leaving: a   291
      descriptive model
A1   The structure of education in the Flemish community   372
      of Belgium
A2   The structure of education in Ireland   376
A3   The structure of education in the Netherlands   380
A4   The structure of education in Portugal   388
A5   The structure of education in Spain   395
A6   Scotland's educational system   400

List of abbreviations

BITE (Irl)	Ballymun Initiative for Third-level Education
BUP (Sp)	Bachillerato Unificado Polivalente (upper secondary general education)
CIREM (Sp)	Centre d'Iniciatives i Recerques Europees a la Mediterrania
CLB (Fl)	Centra voor Leerlingbegeleiding (centres for pupil guidance – the former PMS centres)
COU (Sp)	Curso de Orientación Universitario (pre-university certificate)
EPP	Educational Priority Policy
ESE (P)	Escola Superior de Educação
ESRI (Irl)	Economic and Social Research Institute
HIVA (B)	Hoger Instituut voor de Arbeid
HSCL (Irl)	Home–School–Community Liaison
HSEP (Sc)	Home School Employment Project
IESE (P)	Instituto de Estudos Sociais e Económicos
ITS (Nl)	Instituut voor Toegepaste Sociale Wetenschappen
IUFM (Fr)	Institut(s) Universitaire(s) de Formation des Maîtres
IVBO (Nl)	Individueel Voorbereidend Beroepsonderwijs
JCEP (Irl)	Junior Certificate Elementary Programme
KMBO (Nl)	Kort MBO (short secondary vocational education)
LCAP (Irl)	Leaving Certificate Applied Programme
LCBEI (Irl)	Limerick Community Based Educational Initiative
LOGSE (Sp)	Ley de Ordenación General del Sistema Educativo
MAVO (Nl)	Middelbaar Algemeen Vormend Onderwijs (general secondary education)
MBO (Nl)	Middelbaar Beroepsonderwijs (secondary vocational education)
O&S (Nl)	Oriëntatie en Schakeling (orientation courses)
OVB (Nl/Fl)	Onderwijsvoorrangsbeleid (Education Priority Policy)

PPA (Sc)	Priority Partnership Area
PMS (B)	Psychological, Medical and Social guidance centres
RCF (Nl)	Regional Reporting and Coordinating Function
SEN (Sc)	Special educational needs
SGP (Sp)	Social Guarantee Programme
SOEID (Sc)	Scottish Office Education and Industry Department
TEIP (P)	Educational Priority Territories
VBO (Nl)	Voortgezet Beroepsonderwijs
WEB (Nl)	Wet Educatie en Beroepsonderwijs (Education and Vocational Training Act)

Introduction

Ides Nicaise (HIVA) and Emer Smyth (ESRI)

Have we given up?

The issue of social inequality has been pushed well into the background in the last 15 years, both in the political discourse and in education research. There has been a clear shift of emphasis from equality of opportunity to the performance of the education system, in terms of both efficiency and labour market demands. Have we given up the ideal of achieving greater equality in education?

The observed shift in the policy debate may be linked to the generally weak position of school leavers in the labour market. Mass unemployment hits this group harder than other groups, because they are newcomers and still have to secure their first job. Early school leavers are not the only ones to have problems here: graduates of secondary and higher education also face difficulties.

Many observers interpret these high levels of unemployment as evidence of the inadequate quality of the education system itself. Schools, they argue, do not keep pace with the demands of the labour market, and turn out 'uneducated' young people, despite the fact that these students have spent between 10 and 15 years at school.

In addition, there is budgetary pressure to cut costs; this has led to calls for greater efficiency in education, as in other fields. Schools have to become more effective, and this effectiveness is usually measured in terms of average pupil achievement. This approach has obscured the inequality of that achievement among pupils.

Although social inequality – and more particularly social exclusion – has re-emerged as an issue in the European education literature as well as the policy debate (boosted by the shift towards social democracy in several member states), it is still often confined to issues of a 'lack of education' on the part of certain groups in preparation for the labour market. Arguably, like all regions in the world, the European Union is challenged by a continuously changing economic and technological environment. Adapting to new markets, new technologies, and new realities implies a need for new productive roles for individuals. Young people who are not prepared for those changes are regarded as being particularly at risk of being excluded in the future. Evidence indeed suggests that individuals without qualifications are four times more likely to be unemployed than those with qualifications (European Commission, 1996). Hence, preventing and combating unemployment requires active measures both in the labour market and the institutions responsible for preparing the future work force; that is, educational institutions.

And yet, this economic function of education is only one of the dimensions of the debate on social inequality and social exclusion. Schools themselves can directly reinforce the social inequality between young people. First of all, school success is essential for the development of young people's self-esteem and citizenship. To the extent that this success is unequally distributed, through a complex interaction with pupils' social backgrounds, education contributes to the propagation of social inequality.

Furthermore, the school itself is the main meeting place for people from different social backgrounds and, for many, their first experience of socialisation – or of exclusion and conflict. Schools are in fact caught up in a paradox: they are supposed to educate their pupils in mutual respect, tolerance, and solidarity, while at the same time preparing them for a competitive economy. Schools that fail to strike the balance between these values soon turn into arenas of conflict where children imitate the unequal, unjust society of which they form a part.

The present picture of educational systems is far from flattering. Schools are blamed for:

> (a) alienating students and teachers; (b) providing low standards and poor-quality educational processes; (c) having differential expectations for students; (d) having high non-completion rates; (e) being unresponsive to students; (f) having high truancy and discipline problems; or (g) not adequately preparing students for the future.... Producing quality, extended care and preventing school dropout in these circumstances is beyond the capacity of many teachers and schools in primary and secondary education. The overriding picture is one of worsening pupil problems, burnt-out or disillusioned teachers, and school organisations under pressure. (Day et al, 1997, pp 9-12)

Attempts to remedy these problems have already been made in most member states of the European Union. Governments are developing new educational strategies in order to improve the quality and effectiveness of schools. However, these attempts have not, in general, been focused on children from socially excluded families, although it is quite clear that they are among the most vulnerable groups in education. In some countries, virtually no progress has been made. In some cases, budget cuts and legislative restrictions over the past 15 years have even meant setbacks in innovative strategies; in others, effective structures that had been set up by previous governments have been gradually eroded.

The target group: children in poverty

Who are we talking about? The target group of our research is often referred to using concepts such as 'children at risk', 'the poor', and 'the socially excluded'. Let us briefly examine some definitions of those concepts given in the literature and discuss the relations between them.

The term 'children at risk' refers to:

> children and youth who are in danger of failing at school, in their social life, or in making a successful transition to work. Educational, social and vocational failure are predictable to some extent by a range of factors, including poverty, ethnic status, family circumstances, language, type of school, geography and community. Thus the term 'at risk' refers in a general sense to children and youth from disadvantaged backgrounds. (Day et al, 1997)

However, the term has a more predictive (and thus possibly preventive) sense, because it identifies 'risk factors' that become problematic only in conjunction with adverse events (OECD, 1995b). Such risk factors are said to act in a cumulative, multiplicative way: "two factors predict a four-fold, while four factors predict a ten-fold likelihood of failure" (OECD, 1995b, p 5). On the other hand, one can list a number of 'protective factors' (such as secure attachment by children to their parents) that reduce these risks (Pugh, 1998; Nisolle and Vanden-Bosch, 1991).

The second term on our list, 'poverty', covers an equally broad spectrum of aspects of disadvantage, with varying intensity and duration. In the past, poverty was mostly interpreted in a purely material sense, as a shortage of the goods and services needed to physically enable someone to lead a dignified life. Contemporary poverty is obviously more than that; it is also a lack of opportunities to participate in education, the labour market, and cultural and political life. In other words, poverty is an accumulation of deprivations in various dimensions of social life. Moreover, it is to some extent relative, depending on the living standards of the surrounding society: some situations of shocking poverty in Belgium are not necessarily regarded as equally extreme in Portugal. Increasingly, attention is also devoted to the time patterns and intensity of poverty. Ashworth et al (1994), drawing on panel data, distinguish between six time patterns, ranging from 'transient' and 'occasional' to 'chronic' and 'permanent' poverty. Whereas 38% of all American children are faced with poverty at least once in their childhood[1], 4% experience chronic or permanent poverty. The latter are predominantly black and have poorly educated parents. Needless to say, education plays an overwhelming role in the reproduction of chronic and persistent poverty between generations (Kolvin et al, 1990; Duncan et al, 1994; Garrett et al, 1994).

The definition propounded by the French Economic and Social Council synthesises very clearly the multidimensionality and time dimension of poverty: "Deprivation points to the absence of one or more certainties (particularly the certainty of income or employment) which enable people to take up their professional, family or social responsibilities and to exercise their rights." The uncertainty that results from this can vary widely in scope and duration and can have more or less serious and definitive consequences. Deprivation can lead to poverty (Wresinski, 1987, pp 5-6):

- if it is situated in several fields (not only is the level of income low, but there are also problems in the area of education, housing, healthcare, etc.);
- if deprivation manifests itself over an extensive period;
- if the chances of independently finding solutions to the current problems, in the short run, are small.

This definition situates genuine poverty at the end of a continuum and already gives an indication of some of the processes which generate and reinforce it. The interaction between different deprivations and the time dimension play an important role here.

Children in poverty: some European statistics

In international statistical comparisons, the measurement of poverty is mostly based on income distribution data. Poverty thresholds are supposed to vary with family size, but also with the average living standard in a country (taking into account that poverty has to be determined in relation to the norms that are generally accepted in each country). The poverty threshold is thus defined as 50% of the median net disposable income (or consumption) per consumption unit in every country (household income being corrected for family size by division through the corresponding number of consumption units).

The average poverty incidence ratio in the Union was thus estimated at 10.3% between 1984 and 1987 (Hagenaars et al, 1994). By 1993, it had risen to about 17%. This means that 57 million people living under the poverty threshold were counted in the former 12 member states. Thirteen million of them (or one in five children in the EU) were younger than 16 (Eurostat, 1997a). Single-parent families and large families with young children face particularly high poverty rates (although they constitute relatively small minorities). Other risk groups include the elderly and young one-person households.

The overall poverty rates in the six countries covered by this study range from 13% in Belgium to 26% in Portugal. Child poverty varies between 15% in Belgium and 32% in the UK. These statistics indicate that children are among the main victims of poverty. Further details are found in the Appendix.

Many people would see poverty and 'social exclusion' as related; but it is now widely accepted that, although exclusion includes poverty, poverty does not cover exclusion. According to Andersen, the "broader notion of exclusion allows the extension of the concept to groups that suffer from non-material forms of deprivation and that can not be rightly considered as poor. In this sense, the notion of social exclusion is wider than that of poverty." (Andersen, 1995)

In recent years, the European Commission has increasingly replaced the term 'poverty' with 'social exclusion' in order to account for non-material aspects and to emphasise the structural causes behind poverty (the processes of exclusion). These arguments are, of course, legitimate. However, a possible drawback of this shift in terminology is that many other forms of social exclusion are covered by the same concept (discrimination against migrants, the handicapped, or women; marginalisation of drug addicts or ex-offenders, and so on) and, hence, that the political debate and actions focused on poverty may be diverted away from their original objectives.

In what follows, these three concepts (at risk, poor, and socially excluded) will be used, acknowledging that they overlap to a large extent. Yet the focus of our research will be on poverty, in the sense of multidimensional and persistent deprivation, as explained above.

At the same time we have to concede that poverty in this sense is difficult to measure. In practice, rough, indirect indicators generally have to be used (such as an income below a certain threshold or the lowest socio-professional categories), behind which the true facts about poverty can only be guessed at. The reader will note that our statistics sometimes tell more about social inequality than poverty or social exclusion. This is of course justifiable to the extent that poverty and social exclusion are extreme expressions of social inequality; but it is sometimes also a makeshift solution where data on the most disadvantaged groups are not available. In our view it is better, then, to use rough data than to be unable to present any empirical material at all.

Purpose and scope of the study

It has to be acknowledged that some convincingly positive experiences do exist in combating social exclusion within education. Schools that have increased their understanding of children and their families' conditions, schools that have involved the family and the local community in their educational strategies, and schools that have adapted their curricula and methods to specific social and cultural environments appear to enhance substantially their chances of educational success, and appear to bridge the gap between the poorest and mainstream society – at least to some extent.

This research will not concentrate on mechanisms of educational failure and exclusion. It will instead try to identify strategies for success and examples of good practice. The scope of the exercise is rather broad and ambitious. The term 'strategies' encompasses nationwide programmes as well as regional or even small-scale local pilot projects. We will consider selective strategies targeted at disadvantaged children within a school, as well as strategies involving the entire school system, provided the latter aim at greater equality. The strategies may include measures focused on environmental factors (such as healthcare, cultural activities with parents, and so on) as well as purely educational reforms. Lastly, we will not limit our research to the age span at which young people leave school prematurely; we will instead examine actions on different levels of education, from pre-school projects to the transition to tertiary education or the labour market. As we shall see, preventive action should start at the earliest possible age.

Educational strategies in favour of socially excluded children have been tried out and evaluated in a rather fragmentary way in Europe. Our intention is to collect, reinterpret and order this information and to make it available on the European level. Our analysis will contain critical discussions of basic strategies and policy measures, ordered according to a common framework and based on cross-national comparative evidence. It will be mainly built on existing and ongoing research from various disciplines (education, psychology, sociology, economics, anthropology, and criminology).

The geographical scope of our research coincides more or less with the composition of the research network. Institutes from Flanders, the Netherlands, Scotland, Ireland, Catalonia, and Portugal participated in this project. The six countries (or in some cases autonomous communities or regions) in question occupy a prominent place in the research; however, this does not prevent interesting experiences from other countries being brought into the discussion occasionally.

The selection of the six countries/regions mentioned above is thus to some extent arbitrary. No attempt was made to show a genuinely representative picture of educational systems in Europe. However, as can be noted from the review in the Appendix and from the following comparative figures, our 'sample' reflects a great deal of the diversity in systems and policies within the EU.

First, the countries differ in their degree of educational participation at the second and third level. Figure 1 indicates the proportion of the population with at least upper secondary education in the six countries. It should be noted that the definition of 'upper secondary' education differs from country to country, and variation may reflect definitional as well as substantive differences.

It is clear from Figure 1 that the proportion of adults with at least upper secondary education is highest in the Netherlands, followed by the UK, Belgium and Ireland, with relatively low levels in Spain and Portugal. Comparing those aged 25-34 with all adults, however, indicates that, in spite of their relatively low levels of second-level completion, Portugal and Spain have recently experienced a substantial growth in this area. The six study countries reflect the range of educational attainment across the European Union, with only Germany having a higher level than the UK (OECD, 2000). Variation is likely within as well as between countries, with the UK, Belgium, and Spain having substantial national and regional differences in their educational systems.

Figure 1: Proportion with at least upper secondary education, 1998

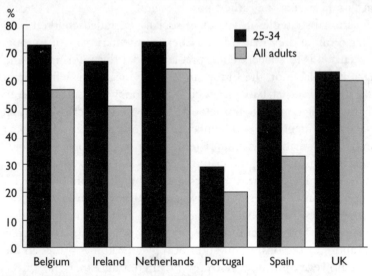

Source: OECD, *Education at a glance*, 2000

Figure 2: Participation in education by age, 1998

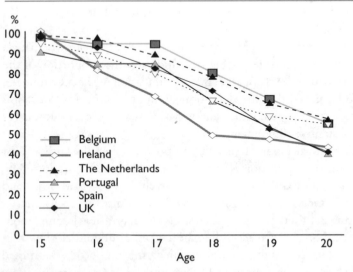

Source: OECD, *Education at a glance*, 2000

Figure 3: Education participation by type of curriculum, 1998

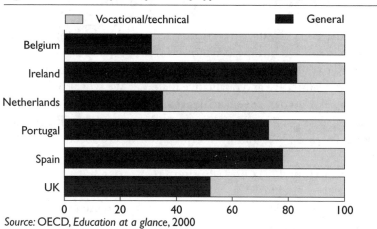

Source: OECD, *Education at a glance*, 2000

Figure 2 indicates the level of educational participation among a younger age group. The data presented in Figure 2 are based on enrolments and do not differentiate between full-time and part-time participation. They may, therefore, underestimate the degree of non-participation due to 'illegal' school dropout and persistent truancy. Participation among those under 18 is highest in Belgium and the Netherlands. Ireland has relatively high participation among those below 18 years of age, but educational participation among the older age groups is relatively low (see also OECD, 2000). The decline in educational participation as age increases is particularly marked in the UK, with sharp declines evident after the age of 16. Spain and Portugal occupy an intermediate position among the study countries.

In addition, the six countries differ in the extent of differentiation in their educational systems; that is, whether the systems are comprehensive or allow for a division into different 'tracks' such as academic and vocational. The extent of variation in the six countries mirrors that in the European Union as a whole. Figure 3 indicates that the Dutch and Belgian systems are highly differentiated, with over two thirds of upper secondary students taking part in vocational/technical courses or programmes. In contrast, the majority of students in Ireland, Spain, and Portugal follow general academic programmes. The degree of educational differentiation may impact on the degree of social differentiation in educational outcomes, since it has been argued that, in such systems, working-class and minority pupils are more likely to take the lower-status vocational tracks (Shavit, 1984).[2]

Structure and methodology of the book

In the first part, a **status quaestionis** will be sketched for different member states of the European Union, as well as some other countries, with regard to the educational situation of the target group, on the basis of available quantitative and qualitative material. We will also develop a **common framework for classification** of policy measures and pilot projects addressing the problems that affect the education of the socially excluded, based on a common interpretation of the mechanisms that (re)produce social exclusion in education.

Parts two to four will consist of a **thematic, cross-national** analysis of the strategies identified in Chapter 2. The aim is to analyse the effectiveness and the key factors of success of some representative set of measures and pilot projects for each of the basic strategies identified in the first step. Drawing on previous research and depending on the availability of research results, several criteria will be used to examine the educational, social, and economic effects of these measures and projects (for example, equalisation of outcomes in terms of cognitive and social skills, repetition of years, dropout, deviant behaviour, transition to further education or work, and so on).

In the final chapter, **conclusions** will be drawn with respect to the relative success of different approaches. This will lead to policy recommendations (including priority issues for further research) in the educational war against poverty. Implications can also be found for practitioners in the field, within the existing institutional setting.

The research was carried out by a multidisciplinary team from six institutions: Centre d'Iniciatives i Recerques Europees a la Mediterrània (CIREM), Barcelona, Spain; Economic and Social Research Institute (ESRI), Dublin, Ireland; Instituut voor Toegepaste Sociale wetenschappen (ITS), Nijmegen, the Netherlands; Instituto de Estudos Económicos e Sociais (IESE), Lisbon, Portugal; the Strathclyde Centre for Disability Research (SCDR) and the Centre for the Child and Society (CCS), both from Glasgow University, Scotland; and the Hoger Instituut voor de Arbeid (HIVA), Leuven, Belgium.

To begin with, the research team produced a series of (unpublished) 'national papers' based on the common framework announced above. Then, every institute was given responsibility for two or three cross-national, thematic chapters. Although these chapters have been signed by their main authors, they are the result of intensive exchanges of information, collaboration, and group discussions during five joint seminars, while our Scottish and Irish colleagues (Sheila Riddell, Emer

Smyth and Kay Tisdall) helped with the final editing of the text. In this sense, the whole team contributed to the content of every chapter.

The research was coordinated by HIVA and supported by the Socrates Programme of the European Commission, an action programme in the field of education which has various objectives, one of which is equalisation of opportunities and the fight against social exclusion. The views expressed in this book are those of the authors and do not commit either the European Commission or the national authorities concerned.

We owe a special word of thanks to the Socrates unit of the European Commission for their trust in our services; to Ms Ivette Betancourt, a fellow researcher from Venezuela, who stayed a few months with HIVA and helped us with the preparation of the project; to our Maltese colleagues, Professor Joseph Mifsud, Joe Cauchi, Carmel Cefai, Joseph Xerri, Emanuel Sciclina and others, for hosting one of our seminars and for the stimulating exchanges; to all colleagues, schools and project promoters who received us or participated in seminars; to our translation office, Alfabet; and, last but not least, to all secretariats of the participating institutes for their professional support.

Notes

[1] That is, between 0 and 15 years of age

[2] The adjective 'lower status', as applied to vocational tracks, is not meant to express a value judgement on the part of the authors; rather, it reflects the unequal esteem accorded to these tracks and their limited perspectives of access to higher education.

Part One:
A status quaestionis

ONE

The educational situation of disadvantaged children

Emer Smyth and Breda McCabe (ESRI)

This chapter presents background information on the educational situation of socially excluded children and young people. The first part of the chapter briefly outlines some of the explanations proffered for the persistence of educational inequality in most European countries. The second and third parts examine the relationship between socioeconomic background and educational outcomes in the six participating countries: Belgium, Ireland, the Netherlands, Portugal, Scotland and Spain. This discussion provides the context for the analysis of educational policy measures to tackle social exclusion presented in the following chapters.

The causes of educational inequality

Research on socioeconomic background and educational outcomes

International research has indicated a consistently significant effect of social background on educational outcomes (see, for example, Coleman et al, 1966; Bourdieu and Passeron, 1970; Jencks et al, 1972; Halsey et al, 1980). Comparative studies have shown that the pattern of association between social class background and education tends to be similar, even in countries with very different educational systems (Shavit and Blossfeld, 1993; Ishida et al, 1995). Parental education has a similar association with children's education, with children of university-educated parents having higher rates of educational attainment (Shavit and Blossfeld, 1993) and higher literacy levels (OECD, 1997a). The effect of social background has been apparent in relation to both the level of education reached and academic performance at various stages within the educational system.

Socioeconomic background is shown to have a stronger effect at earlier stages of the educational process, declining in relative terms as students move through the system (Shavit and Blossfeld, 1993; Raftery and Hout, 1993). Two explanations have been advanced for this pattern. First, the life-course hypothesis proposes that older students are less dependent on family resources, both cultural and economic, in making decisions about continued educational participation (Shavit and Blossfeld, 1993). Second, others have argued that this process reflects selection effects since those working-class students who do go on to higher education are likely to be atypical of working-class students within the educational system (Mare, 1980).

In comparison with social class and parental education, other dimensions of socioeconomic background (such as parental unemployment, family income and 'poverty') have been relatively neglected. These dimensions tend to be correlated with social class and parental education; for example, those from the unskilled working class and/or those with low levels of education are likely to experience disproportionately high unemployment rates and higher levels of income poverty. Some researchers have argued that these dimensions may have little independent effect on educational attainment, once other background factors are taken into account; in the Netherlands, for example, Dronkers (1994) found that fathers' unemployment or non-employment had little direct effect on children's educational outcomes. Other researchers, however, have found that weak labour force attachment (Guo et al, 1996), low income (Mare, 1980; Nicaise, 1999) and poverty (Haveman et al, 1991) have significant direct negative effects on children's educational outcomes.

In spite of the considerable expansion in educational participation experienced by many countries over the second half of the 20th century, there has been a remarkable consistency in the relationship between social background and inequality in educational outcomes (Shavit and Blossfeld, 1993; Breen and Whelan, 1996). Among countries for which comparable data are available, only Sweden and the Netherlands have shown any consistent tendency towards increased equality of educational participation between the different social classes (De Graaf and Ganzeboom, 1993; Jonsson, 1993).[1] It has been argued that these changes cannot be attributed to educational reform alone, but reflect a more general trend towards the equalisation of life-chances in the two countries (Erikson, 1996).

The causes of educational inequality

The causes of inequality in educational outcomes have been the subject of much debate (see Tyler, 1977). In general, discussion has focused on educational inequality in terms of social class background and gender, with some more limited attention to ethnic differences. Consequently, many studies have failed to identify important differences within the working class in terms of poverty and social exclusion, and little information is available on the educational experiences of the most economically disadvantaged groups. Two sets of factors are seen to influence inequality of educational outcomes: differences between social classes in academic ability/performance ('primary effects'); and differences between social classes in their level of educational participation, controlling for academic performance ('secondary effects') (Boudon, 1974). Differences in academic performance are seen to reflect differing cultural resources in the home environment (Bourdieu and Passeron, 1977), variations in physical wellbeing and nutrition (Atkinson et al, 1983), and/or class bias within the school (see below). However, it has been argued that such ability/performance differences are not large enough to explain existing levels of inequality in educational attainment, nor why children from different social classes but with similar ability levels differ in their tendency to remain in full-time education (Erikson and Jonsson, 1996).

One approach to explaining this pattern is the 'rational choice' model adopted by Erikson and Jonsson (1996; see also Goldthorpe, 1996a). From this perspective, educational choice is regarded in terms of the (perceived) costs and benefits associated with continued participation, with variation in outcomes related to a number of factors. First, lack of economic resources will limit participation if families cannot afford the direct and indirect (opportunity) costs of such participation. The relative costs of schooling are likely to vary according to social class and family income levels. Second, different social class groups differ in their cultural resources. Parents with higher levels of education will have greater knowledge of the educational system, and will be better equipped to help their children with homework and study. Among recent cohorts, the effects of cultural resources (such as parental education) have become stronger than those of economic resources (Erikson and Jonsson, 1996; De Graaf and Ganzeboom, 1993). Third, the perceived benefits of educational participation may differ between class groups. The middle classes have more to lose by not staying on in education, since they risk social demotion, whereas in high unemployment areas, young people from working-class backgrounds may not see much benefit to staying on at school. Fourth, the probabilities of success within the educational system may differ between social groups (Erikson and Jonsson, 1996). Other factors, such as geographical distance from educational facilities, may also affect the relative costs of educational participation. While this issue has rarely been considered in a cross-national perspective, experiences in countries such as Spain and Portugal indicate that geographical marginalisation may reinforce the negative effects of economic disadvantage on educational participation.

Changes over time in educational inequality in Sweden can, therefore, be seen as a result of diminishing social class differences in economic security (through increased equality in income and living conditions) in the context of an educational system which postpones the timing of educational selection (Erikson, 1996). The lack of change in other countries can be seen as the product of persistent inequalities in financial and cultural resources between social class groups, along with differences in the perceived benefits and success rates associated with educational participation (Erikson and Jonsson, 1996). Middle-class groups thus retain an advantage even in the context of radical changes in the educational system; in spite of comprehensivisation in Britain, for example, the middle class retained an advantage through maintaining access to grammar and private schools as well as more prestigious comprehensive schools (Kerckhoff et al, 1997). Raftery and Hout (1993) have suggested that, in the absence of significant changes in the distribution of economic and cultural resources, educational inequality will only decrease when the demand for education among the upper middle classes has been saturated.

Schools and educational inequality

While the above discussion has focused on the factors shaping 'demand' for education, other researchers have stressed the way in which the nature of the educational system and the schooling process may influence the level of educational inequality. Institutional factors, such as the timing of educational selection, the length of various educational routes or 'tracks', the size of the system, and the principles for transferring between levels, may serve to reinforce (or reduce) existing social inequalities (Erikson and Jonsson, 1996). For example, in systems where educational selection into academic and vocational tracks happens very early, differences between social class and ethnic groups in the type of education they receive are likely to be more pronounced (see, for example,

Shavit, 1984). In the Scottish case, where educational reforms increased access to an 'academic' curriculum, there was a significant reduction in socioeconomic inequality within schools, as regards academic performance (Gamoran, 1996).

Reproduction theorists have stressed the way in which the structure and processes within schools serve to reproduce existing social inequality. Bowles and Gintis (1977), for example, have argued that the social relations within schools (with a hierarchical division of labour, alienated work, and fragmentation through competition) 'correspond' to the social relations of capitalist society. This process is reinforced by the class-biased nature of the school curriculum (see Apple, 1982), which draws on the cultural capital of the middle classes (Bourdieu, 1973). Even pupil resistance to the formal school culture may, ironically, serve to maintain existing social class differences (Willis, 1977).

Increasingly, reproduction theory has been criticised for being overly deterministic (see Lynch, 1989). More recent research has focused on the impact of schooling structures and processes on pupil outcomes. Structures such as tracking and streaming are found to increase existing social divisions. Pupils from lower socioeconomic backgrounds are disproportionately located in lower ability streams or lower status vocational tracks (Sorenson, 1987; Shavit, 1984; Jones et al, 1995; Hannan and Boyle, 1987; Nicaise, 1999). Such an allocation process is likely to increase differences in academic performance due to the polarising effect of ability grouping (Hallinan, 1987; Kerckhoff, 1993; Smyth, 1999). Research on school effectiveness has indicated a number of factors, including disciplinary climate, teacher expectations, and pupil–teacher interaction, which are consistently associated with enhanced pupil outcomes (see, for example, Scheerens and Bosker, 1997). However, other analysts have criticised such research for failing to take account of socioeconomic differences within and between schools (Angus, 1993). Recent research on American high schools has indicated that the degree of socioeconomic differentiation within schools, or 'social distribution of achievement', is found to be related to the student composition, teacher quality and interest, disciplinary climate, academic climate and academic organisation within the school (Bryk et al, 1993). Thus, schools can serve to reduce or challenge, rather than reproduce, existing social inequality.

The educational situation of socially excluded children

The following sections present background information on the educational situation of socially excluded children and young people in the six study countries: Belgium, Ireland, the Netherlands, Portugal, Scotland and Spain. These countries differ in a number of respects: the nature of their educational systems (see Introduction); the relevance of different background factors to educational opportunities and outcomes; and the relative importance of various educational outcomes to subsequent life-chances and social exclusion. The selected countries should, therefore, give some indication of the situation of socially excluded children in Europe as a whole.

Which social background factors matter?

Research in a range of countries has indicated that socioeconomic factors, such as parental social class and parental education, are significant correlates of educational success or failure. However, countries differ in the degree to which information on the relationship between family background and educational outcomes is readily available. In the Spanish and Portuguese contexts, policy concerns have focused on the expansion of educational attainment among the whole population, and have consequently neglected the collection of information on the situation of children from disadvantaged backgrounds.

Analysis of the educational situation of children from 'poor' families has proved particularly difficult, given the debate about the definition of poverty and the absence, until recently, of large-scale data sets which contain detailed information on family economic and social circumstances.[2] Therefore, in the following sections, a number of different indicators of socioeconomic disadvantage, such as social class, parental education, and family size, are used to depict the relationship between family background and educational outcomes among children and young people. Other factors, such as ethnicity, are discussed where information is available. However, this issue may be less relevant in certain national contexts because of the very small size of minority groups (for example, in Ireland) or may not be taken into account in data collection. The international literature on educational deprivation mentions a range of other poverty-related background characteristics such as family breakdown, the placement of children in state care, poor health, parental illiteracy, mental distress, language barriers (for example, use of slang at home) and so on, that are correlated with children's educational attainment (for a review, see Nicaise, 1999). However, the definitions differ between sources, and very often no comparable data are available between countries.

Which educational outcomes matter?

The impact of educational outcomes on subsequent social exclusion may differ according to the nature of particular educational systems and their linkages with the labour market. In some systems, the level of educational attainment plays an important role in securing access to (well-paid) employment, while in other systems, examination results or the type of education/training received are more significant. For example, in the Irish context, employers pay attention to exam grades when making recruitment decisions (Breen et al, 1995), while in the Dutch context there is a strong 'match' between the level and type (subject specialisation) of education received and occupational position (Smoorenburg and Van der Velden, 1995). During young people's educational careers, on-going academic performance or grade retention may serve as useful indicators of potential educational disadvantage. The prevalence of being 'kept back' in a particular academic year (grade retention) differs across national systems, ranging from the Irish case, where grade retention is exceptional to non-existent, to the Dutch case, where pupils may be retained once in each year (Eurydice, 1994b). These different educational outcomes, and their relationship to socioeconomic disadvantage, will be considered in the following section.

We will also use some more 'sensitive' indicators of educational success or failure in relation to social exclusion, such as illiteracy among pupils at secondary level, truancy, or referrals to special education. Again, the information about such phenomena is highly illustrative, but fragmentary.

Socioeconomic background and educational outcomes: empirical evidence

This section considers the relationship between socioeconomic background and a number of aspects of educational attainment in the study countries. While the research presented is diverse and not designed to yield comparable measures across countries, it does serve to highlight some of the main issues relating to potential educational disadvantage.

Educational participation

The six countries differ in the level of pre-compulsory (pre-school) education, with particularly low levels in Ireland and high levels in Belgium; 98% of Belgian 3-year-olds take part in early childhood education compared with only 1% of their Irish counterparts (OECD, 1998). In the Belgian case, socioeconomic influences, such as parental education, income and family size, appear to have no significant effect on participation in pre-school education. Only child age and labour force participation were found to be significant factors, with higher participation in kindergarten among older children (aged 5 years) and, surprisingly, among households where one parent does not work outside the home (Nicaise, 1999). Data are not available on pre-school participation by social background in Ireland, the Netherlands, Scotland, Spain or Portugal.

Official statistics indicate that compulsory educational participation appears to be successfully enforced in the six countries (OECD, 1998). However, 'illegal' dropout (that is, before the legal school-leaving age) may be prevalent among certain groups (for example, travellers, ethnic minorities) or in certain national contexts, such as Portugal. In other contexts such as Scotland, non-participation may reflect formal exclusion of pupils by the school, rather than 'voluntary' dropout. The level of post-compulsory participation in second-level education differs across the countries concerned, but there is, to some extent, a degree of convergence in the trends (see Introduction; also see IARD, 1998). In spite of a general increase in the level of education in the six countries, participation remains strongly influenced by socioeconomic background.

In the Dutch case, children from working-class environments, and whose parents have a low educational level, are more likely to leave the first phase of secondary education (MAVO, VBO) and the vocational phase (MBO, apprenticeships) before completion. Among this group, 7% leave the system without any educational or vocational qualifications, compared with 2% in the rest of the population (*Onderwijs Voorrangsbeleid* cohort study). Dropout rates are 12% for those whose parents have a primary education compared to 0.5% among those whose parents have a university education.

The relationship between social background and educational level of school leavers has been apparent in the Netherlands throughout the 20th century. De Graaf and Ganzeboom (1993) indicate that fathers' social class and level of education have had a significant effect on educational success among all cohorts born since 1891. However, these effects, while still significant, have been declining in magnitude over the century (De Graaf and Ganzeboom, 1993; Dronkers, 1992).

Pupils from ethnic minority groups in the Netherlands are much more likely to drop out than Dutch-born pupils (Roelandt et al, 1991), even compared to native pupils from 'poor' families. Thus, the dropout rate without qualifications for pupils of Moroccan origin is almost 15%, and for pupils of Turkish origin almost 7%. There is, however, a large overlap between lower socioeconomic status and belonging to an ethnic minority. Comparing immigrant and native pupils from the same social background, the differences in dropout rates are smaller, but a significant difference remains between the two groups (De Wit and Dekkers, 1996, p 37). In addition to socioeconomic status, other factors have an influence on the relatively low school success of immigrant children: language problems, which result in more negative school experiences, discrimination, age differences, uncertainty about staying in the country, and lack of social participation (Voncken and Babeliowsky, 1994). The dropout rate is highest in the four largest cities: Amsterdam, Rotterdam, The Hague and Utrecht. This may partially reflect the concentration of ethnic minority groups in these areas (Voncken and Babeliowsky, 1994).

In spite of the introduction of free second-level education in 1967 and a general increase in educational attainment among Irish school leavers since the late 1970s, social class differences in educational outcomes are still apparent (see Breen and Whelan, 1996). Second-level completion rates are particularly high among the professional groups, with the vast majority of these young people staying on to the end of upper second-level education (the Leaving Certificate). Conversely, rates of early leaving are highest among the manual (especially unskilled manual) groups; among the 1994 cohort, 8% of young people from unskilled manual backgrounds left school without sitting any formal exam, while this was the case for fewer than 1% of those from higher professional backgrounds (ESRI Annual School Leavers' Survey).

In addition to occupational status, the employment status of parents is significantly associated with patterns of school leaving in Ireland. Young people tend to leave school earlier where there is no adult in the household in paid employment. Another dimension of socioeconomic background – parental education – is also associated with educational outcomes. Young people are much more likely to leave school where their father or mother had themselves been early school leavers. In addition, early leavers tend to come from larger families; those who leave school without sitting any formal exam have an average of 4.9

siblings, compared with 3.7 for those who complete upper second-level education (ESRI Follow-Up Survey of 1985/6 School Leavers).

The pattern of socioeconomic inequalities in educational participation is also evident in relation to the third-level sector. Those whose parents are unemployed are significantly underrepresented among entrants to higher education, as are those from semi-skilled or unskilled manual backgrounds (Clancy, 1995). It is estimated that in 1992, 89% of those from higher professional backgrounds went on to full-time higher education, compared with 13% of those from unskilled manual backgrounds. Furthermore, the more prestigious the sector and field of study, the greater the social inequality in participation levels (Clancy, 1995).

Data on the Scottish context indicate that young people are more likely to stay on in school when their father is in full-time employment or retired. A similar pattern is evident in relation to mothers' employment status, with lower staying-on rates among the children of unemployed mothers (SOEID, 1996b). In addition, children from larger families are more likely to leave school before the completion of second-level education. Differences in post-compulsory and third-level participation are evident between social class groupings; those from professional backgrounds are more than twice as likely as those from semi-skilled or unskilled manual backgrounds to stay on in post-compulsory education (75% versus less than 35% – Paterson, 1992). However, there is some evidence that these class differentials have narrowed somewhat over time (Paterson, 1997a; 1997b).

Entitlement to free school meals has been a frequently employed measure of disadvantage within the Scottish educational system. Analyses indicate that absenteeism and exclusion rates are higher in the more disadvantaged local authorities (that is, those with a higher proportion of pupils entitled to free school meals). A lower level of third-level participation is also evident in the more deprived urban areas considered Priority Partnership Areas (HMI, 1996).

School dropout in Belgium (Flanders) can be defined in the following ways. First, there are students who leave school before the end of a cycle (lower secondary or upper secondary) but who may return to another school or educational institution after a period of time. Students from single-parent families and those living in institutions show the highest probability of this type of dropout; children from non-Belgian families and with inactive fathers are also overrepresented in this group (Douterlungne, 1994). Second, there is a group of young people who leave school without any qualification. In Flanders, 3.6% of school leavers (aged 18-25) have no degree beyond primary education, and another 16.4% have just finished lower secondary education. The corresponding figures for the French-speaking community of Belgium (7.2% and 27.2% respectively) are even more dramatic.[3] The third definition refers to the group of 'illegal' dropouts who leave before the official school leaving age. Little is known about this group, almost by definition. Their number is estimated between 0.9% and 3% (Van de Velde et al, 1996a) of the reference population. Boys form the vast majority of these dropouts. According to a 'guesstimate' made by Van Calster (1991), their number amounts to over 20% among children of immigrants; but youngsters from poor families – and particularly travellers' children – are also said to be at high risk of dropout.

Nicaise (1999) has found that, before the school leaving age was raised to 18, participation in upper secondary education in Belgium was significantly influenced by fathers' educational level, parents' employment status, and the cost of education,[4] although other background factors, such as income level and family situation, had no significant direct effects. In contrast, participation in higher education is significantly related to family income, family size, and higher education among parents.

The lack of detailed information on the composition of school leavers in Spain by social class, regional origin and school type is a reflection of the generic and diffuse nature of recent equal opportunity policies. Such policies have been more concerned with improving the general level of educational attainment than with assessing socioeconomic variation in this area. Data from 1981 indicate that the children of white-collar professionals were twice as likely as working-class children to be in school at 16 years of age (Carabaña, 1993). Moreover, the gap between the two classes widened as they climbed the educational ladder; the former were three times as likely to reach the upper secondary level, and six times as likely to go to university, as the latter (see also Justel and Martinez Lazero, 1981). The period since 1981 has seen a process of democratisation in access to education. However, it is difficult to assess the extent to which educational inequality has changed over this period.

One of the few existing studies was conducted by Fundación Encuentro. The social class structure of secondary school students hardly varied between 1981 and 1991, although pupils from working-class families constituted the largest group as well as the one with the fastest growth rate. Nor has the social class composition of university students altered very much. Thus, it appears that increased opportunities have been distributed in a uniform fashion, thereby maintaining the initial unequal structure that existed in 1981. Working–class children have stayed on at secondary school for longer, but a large number of them do not continue their education. At third–level, participation is strongly influenced by the educational level of parents, and by family income (Mora, 1996).

Patterns of school leaving also differ across the various regions (Merino and Planas, 1996). The economically more backward regions are among the least egalitarian, with a higher than average proportion of pupils leaving school without qualifications, and lower than average percentages completing secondary school and going on to university. The most egalitarian, with the highest rates of school completion, are the northern and the Madrid regions (Martinez et al, 1993).

In the Portuguese context, there are significant regional differences in the proportion of young people leaving school at an early stage, with the lowest rates of school enrolment in the north and centre of the country. This pattern may be linked to the 'pull' away from school provided by employment growth in these regions. However, in the longer term, these young people are likely to be particularly vulnerable to the effects of economic restructuring due to their lack of formal qualifications. School enrolment rates are particularly low in areas of the country with high levels of poverty (Ferrão and das Neves, 1992). In addition, pupils from an ethnic/cultural minority group are more likely to drop out of school.

Grade retention

In some educational systems, grade retention, or 'repeating' one or more years within school, is taken as an indicator of educational underperformance. In other systems, such as Spain, grade retention is seen as a means of promoting educational success. However, the implications of repeating will differ significantly for different social class groups, and between the poor and the non–poor. The Belgian, Dutch and Spanish systems are ones in which grade retention is commonly used. In the Irish and Scottish cases, pupils are permitted to repeat years only in very exceptional circumstances, apart from the final year of school. In the latter cases, therefore, other measures of underperformance, such as exam results, are of greater importance.

Data on pupils in the first year of primary education in Flanders indicate that rates of repeating vary according to the socioeconomic background of the family. The main finding to emerge is the demarcation line between children from the lowest classes (with an economically inactive father, or where parents have no qualifications, or are in the very lowest income category) and the rest of the population. Comparing students who have repeated at least one year in lower secondary education with others, the pattern is very similar to that found at primary level. Children from low-income families, with unemployed fathers or mothers who have not finished primary school, show particularly high rates of repeating at lower secondary level (Nicaise, 1999). If one could identify children from poor households separately, the contrast would no doubt be much sharper. Two small samples of children from Belgian families living in persistent poverty illustrate this strikingly: 64% of pupils in primary and secondary schools had resat at least one year, while 30% had resat two or more years (Nicaise, 1999).

A relatively high proportion of students repeat at least one year in the Spanish educational system, although the proportion has fallen somewhat between 1984 and 1994. At primary level, almost one-third of pupils repeat one year, with a further 11% repeating two years. At lower secondary level, 15.5% of all 11-year-olds and 26% of all 13-year-olds have repeated at least one year. The latest available data (for 1994) show that 43% of those still in school at the age of 16 have repeated at least one year of school. Unfortunately, no information is available on the social background of pupils who repeat school years in Spain.

In the Portuguese context, pupils from ethnic/cultural minority groups are more likely to repeat years than others. However, no information on the pattern as it relates to social class or poverty level is available.

Academic performance

Due to the absence of national examinations at primary level, little systematic information is available on the impact of socioeconomic background on pupil performance within primary schools in Ireland. However, survey data have indicated that parental unemployment, social class, and living in a disadvantaged area have significant effects on literacy levels and on performance in ability tests (Kellaghan and Brugha, 1972; Fontes and Kellaghan, 1977). Performance in nationally standardised examinations (the Junior and Leaving Certificates) is significantly related to socioeconomic background. Underperformance in these examinations is more evident among pupils from working-class backgrounds, those with parents who are unemployed, those whose parents have lower levels of education, and those who come from larger families. In addition, the social class mix of the school attended has an effect on pupil performance over and above that of the pupil's individual social background. That is, pupils tend to underachieve when they attend schools with a higher proportion of pupils from disadvantaged backgrounds. Over half of the variation in exam performance between schools is explained by socioeconomic variables; that is, most of the difference between schools in the average exam performance of their pupils is due to pupil composition factors. While socioeconomic factors have a significant effect on the variation in performance among pupils within schools, it should be noted that there is still a relatively high degree of variation in exam grades obtained when background is controlled for (Smyth, 1999).

Young people in Scotland achieve better grades in the Standard and Higher exams when their father is in paid employment or retired, a pattern that is also evident when mothers' employment status is considered; 21% of school leavers with unemployed fathers obtain no qualifications, compared with only 5% of those with employed or retired fathers (SOEID, 1996a). In addition, children from larger families are found to achieve fewer qualifications than other children; 17% of young people with four or more siblings obtain no qualifications, compared with a mere 3% of only children. Aggregate analyses indicate that exam grades are lower in areas with more disadvantaged pupils (Scottish Office, 1997b). A pattern of pupil underperformance is also evident from data on schools in deprived urban areas (HMI, 1996). Other research has indicated that neighbourhood deprivation is negatively associated with pupil performance, even when pupil ability, family background and schooling characteristics are controlled (Garner and Raudenbush, 1991). There are indications that educational underperformance among children in care is particularly marked, although little research has been carried out on this issue in Scotland.

In the Belgian context, secondary school entry test scores in Dutch and mathematics are found to be significantly related to socioeconomic background (Bollens et al, 1998). Labour market status, educational level and parental income explain 25% of the variance in pupil test scores. In addition, a contextual effect is apparent, with lower test scores found among pupils in schools with a high proportion of low-income pupils. It can be concluded from these results that socioeconomic background has a very strong influence on educational performance in Flanders.

Lack of qualifications has a formal policy definition in the Netherlands. Since the early 1990s, a target level has been set in which every young person should successfully complete a short (two year) vocational training course. This minimum level is termed the 'starting qualification'. Under this scheme, any pupil who finishes their education without a starting qualification, even if they have obtained a VBO or MAVO qualification, is considered an 'early educational leaver'. According to this definition, around 98,000 young people, or 43% of all school leavers, leave school without a starting qualification each year (Hövels et al, 1996). As indicated above, leaving school without starting qualifications is more prevalent among young people whose parents have a low level of education, are engaged in manual work, or are not currently employed. Within schools, academic performance is significantly related to social class, language use at home, family size and birth order (Van Eyken, 1988; Dronkers and Kerkhoff, 1990). Children from poor families are found to have lower school performance, a pattern that is partially attributable to the greater incidence of health problems in this group. Furthermore, the social composition of both school and neighbourhood represent important influences on educational achievement (Dronkers and Schijf, 1984; Meijnen, 1987).

The Spanish educational system has relatively high rates of educational failure. In 1993, 84% of pupils obtained the primary school leaving certificate, although universal completion of primary schooling is only a recent phenomenon. Within primary school, a substantial minority (28%) of students fail their exams. At secondary level, 57% of 17-year-olds managed to successfully complete BUP (secondary pre-university level) in 1994, while 68% of all 18-year-olds successfully completed COU (one-year upper secondary level). Again, the failure rate is relatively high within the secondary system; only 42% of pupils enrolled in BUP first and second years (15- to 16-year-olds) passed their end-of-year examinations on first sitting, while this was the case for only 53% of COU students. A lower proportion of school leavers obtain vocational qualifications (FP-1 and FP-2) with a graduation rate of 52% for FP-1 and 38% for FP-2 students. Unfortunately, no information is available on the socioeconomic characteristics of pupils who experience educational failure, although young women appear to attain higher qualifications than young men.

Research in Portugal indicates a relatively high degree of educational failure in basic education. Rates of failure vary significantly by socioeconomic background, with 45% of those with unemployed fathers failing the first phase of the first cycle, compared with only 7% of children of directors/managers. Other research indicates lower educational performance among working–class pupils in relation to science subjects (Morais et al, 1992; Domingos, 1989).

Socioeconomic background can continue to have a significant effect on the possession of basic skills, including literacy, even well into adulthood. Four of the study countries – Belgium (Flanders), the Netherlands, Ireland and the United Kingdom (including Scotland) – participated in a recent cross-national survey of adult literacy levels (OECD, 1997a). It was found that differences in fathers' educational background have an impact on literacy levels among adults, even controlling for their level of education. An earlier survey by the International Educational Association had shown that illiteracy persisted even among 14-year-old students. The socioeconomic status of those with the lowest literacy scores was considerably below the population average (IEA, 1991).

Type of education

While type of education per se does not reflect educational disadvantage, such disadvantage may result where different educational routes have different statuses and varying implications for subsequent labour market exclusion.

In the Belgian context, first-year pupils in the 'B' (pre-vocational) stream tend to come disproportionately from lone parent families, have poorly educated parents, and have fathers belonging to the category of unskilled or semi-skilled manual workers (Van de Velde et al, 1996a). In the third year, social background variables continue to have a significant impact on educational track, even after prior academic ability is controlled for. In addition, children of working–class and poor families are extremely overrepresented among pupils in special education: roughly half the children from persistently poor families spend part of their youth in an institution (Nicaise and De Wilde, 1995). These institutions are often linked to a particular school for special education, where the children are then enrolled more or less automatically. Even excluding special medical educational establishments, around 40% of young people in Flemish special youth care institutions are placed in special education (Hellinckx and De Munter, 1990). Looking at the same phenomenon from a different angle, Goffinet and Van Damme (1990) found that 77% of the pupils in special education are children of working-class families and marginal workers.

Data from the Scottish context indicate the overrepresentation of children from low-income families among those in special education.

In 1996, over two thirds of those in special education were entitled to free school meals (an indicator of low income) compared with one-fifth of those in mainstream schools (Scottish Office, 1996d).

The Dutch educational system is highly differentiated into academic and (various types of) vocational routes. Immigrant pupils are greatly overrepresented in lower level vocational programmes such as IVBO and, to a lesser extent, VBO. Newcomers in particular (mostly refugees) mainly enter education at the IVBO level, where special programmes have been developed for the initial reception of these children into the Dutch education system. Pupils from lower socioeconomic environments are overrepresented in both school types.

In contrast, the Irish system is relatively general in orientation. At second-level, however, there are some differences in social composition by school type, with working-class and lower-ability pupils disproportionately concentrated in vocational schools, while secondary (more academic) schools tend to 'cream off' middle-class and higher-ability pupils (Hannan et al, 1996b).

No data are available on variations in type of education by social background within the Spanish and Portuguese educational systems.

The implications of educational disadvantage

The previous sections of this chapter confirmed the link between social background (and poverty in particular) on the one hand, and educational opportunities on the other. However, the real tragedy is that the broken educational career of underprivileged children is, in turn, translated into poverty in the next generation. Table 1.1 shows that the risk of poverty in families where the head of the household is poorly educated is many times that of households with a better educated head. Poverty here is measured in terms of income per consumption unit, where the poverty line is defined as 50% of the average disposable income in each country.

The causal link between level of education and risk of poverty takes in various interim factors: the poorly educated are particularly at risk of being unemployed (see Figure 1.1). If they are in employment, they earn considerably less and have less stable statuses (part-time, temporary, and so on). A similar pattern is observed if the level of training is measured in terms of literacy rather than qualifications.

A poor educational career has direct consequences beyond the labour market position of the individual as an adult. The International Adult Literacy Survey (OECD, 1997a) also contains a series of references to

Table 1.1: Poverty and education of household head in the six study countries

	PI	FP		PI	FP
Spain			*Belgium*		
None	47.7	10.8	No education/unknown	26.5	3.9
Less than primary	31.1	43.6	Primary	12.2	50.6
Primary	14.0	37.2	Lower secondary	6.0	26.0
Lower secondary	9.2	4.7	Upper secondary	3.8	13.3
Upper secondary	4.5	2.2	University	2.6	3.1
University or equivalent	5.1	1.1	Higher	1.7	3.0
Higher non-university	1.6	0.3			
			The Netherlands		
Portugal			Primary	19.5	45.9
None	61.9	36.8	Lower secondary	5.3	16.3
Less than primary	46.1	11.6	Upper secondary	4.9	30.4
Primary	21.4	48.1	Upper technical/vocational	1.6	5.1
Lower secondary	7.7	2.4	University or equivalent	1.4	1.6
Upper secondary	4.4	0.7	Not specified	24.3	0.7
Lower technical/vocational	1.6	0.1			
Upper technical/vocational	0.0	0.0	*United Kingdom*		
University or equivalent	2.2	0.3	Unknown or in education	24.0	1.3
			Education ended before age 14	45.1	6.7
Ireland			Education ended at age 14	29.1	46.9
Still receiving education	10.9	0.4	Education ended at age 15	15.5	21.6
Education ended at age 13	31.0	5.5	Education ended at age 16	12.8	16.5
Education ended between			Education ended between		
13 and 18	17.7	93.0	17 and 20	6.7	5.9
Education ended after age 18	1.7	1.1	Education ended at age 21 or over	2.1	1.1

PI =poverty incidence ratio (% poor within the subpopulation); FP = fraction of the poverty population (% of poverty population in given subgroup). See Chapter 1 for a discussion of these ratios.

Source: Hagenaars et al 1994, tables A.2.1. The poverty line used is 50% of the average equivalent expenditure, using modified OECD equivalence scales

literature, together with new data on the additional effects of education on social inclusion or exclusion. For example, people with a better level of literacy enjoy markedly better health because they are better informed of risks and can make more effective use of healthcare, and because their living environment exposes them to fewer dangers. Furthermore, better educated citizens are also less likely to display socially maladjusted or criminal behaviour.

Finally, the highly educated also make better use of continuing education. Figure 1.2 reflects the 'adjusted odds ratios'[5] of different

Figure 1.1: Unemployment by level of education, 1998

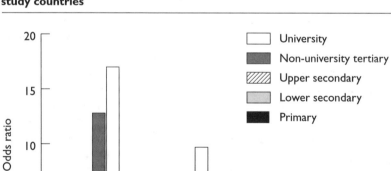

Source: OECD, *Education at a glance*, 2000

Figure 1.2: Adjusted odds of participation in adult education in four study countries

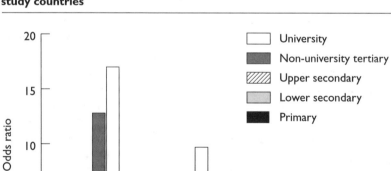

Source: OECD (1997a, p 95, 182)

educational categories as regards their participation in adult education. In Flanders, for example, university graduates participate 17 times more in adult education than people with just a primary school certificate. This may seem contradictory because they have a relatively lower need for this education. However, on the one hand, they see further education as more attractive as a result of their positive experience of school and, thanks to their prosperity, they can allow themselves a greater investment in human capital; on the other hand, the range of education available to adults is perhaps insufficiently suited to those with the lowest levels of education. However this may be, it is disconcerting to have to note that the exclusion of the socioeconomically weakest children at school results in an even greater wedge being driven between rich and poor in adulthood.

Conclusions

A review of research in the study countries indicates that not enough is known about the particular educational experiences of the most economically or socially disadvantaged groups in society. However, available information does indicate the persistence of considerable socioeconomic inequalities in educational outcomes in the study countries. Casual information suggests that children from the poorest families are at great risk of failure and referral to special education from the very start of their school careers. In secondary education, they are faced with persistent illiteracy, high rates of grade retention, streaming towards the least profitable study fields, demotivation and early dropout.

Educational underachievement has significant consequences for subsequent life-chances, resulting in cumulative educational deficits in adulthood, lower earnings, higher unemployment, poorer health, and increased likelihood of deviant behaviour and dependency throughout life.

The importance of policy intervention to prevent or redress such educational inequalities is, therefore, particularly evident. However, different perceptions of the causes of educational inequality call for different sorts of solutions. Perspectives that emphasise the relative 'costs' associated with educational participation would suggest a focus on equalising opportunities more generally, perhaps through financial support to families and/or pupils. Conversely, perspectives that focus on the role of the school in reproducing social inequalities would appear to suggest a more radical rethinking of the educational system and the purposes of schooling. Educational policy is thus informed, implicitly or explicitly, by particular perspectives on how inequalities in educational outcomes come about. A typology of educational strategies relating to social exclusion is presented in the next chapter. The following chapters of the book discuss some of the measures taken by different educational systems to address educational disadvantage.

Notes

[1] Recent evidence indicates some tendency towards an equalisation of educational opportunity in Germany (Müller, 1996), albeit with a higher level of inequality than in Sweden or the Netherlands (Erikson and Jonsson, 1996). In addition, there is some evidence of a decline in inequality of educational outcomes in Scotland during the early 1980s (Gamoran, 1996; Paterson, 1997a).

[2] While the European Community Household Panel survey has facilitated the development of comparative research on poverty, it is less suitable for analysing educational outcomes among socially excluded children and young people; information about the current educational attainment of school-going children is not available, and no information about the social background of adults is recorded.

[3] Estimates from HIVA, based on the Socioeconomic Panel of the Centre for Social Policy (Antwerp).

[4] Direct and indirect cost; that is, including earnings forgone while studying.

[5] The odds have been corrected for differences in age and gender and expressed in relative terms, where the participation score for individuals with primary education is set equal to one.

TWO

Strategies to reduce educational inequality: a general framework

Ides Nicaise (HIVA)

In this transnational study we will seek to order and analyse the relevant but rather diffuse experiences of different countries as systematically as possible. The first requirement is obviously a common frame of reference. In this chapter, a typology is proposed for education strategies,[1] to serve as a framework for the analyses performed in subsequent chapters.

Various criteria can be used in formulating this typology: types of stakeholder (policymakers, parents, teachers, schools, and so on), stages in educational curriculum (pre-school, primary, and so on), nature of the strategies, policy level (national versus local), and so on. We decided to adopt a double key for our reference framework, consisting of the two latter criteria. Each of them will be discussed in greater detail below.

First criterion: 'nature' of the strategy (equal opportunity, equal treatment, equal outcomes)

The nature of the strategies discussed below corresponds to the different nature of the various causes of educational exclusion. As we saw in the previous chapter, the literature on educational inequality suggests a basic distinction between obstacles on the 'demand' side of education (which can be referred to as 'unequal opportunities' depending on the socioeconomic environment of the pupil) and on the 'supply' side ('unequal treatment' or 'discrimination' on the part of educational institutions). The former group of factors are related to the socioeconomic handicaps of pupils from poor families: material or cultural deprivation, poor health, unstable family relationships, lack of social and cultural capital, and so on (that is, factors which are more or less 'exogenous' to the education system). The latter group have to do with the education system itself, or more precisely, the way in which educational institutions and their agents (teachers, counsellors, school principals) contribute to prejudice against pupils from lower social backgrounds.

The distinction does not imply that education policy has no impact whatsoever on the former group, the environmental circumstances. Rather, it helps in classifying strategies to promote educational equality. For example, financial incentives within education can help overcome the (exogenous) material obstacles to a successful school career, even though the education system is not responsible for the latter. Thus, we will consider two types of strategies: those aimed at ensuring **more equal opportunities** (or **more equal access**), and those aimed at **more equal treatment** within education itself.

Besides being 'demand-focused', equal opportunities strategies will, typically, also be multidimensional and multidisciplinary in nature. Given the multiple causes of unequal opportunities (financial, physical, cultural, social, emotional, and so on), only multifaceted responses will effectively combat this source of educational disadvantage.

'Equal treatment strategies', on the other hand, focus on the elimination of discriminatory behaviour within the education process at school. They are thus typically 'supply-centred'; that is, they concentrate on what happens within the school or classroom. A great emphasis will be put on the role of communication, because the lack of communication between the school and the home environment of pupils proves to be a major source of prejudices and discrimination.

Over the years, the emphasis has shifted back and forth between both types of strategies, often accompanied by ideological debates on the causes (structural or otherwise) of educational inequality (Silver and Silver, 1991; Connell, 1994). In our view, controversies of this type are of little use, since both types of cause have structural roots: outside the education system in one case, and within it in the other. Moreover, both types of mechanism interact with each other. In the light of this, it would be naive to tackle the problems using one-sided strategies.

A third, somewhat hybrid approach can be added to the list: strategies for 'more equal outcomes'. These are based on the conviction that equal treatment in itself will not be sufficient to restore the balance in favour of young people from the most disadvantaged backgrounds; rather than 'non-discrimination', they imply 'positive discrimination'. Part of the purpose of education is, after all, to help *reduce* social inequalities, not to reproduce them as neutrally as possible. In this way, equal outcomes strategies are much more proactive ways of combating exclusion than the other approaches. Educational priority policies (consisting mainly of extra funding for schools with a concentration of disadvantaged students) are a standard example of this approach.

The term 'equal outcomes' sometimes meets with resistance from critics who fear that it could lead to a 'levelling down', or at least a redistribution of the resources and opportunities away from the more able students towards the weaker pupils. Similarly, 'positive discrimination' is rejected by some out of fear of other forms of arbitrariness or even discrimination against highly achieving pupils. The first answer to these objections should be that positive discrimination must indeed not be arbitrary, but must in fact serve to remove the obstacles threatening the educational development of certain target groups. Moreover, it must be remembered that education policy is not a 'zero sum game': giving more to one group does not necessarily mean taking something away from another. Positive actions in favour of socially disadvantaged groups can, in fact, lead to reductions in repeated years, special education, and so on, leading to a substantial reduction in the net added costs of these actions or, in the best case, eliminating them altogether and turning them into a gain (Levin, 1989; Nicaise, 1999). We can therefore expect that equal treatment strategies are more likely to lead to 'levelling up' than 'levelling down'. The term 'levelling' can in fact (unfortunately) not be interpreted in absolute terms, since education is unable to rectify the enormous burden of social inequality on its own.

Equal outcomes strategies in fact combine elements of both previous types of strategy. However, unlike equal opportunity strategies, they are focused on *outcomes* rather than *access*. In this sense, they can also be characterised as 'ex post facto', remedying strategies. For example, targeted pre-school programmes and second-chance schools are two types of compensatory programme. However, pre-school programmes can be regarded as a typical equal opportunity approach because they contribute to a more equal start in primary school; whereas second-chance provision aims at equalising outcomes.

Contrary to the equal treatment approach, equal outcomes strategies discriminate positively in favour of disadvantaged groups. Hence, they are also more targeted on the specific needs of minorities than equal treatment strategies.

When reviewing examples from the six countries represented in our research network, we end up with the following checklist of strategies (for a more detailed overview, see Tables 2.1 to 2.3).

Equal opportunity strategies

- (Extension of) Compulsory education: as the spontaneous demand for further education has declined, public authorities have tried to impose a minimum participation on every individual. The minimum school leaving age has been raised in nearly all EU countries over the last 15 years. In some countries, on the other hand, the law guarantees each young person a set of (extra) educational services as a counterpart of these minimum requirements (as we shall see, for example, with the Scottish Education Act and the Spanish Social Guarantee Programme).
- The enforcement of compulsory education is not without difficulties: premature dropout and truancy have become serious problems. Hence, several governments have launched special measures to register and monitor school attendance, to encourage pupils and parents to comply with the measures, and to prevent dropout. Examples are the 'Well-prepared Start' programme in the Netherlands and the 'Education for All' programme in Portugal. Of course, dropout prevention is a more or less explicit objective of many other types of intervention, such as alternative curricula or integrated services to pupils and families, which will be dealt with in other sections.
- National governments have introduced a wide range of financial assistance measures for low-income families: grants, loans, means-tested educational provision (tuition fees, transportation, meals, clothing, book grants, and so on), special measures relating to family allowances, and tax credits (as far as they are related to education and to disadvantaged groups).
- Equal opportunities are also promoted through the provision of a wide range of integrated services (psychological, social, cultural, medical, material, and so on) for disadvantaged pupils, often organised and delivered at the local level. These services aim at improving the general conditions for effective participation in education, mostly in close collaboration with parents and other actors in the neighbourhood. Some attractive examples are found in the Flemish primary schools that were sponsored for some time by the King Baudouin Foundation and the Dutch Extended School Day experiment.
- One of the most effective strategies in promoting equal opportunities has been the development of pre-school stimulation programmes for disadvantaged groups.[2] The Irish 'Early Start', and its preceding local experiments, the Rutland Street and Kilkenny projects, are

undoubtedly the most outstanding examples of this kind in Europe. However, other interesting lessons can be drawn from the 'travelling pre-schools' in isolated rural areas of Spain and from various local projects with babies and toddlers in other countries.

Equal treatment strategies

- In order to combat selectivity, socially biased failure, streaming, and creaming mechanisms, there is a great need for curricular reforms in the sense of comprehensivisation, more relevant learning contents for everyday life, and less discriminating certification strategies. The recent major reforms in Portugal (1989) and Spain (1990) went a long way in this direction.
- Note the distinction between reforms of the general curriculum (covering all students and thus improving equality) on the one hand, and the development of flexible, alternative curricula for pupils with special needs on the other. At this point we will deal only with the former type of curricular reforms, as the latter actually implies a different treatment of disadvantaged groups with a view to equalise educational outcomes. Flexible, alternative curricula will therefore be discussed in the context of 'equal outcomes strategies'.
- Besides curricular reforms, it is worth studying the (potential) impact of some alternative pedagogical approaches (active and constructivist schools, accelerated schools, communities of learning, and so on) on the educational success of disadvantaged children. Experiments in Belgium and Spain suggest that such approaches may be of particular interest for these children; paradoxically, however, their access to such schools is often problematic because of institutional and financial barriers.
- Discriminatory behaviour is often due to social prejudices resulting from the ignorance of teachers (and indeed, of the entire school staff) with regard to social exclusion. Teacher training can play an important role in helping teachers to recognise and understand the processes and victims of social exclusion, and to respond appropriately and effectively.
- Combating discrimination calls for more intensive communication between schools/teachers on the one hand, and parents/local communities on the other. Some interesting experiments have been carried out recently, ranging from home-school-community liaison in Ireland and a school-environment link project in Portugal, to parents' groups and sensitisation campaigns among pupils in Belgium.

- The last type of equal treatment strategy consists – somewhat paradoxically – of categorical measures; that is, specific services being offered to groups with special needs, with a view to their integration into mainstream education – intercultural education, special services to traveller children (well developed in Portugal, Ireland and Scotland), and inclusive education for children with special educational needs.

Equal outcomes strategies

- As disadvantaged groups need greater investments to attain a given outcome, most member states in the EU have now adopted one kind or another of educational priority policies; that is, extra funds for schools faced with a concentration of children at risk. Educational priority funding has 'territorial' and 'categorical' variants; in some countries, both variants coexist (the Netherlands, for example).
- Positive discrimination in favour of marginalised groups can take the form of differentiation; that is, extra learning support within schools or classes (remedial teaching, differentiation within the classroom, direct learning support to pupils, teacher counsellors, and so on).
- Finally, a range of alternative curricula, transition systems and second-chance schools have been developed in order to ensure maximum access to recognised (if possible, standard) qualifications for socially disadvantaged students, mostly at upper secondary level: alternating forms of vocational education combined with work experience, apprenticeship systems, modular programmes, and remedial programmes or lower level certificates for students who fail in mainstream programmes.
- The demarcation line between flexible curricula (aiming at equal outcomes) and streaming (a form of social discrimination) is sometimes a very thin one. 'Flexible curricula' should ideally lead to standard (mainstream) certificates. The integration of specific 'sidetrack' certificates into the national qualification structure is a rather second-best solution, which cannot really be regarded as an 'equal outcomes' strategy. Empirical evaluations are needed in this context, more than anywhere else.

Second criterion: educational policy levels (macro, meso, micro)

In addition to the main criterion relating to the nature of the strategies, we also wish to take explicit account of the policy level at which a measure or project is developed. We are well aware that a great many valuable initiatives are being taken on the field which have not yet been incorporated into general education policy. Thus, the distinction between the different levels is, in the first place, a means of ensuring that 'grassroots initiatives' are not forgotten, although we do not by any means claim to depict a representative sample of the latter.

It is of course quite possible that certain strategies can best be implemented at the micro level (for example, integrated service delivery), while others are more suited to the macro level (for example, statutory education).

The term 'macro level' is defined here as the highest education policy level. This may be the national level (as in Portugal, the Netherlands and Ireland), or the level of an autonomous community or region (as in Scotland, Flanders and Catalonia). The 'meso level' refers to lower level authorities, such as municipal authorities or regional centres, networks or partnerships (often also involving a variety of stakeholders), or Local Education Authorities in Scotland. Sometimes we are dealing with a collection of local projects under the auspices of the national government; the distinction from the macro level in this case lies mainly in the fact that the national regime is not generally binding (as in the case of experiments in a number of schools). Finally, the 'micro level' refers to isolated initiatives in individual schools or classes. Even where these are subsidised by a national or lower public authority, these initiatives are typically 'bottom-up'.

Synoptic tables

Tables 2.1 to 2.3 classify a number of examples of measures, programmes and projects in the six EU member states included in the study, using the double classification system outlined above.

It has to be admitted that some programmes are hard to classify unambiguously. Whereas a 'strategy' is an abstract set of well-defined, logically integrated targets and methods, a real-life 'programme' or project can have more than one rationality. It can combine elements from different strategies. When classifying national programmes by strategy, we can either isolate 'pure' elements from programmes that belong to a single strategy, or refer to the programme within the different strategies to which it belongs. The in-depth analysis of each programme will be classified under the strategy where it fits best.

The same comment applies for the distinction between policy levels. Sometimes a policy framework is created at macro level, which is implemented locally in many different ways. Depending on the context, we shall therefore discuss some initiatives at different levels.

Notes

[1] Some more holistic strategies encompassing educational measures are also studied.

[2] General pre-school provision (such as daycare centres, nurseries or infant schools) will not be analysed in our study, unless they include special services for socially excluded children.

Table 2.1: Synopsis of relevant measures, programmes and projects aimed at more equal opportunities

Type of strategy	Macro-level	Meso-level	Examples at micro-level
Compulsory education	B: 1983: school leaving age raised to 18 IRL: School leaving age raised to 15 in 1972, to 16 in 1997; School attendance officers NL: Compulsory Education Act (1969, amended 1994) NL: 'A well prepared start' (EGVS) P: 1986: school leaving age raised to 15 (if 'basic school' finished) P: Education for All Programme ES: 1990: school leaving age raised to 16 (LOGSE) Sc: 1980: Education (Scotland) Act – as amended 1981: Special Educational Needs Sc: Exclusion and non-attendance – Scottish initiative on attendance and absence Sc: Early years provision	B: Dropout prevention projects at regional level NL: Regional reporting and co-ordination function (RMC) Sc: Youth Strategies Lothian Region/Edinburgh City Council	
Financial and material assistance	B: Free education at primary and secondary levels IRL: Free education at all levels B: Study grants at secondary and tertiary level IRL: Book Grant and Rental Scheme, Back to School Clothing Allowance, Local Authority Higher Education Grants, ESF Training Grants NL: Study grants and loans at tertiary level P: Financial aid via School Social Assistance P: Free milk, subsidised school canteens, accommodation for students Sc: Free school meals/clothing allowances	IRL: Free school meals IRL: Local initiatives including financial aid (BITE, LCBEI, TAP) ES: Grants for lunches and books (Compensatory programmes)	

Table 2.1: Synopsis of relevant measures, programmes and projects aimed at more equal opportunities (continued)

Type of strategy	Macro-level	Meso-level	Examples at micro-level
Integrated services for disadvantaged pupils in mainstream education	B: 'School guidance centres' for psychological, medical and social assistance NL: Schools advisory service NL: Guidance bureaus NL: Support structure P: School social assistance P: Pedagogical support ES: Multidisciplinary Service Teams Sc: 1995 Children (Scotland) Act Sc: Extended support within Further Education	B: King Baudouin Foundation's network of projects in primary education B: Magnet schools (Antwerp) IRL: Locally integrated projects (Galway, Limerick) IRL: Cultural and financial intervention projects (BITE, LCBEI, TAP, Peter Pan) NL: Homework projects NL: Extended Schoolday P: Educational animators Sc: Local authority children's service plans Sc: Home-School-Employment Partnership (Paisley)	IRL: Jobstown Education and Training Strategy (JETS) P: Local school transport initiatives Sc: Pilton Early Intervention Programme
Early intervention	B: Extended care (see equal outcomes strategies) IRL: Early Start Programme Sc: Early Intervention Programmes (see equal outcomes strategies)	ES: Maternity Centres ES: *Casas de los niños* ES: Travelling pre-school	B: Poverty projects for toddlers (Kind & Gezin) IRL: Rutland Street Project, Kilkenny Project NL: *De Koffiepot* Sc: Pilton Early Intervention Programme

Table 2.2: Synopsis of relevant measures, programmes and projects aimed at more equal treatment

Type of strategy	Macro-level	Meso-level	Examples at micro-level
Curricular reform and certification strategies	B: Renewed Primary Education (1980s) B: Renewed Secondary Education (1970s)/Unified structure (1990s) B: Renewed Vocational Education IRL: Junior Certificate IRL: Foundation Levels IRL: Leaving Certificate Vocational Programme NL: Basic Education NL: 'Programmes' in secondary education NL: National Qualification Structure P: Framework law on educational system ES: Comprehensive stage in secondary education (Educational Reform Act – LOGSE) Sc: Standard Grade Sc: 5-14 curriculum Sc: Higher Still	B: Middle schools	IRL: Jobstown Education and Training Strategy (JETS)
Pedagogical innovations		B: Experience-based Nursery Education	B: De Buurt (Gent) ES: Communities of learning
Teacher training			

Table 2.2: Synopsis of relevant measures, programmes and projects aimed at more equal treatment (continued)

Type of strategy	Macro-level	Meso-level	Examples at micro-level
Parent-school-community relationships	IRL: Home-School-Community Liaison Scheme IRL: Visiting Teacher Service for Traveller children	See 'integrated services' (often with active participation of parents) B: Tapori campaign Limburg B: School Community Action P: School-Environment Link Project Sc: Partnership in Education Project (Strathclyde) Sc: Home-School-Employment Partnership (Paisley)	B: Renovation Project Kortrijk IRL: Clondalkin Area Parents in Education (CAPE) Sc: Home-School–Parent Project (North Ayrshire PPA)
Categorical measures	B: Integrated education for disabled pupils B: Intercultural education IRL: Visiting teacher service for traveller children; pre-schools for traveller children; special schools/classes and Junior Training Centres for traveller children NL: Going to School Together Again (WSNS) for disabled pupils NL: NT2 (Dutch as 2nd language) for immigrants P: Entreculturas P: Travelling nursery school ES: Support teachers / therapeutic pedagogy teachers Sc: Ensuring education for Travellers' children in Scotland	B: Non-discrimination charters P: Gipsy mediators (Go to School Project); Nómada Project P: Isolated Schools Project Sc: Scottish Travellers' Education Project	B: Pilot project for gypsy children (sponsored by King Baudouin Foundation) Sc: Positive Action Project for Traveller Children (Armadale Academy)

Table 2.3: Synopsis of relevant measures, programmes and projects aimed at more equal outcomes

Type of strategy	Macro-level	Meso-level	Examples at micro-level
Educational priority in school funding	B: Educational Priority Policy (EPP) B: Extended Care (EC) IRL: Assistance to Disadvantaged Schools IRL: Breaking the cycle NL: Educational Priority Policy (weighting rule) Sc: Early Intervention Programme	B: Educational Priority Areas (EPA) Limburg IRL: Demonstration Programme on Educational Disadvantage NL: Educational Priority Policy (regions) P: Educational Priority Areas (TEIP) Sc: Educational components of Priority Partnership Programmes/Regeneration Programmes	NL: Educational Priority Policy (projects)
Differentiation within schools/classes	NL: Pupil counselling IRL: Remedial teachers ES: Curriculum Diversification Programme IRL: Teacher counsellors Sc: Extended support in Further Education (cf integrated services) Sc: Learning Support/educational psychologist support	B: Learning Support Project Sc: SuccessMaker Project (North Ayrshire PPA) Sc: East Dunbartonshire Council Network Support	B: Differentiation projects within the classroom IRL: Basin Street Project
Alternative curricula and second chance provision for at-risk groups	B: Part-time vocational education (PTVE) IRL: Junior Certificate Schools Programme IRL: Leaving Certificate Applied Programme IRL: Youth Reach NL: KMBO (short secondary vocational education) P: Alternative Curricula P: Apprenticeship ES: Social Guarantee Programme ES: Apprenticeship (abolished); Workshop Schools	IRL: Youth Encounter Projects NL: Free Port Rotterdam NL: Practical schools NL: Remedial projects NL: Educational-work projects	

Part Two:
Equal opportunity strategies

THREE

Learning duties and learning rights

Mia Douterlungne and Ides Nicaise (HIVA)

Traditionally, the most important way of promoting equal opportunities in education has been (the extension of) compulsory education: public authorities try to impose minimum participation on every individual as a way of ensuring the socialisation of young people and avoiding dependency in adulthood. While this tendency still persists today (there are obvious signs of ongoing pressure on jobless school leavers) the emphasis appears to be shifting in recent debates from learning duties (compulsory education) to 'learning rights'. In this chapter, we describe and discuss the issues on this subject.

Trends in compulsory education

The duration of compulsory education in the European Union varies from 8 years (Italy), 9 years (Denmark, Greece, Ireland, Austria, Portugal, Finland, Sweden and Norway), 10 years (Spain, France), 11 years (Luxembourg, England, Wales and Scotland) to more than 11 years if years of part-time schooling is taken into account (Belgium, Germany, the Netherlands and Northern Ireland). Compulsory education most frequently begins at the age of six but it has recently been lowered to the age of four in Luxembourg, where attendance in the last year of pre-school education is compulsory, and in Northern Ireland. In Denmark, on the other hand, it begins at age seven.

Over the decade 1984-94, almost half of the countries extended compulsory schooling by one, two or three years. They did this either by raising the school leaving age – which for full-time education is now usually 15 or 16 years – or by lowering the starting age, generally set at 5 or 6 years. In general, such extensions took place within a comprehensive curriculum.

A political debate is still going on in some countries concerning the school starting and leaving age.

In Belgium, for example, some policy makers have recently advocated

Figure 3.1: Length of compulsory education in the European Union

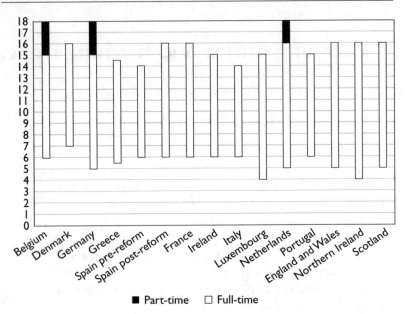

■ Part-time   □ Full-time

Source: European Unit of Eurydice

lowering the compulsory school leaving age from 18 to 16. They have even questioned the effectiveness of part-time compulsory education (16-18 years); many young people opting for part-time education are said to be demotivated and tired of school. Opponents of lowering the school leaving age draw strength from the fact that there is no alternative for those youngsters on the labour market, that they need an adequate qualification, and that policy has to provide better education for these young people, rather than turning them out on to the street. The idea of lowering the starting age from six to five years was another view put forward by politicians who are particularly concerned with social inequality. They stressed the importance and effectiveness of pre-school programmes, especially for disadvantaged children. This debate is still ongoing.

In Scotland, the debate currently focuses on the latter approach. Local authorities are under no obligation to provide early years services for all children, although, since 1996, they must provide services for children in need. In recent years, all parents of 'pre-school' children (that is, 3½- to 4½-year-olds) received a 'nursery voucher', but this was replaced in Autumn 1998 with a guaranteed pre-school place (to be offered by private organisations or local authorities) for all children. In fact, a constant trend of extending the duration of compulsory schooling has become apparent, from which it may be concluded that keeping children at school for a maximum number of years is considered a good thing in itself. A wide variety of motivations underlie this trend.

Aims of compulsory education

How can a measure at macro level like (the extension of) compulsory education be justified? The following arguments can be derived from an OECD report (OECD, 1983, p 13 ff):

- A 'merit good' argument: "With a compulsory school system, new knowledge can reach the young directly; without it, it can only reach them indirectly and informally through the existing adult population, the majority of whom by necessity are committed to life-styles based upon the old knowledge." It is evidently assumed that (some) parents underestimate their children's educational needs for their future lives. Although this argument sounds slightly paternalistic, it can be assumed that it applies in isolated backward regions or in developing countries.
- Socialisation of young people: "Without the skills of literacy made widespread by the compulsory schools, the effectiveness of the mass media as instruments of change would also be greatly diminished." Or further: "The schools are also a vital force in ... maintaining social stability ...." In other words – and this has undoubtedly been the argument in Belgium – the community wishes to avoid the burden of inadequately educated citizens, who are likely to become permanently dependent and to function poorly (or even antisocially) in an ever more complex world.
- An implicit but rather unexpected argument in the OECD report is that compulsory schooling for young people also imposes an obligation on schools to provide education. Compulsory schooling is used as a means to prevent certain young people being excluded from schools prematurely: "In particular, attempts are made to assist children who, because of their race, sex, background or environment, have special difficulty in becoming integrated into schools and society and sharing on equal terms its opportunities."

A study by Eurydice tried to compare the aims of compulsory education in the member states of the EU (Eurydice, 1994b). The aims were grouped into six core themes, inspired by the OECD (1983) categories, but adjusted to the actual responses of the European countries. They were: equal social opportunities for all citizens without distinction; basic education for the population; promoting both stability and social change; preparing children for adult life; acquiring the motivation to continue learning and to prepare for a changing world; and the wellbeing and personal development of the individual.

From the point of view of this study, the first aim mentioned above needs more clarification. Most European Union countries aim to achieve genuine equality of opportunities, to avoid exclusion on social, economic, physical, psychological or any other grounds, and to practise positive discrimination wherever it is considered necessary. The OECD states that, although the declared objective of education systems apparently continues to be the same as it has always been, there has been a qualitative change which is reflected more in initiatives designed to compensate for inequalities than in declarations of principle. Among the stated aims of some countries, we find some which may be considered to espouse the spirit of equal opportunities: free access to education and equality within the education system in Belgium and Greece; protection of the right to education and democratisation of the system in Spain; the concept of education as a public service in France; the right of all citizens to education and the duty of the government not to discriminate in Italy; the right to education and priority for compensating for individual and regional inequalities in Portugal; and free schooling to guarantee the right to education in Scotland.

The policies adopted in Belgium, Spain, Luxembourg and Portugal – that is, the extension of compulsory education in terms of both pupil numbers and duration – are very much the result of an aspiration to equality. The Nordic countries, which have a long tradition of organising their education systems in a single all-embracing structure involving the whole of compulsory education, feature as pioneers in this respect.

Nevertheless, it cannot be denied that the trend to extend the duration of compulsory education is also strongly influenced by economic developments and the collapse of the youth labour market.

Policies relating to school attendance: enforcement of the Act

Not surprisingly, several countries are battling against school truancy and early dropout, in the sense that youngsters are leaving school before the end of compulsory education. The problem is particularly acute among disadvantaged pupils. The link between absenteeism from school and educational disadvantage is well established and proved in several studies (Thorpe and Malcolm, 1994; Douterlungne, 1994). National governments are trying to achieve an effective registration, reporting, and compulsory education enforcement system.

In the Netherlands, the 1969 Compulsory Education Act was not well suited to the developments of the 1980s and 1990s. Truancy and dropout among children of compulsory school age obstinately persists. The former Compulsory Education Act provided too few options for the effective enforcement of the Act. The call for an appropriate compulsory education policy thus became louder. Further to the policy memorandum on truancy in secondary education (Ministry of Education, 1986), a working group was set up to establish an inventory of the difficulties encountered in implementing the Act. As a solution, the working group pointed out the need for better cooperation between local councils, education authorities and support services, and among local councils themselves. In subsequent years, the fight against truancy and dropout has increasingly moved to the forefront of education policy. The need for better enforcement – in particular, with stronger intervention by the authorities – increased. Finally, this resulted in an amendment to the Compulsory Education Act in 1994. The amendments do not relate so much to the nature and extent of compulsory education itself, but mainly to the enforcement of the Act. Some important points in this new Act are (Van Rossum and Van Tilborg, 1996b):

- more supervision of schools and children of compulsory school age;
- greater responsibility for those concerned (schools, parents, children);
- the young people themselves can be punished (including legal penalties);
- increased penalties for parents who fail to comply with the law;
- the role of the Education Inspectorate (supervisory government body) has been strengthened;
- the position of compulsory education officers has been strengthened within the municipal administration, including making the local council (mayor and councillors) directly accountable; for example, the local council is required to draw up a policy plan each year and to issue an annual report.

The Regional Reporting and Coordination Function (RCF) is responsible for identifying those who leave before the end of the compulsory stage, particularly those without a starting qualification for the labour market. The objectives of the 39 RCFs are to:

- ensure an effective registration of early or unqualified leavers, implying a harmonisation of procedures and instruments;
- take stock of existing programmes to tackle early leaving;
- act as an information point on, and clearing house for, such programmes;
- coordinate activities of relevant actors;
- pool staff and resources in combating unqualified leaving.

In Belgium (Flanders), genuine school dropout is estimated at 2-3%. A survey of more than 4,000 young people aged between 11 and 18 reveals that the level of truancy in 1996 had decreased compared with 1994. Yet the truancy rate among 17- to 18-year-olds was still 7.5%. Truancy is more common among boys than girls and in vocational rather than general education (Youth and Health Survey, 1996). Another survey found that study results and falling behind with studies were strongly correlated with frequent changes of school (Department of Education, 1998). During a conference about the evaluation of the extension of compulsory education (1995), the Minister of Education announced better centralised registration of school attendance. Nevertheless, he claims that the school is responsible for each pupil and it is the school that bears responsibility for ensuring that children attend. In order to resolve the causes of school dropout, he pointed to the necessity of networking with social welfare organisations. In order to achieve this, he promised to cooperate with the Ministry of Social Welfare (Stichting Coens, 1995).

At the regional level, a pilot project has been running in Brussels since 1992 to prevent early dropout (in the sense that early dropout is a breach of the law on compulsory education) and this project is now being replicated in five other regions. It is based on:

- partnerships with parents in order to strengthen their involvement with the day-to-day functioning of the school, to provide them with educational support and to gain a better understanding of the background and problems of students;
- collaboration with social services and informal networks, in order to bridge gaps with hard-to-reach groups;
- individual guidance for young people, aimed at helping them

overcome learning problems and guiding them adequately in their decisions regarding choice of study.

In Ireland, school attendance is enforced by School Attendance Officers whose role is to identify problem attenders by visiting schools regularly and by constantly monitoring attendance records (Department of Education, 1994).

In Scotland, schools have a responsibility to ensure the attendance of enrolled children, which involves keeping attendance records for each morning and afternoon session, and detailing all authorised and unauthorised absence of pupils. Education authorities have the power to enforce the statutory requirements on school attendance by issuing attendance orders, by referring children whose attendance is unsatisfactory to the reporter to the Children's Panel, or by reporting parents of children who do not attend to the Procurator Fiscal, with a view to prosecution.

Statistics about non-attendance at school usually make no distinction between truancy and temporary exclusion (the latter still occurring rather frequently in Scotland). Rates of non-attendance appear to be higher in socially disadvantaged areas. There is a significant positive correlation between the percentage of children entitled to free school meals (an indication of disadvantage) and the rates of absenteeism and temporary exclusion (Scottish Office, 1996).

Within the education system, considerable attention has been paid to non-attendance. Policy responses have again required schools to tighten up their recording and reporting systems. Schools' non-attendance records are now published in 'league tables', which have the overt aim of encouraging 'market forces'; that is, parents can use the information to help them decide where to send their children, which in turn encourages schools to maintain a low non-attendance rate.

The Scottish Office has increasingly emphasised the need for inter-agency cooperation. This is demonstrated in policy documents issued both before and after the 1995 Children (Scotland) Act. This Act continues the Scottish system of children's hearings. Non-attendance at school is among the grounds for referral to the system, and educational concerns can arise during the proceedings. Non-attendance at school is a moderately frequent reason for referral to the children's hearing system; it accounted for 8.8% of referrals in 1995. According to Hallett and Murray (1998), this procedure does not work well; truancy cases are often referred at a stage when patterns of non-attendance are entrenched and there are disputes between social work departments and the education service about where responsibility for the problem lies. Further, the resources are often not available to address non-attendance properly.

In Spain, absenteeism from school was rather frequent among the 5-9 and 12-14 age groups. Programmes were launched in the 1980s in a great number of towns, focusing on school attendance. They were promoted by local organisations, with schools, social services and the local police cooperating to detect truancy. Nowadays the problem hardly exists; programmes for the prevention of absenteeism are rare and limited to non-residents and social groups at risk.

Portugal experienced a process of mass education at a relatively late stage in the European context, at least at the formal level. In 1964, the duration of compulsory education was increased to six years, and it was only changed to nine years in 1986. However, compulsory education revealed cumulatively high rates of non-completion due to the high level of school dropout. In 1991, the Education for All Programme (PEPT) was set up. Its chief objective is to ensure equality of treatment for minority groups, whether they are ethnic groups or those who are handicapped in a way that makes the learning process more difficult. The programme is primarily concerned with the achievement of universal access to compulsory education and consists of six measures:

- statistical follow-up of school attendance and school dropout;
- social mobilisation for schooling;
- social initiatives to promote schooling;
- monitoring of the internal factors for success at school;
- monitoring of the external factors for success at school;
- resource centres for schooling.

The 'Education for All' project focuses primarily on the monitoring of the situation and of initiatives and legislative proposals. However, in the context of the 'social initiatives to promote schooling', it also supports intervention projects.

The mixed effects of compulsory schooling laws

Effects on educational participation

In order to ensure genuinely equal opportunities, the first condition that must be achieved is a state of full participation for the entire population, at least during the compulsory phase. According to the

Table 3.1: Educational participation among 18-year-olds, 1995 (%)

	In education or training and non-active	In education or training and active	Not in education or training and active	Not in education or training and non-active
EU	59	17	19	5
Belgium	88	3	7	2
Denmark	30	60	8	2
Germany	48	39	10	3
Greece	68	3	22	7
Spain	66	6	23	5
France	84	7	7	2
Ireland	64	7	26	3
Italy	70	2	21	7
Luxembourg	72	6	19	3
The Netherlands	41	42	12	5
Austria	41	29	29	1
Portugal	60	5	28	7
Finland	54	29	15	2
Sweden	70	1	25	4
United Kingdom	27	29	38	6

Source: Eurostat, Labour Force Survey

Eurydice report, this objective has already been achieved in all countries of the European Union.

In fact, throughout the EU, young people are gradually spending more time in education, taking longer to cross from school to work, and waiting longer before starting families. A study by Eurostat (Eurostat, 1997b) states that in 1995, 59% of all 18-year-olds were exclusively in education or training. The highest figure was recorded in Belgium (88%), the lowest in the UK (27%).

Research in Belgium on the effects of the extension of compulsory education on participation rates showed that this measure has had the greatest impact on youngsters from the lowest social classes. The extension of the compulsory education period in Belgium was not particularly revolutionary in overall terms, since the participation rate of 16-year-olds was already 84% when the new law was introduced, and was rising spontaneously year by year. For the lowest social classes and for the poor in particular, however, the 1983 intervention had important consequences: prior to this time (in 1981), 30% of 16-year-olds whose father had no school qualification had already left school (Van de Velde et al, 1996a). At a stroke, the raising of the school leaving age made this impossible.

However, despite the seemingly positive effects of compulsory education laws in terms of participation rates, the issue remains highly controversial. Critics have pointed at poor economic returns, perverse distribution effects and problems with demotivation among pupils.

The differential rate of return on education

A first series of criticisms concerning the extension of compulsory education has been put forward by economists.

Harmon and Walker (1993) compared the marginal rate of return on education (in terms of income) for young people aged 16 before and after the raising of the school leaving age in the UK in the mid-1970s. The rate of return for girls remained unchanged; for boys, however, the return on the extra year after the raising of the school leaving age was significantly lower and was actually totally cancelled out by the loss of labour market experience which accompanied it.

The key question from our perspective is whether the extension of compulsory schooling is actually a profitable investment for the most deprived young people, rather than for the average young person. In the Belgian case, there are a number of indicators that do not lead to a particularly favourable answer. First and foremost, we may wonder whether the government was aware that it was imposing severe additional costs on the young people concerned and their families when raising the school leaving age in 1983. Even after the deduction of subsidies (child benefit, tax-deductible items, student grants), a year's full-time study in higher education cost an average of Euros 6,370 in 1985-86. While most of this is an indirect cost (forgone earnings), it undoubtedly impacts very strongly on the families concerned. If we then add the fact that nowhere is the risk of school failure higher than in this group, plus our finding that even a higher secondary education qualification has a zero return for people from the poorest families,[1] there is a risk that the scales will quickly be tipped in the wrong direction (Nicaise, 1999).

Leapfrogging between social groups

Another perverse social effect was brought to light by Lang and Kropp (1986) on the basis of time series analyses for the US. They observed that increases in the compulsory schooling period also led to a leap in the educational participation of better-off youngsters beyond the school leaving age, so that the envisaged aim of levelling out the distribution of education was not achieved. In this sense, they contradicted the prediction by Blaug et al (1982) that the raising of the school leaving age in Britain (in 1972) would equalise earnings within age cohorts in the long run. The findings of Lang and Kropp are in line with the 'signalling' theory, which states that individuals invest in education in order to strengthen their relative position on the jobs market, rather than because of the content of the education itself. This immediately places a question mark alongside the third motive for raising the school leaving age cited above (levelling out of opportunities).

Educational bottlenecks

Social scientists (Van de Velde et al, 1996a; Vettenburg, 1995; Svendsen, 1996) have pointed to the lack of motivation among pupils and the problem of school failure, and placed the blame on the school environment and its methods, which are too cognitive; they fail to make the link between the school world and the interests of youngsters, especially from the lower classes (see Chapter 8).

The difficulty in providing extended education under optimum conditions for pupils who are often school-fatigued has renewed the debate on patterns of compulsory schooling, which can be very diverse and must accommodate the entire population, according to specific age groups, in a way that is both equitable and appropriate to a wide variety of circumstances and abilities. In fact, there is general consensus that the extension of compulsory education cannot be effective on its own. The Eurydice report (1997) mentions – somewhat optimistically – that in terms of quantitative participation, the goal has nearly been achieved by all EU countries, but it admits that more attention is needed for the quality of education: "Efforts must now be focused on achieving quality education for all."

The shift from quantity to quality

The Eurydice Report (1997) mentions that, with only a few exceptions, compulsory education has not undergone radical structural changes anywhere.

> However, secondary education is more subject to reorganisation than primary education, which is more stable and satisfactory.... Secondary education has evolved from being a level designed for a social elite, leading subsequently to higher education, to being a system of general

education for the entire population. This important fact has necessitated a substantial change in perspective, with a move away from a high level academic approach towards a totally different one to provide a satisfactory general education for all pupils. This has entailed trying out various formulae to accommodate all pupils without lowering the standards of the most capable; to maintain a satisfactory link between primary and lower secondary education on the one hand, and lower secondary and post-compulsory education on the other; and to include the latest scientific and social advances in the curriculum at this level, without losing sight of its vocation of providing education for all. (Eurydice, 1997, p 62)

Related curricular reforms

Since curricular reforms will be discussed in greater depth in Chapters 7 and 14, we will confine ourselves at this stage to a very brief overview of some measures that were directly related to the extension of compulsory schooling.

The most common structure for compulsory education – towards which many countries have evolved – is a division into two main stages: primary and lower secondary education. However, one group of countries has opted for a single curriculum of compulsory education, followed by an upper secondary level.

Two other contrasting phenomena have also occurred: the consolidation of a common curriculum in some countries and a partial diversification of the common core syllabus in others. In general, depending on the point of departure, a trend can be observed towards a balance between a common core curriculum and diversification, as well as the replacement of short, rigid time divisions (such as those of school years) by broader and more flexible divisions (cycles or stages).

In Scotland, compulsory schooling takes place within comprehensive schools, which are attended by children of all abilities.

In Belgium, the extension of compulsory education was accompanied by other measures designed to help prevent pupils repeating years and to increase the quality of education, particularly for the most school-fatigued pupils. The main examples of such measures are the renewal of vocational education and – more importantly – the organisation of part-time education. Renewed vocational education contains elements such as thematic and project learning, integration of theory and practice, the 'workshop class', and so on, with the main aim of increasing the involvement of pupils (see Chapters 7 and 14).

In Ireland, the 1990s have been a period of rapid curricular reform, with the development of new second-level programmes and assessment procedures to cater for groups that were previously marginalised within the education system. The main objective has been to tackle biases within the pre-existing system.

Related changes in assessment practices within compulsory education

Since the extension of universal compulsory education, failure at school – which initially was an educational phenomenon without any real social consequence – is increasingly perceived as a major social problem. "More than ever, failure at school begets social failure, which means a life of uncertainty, marginalisation and dependence on the structures of social assistance" (Bernard Charlot, 1990). In passing their 1989 resolution on combating school failure, the education ministers of the European Community recognised the existence of a major common problem.

A European study (Gordon, 1990) shows that, between 1986 and 1987, out of just over five million young people aged 15-16, approximately 550,000 did not obtain any certificate at the end of their compulsory education, or did not complete their education normally. This is equivalent to 10-12% of pupils being excluded from the education system at the end of compulsory education. It appears, therefore, that each year, between 70,000 and 100,000 young people leave education with no vocational qualification whatsoever.

Most countries support a single qualification at the end of compulsory education. Many countries have reformed their systems of examination, assessment, and certification at the end of compulsory education, with the aim of removing any possible discrimination which can, at such an early stage, have a dramatic influence on young people's academic and professional future. On the other hand, in countries where compulsory secondary education is diversified, the qualifications awarded at the end of this period of schooling differ according to the subjects studied and, consequently, provide access to different branches of post-compulsory education.

Another trend is the evaluative cultivation of success: the school's task is not to construct hierarchies of excellence, but to stimulate the greatest number of pupils to learn as much as possible at their own pace.

Figure 3.2: The proportion of children leaving secondary education with no qualifications

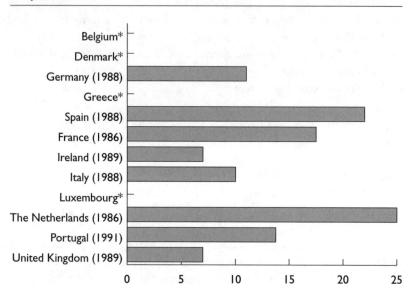

*no data available

Summative assessment should therefore be based on reference criteria; that is, it should assess the pupil in relation to the skills to be mastered.

In Belgium (Flanders), one of the main conclusions to be reached 10 years after the extension of compulsory education (Stichting Coens, 1995) was the need for a 'pedagogy of success' for youngsters. The Minister of Education decided to launch research and an experiment on course modelling in vocational education.

The idea of integrated service-provision is another way of raising the chances of success and increasing pupils' sense of wellbeing. Examples include homework classes, the development of social services, the provision of sociocultural activities, and so on. See Chapter 5 for a more detailed discussion.

The shift from duty to right

As discussed in the previous subsection, the issue of compulsion inevitably raises the question of educational rights. If society imposes duties on young people, what does it offer in return? Is there something akin to a 'right to learn', beyond the mere 'access' to education? What this refers to is more than the abolition of physical or financial thresholds: the question is whether there can be some form of commitment on the part of society to offer adequate services and to ensure *effective* education.

Duties of public authorities, schools and parents

As previously stated, when talking about compulsory education, the other side of the coin is an entitlement to education on the part of children. Some categories of children were excluded from education in the past – for instance, disabled children in Greece, or travellers' children in Ireland. In Scotland too, disabled children were often denied access to schools prior to 1975.

The question of whether schools can refuse to enrol candidates is an important issue from the perspective of social exclusion. In Belgium, many schools use subtle forms of obstruction which hinder the access of pupils with learning or behavioural difficulties. This results in major problems of segregation or even complete exclusion from the education system. Bollens et al (1998) found that the proportion of pupils with learning difficulties[2] ranged from 0% in some secondary schools to 88% in others (not including special education). A survey in Leuven revealed that out of a secondary school population of 14,500 students, 83 were excluded from any school, while 22 were permanently absent (which suggests that schools tacitly accepted their dropout) (Hedebouw, 1997).

While no measures have so far been taken to combat these forms of segregation and exclusion, ethnic discrimination in schools has been restricted through public intervention. Since 1995, 'non–discrimination charters' have been concluded between schools at local level. Whereas the conclusion of charters itself is imposed by law, decisions regarding minimum and maximum quotas of children from ethnic minorities are left to the negotiating partners. No formal evaluation of this measure has as yet been carried out, although it can be expected to some extent to have levelled out the differences in the ethnic composition of schools. One perverse effect is that, in a limited number of cases, young people from ethnic minorities have been refused in all schools within their own district, as all schools appeared to interpret their commitments in a minimalist way.

The 1980 Scottish Education Act stipulates that each of the 32 local authorities has a duty to ensure that adequate and efficient school education is provided for its area, beginning with compulsory education for children of school age (5-16 years). Parents or guardians are legally responsible for ensuring that their children of compulsory school age receive "adequate and efficient education", but they need not do so by sending them to state schools. Children themselves still have no direct right to education. Yet, the 1981 Act amending the 1980 Act strengthens the principle that local authorities have a duty to provide "adequate and efficient" education for *all* children in their area.

On the other hand, school exclusion is also regulated by law: a pupil may be excluded from school in cases where the authority is of the opinion that the parent of the pupil is refusing or failing to comply, or to allow the pupil to comply, with the rules and regulations or the disciplinary requirements of the school, or the authority considers that, under all circumstances, to allow the pupil to continue his attendance at the school would probably be seriously detrimental to order and discipline at the school or to the educational wellbeing of the pupils there. Procedures require the school/authority to notify the parents of the decision to exclude on the day of exclusion. Parents have the right to appeal (as does the child, at age 16). Information on the exclusion must be recorded in the pupil's progress record.

Munn et al (1997) found considerable disparities between schools regarding their levels of exclusion. It appeared that, even when the student intake was fairly similar, schools took different approaches to exclusion. The Scottish Office has now issued new guidance seeking to ensure more equal treatment across schools and to improve the recording and reporting of exclusions. The Scottish Office has also set up a supportive network for schools.

The right to extra support for pupils with special needs

Rather than using medical categories of disability, as was previously the case, the 1981 Act in Scotland established a new category of 'special educational needs'. This was a deliberate attempt to move away from medical categorisation and towards a recognition of the interaction between the individual child and the school in creating 'special educational needs'.

'Special Educational Needs' (SEN) has a particular definition under the 1980 Education (Scotland) Act as amended. Children have SEN if they have "a learning difficulty which calls for particular provision to be made for them" (Section 1(5)(d)). A learning difficulty is said to be present if children:

- have significantly greater difficulty in learning than the majority of those their age; or
- suffer from a disability which either prevents or hinders them from

making use of educational facilities of a kind generally provided for those of their age in schools managed by their education authority; or

- who are under the age of five years are or would be likely, when over that age, to have a learning difficulty as defined above, if provision for special educational needs were not made for them.

Education authorities must identify those children who have "pronounced, specific or complex special educational needs which require continuing review", and must open and keep a Record of SEN for any such child who is found to have such needs, after assessment. Details are laid down in the legislation in relation to parents' requests, appeals, assessments, and so on.

Despite the rhetorical shift from individualising medical categories to 'special educational needs', SEN provision continues to identify the 'problem' with the individual child (see, for example, Armstrong et al, 1993; Fulcher 1989). In the late 1980s, the recording process often seems to have been used as a means for children to gain access to segregated schooling, rather than for support in mainstream schools (Thomson et al, 1990). The inclusion movement has since gathered force and Thomson et al (1995) found that children starting out in mainstream schools now tend to remain in them after recording.

Legally, education authorities have a duty to meet the special educational needs of children, even if the children do not have Records. The Warnock Report (Department of Education and Sciences, 1978), which instigated the changes in special education, suggested that one in five children would have special educational needs at some time during their schooling; yet only a small percentage of the total school population have Records in Scotland (1.4% in October 1993 [Scottish Office, 1995]). Only 68.3% of children in special schools had a Record (Scottish Office, 1995b). Thomson et al's (1995) national sample of Scottish Records revealed considerable disparity between local authorities regarding numbers recorded, with the largest differences appearing for young people with 'emotional and behavioural difficulties'.

These differences can be important. Children with Records have a stronger guarantee that services will be provided. Commentators in England and Wales have been particularly concerned about children with SEN who are not recorded. With devolved school management, grant-maintained ('opted-out') schools, and increased competition between schools, children without Statements (the Scottish equivalent of Records) risk being expensive and hence unpopular students for schools. In Scotland, greater risks may be presented by hard–up, smaller local authorities after local government reform and budget cuts. In either case, unless one has a legal right to services through having a Record, some students' special educational needs may not be met through supportive services. Reference has been made to the comparative educational qualifications of children with and without Records. There is little doubt that, as a group, children from special schools/departments leave school with fewer qualifications than the average pupil. Whether this fact represents the capabilities of children with Records, or the suitability of their schooling, is as yet impossible to determine.

The search for guaranteeing a minimum qualification

In some countries, the discussion on the duration of compulsory education does not concentrate on the age of students but rather on the conditions for school leaving in terms of attainment. These can be described as indirect ways of extending compulsory education. Examples in our study are Portugal, Spain, Scotland and the Netherlands

In Portugal, children are obliged to go to school between the ages of 6 and 15, but there is still serious debate about the outcome of that compulsory schooling: are the youngsters ready to enter working life? In accordance with the principles defined for the vocational training policy, all those who leave school without a vocational qualification – that is, those who have not attended technical secondary education, nor a vocational school, nor gone through the apprenticeship system – should have access to one year of vocational training, leading to a qualification, before entering working life.

In Spain, the 'social guarantee programmes' have a triple objective: they aim to guarantee those affected an elementary level of specific professional training, allowing them to gain access to working life. They can also promote educational reintegration by offering entrance exams for certain certificates. Finally, they aim to develop and strengthen the personal maturity of pupils.

In Scotland, the 'Skillseekers' programme is a national training initiative designed to encourage young people aged 16-18 to gain qualifications in the workplace. Each 'skillseeker' receives a training credit which they can use to purchase their own training. Training is provided by an employer or training provider. Employers are given financial assistance towards the costs associated with training a 'skillseeker' and the training provided must lead to a nationally recognised vocational qualification. Although the Skillseekers programme is constantly monitored, a critical evaluation has yet to be conducted. However, the point has been made that those people entering Skillseekers with Special Training Needs status are often trained within the college or workshop rather than in an employer-based environment. Such isolation within the workshop or college training environment, it has been suggested, does little to promote an individual's employability (Riddell et al, 1997).

In Belgium, following the EU employment guidelines approved at the 'Luxembourg Summit' in November 1997, the government launched a 'training guarantee plan' for young jobless people. This plan states that any young person without an educational qualification who has not managed to find work after six months of unemployment will be offered additional work-oriented training, which they will be obliged to accept on penalty of sanctions in the form of a cut in unemployment benefit. However, this plan has already met with fierce criticism, from the research community among others, using much the same arguments as those regarding compulsory schooling itself. Mandatory training programmes appear to be ineffective, stigmatise the target group, and enhance the risks of social exclusion through sanctions (Nicaise, 1998).

In the Netherlands, a 'quality offensive' has been going on for some time, with ideas on both compulsory and adult education focusing sharply on the achievement of commercial-style 'returns'. A key objective of recent policy proposals and efforts relating to vocational education is to guarantee a basic qualification for every student. The achievement of a 'starting qualification' is the aim, not only for those of compulsory schooling age, but also for those who leave school early, are unemployed, or who run the risk of being excluded from the labour market because of an inadequate level of training. This objective is stated explicitly in the policy document, *A well-prepared start*, and in the Education and Vocational Training Act (WEB) which came into force on 1 January 1996. Two lines of approach are used: the development of a national vocational and adult qualification structure, and the introduction of regional training centres, which offer a range of different courses and learning paths. Scientists support the policy makers' commitment to a basic qualification for everyone. Several observers, however, have questioned the feasibility of such an aim and even the need for it. They have advocated 'more realistic' approaches through the creation of curricula giving access to qualifications below the general standard for particular groups, and/or the development of more flexible transition paths between school and work. Educational experts strongly emphasise the search for different ways (in-school and out-of-school) of achieving this qualification. The importance of individual route counselling –

made-to-measure education – is emphasised here (Hövels et al, 1994; Tesser and Veenman, 1997).

Conclusion

As a macro-measure, compulsory education is defended from several perspectives: equal social opportunities for all citizens without distinction; basic education for the population; promoting both stability and social change; preparing children for adult life; acquiring the motivation to continue learning and to prepare for a changing world; and ensuring the wellbeing and personal development of the individual.

Over the last decade, almost half the countries of the European Union have extended compulsory schooling by one, two, or three years. In fact, there is a continuing trend to prolong the duration of compulsory schooling. In some countries, political debate is still raging over the school leaving age and even further measures with respect to unqualified school leavers are being considered. It cannot be denied that this trend is strongly influenced by economic development and the collapse of the youth labour market. On the other hand, the idea of lowering the school starting age – from six to five in Belgium, for instance – was another approach advocated by politicians who were worried about social inequality. Despite the tendency to lengthen the duration of schooling and the observed effects on educational participation, the issue of the duration of compulsory schooling remains highly controversial.

Several countries are struggling with school truancy and early dropout. Rather than tackling these problems through educational reforms, national governments tend to rely on measures relating to registration, reporting and compulsory education enforcement systems. It is apparent that increasing the control of school attendance can lead to different strategies; one involving enforcement and penalties, and one entailing more care for the group in the sense of partnerships with parents, collaboration with the social services and informal networks, individual guidance for young people, and so on.

None of these measures has challenged the value of extended compulsory schooling as such. Nevertheless, criticisms are formulated from different scientific angles. Economists point to the differential rate of return on education; young people from disadvantaged families have to give up proportionately more in order to take part in education, and derive less from it later in terms of their position on the labour market. Social scientists point to the 'leapfrogging' phenomenon among young people from different social backgrounds, while educationalists draw attention to the motivation and school fatigue problems affecting groups of young people who are unable to find their way in the education system. No statements are made regarding the optimum length of compulsory schooling – all conclusions, however, lead to the observation that the extension of compulsory education cannot be an isolated measure. Efforts must be focused on achieving quality education for all.

The debate acquires a new dimension if we start with the question of whether compulsory schooling should be seen more as a right than as a duty for every child. The emphasis then has to lie more on made-to-measure education, in which every child, every individual, is equipped to make his way in society.

A good example of a policy which strengthens the right to compulsory education is the Education Act in Scotland. Under this Act, local authorities have a duty to ensure that adequate and efficient school education is provided in their area, including the registration of special educational needs and the development of adequate services to deal with them.

The extension of compulsory education needs to be accompanied by qualitative reforms. Some countries, following the Scandinavian model, develop a single curriculum within compulsory education, in which everyone follows the same courses. Other countries try to strike a balance between a common 'core' of education, and diversification.

Failure at school is increasingly perceived as a major social problem. Too many young people are still leaving the compulsory education system with no vocational qualification whatsoever. Many countries have reformed their systems of examination, assessment, and certification at the end of compulsory education in order to remove any possible discrimination. Another trend is the evaluative cultivation of success: schools have to assess the pupil in relation to the skills to be mastered. In Belgium, one of the main conclusions to be reached 10 years after the extension of compulsory education was the need for a 'pedagogy of success' for youngsters. The government launched research and an experiment on course modelling in vocational education.

In some countries, much concern is expressed about the school leaving conditions in terms of attainment. These can be described as indirect ways of extending compulsory education. Once again, we observe a tension between measures which tend to emphasise the 'duty' aspects, and measures which stress the right of every individual to a qualification. Young people tend to be compelled in some countries (Belgium, UK,

Denmark), or, rather, encouraged in other countries (the Netherlands, Portugal, Scotland), to obtain a vocational qualification at the end of their compulsory schooling, which will improve their chances on the labour market. An example is Portugal's 'social guarantee plan'; under this scheme, the person in question is guaranteed an elementary level of specific training, allowing him to gain access to the jobs market.

To summarise, compulsory schooling as a macro-measure for equal opportunities cannot stand alone but needs to be backed up by measures concerning the quality of education. At the same time, a new balance needs to be achieved between the rights and obligations of young people.

Notes

[1] See Chapter 3 of Nicaise (1999). A zero return does not mean that a higher secondary education diploma produces no additional income. Rather, this additional income, spread over the rest of the life cycle, is barely enough to recoup the investment without interest – even assuming that the risk of school failure of pupils from poor families is equal to the average risk of failure.

[2] Learning difficulties were defined as entrance test scores in maths and language falling more than one standard deviation below the population average.

FOUR

Financial and material assistance for low-income pupils

Ilse Vleugels and Ides Nicaise (HIVA)

This chapter gives an overview of financial or material support measures for pupils in different countries and their effectiveness in securing equal opportunities for children from economically disadvantaged families. The aim is to identify the various strategies, to make cross-national comparisons, to analyse some critical issues, and to describe examples of good practice which may be transferable to other member states.

In summarising the existing financial/material support measures, a distinction is made between:

- pre-school education level (nursery schools or daycare centres);
- the compulsory education level, which lasts for 9 to 12 years (primary and lower (sometimes also upper) secondary education level – see chapter 7);
- the post-compulsory secondary education level (mostly between the ages of 16 and 19); and
- higher education.

A description of material and financial support measures

Pre-school level

The degree to which pre-school education is organised at national level varies widely from country to country (see Chapter 6). For this reason, support measures for children of less well-off parents can also vary widely, as can their general applicability. The first question, then, is: which countries have a national system of pre-school education, and is this free? Second, we come to the question of the extent to which special facilities exist for children from disadvantaged families.

As a general rule, it can be said that daycare services (for children aged 0-3 or 4) are not free; parents usually pay a contribution in proportion to their income. Nursery education, by contrast (organised by the Ministries of Education) is usually free, at least in principle. The discussion below is limited to nursery education; an analysis of the financial aspects of daycare would require a separate study.

Non means-tested support

Flanders has a highly developed pre-school education system (from the age of 2½); the law guarantees that this education is free to parents, although it is not compulsory. This means that no enrolment fees are payable and that all school facilities are free in principle. In practice, however, parents' expenses for transport, school trips, and so on, equal a yearly contribution, expressed in 1998 prices, of approximately 125 Euros per pupil, or 10% of the total educational costs (Van Hooreweghe et al, 1989). There are no specific refunds for these educational costs. In spite of this, participation by children in pre-school education is very high: 78% of children aged 3 attend school, and at age 5 the figure is 98%. Research shows that the decision of whether to participate is not influenced by the socioeconomic position of the parents (Nicaise, 1999).

Ireland has no national pre-school system, but does have a system of 'pre-primary education' whereby children aged 4 and 5 can enter primary education before the compulsory age of 6. Around 65% of 4-year-olds and almost all 5-year-olds join this system. The same early entry into primary education from age 4 is also common in the Netherlands and Spain. Most Spanish (state) schools take children from the age of 3; attendance rates are very high. Pre-school education in these state schools is free. Subsidised private schools, however, cannot be guaranteed to be free, due to a lack of resources for these schools.

In January 1997, the Portuguese Government introduced a programme for the expansion and consolidation of the pre-school education system, the primary objectives of which are the expansion of the public network (there is also a social welfare network and a private network) with a view to guaranteeing free pre-school education, and the establishment of new regulations governing the various pre-school education networks. The aim is to achieve a significant increase in the rates of attendance in pre-school education by the end of the decade. In 1990, the rate of enrolment in pre-school education (lasting three years) was no more than 30% (GEP, 1992).

The Scottish pre-school system is presently in the midst of sweeping changes. Until now, places for children aged 3-4 in nursery schools and day nurseries have fallen far short of demand (compulsory education starts at the age of 5). In rural areas, this situation is particularly problematic. Where the offer is satisfactory, the publicly funded pre-school education is free of charge except for small charges for activities, visits, and so on. For children in need, most charges are met. In 1996, 38% of all children aged 3-4 were enrolled in a nursery school or day nursery session, made up of 20% 3-year-olds and 53% 4-year-olds (SOIED, 1997). If the offer of places in nursery schools or sessions is insufficient, priority is given to the enrolment of 'children in need'. In day nurseries, priority for admission is given to children of single parents, children who have been neglected or abused, and children from families whose difficulties may be eased by the day nursery placement. By the winter of 1998, however, the government was committed to the provision of a quality part-time pre-school place for every child in their pre-school year (age 4) (SOEID, 1997). As a result of the part-time character of the pre-school places, the system is not completely free of charge to parents as they are obliged to combine different types of places (free of charge and others).

Apart from offering pre-school education free, some countries also offer free goods or services through schools, which can be of great importance for disadvantaged children.

In Portugal, for example, free school milk is distributed to all pupils in nursery schools, basic education schools of the 1st and 2nd cycles, media-assisted basic education schools, and institutions offering special education. In practice, however, not all schools participate because of problems of transport, storage, or the lack of auxiliary personnel to implement the measure (see Cabral, 1981). In 1991/92, 85.1% of schools served free milk to 68.8% of the total population of children. Moreover, situations of educational disadvantage are more likely to be found in schools 'at a geographical disadvantage'; that is, for which there are access or logistical problems (Bruto da Costa, 1988).

Means–tested support

According to our study, the only countries operating means-tested grant systems for pre-school education are Spain and Portugal. In Spain, grants are provided every year for pre-school children aged 3, 4 and 5 who are enrolled in private schools if their parents do not find a place in a public (free) school and whose family income does not exceed established ceilings (Eurydice Eurybase, 1996a). The grants for pre-school children in Portugal come under the 'School Social Assistance' scheme, which is discussed in the next subsection. The priority given to enrolling 'children in need' in Scottish day nurseries (see above) must be mentioned here as well.

Compulsory (primary and lower secondary) education: to what extent is free education guaranteed?

Non means-tested support

In Belgium, Spain, the Netherlands, Portugal, the UK, Ireland, France, Finland, Sweden, and Norway – and probably in most other countries in Europe – free education is guaranteed by law. Nevertheless, certain costs are passed on to parents and not always in proportion to the financial capacity of these parents. This is often the case with complementary services such as lunches, transportation to and from school, and board.

In France, for example, items explicitly excluded from the regulations on free education are third-party insurance, the cost of child-minding, and school lunches (Eurydice Eurybase, 1996b).

In Spain, books, clothing and personal study supplies are not included in free compulsory education, which is guaranteed by law and applies in both public and private subsidised schools (since 1985). Transportation is free of charge only when pupils have to commute because of a lack of schools in their own area. Families from lower socioeconomic classes usually prefer public schools for their children because private subsidised schools usually charge extra for school uniforms, activities outside school, sports, and so on.

Portuguese schools charge parents for all 'complementary services' (lunches, transportation, school materials, and so on), but a means-tested support scheme compensates low-income families (see next subsection).

In Scotland, too, parents may need to pay for transportation, meals, equipment and school trips, despite the legal obligation of local authorities to provide free education to all children in their areas.

Two reports highlight the hidden costs associated with 'free' education in Ireland (Murphy-Lawless, 1992; Carney et al, 1994). These costs include books and stationery, lunches, school uniforms, physical education and sports equipment, extracurricular activities and school trips, transport, and so on. In addition, at second level, voluntary secondary schools (but not the other school sectors) may request a 'voluntary contribution' from parents towards the running costs of the school. The amount requested and the proportion of parents who pay this amount does tend to vary from school to school. It has been found that the weekly cost of education rises as the child moves up through the educational system.

A similar situation is found in the Netherlands, where primary schools ask for a voluntary contribution of about 45 Euros from parents for school trips, Christmas presents, and so on. This contribution can differ between schools. In fact, many parents do not know that they can 'opt out' and schools are often in no hurry to suggest this to them. Some hard-up parents allegedly prefer to pay in order to avoid stigmatisation.

In Italy, lower secondary education is free of charge except for some services such as canteens and school buses provided by municipalities, which impose small charges. Moreover, textbooks are generally not free in Italy (Eurydice Eurybase, 1996c).

In Flanders, notwithstanding legal statements on free compulsory education, average 'private direct study costs' (outlays for school attendance borne by parents, expressed in 1998 prices) are estimated at about 250 Euros per year in primary school (Van Hooreweghe et al, 1989) and 500 Euros at secondary level (Denys, 1987). This amount comprises the costs of transportation, meals, cultural, sports and other day trips, clothing, and so on. In an attempt to control these costs, the new law on primary education – passed in 1996 – provides a procedure for complaints and sanctions when schools impose excessive costs on parents.

In Finland, on the other hand, the no-cost nature of compulsory education (and even upper secondary non-compulsory education) includes free textbooks, materials and free daily meals for all students. They are entitled to free transportation over any distance of more than 5 km (Eurydice Eurybase, 1996d).

In passing, we must point out that European exchange programmes are becoming increasingly well-established in schools. The costs associated with these exchanges are high for the parents involved. Although some schools have found ways of reducing the contributions made by less well-off parents, this problem deserves further attention, both in terms of cost price research and within the Socrates programme itself, at the EU level.

Means-tested support

In the following summary a distinction is drawn between financial support organised within the educational policy domain and financial support as part of a country's social security or national assistance system; finally, we shall discuss some examples of material support.

Financial support for general study expenses

Flanders operates a system of means-tested student grants at secondary level. An extension to primary education is advocated in the General Report on Poverty (ATD-Fourth World et al, 1995). At the same time, however, there is ongoing discussion concerning the role of grants versus other forms of intervention; some people argue that study grants for young people under 18 are contradictory to the constitutionally guaranteed free access to compulsory education, which should normally imply that participation in primary and secondary education is free. For this reason, policy makers are resisting the idea of introducing grants for primary schools; some would even prefer to abolish the existing grant system in secondary education.

In Spain, compensatory education programmes provide financial support for 3- to 19-year-old pupils from poor backgrounds, recent immigrants, and some groups of the travelling population of gypsy origin. Financial grants at national level are established for compulsory schooling, covering lunch in school canteens, transportation, textbooks, and other school materials needed by the pupils. These grants are meant for a broader group of economically disadvantaged children. Free transportation and meals are also provided for children from isolated areas. Complementary financial grants are provided by local bodies. These usually cover those people on the fringes of general social welfare networks (non-residents, those not registered in the census, and so on), as these individuals are more easily identified and traced by local social services.

School Social Assistance in Portugal includes financial support to encourage attendance at pre-school, primary and secondary education. The various types of assistance awarded are designed to help with the buying of books or other school material considered indispensable for school attendance, to support accommodation commuting expenses incurred as a result of the distance of the school from the pupil's usual place of residence, and to subsidise transport for the handicapped. This measure can be of fundamental importance for the full achievement of universal education, in that it gives support where there are unsatisfied basic needs which could impede school attendance.

The number of pupils benefiting from assistance illustrates the importance of School Social Assistance as a measure supporting attendance in basic education in general, and attendance in the 2nd cycle in particular, as this is when the attendance costs (of school material, meals, and so on) increase considerably. Despite the fact that the assistance

Table 4.1: Number of pupils in the state system who benefit from socioeconomic assistance measures (state education system – continental Portugal) in 1991/92

	No. of beneficiaries	No. of pupils in state education	Coverage rate
Pre-school	3,263	87,655	3.7
1st cycle	92,683	565,193	16.4
2nd cycle	76,964	271,856	28.3
3rd cycle	55,117	379,206	14.5
Secondary	17,334	281,867	6.1

Source: DEPGEF (1995)

covers a wide range of needs, 96.6% of the funds granted to pupils in the 2nd and 3rd cycles of basic education, as well as in secondary education, centred on support for the acquisition of books and school material.

In the Netherlands, no such system of direct financial support to children and their parents exists at primary school level, as this education is in fact virtually free. In general, the financial support for low-income pupils is given to schools or communities, allowing them to work out measures for the economically less well-off (for example, within the 'Educational Priority Policy').

Financial support via the country's social security or national assistance system

In France, a 'new school-year grant' is paid by the family allowance fund at the beginning of each school year to families whose resources do not exceed a certain ceiling for each child between 6 and 16. Luxembourg also provides an additional grant via child benefit at the start of each school year, but this is universal and not income-related (EC, 1996).

In some countries (such as Belgium and the Netherlands), aid can also be provided through the public assistance system for specific study costs such as cultural trips, the cost of books, and so on. The municipality covers the cost of these specific supplementary benefits. The problem is that many people do not apply for this aid, which remains underused; moreover, the nature of the aid and the degree to which it is used varies fairly widely between municipalities.

In Portugal, the guaranteed minimum income is obviously not an outright educational measure, but it has produced effects in the education sector, particularly as far as completion of compulsory education is concerned. The integration contract[1] for a family with children of school age who do not attend school or who have a high level of absenteeism always includes an agreement on the conditions for the children attending school. In these cases, the parents are made responsible for the children receiving compulsory education, and they could forfeit the financial assistance if their children do not finish school. In addition, other assistance measures for successful completion of school attendance can be mentioned within the scope of the 'complementary support' measures of the integration programmes.

A scheme funded by the Department of Social Welfare in Ireland is the Back to School Clothing Allowance, which was initiated in 1990. The aim is to assist low-income families with the costs incurred on their children's return to school. To be eligible for the allowance, parents must already be in receipt of social welfare benefits; the allowance, therefore, is not tied to attendance at a specific school as many other initiatives are. Almost 120,000 families recieved this allowance in 1994, with total expenditure by the Department of Social Welfare in the region of 14 million ECU.

Material (in kind) support schemes

Book grant and rental schemes are provided in the Irish educational system (at primary and secondary level). Their aim is to help pupils who are in the greatest need of assistance; that is, those whose parents are dependent on social welfare, receive low income from employment or are experiencing hardship due to illness. A total of 3,715 schools are involved in the scheme, catering for almost 320,000 needy children, with the Department of Education providing in the region of £5.1 million in funding.

In France, local authorities can charge special rates for lunches and child-minding after school hours, depending on family income. They can also provide free school textbooks and individual supplies. All this is called indirect aid (Eurydice Eurybase, 1996b).

The provision of free school meals for pupils in primary schools in Ireland began in 1914. School meals are not, however, universally available, and provision is concentrated in designated areas, usually confined to urban areas and the Gaeltacht (Irish-speaking) districts. In 1994, some 411 schools participated in this second scheme under the auspices of the Department of Social Welfare.

In Scotland, too, a system of free school meals and milk entitlement exists in primary and secondary education. Unlike in Ireland, in Scotland there is a statutory entitlement for all children whose parents are unemployed and receiving Income Support or the income-based Jobseekers' Allowance. It is used as an indicator of disadvantage by local

Table 4.2: Coverage of the pupil population with school canteens in Portugal (%)

Education level	Coverage of the pupil population	1991/92
1st cycle	No of school canteens	2.9
	Average no of school meals	3.4
2nd, 3rd cycle/secondary	No of school canteens	37.1
	Average no of meals for 2nd cycle pupils	28.6
	Average no of meals for 3rd cycle pupils	15.6
	Average no of meals for secondary school pupils	11.2

Source: DEPGEF (1995)

education authorities and schools when allocating additional resources such as learning support. Besides the free milk and meals, local authorities also provide free transportation and free clothing to children from parents on incomes below a certain level (SOEID, 1997).

The Portuguese School canteens are, like free school milk, another component of a policy of guaranteeing proper nutrition for all pupils, and it has been stipulated that they should primarily serve those benefiting from the financial support of the School Social Assistance system. Unfortunately, information on this measure is very scarce. According to Bruto da Costa (1988), until 1984/5 the number of pupils in the 1st cycle of basic education who received meals in school canteens was practically nil; however, it should be noted that in many schools in Portugal, the 1st cycle is taught either in the morning or in the afternoon. In the 2nd and 3rd cycles of basic education, as well as in secondary education, the number of schools served by a school canteen is higher.

In some parts of Portugal it is still impossible to make the home–school–home round trip in one day. In such cases, the state has established an accommodation policy targeted at pupils in basic and secondary education. The pupils can be accommodated in establishments belonging to the national network of student residences (which, in 1991/2, consisted of 47 residences) or placed in private accommodation. With the improvement in physical accessibility in the country and the improvement of school facilities, the number of pupils in accommodation is decreasing. In 1981/2 (according to Bruto da Costa, 1988), the number of pupils in residences was 4,800. In 1991/2 (according to the DEPGEF, 1995) there were fewer than 3,200.

In the Netherlands, some municipalities provide free transport for immigrant children to specific schools (teaching Dutch as a second language), or parents at least receive a contribution to transport costs.

The transition from compulsory to post-compulsory education level (15/16-18 age group)

The key question here is whether free access to education is still guaranteed after compulsory school age. If other measures apply, how selective are they? Are they of a different nature?

Non-means-tested support

In Flanders, the constitutional principle of free access to education – already discussed above – applies until the age of 18, which coincides here with the end of compulsory (and secondary) education. In Ireland, free further education has also been guaranteed for all categories since 1967. In Spain too, according to a law passed in 1987, the principle of no charge is applicable at the post-compulsory (upper secondary) level.

The maximum age limit for child benefit was raised in Ireland in 1995 from 16 to 21, if the young person continues to attend full-time education during that period. This brought Ireland into line with other European countries, where child benefits were already paid up to the age of 18 (such as Spain, Denmark and the UK) or longer (the Netherlands, 22; Belgium and Portugal, 25), provided the young person concerned is in full-time education.

Apart from the differences in maximum age limits, wide variation is observed across Europe in the amount of monthly child benefit, which is not always sufficient to cover study costs as well (EC, 1996).

Means-tested support

Education in the Netherlands is free up to the age of 16 (the end of compulsory full-time schooling). Thereafter an annual 'education contribution' (tuition or course fee) applies to cover the costs of books, travel expenses, and so on, which is payable by students who remain in full-time education in a state-subsidised school. In the 1997/8 school year this contribution amounted to approximately 680 ECU annually. For youngsters aged between 16 and 18 in full-time education, the Study Fees (Financial Assistance) Act (WTS) applies. This Act provides for a transfer to parents equivalent to the full statutory parental contribution of 680 ECU. Sometimes a supplementary payment of about 350 ECU is given to cover study costs. The amount and structure of the total grant depends on parental income. About 40% of the total amount of 'education contributions' that the government collects annually are redistributed in this way.

The Spanish national government provides annual scholarships and student grants for students in intermediate, post-compulsory secondary education (as well as university students). Two types of aid exist: general grants and special scholarships awarded for outstanding academic achievement only. To be eligible for the general aid, the student must meet minimum academic standards (as opposed to grants in compulsory education), and the aid is only meant for students whose family income is insufficient to cover the costs of education for family members. The grants are supposed to cover the costs of travelling, urban transport, accommodation, materials and tuition fees (Eurydice Eurybase, 1996a) (see above).

In Scotland, students aged 16–18 studying on a full-time course may continue to claim their child benefit and are entitled to apply for a small bursary to cover some expenses such as travel and books. Those not eligible for the normal state benefits may apply for a college bursary. This is means-tested but may be worth a maximum of about 29 ECU per week. Where there are fees to be paid, these are paid by the college if the person is on benefit or entitled to a bursary. Fees vary, but may be as high as about 470 ECU for a one-year full-time course.

In Ireland, a number of locally based initiatives, including the Ballymun Initiative for Third-level Education, the Limerick Community-Based Educational Initiative and the Trinity Access Project, have attempted to address this issue by including financial aid as part of a multistranded approach to promoting educational access. These three initiatives combine financial direct and indirect support with cultural interventions.

Examples of good practice

The Ballymun Initiative for Third-level Education (BITE) scheme

The Ballymun Initiative for Third-level Education (BITE) scheme began as a pilot programme in 1990. The aim of the scheme is to increase participation rates in third-level education among students from disadvantaged areas, and therefore contribute to breaking the cycle of deprivation and poverty. It is believed that young people from lower socioeconomic groups will persevere in the full-time education system throughout both the second and third level, if they are encouraged and supported through economic and cultural interventions. BITE is funded by the Irish American Partnership (IAP), the Ballymun Partnership and the Department of Education. The programme targets academically able students and supports them through a two-tiered approach. Economic intervention takes the form of both direct and indirect financial assistance. Direct financial assistance (in the form of a grant) begins at second level (with 73 second-level scholarships funded in 1997), as it was felt that starting such intervention at third level was inadequate. Financial assistance is also targeted at third-level students, with 54 students receiving scholarships in 1996/97. Indirect financial assistance is provided through an annual subsidy to the existing book fund. In addition, students are provided with summer employment by local employers if they experience difficulties in obtaining work. The second strand of the programme involves cultural interventions, designed to create a community climate in which educational values will be understood and appreciated. The task therefore is to change attitudes among both parents and students who would not normally consider the completion of second-level education, let alone third-level, as part of their aspirations. These cultural interventions take the form of a liaison with both primary and comprehensive schools in the Ballymun area, provision of parent groups, evening study facilities, extra tuition schemes, summer schools, and promotional literature. In addition, a school-based coordinator liaises with the admissions office of Dublin City University (its associated university). DCU and BITE have established special entry requirements for BITE students to specified courses in the university.

The Limerick Community-Based Educational Initiative (LCBEI) scheme

The Limerick Community-Based Educational Initiative (LCBEI) scheme began in 1990 and aims to increase third-level participation among students who have the academic ability and motivation to complete third-level education, but would be prevented from doing so for financial reasons. Funding for the scheme comes predominantly from the Irish American Partnership and the Department of Education. Three schools are involved in the programme and, again, a two-pronged approach is adopted, providing both financial and cultural interventions. Direct financial assistance only begins at third level, taking the form of a grant. Previously, grants were awarded to primary-level pupils but, as a result of financial constraints, this is no longer in effect. Cultural interventions include such measures as the provision of a newsletter, educational tours, and a programme for gifted children at primary level. At second level, language tutorials, career guidance and parenting courses are also provided. There are at present no special entry arrangements with the University of Limerick (the local university) although this issue is currently being negotiated.

The Trinity Access Project (TAP)

The Trinity Access Project *(TAP)* was initiated in 1993 and seeks to assist and encourage talented second-level students from socioeconomically disadvantaged areas to continue to third-level education. TAP has a broader target area than BITE or LCBEI, encompassing seven schools in Dublin. The programme is funded by Trinity College, Dublin (TCD) and the Department of Education. The two-tiered approach of economic and cultural intervention is also evident in this programme. Direct financial assistance is given to schools, and this assistance must be spent on educational activities. Indirect financial assistance is given to the students, for example, through the payment of examination fees and purchase of school books. Such awards are given not just on the basis of academic achievement but also on the effort students have made. Cultural intervention can take the form of parents' evenings, visits to higher education establishments, a summer school, and study skills courses. Voluntary support from the staff and students of TCD is provided through tutorials and group work. Unlike BITE, there has been no change in the entrance criteria or admissions policy of TCD for students supported under the scheme. An evaluation of the scheme is currently underway and an interim report is due for completion shortly.

Higher education

Under pressure from budget restrictions, increasing financial thresholds in access to tertiary education seem to be generally accepted throughout Europe. Ireland is a notable exception in this regard; since 1996, free third-level (and further) education has been guaranteed by law in this country. Other countries have turned to various systems of student support to compensate low-income students.

The different support systems for students in higher education in Western Europe can be roughly divided into two groups of countries: one group where financial support for students is provided to parents and depends (largely) on parental income, and another group with (more or less) 'parent-independent' support systems (DSW, 1997). Belgium, Ireland, Spain, Portugal and Scotland fall into the first category, as do France, Germany and Italy. The Scandinavian countries form the second group. The Netherlands fits into both groups.

A number of countries with parent-dependent student support impose a statutory maintenance duty on parents for their children (aged 18 and over) who are in higher education. This is the case, for example, in Belgium, Germany, France and Italy. It is reflected in, among other things, the high upper age limit for child benefit, which corresponds to the normal graduation age in higher education, and in ongoing tax benefits or exemptions which are not tied to age. The exceptions are Spain and the UK: here, there is no statutory obligation, and child benefit stops at the age of 18.[2]

This statutory maintenance duty does not apply in the Scandinavian countries either, with their parent-independent student grant system. Here too, child benefits stop at the age of 18 (age 20 in Sweden).

A further feature of parent-dependent grant systems is that the size of student grants depends on the income of the parents; these grants are generally provided in addition to child benefit and not everyone is eligible. By contrast, in the Scandinavian countries, the student grant replaces child benefit for all full-time students in higher education, and is designed to meet the full maintenance needs of the student. Generally, more than 50% of students in higher education receive this grant (all full-time students). In Denmark the figure is 80%, in Sweden 77%, and in Finland 58%. The percentage is generally lower in the parent-dependent grant systems (25% of students in higher education, or lower). In Ireland, where there is no child benefit over the age of 21, 40% of students still receive financial support. In Spain, where there is no child benefit over the age of 18, the percentage is 'only' 20%.

The system in the Netherlands is a mixture of these two archetypes. From the age of 18, students in higher education receive a 'basic grant' which is largely parent-independent.[3] This basic grant is received by 95% of students. In addition, supplementary support is available to help meet the costs of study; the size of this grant *is* dependent on parental income. Students can also take out a low-interest loan, which again is parent-independent.

A further important distinction is that, in systems where parents have a statutory obligation to continue supporting their children during their studies, grants are paid for only a limited period (one year, for example) and usually under strict conditions. Follow-up grants generally depend on success in end-of-year or sessional examinations; failure results in the grant being withheld. This is the case in Belgium, France and Austria. In Italy, the maximum number of student grants to be paid is even fixed in advance for each university, thus reinforcing the importance of academic achievement as a selection criterion. Only 2.4% of students in higher education in Italy receive a grant.

Under the Scandinavian system, by contrast, grants are generally paid for the full term of study. In Denmark, for example, students receive 70 monthly grants (or 'vouchers') at the start of their studies. This includes a built-in reserve of 12 months over and above the normal duration of the study. Students decide for themselves over what period these vouchers are used and thus also how they spread their studies over time. This system also allows for changes of course; students simply take their remaining vouchers with them.

In parent-dependent systems, finally, the main emphasis is on study allowances. Grants can, in some cases, be converted into loans if the student fails their examinations (in France, for example). In Ireland, it is possible to take out a student loan on the private market, which is totally separate from the student grant. In countries with a parent-independent student support system, both systems – grants only and combinations of grants and loans – are found.

The impact of financial and material support: evaluation

Compulsory education

Generally speaking, little is known about the impact of these school expenses on poor families. According to a memorandum from the Belgian department of ATD-Fourth World (1999) the consequences are much more harmful than hitherto suspected. The shame of not being able to pay takes a heavy toll on the parent/school relationship. In addition to the shame felt by parents and the children themselves, which leads to avoidance of contacts with the school, schools react with a lack of understanding and thoughtless humiliation (malicious reminders, ever-increasing bills, the withdrawal of some extra-school services). The pupils themselves often bear the brunt: they are punished and excluded from certain activities (sometimes the most interesting and stimulating) and are therefore looked down upon by their peers and feel left behind. Sometimes they also lack the required educational resources. Often, the consequences are absenteeism, a dislike of the school, and inadequate choices of school and course. Some cases have even been reported of parents sending their children into special education because this is better subsidised and costs them less.

Apart from the direct additional expenditure on the school, the indirect costs of education (the sacrificed income of young people) also take their toll. In Portugal, premature dropout by school-age students is still a major problem. This occurs chiefly among the lower social classes and is related, among other things, to seasonal labour by children in poorer rural areas (Ferrao and das Neves, 1992). The call of the labour market is also strong in more industrialised areas, such as Vale do Ave in the north of the country, where children are still being employed in the textile industry. Concerns about this problem are reflected in strategies geared to increasing access to compulsory education. In Portugal, making the guaranteed minimum income conditional on school attendance by children appears to be proving effective. According to the data available in September 1997, which as yet only refers to the pilot projects covering approximately 20% of the resident population, 1,244 young children

Table 4.3: Summary of financial and/or material support for pupils in different countries

Pre-school education (nursery schools)	Compulsory education	Post-compulsory education (15/16-18 age group)	Higher education (18+ age group)
Non-means-tested financial/material support	*Non-means-tested financial/material support*	*Non-means-tested financial/material support*	* Student maintenance grants (DK, Sw, Fi, No, NL)
- Free education in comprehensive schools: (Be (Fl), Po, NL, Sp, Fr, Sw, Fi, No):	- Free compulsory education (in B(Fl), Fr, Sp, It, Po, Fi, NL, Scotl, Irl, Sw, No)	- Free education: Irl, Be	* Vouchers: DK
But: in Sp, only in public schools in Scotl, only part-time places	But:		* Full term of study
- Free milk: Po	- B (Fl) except: transport, meals, childminding		* Free education: Irl
- Free transport if dist. >Xkm: Be (Fl), Fi	- Fr except: insurance, childminding, meals		
- Sp. except.: meals, transport, board, etc	- It except: textbooks, transport, meals, etc		
	- Sc except: transp, meals, equipment, trips		
	- NL except: School trips, presents, etc		
	- Free accommodation: Po		
	- Free transport if dist. >Xkm: Be (Fl), Fi		
	- Study grants: Fi (only secondary education)		
- Grants or means-tested support	- Grants for textbooks: Irl, Po	- Exemption from tuition fees: NL	* Student grants in addition to family allowances: B, Fr, D
	- Rental schemes for books: Irl	- Grants for school-related Costs: Be, NL, Sp	* Student grants replacing family allowances:: Sp, Irl, UK
* In Sp: in private schools if public school places are not available	- Free meals: Irl, Po, Scotl.	- Combination of financial and cultural intervention:	* Selection on academic standards/results: (It, Sp)
* In Scotl: priority to enrolment of 'children in need'	- Irl: only schools in some areas	Irl (three pilot projects)	* Annual review based on study results / (B, Fr.)
* In Po: School Social Assistance Scheme	- Scotl: children from families on unemployment benefit	- Scotl: grants, college bursaries no entry fees	
	- Po: children with social assistance		
	- Support for pupils from families on		
	- Income Support: Irl, Fr, NL, Po		
	- Irl: back to school clothing allowance		
	- NL: extra municipal support		
	- Fr: extra family allowance (6-16 years)		
	- Po: via integration contracts		

Be (Fl): Flanders-Belgium; NL: Netherlands; Po: Portugal; Sp: Spain; Fr: France; Fi: Finland; No: Norway; Sw: Sweden; It: Italy; Irl: Ireland; DK: Denmark; Scotl: Scotland

and adolescents out of 11,842 assisted families had returned to compulsory education. A further 827 had begun to attend continuing education, having already passed the age limit for compulsory education.

This chapter has already shown that the statutory guarantee of free compulsory education is the most important financial policy instrument in promoting equal opportunities. In many countries, however, application of this principle remains problematic, first and foremost because the limits of what is and is not covered are variable (school transport, books, insurance, extracurricular activities, and so on), but sometimes also because the working resources of the schools are inadequate. As a result, with a view to combating poverty, supplementary income-dependent support either in cash or in kind often remains indispensable.

All too often, student grants in compulsory education are regarded as superfluous. Opponents of student grants argue that grants have lost their role, since school attendance is now enforced by other means. However, the role of student finance does not in fact end with the participation decision itself: the grants must also help students and their families to make sufficient home investments for an optimum result. This means full participation from a qualitative point of view (availability of the required time and equipment, participation in extracurricular activities, and so on), a free choice of study (including access to 'more expensive' or more cost-sensitive disciplines) and a reduction of the risks related to failure. Little research has been carried out to date on such effects of student grants. The results of a multinomial logit model for study orientation in Flanders (Nicaise, 1999), for example, suggest that student grants in secondary education, even without differentiation in the amounts according to discipline, could to some extent stimulate transfer to technical or general (rather than vocational) education (because the demand for those disciplines is more cost-sensitive).

Admittedly, student grants do not always reach those who most need them. In Flemish secondary education, for example, it has repeatedly been observed (Cossey et al, 1983; Van Brusselen and Nicaise, 1993) that about one in four potential beneficiaries do not claim their grant. Moreover, this lack of take-up is concentrated among the least well-off families. Lack of information is but one (and perhaps not the major) cause: despite their legal entitlement, some potential beneficiaries appear not to believe that they have a right to a grant or are ashamed to claim their benefit. This indicates a need for repeated information campaigns.

On the other hand, problems arise with the families of self-employed workers whose taxable income is often underestimated. A legal correction was introduced into the Flemish grant system in 1991, whereby the value of the home occupied by the family is used as an additional wealth indicator. Despite some (avoidable) deficiencies, this correction has brought about a notable decrease in abuse (Vos and Nicaise, 1993).

Precisely in order to circumvent the social ineffectiveness of bureaucratic systems, several countries provide support in kind, often distributed by the schools themselves, since they are supposed to know better which families need help. Yet similar problems exist with this system. A critical concern about free school meals in Scotland is the stigma attached to them. Research has demonstrated that many children do not take up these meals because of the stigma. In Ireland, the system of free meals at school has also been criticised on a number of grounds, including the fact that it is considered out of date, the poor quality of the meals, the administrative procedures involved, and the fact that the school decides whether to apply for the scheme, and therefore parents may not know that their children are eligible (Kellaghan et al, 1995). Similar criticisms have been aimed at the Irish book grant and rental scheme, particularly as regards the identification of 'needy children', with questions raised as to whether or not eligible families are receiving assistance. In the past, there has been a great deal of variation between schools as to how the scheme has been administered; attention has been drawn to the practice among some schools of using the financial assistance received to benefit all pupils rather than to specifically target those defined as 'needy' (ESF Programme Evaluation Unit, 1997; Kellaghan et al, 1995). This problem does not exist with the Back to School Clothing Allowance, which is not tied to attendance at a specific school. However, it has also been observed in other countries, as in the case of Portuguese free milk provision (Bruto da Costa, 1988).

The transition from compulsory to post-compulsory education level and higher education

An evaluation of support during the period of post-compulsory education first of all involves an examination of the quantitative effects, specifically on the extent and distribution of participation in upper secondary and higher education. One example of such quantitative objectives is found in Spain, which sets itself the primary objective of raising the education participation rate, rather than introducing positive discrimination or objective assessments of effectiveness among those most in need. This is an important policy option, though obviously not the only possible one.

The effectiveness of student grants as an incentive to participation in post-compulsory education has been adequately demonstrated. In a separate publication (Nicaise, 1999, Chapters 4 and 6), the authors present a summary of the international literature on this subject. For Flanders, logistic regression analyses were applied, in which the probability of participation and choice of study are related to a range of socioeconomic determinants, including the direct and indirect costs[4] (after deduction of direct and indirect subsidies[5]). For every 1% decrease in the (combined direct and indirect) cost, the participation in upper secondary education increases by 1.5 percentage points, and in higher education by 1.6 points.

An important issue in connection with student financing – mainly at tertiary level – relates to the choice between student grants and student loans. Based on the argument that education is partly a private investment, and in order to promote efficient student behaviour, some observers call for grants to be replaced by 'soft' loans. A number of comments can be made regarding this issue:

- A 'pound for pound' conversion of grants into loans will undoubtedly reduce the demand for education. This means that substantially higher amounts would have to be extended in loans in order to achieve the same effect as grants in terms of equality of opportunity.
- In order to limit their debts, students might attempt to finance their studies in another way, for example via part-time work. This would reduce their chances of success and mean that student loans could generate precisely the opposite effect to that desired in terms of efficiency. Moreover, working students often tend to poach jobs from poorly skilled workers and apprentices.
- It must be remembered that education is by its very nature a riskier enterprise than other forms of investment. The administration costs, losses and lawsuit costs for the government in the event of non-reimbursement by beneficiaries are high in such systems.

For deprived groups, therefore, the literature tends to argue more in favour of the traditional system of student grants (Schwartz, 1985; Ehrenberg and Sherman, 1987; Nicaise and Winters, 1988; Barr and Falkingham, 1993).

Caution should be exercised, particularly as regards the efficiency argument mentioned above (when making support conditional on achievement or future reimbursement). Inequality of opportunity boils down to the fact that the poor 'pay more' for the same quantity of education, in terms of the repetition of years among other things. Many student finance systems impose conditions in this area which result in de facto discrimination against deprived students. Until recently, for example, students in Flanders would lose their grant if they had to repeat a year, with the result that the most deprived students were subject to double sanctions. This condition has since been abolished within the compulsory education system, but remains in effect in higher education. In the French community of Belgium, only one year can be repeated with a grant in secondary education, upon special request. Minimum academic requirements also apply in the Spanish grant system (at secondary and tertiary level) and in the Italian and French third-level grant systems.

Purely financial incentives have sometimes been criticised as inadequate in assisting students from disadvantaged backgrounds to attend university or other third-level institutions (Lynch and O'Riordan, 1996). An interesting approach in light of this is the linking of financial or material support to sociocultural intervention aimed at encouraging transfer to further education. Some Irish initiatives of this type, albeit on a limited scale, are referred to above.

Evaluations of the Ballymun Initiative for Third-level Education carried out to date indicate that the programme has been successful in creating a positive view of third-level education. The numbers of pupils continuing on to the third level has increased, but there has been little or no improvement in the number of pupils taking higher level papers for the Leaving Certificate. The performance of students who have proceeded to third-level education compares favourably with that of traditional entrants. On a less positive note, it has been argued that, due to the costs and labour time involved, the scheme would be difficult to implement on a national level (Lynch and O'Riordan, 1996).

Evaluations of the Limerick Community-Based Educational Initiative again point to the progress made in creating a positive view of third-level education among young people in the area. Participation in third-level education has improved and performance compares favourably with traditional entrants. Since 1990, 66 students have completed (or are completing) courses in an area where previously only one or two pupils would have done so. However, the applicability of the scheme at national level has also been questioned in this case (Lynch and O'Riordan, 1996).

Conclusions

In most European countries, free compulsory education appears to be the chief policy instrument in removing the financial barriers to educational participation. It is not clear, however, to what extent free pre-school and compulsory education has been achieved in practice. There is an obvious need for further comparative research on this subject.

Income-dependent support in kind (such as transport, meals, school uniforms and books) is still widespread. The advantage of this form of support is that its distribution is highly decentralised and that it goes directly to the children concerned (rather than their parents). Disadvantages may be that schools fail to offer these services, resulting in failure to take up the support. In addition, this form of support may have a stigmatising effect, and schools sometimes display a somewhat arbitrary approach in assessing who is in need of help.

Income-dependent financial support for low-income families remains a useful 'extra' in meeting school expenses such as transport, durable school equipment, extracurricular activities, and so on. In Spain, Portugal and Scotland, this support is available from pre-school education onwards; France and Ireland provide support from the start of primary education and Belgium from lower secondary education; in other countries, it is generally available only in post-compulsory or higher education.

The effectiveness of student grants can be both quantitative (after compulsory education) and qualitative ('fuller' participation and choice of study). The advantages of national student grant systems are the greater objectiveness of the awarding criteria and the anonymity of the administrative procedures, which helps to avoid any stigmatising effects. On the other hand, lack of take-up is a problem because people are unaware that they are eligible for support or because they are ashamed to accept it. This highlights the need for supportive information campaigns. The correct determination of the income criteria used to assess eligibility for support is also not without problems.

In some countries, income-dependent support is linked to academic achievement (for example, support that is dependent on success in annual examinations, a predetermined maximum number of grants, and so on). From a social perspective, such a system is best avoided – especially in secondary education – since the risk of failure for students with equal innate capacity is greater among those from lower backgrounds.

On the other hand, linking financial and material support to cultural intervention, perhaps further supplemented by individual social and educational help, may be desirable as a means of reaching the most disadvantaged groups.

Notes

[1] The entitlement to a minimum income is subject to the conclusion of an 'integration contract'.

[2] For Scotland, however, the statutory obligation exists, but the child benefit does not.

[3] It is not related to the income of the parents, although it does depend on whether or not the student lives in the parental home.

[4] The indirect cost of education consists of forgone earnings while attending school.

[5] Examples of indirect transfers are family allowances, tax deductions and subsidised services such as cheap accommodation or cheap meals.

FIVE

Integrated services for disadvantaged young people

Kees Meijer (ITS)

Educational disadvantage is a complex problem. It can have multiple causes at individual, family, and community levels that often interact with each other. For example, research by the Organisation for Economic Cooperation and Development (OECD) found the following individual and family risk factors, among others: long-term unemployment and poverty in the family; a migrant, ethnic or linguistic minority status; inadequate housing; low educational attainment characterised by repeating classes and home–school breakdown; an often 'negative' choice of vocational training at the end of primary education and/or a secondary education track leading to early dropout with no qualifications. Community risk factors include limited healthcare and leisure facilities, and the use of many different first languages among school friends. If a young person does find a job, it is often short-term, offers few opportunities for continuing training, and is highly likely to lead to future unemployment – thus closing the cycle of disadvantage (for further discussion, see Evans, 1995).

With such multiple and interconnected causes, a piecemeal approach is unlikely to address young people's educational disadvantage successfully. Improving local education and training provision without, for example, simultaneously promoting employment options and enhancing the quality of housing will ultimately not erase the educational disadvantage. Instead, integrated approaches are required; approaches that address both individual young people and services by creating:

- coordinated transitional pathways: to consider young people's needs over time, both within the day (home, school, play) and throughout their lives (transitions from primary to secondary to post-secondary education and training);
- integrated services: to address organisational arrangements, made at local/regional level, to ensure that the 'transitional pathways' are

delivered in a coordinated and integrated way. More generally, integrated services "… maximise the possibilities that children and their families could obtain the services to which they are entitled or which they need". Such services must be "… conveniently located, accessible and offered in a way that facilitates addressing the needs of the entire family" (OECD, 1996a, p 8).

The objectives of integrated services

Five tenets underlie and connect these two aspects of integrated approaches:

1. All young people must be adequately prepared for adult and working life. All young people should be able to acquire the 'equipment' they need to enter adult and working life successfully at the end of the education and training process (see also OECD, 1996b, p 39). What precise 'equipment' young people should acquire is much debated in the literature, but the following core skills are generally recognised:
   - Basic skills, knowledge and attitudes: literacy (mother tongue and, preferably, one or more other languages), numeracy and a sufficient understanding of the physical, social, cultural and historical environment to be able to take part in it.
   - Life skills: skills, knowledge and attitudes necessary for independent living, such as confidence, self-awareness, self-development, time and money management, health and hygiene issues, and so on.
   - Core skills or transferable skills: skills necessary for success in the workplace, such as communication (oral and graphical), information technology, problem-solving abilities, being able to work together with others, learning-to-learn skills, and so on.
   - Job/vocational skills: the broad set of competencies necessary for employment as well as for continuing training.
2. Processes to acquire the skills necessary for adult and working life should take place in appropriate social and physical circumstances. Children should be reared, educated and trained in safe and stimulating environments. Young people need to be trusted, respected and have the opportunity to build up self-esteem and motivation.
3. Such circumstances are created through the interactions between the home, the school and the community. The three environments of home, school and community have significant actors:

- the home: the parents and other family members;
- the school/training college: teachers in schools, trainers and other staff in training institutions, tutors in firms, and so on;
- the community: local and regional services, such as health services, social services, guidance services, community development agencies, and so on.

The older the young person becomes, the more they themselves become the fourth actor.

4. In cases of imbalances between the 'contributions' of the main actors, more individualised pathways should be provided. In most cases, interaction between the three main environments goes relatively smoothly. In a situation of (potential) social exclusion, however, interaction may not be so smooth. For example, parents with negative feelings towards the educational system may not wish to participate in school activities. Doing homework in a house with little, if any, free space is not easy. When money is scarce, parents may not be able to fund hobbies or cultural activities for their children. With disrupted interactions between the three environments, young people can find it difficult to negotiate successful pathways – which leads to the next tenet, below.

5. Integrated approaches must have effective mechanisms for identifying those who need extra support and coordinating the delivery of services. A pathway can be 'customised', with integrated supportive services, to 'restore' the balance between the contributions of the main actors. To be effective, an integrated approach needs to:
    - identify all those young people who need additional support;
    - develop customised transitional pathways and provide the required extra support;
    - coordinate or network all relevant local or regional services.

In the countries[1] participating in this study, integrated approaches attract increasing attention. In this chapter, three questions will be asked in relation to countries' experiences. First, which services should be involved in integrated approaches, and which kinds of activities should the services provide? Second, which integrated approaches are already being implemented and how is the networking/coordination arranged between the respective services and organisations? Third, what is the coverage and effectiveness of current models and how can integrated approaches be further improved?

Table 5.1: Partners to be involved in the provision of integrated services

- Education	- Community/cultural groups
- Social/welfare services	- Employment services
- Health services	- Police/criminal justice service
- Youth services	- Housing services
- Parents of children at risk	- Employers/companies

Source: Based on Hurell and Evans (1996, p 80)

Building up an integrated approach: partners and content of the activities

Which partners should be involved in integrated approaches? Ten groups are listed by Hurell and Evans (1996), following research on 14 countries (see Table 5.1).

These partners, according to Hurell and Evans, should work together in planning and implementing activities, ensuring a balance between the contributions from the home, the school and the community. Such joint working should provide young people with the full academic and practical 'equipment' they need as adults.

For an effective integrated approach, these partners would need to provide services that address the individual, family and community risk factors listed at the beginning of this chapter. A series of intervention areas is described below, illustrating the wide variety of possible activities; these are summarised in Table 5.2.

The cases described cover local- or regional-level experiments, which are mostly provided outside regulated mainstream provision. Whenever available, evaluations of such experiments are summarised.

Table 5.2: Content of the activities

2.1:	Supporting parents as educators
2.2:	Homework clubs
2.3:	Healthcare
2.4:	Recreation and sports
2.5:	Cultural activities
2.6:	Language development
2.7:	Liaising with socioeconomic actors

Supporting parents as educators

For an in-depth discussion of home–school–community relationships, the reader is referred to Chapter 10. At this point, a few examples of liaising activities will be mentioned, emphasising their role as part of a multi-service approach.

Mutual trust is a prerequisite for effective partnership between parents and schools. Partnerships change and develop as the young person moves through the different phases of the educational process.

At pre-primary and primary levels, contact between parents and the school has frequently been the priority in countries' experiments. Apart from better communication, some projects aim at offering services to parents which reinforce their role as educators. In Flanders, for example, an experimental network of nursery and primary schools, supported by the King Baudouin Foundation, sought to improve intercultural understanding and to encourage better participation by ethnic minority parents in school activities. Teachers were encouraged to visit all pupils at home twice a year; an open-door policy in the nurseries and primary schools sought to bring parents into the schools. Parents could take part in language courses, received guidance on how to support their children's homework, and were involved in organising sociocultural activities.

In secondary education, the emphasis shifts partly to widening the service support to the students themselves, as well as parents. For example, the Scottish Home-School-Employment Partnership (HSEP, 1991–98) aims to enhance the educational achievements of young people living in a small, disadvantaged area to the south west of Glasgow. HSEP offers direct educational help for young people through homework clubs and residential work, and aims to raise young people's expectations of education through such means as work experience, college and university visits, and group work across the different school years. It seeks to improve school attendance through additional attendance reports to parents, and to involve parents in their children's learning through curriculum workshops for parents. HSEP also tries to improve inter-agency cooperation by such means as work-shadowing among different groups of professionals (for example, teachers shadowed HSEP staff when they visit young people's homes). A more in-depth description and analysis of HSEP is found in Chapter 10.

The third and probably most important challenge is ensuring that young people continue their education careers after the end of compulsory schooling, by entering post-compulsory provision. A series of good examples from Ireland have already been described in Chapter 4 (BITE, TAP, LCBEI).

Homework clubs

The physical resources to undertake homework (such as dictionaries, atlases, and computers) may be scarce in some households. To remedy such scarcity, and to provide immediate support and feedback, young people can be offered alternative opportunities. In the early 1990s, 20 such out-of-school homework projects were organised in the city of Utrecht (the Netherlands) for lower secondary students, as part of a broader social renewal programme. Projects were run by trained and coached volunteers, in small catchment areas, and provided homework support as well as pastoral care. Separate groups were sometimes held for specific young people, such as young women, Moroccan and Surinam youth. Eighty per cent of the participating young people were migrants.

Evaluation studies suggest that the projects have had a positive impact. Participating young people reported that, as a result of the educational discipline and support provided by the projects, they continued with formal education. Qualification levels of participants were at or above average (in comparison with national data) two and a half years after they left the projects.

While the Dutch experiences suggest that homework support has some positive effects, the question has been raised as to which organisation – schools or other – should provide homework support. Schools generally perceive homework support as part of their task, but often lack the human resources to provide it. If other organisations take on homework support, however, schools may be suspicious and hesitant to cooperate. Such a response has been noted in Flanders, and concerns have been voiced that organisational involvement lessens parents' participation in their children's school activities. To meet such concerns, parents could be supported and coached to help support their children's homework. Such support and coaching could be provided through discussion groups, training, and/or home visits by teachers.

Healthcare

Disadvantaged children's education is often hindered by physical or mental health problems, such as poor hygiene, nutritional imbalances, lice, chronic diseases, stress and lack of sleep, or simply by inadequate treatment of common illnesses. Schools are often reluctant to take direct action in such matters due to lack of means, or because they fear interference with parents' responsibilities. Nevertheless, some Flemish schools involved in the network sponsored by the King Baudouin Foundation (see above) decided that they should treat health problems internally. Rather than intervening in individual situations, they set up projects in which the parents were involved, discussion groups, and so on, often involving all pupils in order to avoid stigmatisation.

Recreational and sports opportunities

Since 1993, the Flemish Fund for the Integration of the Disadvantaged (currently Social Impulsion Fund) has supported a 'magnet school' near Antwerp; this was set up to undertake activities that would be more inclusive of children from *all* socioeconomic backgrounds. In addition to homework and study support, and a borrowing service for books, journals and games kept within the school library, extra attention was given to sports. Sports activities are expected to improve students' health, help them develop team skills, and allow some of the less academically gifted to experience another form of success. Furthermore, these activities hope to build a positive image of the multicultural community in the region. It is interesting to note that sports can, to some extent, be 'substituted' for lectures with surprising success, particularly for disadvantaged pupils. Experiments showed that pupils for whom afternoon lectures were replaced with sports performed equally well at examinations in comparison with a control group (Van Assche, 1988; Vettenburg, 1992).

Cultural activities

A range of resources now provide access to information outside mainstream educational settings. Television, the Internet, books, magazines and journals provide additional alternative views on social, cultural and political issues. Communities may have cultural resources such as museums, theatres and galleries. A number of pilot projects perceive educational advantage in young people accessing such alternative views and resources: for example, the Limerick-based Educational Initiative, already mentioned in the previous chapter. The King Baudouin Foundation sponsors arts projects in 20 primary schools in Flanders – 'magnet schools' situated mainly in disadvantaged districts – with a view to encouraging intercultural exchanges, developing skills other than those of a cognitive nature, and improving the team spirit among children as well as relationships with the local community (see Chapter 10). In the Netherlands, 28 primary schools are experimenting with an 'extended school day'. After school hours, children are offered opportunities to take part in educational and cultural activities.

Example of good practice: the Extended School Day in the Netherlands

Since 1992, 28 primary schools have experimented with an 'extended school day'. After school, children are offered opportunities to take part in extracurricular activities such as sports, arts, computer skills, basic science, environmental and nature issues. Activities are organised and led by trained staff from external organisations specialising in such activities. Overall, through providing additional opportunities, the experiment aims to strengthen the links between disadvantaged children, their educational environment, and the local community, and to enhance their cultural capital and social skills in order to raise success rates in school.

An evaluation study was carried out in 1997, involving 20 schools in the cities of Amsterdam, the Hague and Utrecht. The overall conclusions were positive. The children were reported as very enthusiastic about the activities. Most of them had not taken part in this kind of out-of-school activity before; "For them a door to a new world was opened; a world previously unknown to them." According to the teachers and the activity leaders, the children had become more open, more sociable, worked together better and had more self-confidence; "Children now dare to speak before a large group. The attitude with which they enter the classroom has changed; they are now more alert, curious, ask more questions, and look forward towards new adventures." The children also learned to make presentations in the class. All these results, according to the participating schools, had a positive bearing on the children's success in school.

The schools and the supporting organisations were positive about their collaboration. Contacts between them had increased, although the external group leaders would like to have more contact with the teachers. The schools reported that they were organising more classroom activities in which pupils had to present results of their work orally. The support organisations indicated that their understanding of the needs of disadvantaged children had grown. They were now organising more outreach activities to inform parents and other children about their work in the hope that the latter would take part in their regular activities too.

Which factors have made the extended school day a success? According to teachers and group leaders, participants had gained a lot from the experiment.

They could choose freely between activities, which increased their motivation. The activities took place in a 'safe environment'; that is, in small groups and without threatening assessments. Social aspects were strongly emphasised, enabling less academically gifted children to also experience success.

Although the longer-term impact of the project is as yet unknown, all parties involved considered the intermediate results as very promising for participants' future educational success. Based on their experiences, however, the staff of both schools and support organisations indicated that certain questions need to be addressed for any replication of the experiment:

- What is the main objective of the extended school day? Is it educational (providing positive support to children 'at risk' and their parents) or 'custodial' (to make the life of working parents more easy through providing a daycare service from 8 am to 6 pm)? And if it is a combination of the two, where is the emphasis?

- What are the wishes and the needs of the pupils and their parents? Can the school and its potential partners respond to them?

- What are the strengths of the pupils, the school and its environment? Which aspects – for example the presence of support organisations in the 'world of work' – could be capitalised upon? What does one partner have to offer other potential partners in the cooperation process?

- What are the weaknesses of the pupils, the school and its environment? Which (trustworthy) partners should be invited to help remedy these deficiencies? For example, does a club exist in the area providing sports that interest the pupils?

- Does the school have the capacity and willingness to set up a cooperative structure, to 'open up' to the outside world, and to accept contributions from others?

- And, last but not least, does the school team have the motivation and the stamina to launch the experiment and to carry it through for a number of years?

Language development

Education provided in an unfamiliar language creates serious barriers for young people. Initiatives have thus sought to improve young people's oral and written skills in the language in which classes are being taught, should the young people have another first language, with an emphasis on early intervention. The projects developed for children from ethnic minorities appear to be equally successful with native children from disadvantaged backgrounds.

The King Baudouin Foundation in Belgium funds such a project, with a wide range of approaches, to develop the language skills of non-majority language speakers. These approaches include: conversation circles in the classroom; language holidays for migrant children; language classes for parents; narration; cartoons; special resource books for infant school teachers aimed at developing a basic vocabulary; reading and even printing activities; school libraries for toddlers, run by parents; and 'language baths', involving both children and parents (Vettenburg and Thys, 1996).

Liaising with the socioeconomic environment

A Portuguese project seeks to enhance pupils' motivation by ensuring the school curriculum relates to the regional economic realities. The School-Environment Link Project (1987-92) was part of the European Union's PETRA Programme. The Project aimed to establish closer ties between the school and the local community, thus placing value on pupils' backgrounds in their educational experiences and involving the local community as an educational resource. Closer links were established with regional employers as well as social and cultural organisations, in order to enrich the teaching process and to provide better vocational orientation and guidance to the pupils.

While the focus of the various initiatives described above might differ, none are single-faceted. Instead, each initiative seeks to incorporate numerous activities for different actors (young people, parents, teachers and other professionals) in different environments (home, school, community, work). To tackle the overall problem of social exclusion, a multi-agency, multifaceted approach is regarded as necessary.

Providing integrated approaches: a review of institutional structures

The previous section concentrated on local pilot projects. This section considers institutional structures established at the macro level, which can facilitate integrated services and activities. Five questions will be addressed in relation to current institutional structures in participating countries:

- What are the policy backgrounds and developments?
- At what level (national/regional/local) are the services provided?
- Which partners are involved in the integrated approach?

- Which organisation has the primary responsibility for identifying young people in need of support?
- Which organisation has the primary responsibility for coordinating the services involved?

For a comparative overview of countries' institutional structures and policies, see Table 5.3.

Flanders

In Flanders, a single national-level policy for integrated services is presently lacking. Three separate institutional structures provide integrated services at different levels, focusing on the individual child, the school, or the local community. The gaps between the different levels have been criticised, and reforms are being implemented to better integrate these approaches.

On the level of the individual pupil, the centres for Psychological, Medical and Social guidance (PMS centres) are used to screen all children at the end of nursery school and at other key stages in their school careers. This screening enables professionals to identify young people in need of extra support. On request, PMS centres provide guidance and advice services to individual young people and parents.

The centres consist of multidisciplinary teams; however, they have been reproached for taking an overly psychological and individualised perspective on the problems of disadvantaged young people, and not recognising the societal and economic context of young people's lives. As a result, the centres have too little impact on educational processes within schools. A new law has redefined the centres' roles, making them focus their work more on young people at risk and to provide educational 'system support'. Such support would help schools and teachers to design strategies that address the educational and socio-emotional problems of groups of disadvantaged pupils.

Educational Priority Policy (EPP) came into effect in Flanders in 1991. It enables schools to implement group-based integrated approaches for pupils in primary and secondary education who have learning and developmental difficulties for social, economic or cultural reasons. The primary focus is on children from migrant families in disadvantaged areas. A similar policy (Extended Care) has been launched for all pupils with socio-emotional or developmental problems in the transition phase between nursery and primary education.

Table 5.3: Features of Integrated Approaches in six countries

	Flanders	Spain	Ireland	The Netherlands	Portugal	Scotland
Main policy measures relating to integrated approaches	- Educational Priority Policy (1991) - Extended Care (1993) - Pupil Guidance Centres (PMS)	- Act for the Social Integration of People with a Disability (1982)	- Home-School-Community Liaison Scheme (1990) - Youthreach (1989) - Demonstration Programme on Educational Disadvantage (1996)	- Social welfare policy (1994) - Local educational policy (1997)	- Act on the Priority Educational Territories (1996)	- Several cross-cutting integrated approaches exist: eg, the Children (Scotland) Act 1995
Level of implementation	- local level	- local level	- local level	- regional/city level authorities	- local/regional disadvantaged areas	- local level
Main partners involved in the implementation of the policies	- schools - community groups - guidance centres - parents and young people	- education - training - social services - health - judiciary - employment - other specialised services (see text) - parents and young people	in 1: education community groups in 2: training centres in 3: not specified parents and young people	- education training - social services - health - judiciary - employment - parents and young people	- education - training - social services - health - parents associations - cultural groups - recreational bodies - parents and young people	- 'all local authority services': social work, housing, education, leisure, youth services etc. health - voluntary and private sectors - housing associations - police - parents and young people
Coordinating agency	- no single agency	- not specified	for 1: not specified for 2: the national training agency	- secondary level: Regional Reporting and Co-ordinating functions	- the pedagogic council	- the local authority
Identifying agency	- compulsory phase: guidance centres	- multi-disciplinary teams	for 1: the local coordinators for 2: the schools for 3: not specified	- primary level: school health service	- not specified	- Some services are universally provided while others are targeted. Local authorities would typically assess for targeted services.

The Flemish government plans to integrate these support mechanisms into a single policy for schools that have a high percentage of youngsters who need customised care.

Both policies (educational priority and extended care) include collaboration with 'School Community Action'. School Community Action originated in Flanders in the late 1980s. Its aim is to improve the participation and success of disadvantaged groups in the school system, through better communication between parents, neighbourhoods, schools and PMS Centres. These projects are still experimental and lack a firm legal base.

The various schemes are implemented at the local/regional level. PMS centres and Extended Care cover all areas of Flanders; Educational Priority Policies and School Community Actions are implemented in disadvantaged areas.

At present, a coherent policy framework (including responsibility for identification and coordination of services) is still lacking. Developments are currently being discussed that would address these gaps. For example, the Flemish government plans to integrate Educational Priority and Extended Care into a single scheme for schools that have a high percentage of youngsters who need customised care. Logically speaking, one would also expect the PMS centres to be merged with community action centres. However, this measure has not as yet been considered.

Spain

The 1982 Ley de Integracion Social del Minusvalido (Act for the Social Integration of People with a Disability) commissions multidisciplinary teams for special education, consisting of psychologists, educationalists and social workers. The teams are responsible for early detection, diagnosis and guidance with regard to children's special educational needs in the pre-primary and compulsory school stages. The teams work on both curricular and vocational issues, and promote preventive as well as remedial measures.

Each local education area covers several municipalities and has its own team. The teams inform the authorities about the needs for special education resources. They also elaborate service plans and coordinate other services in the same educational area; these include specialised early intervention teams, social services, healthcare, mental health services, youth protection, occupational training centres, and recreational and sports centres.

Unfortunately, the teams do not cover the full population, as they work solely in state-sponsored schools in the pre-primary and compulsory stages. No policy has been defined for children aged 0–6 from socially marginalised or disadvantaged groups. Some isolated rural areas, as well as some densely populated areas, are not well covered. Other deficiencies are the lack of system flexibility and adaptability to the needs of the modern child, and the lack of coordination between governing bodies at the local, regional and national level.

Ireland

Numerous national and regional schemes in Ireland could be classified as 'integrated'. One example is the national Home-School-Community Liaison (HSCL) scheme, introduced by the Department of Education in 1990 to counteract disadvantage. The scheme seeks to increase cooperation between schools, parents and community agencies, to improve young people's education. Nationally, a coordinator runs the HSCL scheme, assisted by a National Steering Committee. The Committee includes representatives from the Department of Education, teachers' unions, parents' associations, and other relevant experts in the area. Locally, school-based coordinators cooperate with local committees.

For a further description and evaluation of the activities implemented in the HSCL scheme, see Chapter 10.

In addition to the HSCL Scheme, two other schemes contain elements of integrated approaches.

- The Demonstration Programme on Educational Disadvantage was launched in 1996 by the Combat Poverty Agency, a state-funded agency designed to combat socioeconomic exclusion. The programme establishes and supports local networks, which seek to develop an integrated response to educational disadvantage within their local areas.
- The Youthreach Programme was introduced in 1989, by the Department of Education and the Department of Enterprise and Employment. The programme aims to 'track' young people who leave school without formal educational qualifications and who have been unemployed for six months or more. It offers such young people a two-year programme that is person-centred, with an emphasis on the development of basic literacy and numeracy skills along with vocational training and work experience. Evaluation studies indicate, however, that the existing Youthreach Programme fails to track all those who leave school without qualifications.

Despite the existence of a number of integrated approaches tackling educational disadvantage in Ireland, there are many pupils from disadvantaged backgrounds who are not covered by these programmes. While some programmes have shown positive outcomes for disadvantaged young people, many programmes have not been systematically evaluated or are awaiting such evaluation. At present, the programmes fall under the authority of several government departments and state agencies, which reduces the potential for a coordinated approach to educational disadvantage. The various programmes could benefit from a coordinating of efforts and the establishment of clear targets to assess their impacts.

The Netherlands

Over recent years, major policy initiatives have sought to address the needs of disadvantaged young people. In all of these initiatives, power has been devolved to the regional/local level.

Since 1994, provinces must develop a consistent, cohesive and preventive youth policy in the context of Social Welfare Policy. Such policies must seek to gain a better understanding of youth problems, take stock of existing provision, improve access to these services, decide which new programmes should be launched, and distribute the available resources over the various services and programmes.

As this is a new challenge for the authorities, they were advised by the Ministry of Health and Welfare to appoint a 'local youth monitor'. The monitor would provide coherent information about young people and the services that cater for them. Special attention must be given to 'at risk' groups among young people.

At the local level, there is an Educational Policy for Disadvantaged Young People. In the 1995 memorandum on 'local education policies', all municipal councils were encouraged to set up appropriate structures to develop educational policies for disadvantaged young people, and related programmes and actions. Legislation was passed in 1997 that requires municipal councils to combat the effects of socioeconomic deprivation. The legislation aims to reduce the number of young people dropping out of formal education, and to ensure that all school leavers acquire at least a diploma based on two years of post-compulsory training.

Given that the problems are more severe in the four large Dutch cities – Amsterdam, Den Haag, Rotterdam and Utrecht – the 'large city' policy seeks to merge various policy areas and to improve education/ training provision. Overall, the 'large city' policy aims to fight social exclusion, reduce the number of early school leavers, improve prospects for unemployed young people, integrate migrants further into the local community, and increase citizens' participation in local/regional developments. More specifically, the educational and training sectors are required to improve attainment levels in primary and lower secondary education, reduce the number of early school leavers by 35%, integrate the world of employment more fully into training activities by creating 15% additional work experience/apprenticeship places, and develop more effective programmes to cater for young migrants or refugees.

Both the social welfare and educational policies seek to integrate strategies relating to family life, education, training and employment. Local policies will have to strengthen the cooperation between education, primary healthcare and health promotion, youth welfare work, work facilities, employment opportunities, the judiciary, the police, and social services. However, no agency has as yet been nominated to coordinate local social welfare policies. The Regional Reporting and Coordination Function could play this role.

At pre-primary and primary level, the school system (including the school healthcare service) bears the primary responsibility for identifying young people who need extra support. As of the start of the secondary education phase, the Regional Reporting and Coordination Function (RCF) is responsible for combating truancy and early school dropout (see Chapter 3). The RCFs began in 1995 and the pilot phase ended in 1997. The term 'function' is used, because no new organisation was set up. The provincial authorities have to decide which of the existing agencies would have responsibility for the new tasks; this could be the department in charge of controlling school attendance, a regional guidance agency, a project, or another body.

An evaluation study, carried out in 1996, indicated that almost all Dutch municipalities took part in one of the RCFs. All RCFs had experienced operational difficulties; for example, with gaining support from other organisations and gaining credibility in the eyes of schools, a lack of quantitative data, and insufficient facilities. Setting up an effective registration system proved more difficult than expected. Discrepancy between the various objectives of the RCFs was seen as a significant obstacle. While registration, stocktaking and information-giving are (relatively) 'neutral' activities, coordinating activities and pooling of resources are not. Other organisations objected to the latter role of the RCFs.

A wide range of support facilities are available for schools, parents and community groups. Over the last few years, steps have been taken to integrate these support measures. At the national level, the policy framework sets standards and general objectives. The regional level forms the heart of the system. Organisations cooperate under the umbrella of the municipalities, while local organisations fit their activities within this framework and make deals with the partners. As many of the schemes described above are still in their developmental stages, no final conclusion about the effectiveness of their delivery can be drawn yet.

Portugal

Since 1993, all primary schools provide pedagogical support to their pupils. Such support aims to prevent dropout and promote better school results. Activities range from differentiated teaching in the classroom to the development of interdisciplinary curricula responding to the needs of pupils, and the provision of extracurricular activities. Schools bear the responsibility for defining, developing, implementing and evaluating the effectiveness of their activities. Additional costs for materials and staff have to be met within the school's own budget.

The Priority Education Territory (PET) Act was introduced in 1996, in recognition of the fact that schools in disadvantaged areas require extra support. The first 34 PETs sought to improve the cooperation between the different levels within the school system, as well as between education and other agencies. Each PET has a partnership between pre-primary, primary and secondary level education providers. This partnership develops an educational project, involving local authorities (municipalities, social services and healthcare bodies), parents' associations, and cultural and recreational groups. Each PET is run by a pedagogic council, with all partners represented. A more extensive description of the PETs is given in Chapter 13.

'Educational animators' were also introduced in 1996, to support the schools in PET areas. The animators deliver extracurricular activities organised by the school. This provision was a joint initiative of the Ministry of Education and the Ministry of Qualifications and Employment. The Ministry of Education saw the animator as an opportunity to support young children and youth that live in underprivileged areas. The Ministry of Qualifications and Employment saw the role as an opportunity to provide work experience for unemployed people, particularly those who had finished a course in social work or in nursery school education. In 1997, there were 425 animators working in 219 schools.

Scotland

Numerous initiatives and policies seek to deliver integrated services, from 'community schools' to 'Social Inclusion Partnerships' based in disadvantaged areas, to health promotion. The most comprehensive provision for children and their families, at least potentially, can be found in the recent children's legislation. The 1995 Children (Scotland) Act legally requires local authorities to prepare, consult upon and publish Children's Services Plans.

In this system, the local authority has to indicate which services it will provide to safeguard and promote the welfare of children in the area who are 'in need'. Such services should, so far as it is consistent with children's welfare, promote the upbringing of such children by their families. Services can be provided to the child, to the child's family, or a member of the family. Assistance can be 'in kind' or, in exceptional circumstances, in cash. In the Act, a child is defined as someone below the age of 18, and is considered 'in need' if and when:

- the child is unlikely to achieve or maintain, or to have the opportunity of achieving or maintaining, a reasonable standard of health or development, unless this is provided for them by a local authority;
- the child's health or development is likely to be impaired significantly, or further impaired, unless such services are provided;
- the child is disabled; or
- the child is adversely affected by the disability of any other person in his family (see Chapter 3).

Such a definition could be interpreted to cover young people at educational disadvantage.

The 1995 Children (Scotland) Act defines local authorities 'corporately' (thus including all local authority services, from education to social services, recreation, and housing). Further, the Act promotes inter-agency working between local authorities and other organisations such as health services and the police. The Act specifies organisations that local authorities must consult with regarding their Children's Services Plans; the explanatory memorandum lists additional services to be considered. For example, when they may provide services for 'children in need' local authorities must consult with the voluntary and private sector, housing associations, health organisations, the police, and organisations representing service users.

While the local authority, by virtue of the Children's Services Plan, has an opportunity to reinforce the planning and working relationships between agencies, much still depends on the willingness of these bodies to cooperate.

As the legislation has come into effect only recently, little can yet be said about its effectiveness. Similar provisions in England and Wales for 'children in need', however, have been criticised for failing to meet their potential for preventive work. Children and families were sometimes receiving 'children in need' services only if they went through child protection procedures; a number of local authorities were prioritising groups of children for whom they had long provided services, rather than basing services on assessed needs. While a lack of coordination between services was often observed in England and Wales, the situation in Scotland looks more promising, given the corporate approach. On the other hand, many local authorities have found it hard to implement their new duties due to financial constraints (see Tisdall, 1997b for more discussion and research references).

Integrated approaches: from a first assessment to further developments

This concluding section will consider the coverage and effectiveness of integrated approaches in the six participating countries, at tackling the problems of youth 'at risk':

- Do the integrated approaches cover the full target group and involve all relevant partners as identified in Table 5.4?
- How effective are these integrated approaches, whether pilot projects or institutional structures?
- What are the options for further development of integrated approaches?

Issue 1: The presence of integrated approaches for young people 'at risk'

Conclusion 1: no country has, as yet, developed the appropriate institutional structure to provide integrated approaches to all those who need it. *All* young people should have the opportunity to receive their education in normal conditions. For those who experience difficulties in mainstream provision, for whatever reason, a more individualised pathway should be provided. Relevant authorities have to plan coordinated transitional pathways – that is, a series of measures enabling the young person to reach the end of the pathway satisfactorily. Following assumption five in the introduction to this chapter, such a system must be able to identify all young people who need additional support, develop holistic transitional pathways and provide the required extra support, and coordinate, or network, all local or regional services that should be involved.

Using this as a benchmark, none of the six countries have mainstream schemes that meet all three criteria (see Conclusion 2, below). In Spain, for example, the teams only reach pupils in the state schools; in Ireland, the Liaison Scheme does not cover all schools, while the Youthreach Scheme has insufficient places. Scotland has the potential to meet all three criteria, but in practice, local authorities have found it difficult to meet all needs due to financial constraints.

Conclusion 2: no country has, as yet, developed an operational system to provide integrated approaches involving all relevant partners. Table 5.4 provides a comparison between the list of organisations which, according to the OECD (1996b), should be involved in providing integrated services, and the organisations actually participating. In most countries,

Table 5.4: Organisations mentioned as being involved in integrated approaches

OECD services to be involved	FL	Esp	Irl	NI	P	Scot	Total
Education/training	*	*	*	*	*	*	6
Social/welfare services		*		*	*	*	4
Health services	*			*	*	*	4
Community/ cultural groups	*		*		*	*	4
Employment service	*			*		*	3
Youth services				*		*	2
Parents for children at risk					*	*	2
Police/criminal justice service					*	*	2
Housing services						*	1
Employers/companies							0
'Other' services							3
Total number of services	10+	4	2+	2+	6	5	8+
Additional services							
Daycare services						*	1
Recreational bodies					*	*	2
Guidance services	*					*	1
Number of services:	13+	5	2+	2+	6	6	12+

Note: + refers to the number of 'other services'

some core organisations are involved in providing integrated services: education and training providers, social and welfare services, health services and community groups. To this nucleus, one or more other organisations are usually added. But neither parents' associations nor youth services form part of the core group (except in Scotland). Parents are still too often seen as 'receivers only' and not as active co-producers of solutions for the challenges they face, which is a trend that should be reversed. Equally, youth services play a significant role in young people's lives (in the countries where they exist), and thus should be fully involved in integrated approaches.

Another body involved in only three countries is the employment service. In Flanders, monitoring is continued during part-time education and, if possible, support is provided. In the Scottish Home-School-Employment Partnership, a close cooperation with the Employment Agencies was essential to ensure a smooth integration of the participants into the labour market.

In comparison with the OECD list, however, some countries have called in additional organisations; daycare provision by the voluntary and private sectors in Scotland, recreational organisations in Portugal, and guidance services in Flanders. With the exception of Flanders, little attention is paid to the provision of educational and vocational guidance as part of the integrated services. A reason for this could be that in some countries, the Netherlands and Scotland for example, such provision is part of the responsibility of the school system.

Conclusion 3: all countries, however, have adopted policies that to some extent promote the full emergence of integrated approaches. What are the prospects for the wider implementation of integrated approaches? Countries can be divided into two groups, in terms of their development of a complete system of integrated services:

• Countries that actively aim to develop a full system of holistic transitional pathways and integrated services. Three countries follow a policy-led, top-down approach to creating such a system. The Netherlands is doing so through its local educational policy (1997) and its local social welfare policy (1994). The 1997 Children (Scotland) Act has the potential to create this type of system, with its corporate definition of local authorities and the new requirements regarding Children's Services Plans. To some extent, Portuguese legislation on Priority Educational Territories also moves in this direction. All these national policies aim to knit together the various resources at the local level. In all three countries, the policy initiatives are recent.

- Countries that promote the more or less gradual merging of existing provision. Flanders, Ireland and to some extent Spain can be included in this group. In Flanders, the new Educational Priority Policy (originally introduced in 1991), Extended Care, School Community Action (launched in the late eighties) and a new role for the PMS centres may combine to form an integrated approach. In Ireland, the Demonstration Programme on Educational Disadvantage is relatively new (1996) but the two other schemes – the Home-School Liaison Scheme (1990) and Youthreach (1989) – are both relatively 'old'.

The prospects for fully functional integrated approaches are probably brighter in the first group of countries, as policy makers are actively promoting and requiring such approaches.

Conclusion 4: all countries have also set up experiments to try out parts of integrated approaches. In Flanders, these experiments have been funded by the King Baudouin Foundation, Educational Priority Policy, Extended Care or other funds for social renewal. In Spain, the multidisciplinary teams cooperate with local services. In Ireland, the Home-School-Community Liaison Scheme is relevant for the younger age range, while for the older age group, Youthreach and the Programme on Educational Disadvantage offer opportunities. In the Netherlands, the new regional social welfare and educational policies form the framework. In Portugal, Priority Educational Territories provide new options. Various pilot initiatives are established in Scotland, often through the various forms of urban regeneration programmes.

The kinds of activities that are organised both within and outside mainstream provision are remarkably similar. The activities focus on offering additional educational, cultural and sports options to young people, and strengthening parents' involvement in the education and training process. On the basis of these experiments, ideas are converging about which key activities are required for integrated approaches.

Issue 2: Effectiveness of integrated approaches

Conclusion 5: no firm conclusion about the overall effectiveness of integrated approaches can as yet be drawn. No overall evaluation results are available on integrated approaches, as all the schemes are either partial or still too new. Furthermore, research on integrated approaches has inherent difficulties with regard to validity, both internal (for example, disentangling cause and effect between different services) and external (for example, identifying a control group).

Conclusion 6: some indications can, however, be given about the effectiveness of specific building blocks of integrated approaches. A number of aspects do appear to yield positive results. Evaluative data from several studies (studies of the cases described above, as well as the large-scale study from the OECD) suggest that decision makers should focus on the following points:

* increasing the involvement of the parents in all phases of the process as this leads to increased parental interest in their children's school careers, a higher retention rate at secondary level, and a higher progression rate to tertiary provision (see Chapter 10 for a more in-depth discussion of these ideas);
* involving cultural and sports organisations, as their activities develop generic learning contexts and understandings that young people need for successful adult and working lives;
* supporting schools in reinforcing the involvement and commitment of parents and developing a positive team spirit, clear leadership and good support staff. These features all have a positive influence on young people;
* maximising the voluntary co-operation between the main players involved, as this leads to an acceptance of each others' expertise and to a greater willingness to cooperate (see, for example, OECD, 1996a, p 77);
* setting up approaches which cover a wide range of services to young people and their parents, as single or limited actions will be less successful. For example, home visits will not work if they are not embedded in a wider approach.

Issue 3: the further development of integrated approaches

In order to make integrated approaches more widely available and more effective, more attention needs to be paid to the following aspects:

Conclusion 7: a clear policy framework with concrete objectives must be formulated. Integrated approaches require complex cooperation patterns between (sometimes unwilling) partners. No misunderstandings, therefore, should exist as to why partners should cooperate.

Ireland, for example, has specific objectives for its extra assistance and the development of home–school links; these categorically aim at reducing the level of dropout and educational failure.... Reducing early dropout is an explicit target of government educational policy with a stated objective of increasing the proportion of 16 to 18 year olds completing senior cycle to at least 90% by the year 2000. In Scotland and the Netherlands (see above), similar quantitative policy objectives are set. Such objectives will allow for a constant monitoring of the success achieved with the integrated approaches.

Conclusion 8: final responsibilities for the coordination of integrated approaches should be allocated to a single body. Integrated approaches can fall apart if final responsibility is not clearly allocated for their planning, decision making and implementation. For example, the RCFs in the Netherlands suffered because an existing organisation was given the responsibility for coordination without the power to act on it. As described above, this led to conflict with other partner organisations who were wary of losing autonomy. The top-led policy approach might reduce such problems. Would organisations in Flanders automatically accept decisions made by a PMS centre, if the centre was given a wider remit? Scotland does have such a policy approach, but the 1995 Children (Scotland) Act allows for services outside local authorities to refuse cooperation if it would "unduly prejudice [their] other functions". Policy needs to close such loopholes if an integrated approach is to be implemented fully.

Conclusion 9: adequate funding must be provided. In Ireland, it was felt that the integrated approach would be hard to implement on a national level due to cost factors. Many Scottish local authorities have found it difficult to implement the corporate, inter-agency approach because of financial constraints. Policy objectives can only be met with sufficient resources.

In sum, both the richness and the opportunities offered by integrated approaches are amply illustrated in this chapter. All countries in the study have moved towards providing integrated approaches, but clearly none have fully achieved them.

Note

[1] For simplicity, the term 'country' will be used to denote the six 'areas' covered in the national reports – that is, Flanders, Ireland, the Netherlands, Catalonia, Portugal and Scotland – realising that in three cases, in geographical terms, this is not correct.

SIX

Early childhood education

Emer Smyth and Breda McCabe (ESRI)

This chapter discusses the provision of early childhood education for children from disadvantaged backgrounds in the six study countries. 'Early childhood education' is used in a broad sense to take account of all educational measures targeted at children under the compulsory school age. Since a high proportion of children under school age attend 'mainstream' primary school in a number of countries, the term 'early childhood education' is more accurate than 'pre-school'. In practice, however, it is often difficult to disentangle educational measures from broader childcare provision. Such provision addresses a diverse set of objectives, including promoting the educational and social development of young children, and/or facilitating the access of parents to employment or training. While some services (such as pre-school provision in mainstream primary schools) are clearly 'educational' in focus, other measures, such as playgroups, often incorporate an emphasis on educational development in the broad sense. In fact, the EU Council Recommendation on Childcare suggests that member states "should try to ensure that ... [childcare] services combine safe and secure care with a broad education or pedagogical approach". Provision in the six study countries entails a combination of these 'welfare' and 'education' functions. The relative balance between these two perspectives, along with the extent to which such measures target children from disadvantaged backgrounds, will be discussed in this chapter.

The first section outlines some of the innovations in provision for young children from disadvantaged backgrounds developed in the United States since the 1960s. The second section discusses the level and nature of early childhood educational provision in the study countries, and the extent to which it targets children from disadvantaged backgrounds (however this is defined). The third section presents some examples of projects that have been designed to target these young children. Conclusions are presented in the fourth section of the chapter.

Background to early childhood intervention programmes

The development of early childhood intervention programmes in Europe and elsewhere has been heavily influenced by the projects initiated in the United States in the 1960s, as part of the 'war on poverty'. These programmes were specifically focused on economically disadvantaged children and were guided by the following assumptions:

- the environmental conditions associated with poverty are often insufficient to promote healthy development in children;
- educational enrichment can compensate for the disadvantages brought about by poverty;
- children will be more likely to experience later success in school if early intervention takes place;
- longer-lasting effects can be achieved by extending intervention into mainstream primary school (Reynolds et al, 1997).

One of the earliest programmes, Head Start, was initiated in 1965 and was a comprehensive child development programme primarily for pre-school age children living below the poverty line. This federally funded programme grew rapidly and is still in existence today. Its aim is to enhance social competence, primary school readiness, health and nutrition, and social-psychological development. Its target is poor children aged 3-5 years and their parents, along with children with disabilities. The programme stresses parental involvement (Reynolds et al, 1997).

Evaluation of the effectiveness of the Head Start programme has been far from controversial. An initial evaluation indicated that the full-year programmes were ineffective or only marginally effective at enhancing children's cognitive development. However, this early study was criticised for failing to take into account the fact that the comparison group was more advantaged than programme participants (Wu and Campbell, 1996). Other research has indicated positive effects in the short term, with higher rates of immunisation, higher cognitive ability, higher school achievement and motivation, and improved social behaviour among participants up to two years after finishing the programme. There is also evidence of lower grade retention and referral to special education services among those who have taken part in Head Start. However, other research indicates that subsidised centres such as Head Start may have larger group numbers and lower quality inputs than centres in more economically advantaged areas (Phillips et al, 1994). It was found that pre-school services tend to be more successful when they are followed by coordinated intervention in primary school (Zigler, 1995; Bryant and Maxwell, 1996).

There is limited evidence for any significantly long-term effects of participation in Head Start (Reynolds et al, 1997). However, one of its earliest projects, the High/Scope Perry Pre-school Programme, was initiated in 1962 for African-American children aged 3-4 years who were living in poverty. It was a two-year programme, involving five 90-minute classes a week, for seven months a year. The programme involved child-initiated learning activities, along with weekly home visits by teachers. Children aged 7-14 who had participated in the programme had higher school achievements (but not IQ scores) than a control group. The High/Scope programme is unusual in that participants were followed up until the age of 27. Evaluation indicates significant long-term effects for programme participants; the scheme has resulted in a higher rate of high school graduation, higher earnings, a lower take-up of welfare, and a lower crime rate. The programme has thus been seen as extremely effective in cost-benefit terms. The success of the programme is related to raised expectations among teachers and parents, which resulted in higher motivation among pupils (Wortman, 1995; Weikart, 1996; Gomby et al, 1995).

In the late 1970s and 1980s, many American states launched pre-school programmes to serve disadvantaged children through public schools (Gomby et al, 1995). Programmes such as the Child-Parent Centers in Chicago have been integrated into the school system, adopting child-centred approaches to social and cognitive development among 3- to 9-year-olds. Evaluation has indicated higher reading and maths scores among participants, although there has been some evidence of 'fading' of these positive effects over the next five years. Participants were more likely to complete high school, and were less likely to experience grade retention or special education, or be arrested in their early teens. Positive effects on school performance increased with length of time spent in, and earlier entry into, the programme (Reynolds and Wolfe, 1997; Bryant and Maxwell, 1996).

A number of other programmes for early childhood education have been introduced in the United States since the 1970s. A review of project evaluations indicates that the majority of studies support the existence of both short-term and longer-term effects. Studies have indicated immediate gains in IQ scores which diminish over the first years in school (Barnett, 1995). However, there has been a good deal of controversy about the reliance on IQ as a measure of programme 'success' (Gomby et al, 1995). The magnitude of short-term effects is related to the intensity, breadth, and amount of involvement with children and their families (Barnett, 1995). In addition, there is substantial support for longer-term effects on children's development, especially in relation to school competence (lower rates of grade retention and referral to special education, for example) (Barnett, 1995). However, the vast majority of empirical evidence comes from model or pilot programmes rather than large-scale interventions, so findings should be interpreted with some caution due to the problems of finding an appropriate comparison group (Reynolds et al, 1997).

Broader family support programmes ('two-generation' programmes) in the United States appear to have inconsistent or only modest effects on children's cognitive development (Bryant and Maxwell, 1996). Evaluation indicates better results from projects which link child-focused activities to parent-focused activities (Gomby et al, 1995).

Early childhood provision in Europe

Childcare policies and programmes tend to emulate features of the social and economic systems in which they arise. It has been argued that the strength of progressive political parties, the relative homogeneity of the population, and the perceived importance of children to a nation's welfare are crucial factors in the development of childcare provision (Lubeck, 1995).

European countries, including the study countries, differ significantly in the level and nature of educational provision for young children in general and for disadvantaged children in particular. Figure 6.1 indicates rates of participation in education among children aged 3 to 6 in the study countries. These figures should be interpreted with some caution since countries differ somewhat in their definition of educational provision[1] and due to the overlap between 'education' and 'childcare' discussed above. It is evident that Belgium has near-universal participation in early childhood education, even though school attendance is not compulsory until the age of six. Participation rates are extremely low among very young children in the Netherlands and Ireland, although rates are high for children aged 4 and 5. In the Irish and Dutch cases, this is accounted for by the high proportion of children who attend 'infant' classes in primary schools before the compulsory school entry age. The Spanish and UK[2] patterns are fairly similar, with a dramatic increase in participation between the ages of 3 and 4. In

Figure 6.1: Educational participation among young children in the study countries

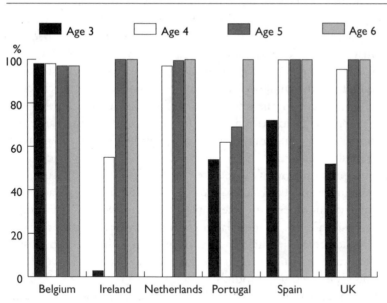

Source: OECD, *Education at a glance* (2000)

contrast, educational participation is relatively low among Portuguese children under the age of 6.

The overall levels of participation in early childhood education have consequences for the situation of disadvantaged children. Given the very high levels of participation among children in Belgium, it is clear that almost all children from disadvantaged backgrounds will experience three years of educational activities prior to entering the compulsory schooling system. The point is reinforced by Nicaise's (1998) research, which indicates that kindergarten participation is not significantly related to parental employment or occupational status. However, the high level of participation among all Belgian children may mean that existing inequalities in educational outcomes between more and less advantaged children are maintained (see Chapter 3), unless specific measures are designed to improve the position of poor children. In the other countries, the lower level of participation among very young children is likely to mean that levels are especially low among children from disadvantaged backgrounds, although such differences have not been subject to systematic investigation in the European context.[3] If, as American research has indicated, early participation is associated with more positive schooling experiences in the longer term, then lower participation among poor children is likely to reinforce their initial disadvantage.

Figure 6.1 indicates the quantity, rather than the quality, of early years provision across the study countries. While there has been no systematic study of cross-national variation in early educational quality, European countries are found to differ in the nature and focus of provision for early childhood education. Most publicly funded childcare for children under 3 is the responsibility of welfare authorities, although there is some educational provision for this age group in France and Belgium. In general, publicly funded provision for this age group is low. For children aged over 3 (and under the compulsory school age), most countries provide two to three years of pre-primary schooling; however, in Ireland, the UK and the Netherlands, children are admitted to primary school early or attend playgroups. Levels of care outside school hours are low in these latter countries (Moss, 1990).

The study countries differ in the nature of early childhood provision and the extent to which specific measures are targeted towards children from disadvantaged backgrounds.

Over time, Belgium has moved from a welfare model of childcare provision, in which provision is targeted at the neediest children, to one of near universal provision (Lubeck, 1995). In the 19th and early 20th centuries, provision focused on reaching children from disadvantaged backgrounds, a policy which had its roots in the charitable origins of pre-schools. As in many other European countries, services are divided between 'welfare' and 'educational' functions, with 'welfare' provision targeted at children under three, and 'educational' provision targeted at those aged 2-6 years. Provision for children under 3 is the responsibility of welfare agencies in each of the three Belgian communities. In Flanders, *Kind en Gezin* (K&G, see below) subsidises and regulates local initiatives by local authorities or private organisations. Some of this childcare (*kinderopvang*) provision is specifically targeted at children living in poverty, and charges are means-tested (see below). Despite this positive discrimination, the use of daycare remains extremely unequally distributed, as the centres tend to favour two-earner families when there is excess demand (Storms, 1995).

Among 3- to 5-year-olds in Belgium, there is a high level of attendance at nursery schools (*kleuteronderwijs*), which are usually part of primary schools. Nursery schools are centrally regulated by the Department of Education but can be run by local authorities or private institutions. Children are taught in groups of 20-25 pupils by a teacher specifically trained in early childhood education. The pre-school curriculum is regulated by a general framework, although it allows for a good deal of discretion at the school and teacher level. The focus is on the development of cognitive, socio-emotional and artistic skills, using a child-centred approach. Research indicates, however, that the nursery school programme is strongly oriented towards the preparation of children for entry into primary school, with about two thirds of the time devoted to educational activities (Delhaxhe, 1989). A study in a French-speaking region indicates that the nature of activities differs according to the children's social background, with less time being devoted to educational activities for working-class children (Quoidbach and Crahay, 1984). Some provision is available for care outside school hours during term time. Apart from nursery schools, which are free, parents pay for other publicly funded services according to income (Moss, 1990).

Until recent years, the level of early childhood provision in Portugal has been relatively low. This must be seen in the context of traditionally low levels of participation in compulsory education. Consequently, educational policy tended to focus on measures to improve pupil retention within the compulsory schooling system rather than on pre-school programmes. Until the mid-1960s, the majority of centres in Portugal for children under six were not concerned with education, and staff tended to lack specific training. Early childhood education was granted greater recognition from the 1970s onwards, with a concomitant increase in the level of provision and the development of specific training for teachers working with young children. In 1997, the government introduced a programme for the expansion and consolidation of the pre-school sector, with the aim of guaranteeing free pre-school provision for all children.

As in Belgium, there is an age-based distinction between welfare and education services for young children, with responsibility shared by two ministries – the Ministry of Work and Social Security (MWSS) and the Ministry of Education (ME). Services for children under three are the responsibility of the Ministry of Work and Social Security, whose kindergartens operate a 'social welfare model' with access depending on family background characteristics and 'need'. Most of this provision is in nurseries, usually run by private organisations. While programmes are intensive, providing services for 10-12 hours per day, their coverage is low (involving about 6% of those under 3 in 1988). For children aged 3 to 5, about half of the available places are provided by education authorities in pre-primary schooling, with the remaining places in public or private kindergartens. These kindergartens use an educational model.

In the case of excess demand for pre-school places, access is decided on the basis of age (with older children given preference), although there are regional differences in pre-school coverage. Pre-school programmes operate six hours per day and close for summer, Christmas and Easter holidays. Public kindergartens (of both types) have two parent representatives on the consulting body. In terms of curricula, general goals and guidelines are provided by the Ministry of Education. Parents contribute to the costs of all services (except schools) according to their income and number of children. There is a general lack of pre-school research in Portugal, and it appears that there are few specific projects for disadvantaged children, with the exception of the Amadora Project (see below) (Bairrão et al, 1989; Moss, 1990).

In Spain, there is a long history of public provision for young children; publicly funded pre-schools for 3- to 6-year-olds have existed since the mid-19th century. Since 1970, provision has been divided into two levels: the first cycle, which covers children under 2, and the second cycle, which covers children aged 3-5. Provision for very young children is heterogeneous, involving daycare centres and work-based care centres; the focus of such provision tends to be custodial rather than educational. The level of attendance of pre-primary schools among 4- and 5-year-olds is very high, with levels also increasing among 3-year-olds in recent years. Such provision is generally incorporated into primary schools, with curriculum guidelines issued by the Ministry for Education. Parents' involvement in the educational process is normally sought. In general, pre-school education has grown rapidly in Spain over the past 20 years. Public provision has become more important numerically (at two thirds of the total provision) than private (usually Church-run) provision, although this varies by region (Palacios, 1989; Moss, 1990). Quality tends to vary between the two sectors, with higher pupil–teacher ratios in the private sector. There is also evidence that children of parents with higher levels of education and/or income tend to have greater access to high-quality pre-school education (Palacios, 1989). While pre-school or nursery centres tend to give priority to lower income families, and although some measures (such as multidisciplinary teams in schools) are designed to provide additional services to this group in the context of mainstream provision, there is no clearly defined policy for pre-school children from disadvantaged backgrounds.

In the Netherlands, compulsory schooling begins at the age of 5. Nearly all children start primary schooling at the age of 4 on a voluntary basis, but there is no pre-primary schooling as such. The main form of provision for children under 4 is the playgroup, with one quarter of 2-

year-olds and half of 3-year-olds attending such groups. Most playgroups receive public funds, but children only attend for five to six hours per week. Among children aged 3-5, half attend primary school, with a further quarter in playgroups. There is a low level of provision of outside school hours care. Parents pay for publicly funded services according to income. The highest level of provision is in urban areas, especially Amsterdam (Moss, 1990). There appears to be no specific pre-school provision for children from disadvantaged backgrounds with the exception of some broader community-based projects (see below).

In the UK (including Scotland), compulsory primary schooling begins at the age of 5, but many 4-year-olds attend primary schools on a voluntary basis. With the exception of schools, services are the responsibility of local authorities and the Department of Health. Local authorities in Scotland are under no obligation to provide early years services for all children, although since 1996 they must provide services for 'children in need' (as defined in the previous chapter).

While as of yet untested by law, 'development' is thought to include intellectual, and thus educational, development. Daycare and after-school and holiday care must therefore be provided to 'children in need' by local authorities. The issue of the quality and affordability of childcare for all children aged under 14 years of age has recently been addressed in a Green Paper, *Meeting the childcare challenge: a childcare strategy for Scotland (1998)*. However, it is too early to assess its impact on policy development for young children in general, and children from disadvantaged backgrounds in particular.

There are publicly funded places for only a very small proportion of children under 3 in the UK as a whole, mostly in day nurseries and family centres. There is also a shortage of low-cost day nurseries in Scotland (Powney et al, 1995). Existing provision is directed at children who are severely disadvantaged or 'at risk'. Among those aged 3-4, a quarter are in pre-primary schooling (usually on a part-time basis) with a further fifth in regular primary school. The proportion of children in pre-school is likely to increase in future years due to the government's commitment to provide a free part-time pre-school place for all 4-year-olds from winter 1998. Playgroups, attended for five hours per week, are the privately funded service which provides for most pre-school children. Most playgroups are run by parent groups (Moss, 1990). The part-time nature of playgroup provision means that most children tend to use more than one service (for example, playgroup plus child-minder) (Powney et al, 1995).

Pre-school provision for children over 3 tends to be educational in focus, with 4-year-olds spending two thirds of their time in activities directly relevant to the primary school curriculum, regardless of the type of centre they attend (Powney et al, 1995). In 1997, the Scottish Office produced a curriculum framework for children in their pre-school year. This framework covers the following key areas: emotional, personal and social development; communication and language; knowledge and understanding of the world; expressive and aesthetic development; physical development and movement. Pre-school education is also subject to inspection on the basis of nationally specified 'output standards'.

In the UK as a whole, there is some evidence that children from socially deprived backgrounds are less likely to receive pre-school education and, where they do so, the quality of care they receive is likely to be lower (Eurydice, 1994c). However, the 1996 Task Force in Scotland recommended a comprehensive intervention strategy with particular emphasis on overcoming the "disadvantages and inequalities of social and domestic background" (SOEID, 1997). The measures which target pre-school children from disadvantaged backgrounds in Scotland are discussed in the following section.

In Ireland, there is limited provision of early childhood services (Hayes et al, 1997). There is also a problem of lack of co-ordination and standardisation among pre-school services, a problem that led to the establishment of a National Forum on Early Childhood Education in 1998 as the basis for the drafting of a White Paper. As in many other countries, there is an artificial divide between 'welfare' and 'education' functions. Less than 2% of children under 5 attend publicly funded day nurseries (Moss, 1990). These are run by private organisations and are essentially a social work service for children who are severely disadvantaged or deemed 'at risk'. Other types of provision include playgroups (usually privately run, although some are run by parents' committees), *naíonraí* (Irish-speaking playgroups) and Montessori pre-schools. The majority of pre-school services charge fees, even those located in disadvantaged areas (Hayes et al, 1997). Although compulsory schooling does not begin until the age of 6, most 4-year-olds and almost all 5-year-olds attend 'infant' classes in primary schools on a voluntary basis. There are significant differences between the educational experiences of 4-year-olds attending pre-schools and those attending mainstream primary schools. First, pupil–teacher ratios are higher in schools, and the availability of play equipment is somewhat lower. However, there is a higher level of training among teachers in schools, and children tend to attend for a greater number of hours. Second, there is a greater educational focus in schools, with pupils spending more time on pre-academic activities, while children in pre-schools spend more time on child-initiated activities (Hayes et al, 1997). There are some specific measures in Ireland designed for children from disadvantaged backgrounds, including the Rutland Street project, the Early Start programme, and centres for pre-school traveller children (see below).

In summary, the six study countries differ in terms of both the level and type of provision for early childhood education. However, a number of common issues are apparent. First, there is in many systems a distinction between the provision focused on 'welfare' and that focused on 'education', a distinction which has obvious implications for the experiences of young children. Second, existing provision tends to be general in nature; children from disadvantaged backgrounds tend to be the focus of 'supplementary' programmes, rather than having their needs addressed within mainstream provision. The nature of provision for children from disadvantaged backgrounds is discussed in greater detail in the following section.

Intervention programmes for disadvantaged children

It is difficult to systematically compare the study countries in terms of the proportion of children from disadvantaged backgrounds and their participation in early childhood education. There are immense conceptual difficulties in cross-national comparisons of poverty rates. However, it is evident that children are overrepresented among those living below the poverty line in the six study countries (Ditch et al, 1998).[4] There are both commonalities and differences between the study countries in the type of pre-school measures available for disadvantaged children. These measures can be broadly grouped as follows:

- structured education programmes for pre-school age children;
- measures designed to achieve flexible delivery of pre-school services to certain groups;
- home-based intervention programmes which focus primarily on the child;
- interventions aimed at both children and parents (and sometimes the wider community).

Structured education programmes for pre-school children

Example of good practice: the Rutland Street project

The best known example of an early intervention programme in the Irish context is the Rutland Street project. The project began in 1969; its basic purpose was to develop strategies to prevent school failure in disadvantaged areas. The project came about as a result of cooperation between the Bernard van Leer Foundation, an organisation concerned with the promotion of innovation in education to meet the needs of the disadvantaged child, and the Department of Education in Ireland. The Department contributed the normal financial provision available to schools, while the special features of the project were funded by the Foundation. The Rutland Street area, located in Dublin's inner city, is one of high unemployment and poverty and low levels of educational attainment. The area was selected in response to demands by teachers and voluntary groups concerning the problem of educational failure in the area.

The development of the project was influenced by a number of the early intervention projects in the North American context (such as Head Start), and by Piaget's work on child development. The objective of the curriculum was to develop skills that would facilitate adaptation by the children to the work of the primary school. This involved the development of skills of perceptual discrimination, the extension of the child's knowledge of the world, the development of skills related to the organisation of knowledge, and the development of language skills. Children were to follow this cognitively oriented, structured programme for two pre-school years. The Pre-School Centre was targeted at 3- and 4-year-old children, catering for 180 children in all. Children attended morning or afternoon sessions lasting two and a half hours, and were taught in groups of 15 by a teacher and a classroom assistant. A cooked meal was provided to children in the middle of the school day.

In addition to the emphasis on child development, the Centre aimed to increase the amount of contact between parents and the school through the establishment of a mothers' club, an advice centre, and regular parent-teacher meetings. This work with parents was also supported by three social workers who conducted intensive casework with some of the most severely disadvantaged families. In 1971, it was decided to develop home-school contacts through a home-based intervention programme. The aim of this programme was to change the teaching style of the mother and increase her confidence in her ability as an educator. It involved 26 mothers being visited at home for an hour each week by one of the home teachers. The focus of each session was on the development of the child's language and communication skills (Holland, 1979; Kellaghan, 1977).

The Rutland Street project was intended as an experimental programme, with ongoing evaluation built into the work of the programme. For the purposes of this comparison, children participating in the programme were compared to a control group of children living in the same catchment area. By the end of the two-year programme, participants showed an increase in their intelligence scores and an improvement in measures of pre-school readiness. In addition, a survey of mothers indicated positive attitudes towards, and satisfaction with, the pre-school, along with greater involvement by the mothers in the education of their children. However, on transfer to primary school, children showed a decline in their intelligence scores over the first three years; this pattern was particularly marked among the children with initially higher test scores. It should be noted, however, that a development gap between participants and non-participants in terms of intelligence scores was still evident. This difference did not translate into advantages in school performance; at the age of 8, the experimental group performed no better on an English reading test than the control group. A separate evaluation of the home-based intervention programme indicated no significant differences in average intelligence between participants and non-participants (Kellaghan, 1977).

The pattern of initial improvement followed by gradual decline was similar to that found in many American evaluations of early intervention programmes (see above). An interesting feature of the Rutland Street project was a follow-up of participants at age 16, in order to assess the longer term benefits of programme participation. This evaluation indicated no differences between the control and experimental groups in subsequent absenteeism from school or in social deviance. However, a number of positive benefits were evident. First, participants reported greater encouragement from home to attend second-level school. Second, participants were more likely to stay on until second-level schooling and to take state examinations. They were more than twice as likely as non-participants to take the Group Certificate, and three times as likely to take the Intermediate Certificate. Furthermore, just under one tenth of the participants took the Leaving Certificate; none of the control group did (Kellaghan and Greaney, 1993). The Rutland Street Centre still serves children in its catchment area, and the experience of the project has been used to develop a structured programme for infant classes in schools in other disadvantaged areas (CMRS, 1992).

The Early Start programme, inspired by the Rutland Street experience, was initiated as a pilot pre-school intervention programme in eight pre-school units (in seven areas of disadvantage) in 1994. It is one year in duration, and is seen as an integral part of the primary education system, targeting 3-year-old children in disadvantaged communities. The aim is to enhance the overall development of the child, to ensure a smooth transition to full participation in the formal education system, and to offset the effects of socioeconomic disadvantage. Under the Early Start programme, learning is seen as a guided journey of discovery, in which children are seen as active agents in their own development.

In 1998, some 40 schools and 1,593 children were involved in the programme, with over two million ECU in total expenditure by the Department of Education. The programme is staffed by trained primary school teachers and care workers, and has an adult–child ratio of 1:7.5. The curriculum emphasises language and numeracy skills and also the development of links between home and the school. Parental involvement is a particular feature of the programme and occurs on three levels: (i) the day-to-day running of the centre; (ii) taking part with their children in the centre's activities; (iii) participation in an advisory group in the centre.

The monitoring of the programme is carried out by a committee composed of parents of the children and representatives of various educational bodies. In addition, an independent evaluation of the programme is being carried out by the Educational Research Centre, but has not as yet been completed (Department of Education, 1995; ESF Programme Evaluation Unit, 1997). While it is too early to assess the potential impact of the Early Start programme, some concern has been expressed concerning its displacement of existing community-based childcare services (often run by local groups of parents themselves) (NESF, 1997). In spite of this new programme, however, the level of public funding available for pre-school provision in Ireland remains very low by European standards.

In Scotland, there have been a number of projects designed to boost literacy levels among young children living in economically deprived areas. A 1992 study of the Pilton area in Edinburgh (which is now part of a designated Priority Partnership Area) had found that 85% of primary four children were over a year behind in their reading age, and 50% were more than two years delayed (Paterson, 1997d). In response to this situation, Lothian Regional launched the Pilton Early Intervention Project and provided additional funding for the employment of extra classroom support, in the form of extra teachers and home–school link staff, the aim being to encourage children to spend more time reading. The project involved additional teaching in the early years, the provision of nursery nurses for the infant classes, and home–link teachers to promote parental involvement in children's learning. At nursery level, the project aimed to improve pupils' knowledge of books, letters, rhyme and phonology. Each nursery involved in the project was provided with a package of relevant books and other materials to assist this process. Home-school link teachers were given the task of supporting parents in their role as educators of their own children. This involved holding workshops for parents on early literacy in both pre-school and early primary years, the development of resources to enable parents to stimulate literacy, and the provision of opportunities for children and parents to work together. Evaluation indicated clear improvements in children's literacy levels over the first three years of the project. The number of primary four children a year behind in their reading dropped from 85% to 45% (Paterson, 1997d). However, it must be said that some children were found not to have benefited from the early intervention initiative. According to head teachers, these included children from the most severely disadvantaged backgrounds as well as those that did not attend regularly. This raises the question as to how far such initiatives reach the most disadvantaged children in communities. There was also some variation between classes, which was likely to relate to individual school and teacher effectiveness (SOEID, 1997; Lothian Region, various years).

A similar project was initiated in Wester Hailes Schools, which provided nursery nurses or classroom assistants in early years classes. These nurses/assistants are actively involved in literacy development, and progress has been reported for participating classes (SOEID, 1997).

In June 1997, the Scottish Education Minister announced that the Early Intervention Programme would be extended to run on a national basis. The programme is designed to run until 2002. Additional funding provided by government and local authority grants provides extra support in schools through the employment of learning support teachers, educational psychologists, classroom assistants, and home-school link personnel. The programme incorporates ongoing evaluation of its effectiveness and value for money.

Local authorities are not specifically required to target schools in disadvantaged areas. However, it seems that it is now established that Early Intervention Programme funding should be allocated to schools on the basis of their socioeconomic status. The number of children receiving free school meals and in receipt of clothing grants have been used as indicators for the selection of schools to participate in the programme. Nevertheless, there is still considerable discretion allowed to local authorities in deciding the nature of funding allocation. This has raised some concern about the programme being inadequately targeted and being used as a general strategy to accelerate the educational curriculum for all (in the context of international educational competition), rather than redistributing opportunities towards the most disadvantaged.

Many of these structured programmes (such as Early Start) incorporate an element of additional funding for disadvantaged areas and/or groups. This approach is also evident in the Extended Care programme in Belgium (Flanders). This policy, introduced in 1993, enables schools to obtain extra staff and resources to develop an educational approach which is geared to the specific backgrounds and developmental needs of individual children with 'learning problems' (poor and non-poor). In allocating additional resources, account is taken of the background characteristics of the pupil population of the school. Additional funds obtained under the programme must be used for additional educational staff and activities in the transition period from nursery (mainly the third year) to primary school (first year). In addition, schools are required to design an action plan which optimises the development of the pupils' language and social skills, the monitoring of pupils, teaching techniques, and cooperation within the school and with parents. Evaluation of the programme indicates that the number of teacher hours spent on extended care has a significant positive effect on pupil progress (Bollens et al, 1998). Other research has indicated that the programme has resulted in greater confidence among teachers in detecting and remedying developmental problems. However, the difficulties of implementing initiatives involving more than one class have been highlighted (Verhaeghe, 1998).

Flexible delivery

A number of countries have developed special provision to reach young children who do not usually have access to, or participate in, early years services. The groups targeted are mainly traveller children or those living in isolated rural communities.

In the Irish context, there are 56 pre-school facilities for Traveller children, catering for 660 children in all. These pre-schools are usually established as a result of initiatives by local committees for travelling people. The Department of Education provides grants for the purchase of equipment, and defrays 98% of the costs relating to tuition and transport. It has been argued that these pre-schools can have a positive role in preparing children for integration into primary school. However, the lack of guidelines for practice and curriculum, along with the absence of systematic in-service training and support for staff, have been criticised (Task Force on the Travelling Community, 1995). A pilot programme providing pre-school services for traveller children (Traveller Education and Support Options) has recently been set up by Barnardo's. While the ultimate aim of the programme is to hand provision over to the traveller community, the project was initially run by qualified members of the travelling community who were employed by Barnardo's. The project uses the active learning approach developed by High/Scope (see above).

In Spain, there are two such programmes: *La Casa de los Niños* and travelling pre-schools. La Casa de los Niños is an educational service aimed at children under 4 years old and their carers. Those living in rural areas without pre-school provision were initially the target for intervention; more recently, however, the service has been extended to working-class urban areas. The objectives of the programme are twofold: for children to socialise and engage in activities with other children; and for parents to exchange information and experiences, in collaboration with educators from whom they receive guidance and support. Centres are staffed by a teacher and an educator, and run by a director in each area. Finance is provided by the Madrid Community and the Town Council.

Travelling Pre-schools (*Preescolar na Casa*) are educational services provided in sparsely populated rural areas. The programme is an educational intervention scheme that works with children under 6 and their parents, with the assistance of systematic and regular guidance by professionals. The programme was initially launched in the region of Galicia in response to low educational participation and academic underperformance. The programme works with the family members; the children are given guidance as to the week's work, but the parents are the ones who actually work with the children. Periodically, meetings with children from other families are organised, for play or to carry out group projects. In 1988/89, there were 543 such groups in Galicia, involving over 2,000 children. The programme has been seen to have positive effects on children's integration into compulsory schooling. However, issues such as the difficulty in involving parents (particularly fathers), and scepticism on the part of 'mainstream' teachers, have been raised.

Travelling pre-schools were also introduced into Portugal in 1993. Their objective is to promote development among pre-school children who live in remote areas with no nursery facilities. The network of nursery school teachers reaches 170 children in 75 localities.

Home-based intervention programmes

In Scotland, the Lothian Region Home Visiting Scheme involved trained teachers visiting the homes of 2- and 3-year-olds for one hour per week to encourage mothers in the educational development of their children. However, concerns have been expressed that the scheme may damage mothers' self-confidence in their own child-rearing practices by failing to recognise and take account of the family's home culture (SOEID, 1997).

In the Netherlands, a home intervention project, using structured activities designed to prepare the child for school, was implemented. Local mothers were involved in training other parents. However, evaluation indicated mixed results in terms of the impact on children. There were positive effects for the development of language skills among Moroccan children, but no effects on other dimensions of child development (Eurydice, 1994c).

A home-based intervention project for disadvantaged pre-school children, similar to the scheme used in Rutland Street, was implemented on a pilot basis in a provincial town in Ireland (the Kilkenny project). For the purposes of the programme, disadvantage was conceptualised in terms of low occupational level, poor housing, and family reliance on social welfare payments. The objective of this programme was to increase the quantity and quality of mother–child interaction, in order to facilitate the development of school-related concepts and skills among pre-school children. The curriculum was centred around perceptual–cognitive activities, imitative play, manipulative activities, and language, and involved 38 hour-long home lessons, spread over a two-year period. An evaluation of this programme indicated no marked advantage for participants in terms of performance in ability tests (Archer and Kellaghan, 1975).

These measures overlap somewhat with the 'two-generation' measures discussed in the following section. However, home-based intervention programmes can be seen as focusing more closely on the promotion of the educational development of the child (by working with the parent), while community-based interventions may also have specific goals for parents, including the promotion of access to training and employment.

'Two-generation' and community-based interventions

In the Belgian context, some poverty projects have been set up by *Kind en Gezin* (Child and Family) for the 0-3 age group, before the start of nursery school. Kind en Gezin is the official body in charge of care for babies and toddlers in Flanders. It runs and subsidises daycare centres, and operates preventive healthcare centres in disadvantaged areas. In addition, specialist nurses systematically visit new mothers and babies at home, particularly when the latter are thought to be at risk. The Pedagogical Training School was set up in collaboration with a voluntary organisation in a deprived district of Antwerp. 'Social nurses' from Kind en Gezin gave training sessions to parents; these initially focused on health information but expanded to incorporate educational issues, with the active participation of parents in practical workshops. Another project is a daycare centre, *De Wurpskes* in Leuven. This centre differs from ordinary daycare centres in that it is embedded in a network of voluntary organisations in a disadvantaged district, it forms part of a set of support facilities for the integration of disadvantaged women into the labour market, and it provides for extra stimulation activities for children and educational support to parents. Parents are closely associated with these activities; group sessions, where parents exchange experiences and receive training on educational issues, are also organised.

The *Koffiepot* centre for work, knowledge, living and wellbeing is a community project in a working-class district of the Hague with a relatively high proportion of immigrants. It is run by the Hague social department, together with local women. Its aim is to promote education and training for both mother and child; to develop job opportunities for local mothers; and to promote the involvement of mothers in the education of their children. The target group consists of mothers and children (up to the age of 4 years) in a specific neighbourhood. The Koffiepot centre is largely subsidised by the Hague municipal council. Women from the neighbourhood can go to the Koffiepot each day with their children. The centre offers a varying range of activities and courses in the areas of education, recreation, art and culture, health, and community structure. It is free of charge. While participation is voluntary, its reach among women in the community is high (Schwab, 1994).

In Spain, maternity/infant centres are directed at both parents and children, but at the former in particular. Some target mothers during the child's first year of life, trying to provide information and training, and allowing mothers a space of their own and a chance to exchange experiences with other mothers. Other services target both mothers and fathers of children under 3 years of age. They have a clear social, educational, and health function. In addition, the *Proyecto Granada* provides parents and children (including those from the gypsy community) with training and cultural and educational activities. Initial results suggest that this project has assisted the integration of children into mainstream schools (Eurydice, 1994c).

Other locally based projects in Spain provide services jointly to parents and children. *Capitulaciones 92* in Granada provides psychopedagogical support to families with children under 3 years of age. Both play and learning activities are provided for children, while training and group meetings are provided for parents. Information on the needs of young children is also provided to other adults in the community. This initiative has been found to have positive developmental outcomes for children. Parents are better trained to stimulate their children's physical, intellectual, emotional and social development. In addition, parental awareness of local services for their children is enhanced. The initiative has since been supplemented by services directed at pregnant women, and a home visiting scheme for families. Elsewhere, *Proyecto Avanzada* has taken an integrated approach to service provision for families, involving the early detection of children and mothers at risk, and support for mothers on an individual or group basis. The existence of multidisciplinary teams (of psychologists, social workers, and so on) in mainstream schools in Spain can also be seen as leading to a 'two-generation' approach.

The Amadora Project in Portugal is a project in which educational, health and social welfare agencies integrate their efforts to respond to the socioeducational needs of at-risk children, and to promote family and community involvement in dealing with social problems. The project has been undertaken in two of the most deprived areas in the district of Lisbon; it is run by the local social security centre and subsidised by the Bernard van Leer Foundation (Bairrão et al, 1989). Similar initiatives, using integrated approaches to the needs of children at risk and the promotion of family and community involvement, have been integrated into general programmes targeted at those experiencing socioeconomic disadvantage (the Integra Programme, for example). A similar approach is taken by the educational animators scheme. This involves the employment of unemployed people in educational (including pre-school) activities in deprived areas.

A new nationwide UK programme, entitled Sure Start, was launched in 1998. This programme focuses on the prevention of social exclusion by working with parents to promote the development of children, particularly those from disadvantaged backgrounds, to ensure school readiness, and building on existing services to provide a range of supports (including educational services, play facilities, and primary healthcare) for children and parents. Contact with parents commences with a visit by outreach workers within three months of a child being born. Services will be available free to low-income families and 'at a fair cost' to better-off families. Sure Start funding will amount to approximately 760 million ECU over three years, with an allocation of 66 million ECU for services in Scotland. It will be targeted at 'areas of greatest need', reaching up to 5% of children under 3 years old and their parents.

Measures to promote parental involvement in their children's education will be discussed in greater detail in Chapter 10.

Conclusions

This chapter indicates the diversity of provision for early childhood education in the study countries. This diversity is also evident among measures designed to target children from disadvantaged backgrounds. While not enough comparable information is available on the effectiveness of these measures, initial evaluations would appear to favour structured educational programmes for pre-school children as the most efficient way of promoting educational development. Programmes which feature flexible delivery have also been found to provide an efficient way of reaching marginalised groups, as evidenced by the Spanish experience. Findings from home intervention projects in the study countries and elsewhere are as yet less convincing, and it is difficult to assess the impact of broader community-based projects, given the diffuse nature of their goals.

In overall terms, however, the level of provision for young disadvantaged children does not appear to be adequate in any of the study countries. Even in Belgium, where overall rates of participation in pre-school services are very high, there are few measures which specifically target disadvantaged children. As indicated by American research, interventions in the study countries appear to be more successful where they occur early in the child's development, and where involvement is maintained throughout the early years of primary school.

A note of caution must be expressed about compensatory education for pre-school children, however. First, in the absence of large-scale interventions at the national level, measures are unlikely to reach all children who could be deemed 'poor' or 'disadvantaged'. Second, such measures are unlikely to fully compensate for all of the disadvantages which result in the inequalities in educational outcomes experienced by these children (see Chapter 1). Third, a number of critics of compensatory education (for example, Bernstein, 1974; Connell, 1994) have expressed the view that more significant structural reform of the educational system is needed in order to address these inequalities, and that the notion of 'compensatory' education can serve to direct critical attention away from schools and the educational system, and towards parents and children. Fourth, given the success of early intervention programmes in raising the literacy and numeracy levels of young children, there is a risk of such programmes being diverted away from their initial objective (equalisation of opportunities), towards boosting overall attainment rates, increasing the children's workload, and making the education system even more competitive.

Notes

[1] In the UK case, for example, children in educational programmes such as playgroups and daycare facilities are excluded, resulting in an underestimate of overall participation (see OECD, 1996a).

[2] Separate figures are not available for children in Scotland.

[3] American research indicates that, in spite of the expansion of federally funded provision for disadvantaged families, pre-school attendance is still highest among children from advantaged families (Gomby et al, 1995).

[4] This definition relates to the proportion living in households with a net annual income below 50% of the net annual income of all households.

Part Three:
Equal treatment strategies

SEVEN

Curricular reforms

Neus Roca Cortés (CIREM)

Curricular reforms encompass broad measures aimed at adapting the educational system to better meet the needs and interests of society. Some reforms are concerned with bringing about more equal treatment of young people through their compulsory education. This chapter outlines recent curricular reforms in the participating countries, their aims and outcomes, their target groups, and their impact on social exclusion. In conjunction with the funding system and the schooling structure, and as a secondary socialisation system, curricular reforms may have a considerable impact on social cohesion and on the distances between social classes in society.

A typology of reforms

Due to the diversity in curricular reforms adopted in the participating countries, the following typology of measures is proposed:

- Modification of the age at which pupils choose their educational track or finish their compulsory schooling.
- Modification of final qualifications: the extent to which certification is unified or differentiated, along with the required contents, will influence the access of young people to further education and employment opportunities.
- Unification, whereby the same curriculum applies to all pupils in any educational institute, in contrast to an earlier emphasis on two-tier schooling (usually, vocational versus academic education).
- Development of flexible curricula, whereby all types of pupils take the same core curriculum, but a pupil has a limited choice of subjects (or subject levels) on the basis of his/her interests and abilities. Three strategies for the creation of more flexible curricula can be distinguished: (i) choice of subjects: pupils choose different subjects which, together with their core subjects, enable them to achieve

specified educational objectives. This requires a good guidance and tutoring system, along with the removal of prior restrictions on subject choice; (ii) choice of subject levels: pupils choose different levels or grades for each of their subjects (or curricular modules), both core and optional, within the framework of the final certificate or qualification; and (iii) curricular adaptation on an individual or group basis, but one which is selected by teachers. This approach involves modifying certain elements, such as objectives, contents, and classroom and school facilities, in order to better address individual differences among pupils. This reform is not 'fundamental' as long as pupils obtain the mainstream certificate. When curricular reforms involve more 'fundamental' changes, they are termed 'alternative curricula'. These three strategies take place at different levels within the schooling system. Subject choice tends to be introduced by the educational administration, and teachers, schools and families must adapt to these changes. In contrast, curricular adaptation depends almost exclusively on the ideas and skills of teachers and specialist advisers. Thus, the application of these strategies depends on very different processes related either to resource provision and management, or to teachers' training and innovation.

- Alternative curricula are programmes with specific contents and methodologies targeted at particular groups of pupils. These may be found within or outside the compulsory or mainstream educational system.

The typology of measures mainly refers to changes in the structure of the curriculum and may (or may not) involve changes in methodology, mode of assessment or programme content. Pedagogical innovations are discussed in greater detail in Chapter 8.

Overview of curricular reforms in the participating countries

This section presents an overview of the curricular reforms and measures introduced in each of the participating countries. These measures are summarised in Table 7.1. The following sections of the chapter include a comparative analysis of the measures, along with a discussion of their effects. Further information on the educational systems in each of the participating countries is provided in the Appendix.

All of the countries participating in this study initiated curricular reforms during the 1980s and 1990s. These measures have been directed

Table 7.1: Curricular reforms and measures

Country	General structure prior to reforms	Type of measures		
		Unification of curriculum	Flexible curricula	Alternative curricula
Flanders	6-18 years: compulsory schooling 6-12 years: primary education Streaming from 12 onwards (type II) or from 14 onwards (type I) up to 18 years: 4 options: General, Technical, Arts and Vocational Special education is segregated	* 1990 Unified Structure (12-18 years)	* Streaming * Autonomous middle schools (Renewed Secondary Education, 1990)	16-18 years: Part Time Vocational Education ('school-fatigued' students from vocational or technical education)
Ireland	6-16 years: compulsory schooling 6-12 years: primary education 12-16 years: some differences between school sectors (secondary, vocational and community/comprehensive) but within same curricular framework Special education is segregated		* 1989 Foundation, Ordinary and Higher Levels in Junior Certificate Programme (12-16 years)	* 1996 Junior Certificate Schools Programme (12-16 years): only applied in schools with high numbers of educationally and socially disadvantaged population 16-18 years: * 1994 Leaving Certificate Vocational Programme * 1995 Leaving Certificate Applied Programme.
Netherlands	6-18 years: compulsory schooling 6-11 years: primary education 12-16 years: three options: general, vocational and prevocational Special education is segregated	* 1993 Basic Education: (12-16 years) New comprehensive educational centres with a curriculum consisting of: 15 common subjects + optional subjects	* 1993 Subject option choice in Basic Education	12-16 years: * Employment Oriented Programme (or Practical School) for pupils with limited academic capacities 16-18 years: - Assistant Training - Forthcoming streaming of higher general secondary education into four major profiles of vocational specialisation

Table 7.1: Curricular reforms and measures (continued)

Country	General structure prior to reforms	Type of measures		
		Unification of curriculum	Flexible curricula	Alternative curricula
Portugal	*6-15 years*: compulsory education *5-9 years*: primary educ. *10-14 years*: two options: general and vocational Special education is segregated	* 1986 Basic Education (*5-14 years*)		
Scotland	*5-16 years*: compulsory education in comprehensive schools *14-16 years*: can try vocational units (two certificates) and Standard Grade Curriculum (3 levels: Foundation, General and Credit)	*16-18 years*: * 1998 Higher Still unified programme (vocational + academic)	* 1980 Standard Grade courses (of 1-7 ability levels) (*15-16 years*)	
Spain	*5-14 years*: compulsory education in a single common school *15-18 years*: secondary education with two options: - Initial and advanced vocational - Baccalaureate (academic option leading to University Education)	* 1990-1995 Compulsory Secondary Education (*12-16 years*) common core + option choice in subjects and in levels	* 1990-1995 Compulsory Secondary Education (*12-16 years*) 50% common subjects 25% remedial work or extension of common subjects 25% optional subjects	* 1997 Curricular Adaptation Units (*14-16 years*) – only for pupils with special educational needs * 1995 Social Guarantee Programme (*16-18 years*)

at pupils over the age of 10, particularly those aged between 12 and 18, by integrating different types of secondary education, by making core curricula more flexible, by extending the period of compulsory education (as in Portugal), or by developing alternatives to school failure among older pupils. It is worth noting that Spain, Scotland, and (very recently) the Netherlands have integrated compulsory schooling for 5- to 16-year-olds into a single track or system, encompassing pupils with special educational needs (except for those with more serious difficulties) into a single curriculum. The previous rigid division into two or three differentiated educational tracks (vocational, academic and/or mixed/general) has been abolished or reduced. However, Ireland, Portugal and Flanders still maintain the distinction between special and mainstream education. In Flanders (and also informally in some schools in Ireland), pupils are streamed or grouped by ability into so-called 'a' and 'b' classes in the first two years of secondary education (12-14 age group). A choice of educational tracks is required at age 14 in Portugal and Flanders; this falls within the compulsory schooling period in Flanders but is considered as post-compulsory education in Portugal.

The curricular reforms carried out over the past decade have resulted in more or less substantial changes in the structure of compulsory secondary education. Available data indicate that all the participating countries have introduced the same two sets of measures: equal treatment strategies among the 12-16 age group (compulsory schooling), and alternative curricular strategies for specific target groups among 14-16 year olds (and sometimes up to the age of 18). In some countries, reforms have also involved primary education, either by integrating the curriculum and extending the schooling period (as in the case of Portugal and Spain), or by integrating special education for pupils with disabilities into a common educational system for all citizens (as in Spain in 1985 and the Netherlands in 1992). All of these measures are intended to prevent or reduce the prevalence of discrimination within the school, in order to bring about the more equal treatment of all citizens.

The major common aims of the reforms to secondary education presented in this book have been to retain as many pupils within school as possible (that is, to reduce the number of early school leavers), to facilitate the transition between academic and vocational options in order to address biases in provision towards more 'academic' students, to reduce the number of school leavers without qualifications, and to facilitate the transition from school to the labour market. In general terms, this means increasing the opportunities for social equality by bringing about educational equality.

Among the measures adopted to achieve these aims, curricular unification and the development of flexible curricula for the 12–16 age group deserve special mention in this chapter. Special measures for the most disadvantaged pupils in compulsory education will be taken into account in this chapter, but will be discussed in greater detail in Chapter 14, together with transition systems and alternative curricula.

Unification of the curriculum in compulsory secondary education

The first measure adopted by all of the participating countries has been to postpone the early social selection between the (more intellectual) academic option and the (more job-oriented) vocational option. They have instead opted for unification of the curriculum in lower secondary education. In terms of Litt's (1980) classification of types of knowledge, the new curriculum should combine, at least for two additional years, theoretical and symbolic–ideological knowledge (stressed in the academic, general or baccalaureate option) and instrumental knowledge (dominating the job-oriented, vocational option). This has involved a move towards a homogeneous curriculum for all pupils, except in Flanders, which has in fact introduced a hybrid combination of comprehensive education and early streaming (the so-called 'unified structure' with 'a' and 'b' classes). In all of the countries being studied, the necessity of selecting between vocational and academic options has been postponed until the age of 16, except in Flanders and Portugal, where it has been postponed until the age of 14. The main aim of this measure is to reduce the social differentiation produced by the educational system. However, it is still possible in all systems for young people to leave school with inadequate qualifications, and differences in the type and level of final qualifications may still result in unequal opportunities for access to adult education or the labour market.

Curricular unification tends to go hand in hand with the development of flexible curricula strategies. However, the relative emphasis on the two approaches tends to vary from country to country. Broadly, there are two approaches: a partial unification strategy whereby pupils have the same curriculum in the first cycle but are segregated into different curricular tracks in subsequent cycles (unification plus segregated option choice); and a flexible curriculum (unification plus integrated option choice) which combines homogeneity and diversity by providing subject option choices integrated into the same school. Partial unification results in social differentiation through the segregation of curricular options after the initial comprehensive stage. Integrated option choice differentiates among pupils in terms of the optional subjects they take, or the levels at which they take subjects.

The available data do not allow us to assess the impact of these different strategies across countries in a systematic fashion. However, a number of evaluation studies indicate the consequences of these reforms in certain national contexts.

Flanders and Portugal have adopted a strategy of partial unification, with a homogeneous curriculum up to the age of 14, when pupils have to choose one curricular track. Both countries distinguish between special and mainstream education, and even within mainstream education there is some differentiation according to ability level between and/or within schools. Some Flemish authors point to the low degree of mobility between certain curricular tracks. An interesting study of this system, which looked at children with equal IQ scores but with different socioeconomic backgrounds, has revealed that pupils from lower socioeconomic backgrounds are more likely to be referred to technical[1] and vocational tracks than are children from higher social classes (Stinissen et al, 1987; Van de Velde et al, 1996a). In this case, streaming within the school militates against the move towards curricular unification. Furthermore, pupils who have experienced learning difficulties in primary school tend to enter so-called 'b' classes in secondary education, which are intended to help them to 'catch up' with their peers. However, Van de Velde et al (1996a) found that over 95% of those who start in 'b' classes remain in this stream and enter preparatory vocational education. These students are much less likely to achieve access to tertiary education. A similar pattern of social differentiation has been observed in Portugal due to lack of access to certain schools.

The development of flexible curricula in compulsory education

The development of flexible curricula deserves special mention, since it involves allowing pupils to make subject choices within the same school, rather than segregating them into different tracks and/or schools. Flexibility is present in two senses: first, pupils have a greater opportunity for transition between different curricular routes; secondly, the curricular framework formally recognises differences among pupils in terms of their interests, abilities and performance.

Ireland, the Netherlands, Scotland and Spain have moved towards a unified curriculum, but with a strong emphasis on the adoption of a flexible curricula strategy. Since the mid–1980s, Scotland has introduced a homogeneous curriculum for the 12–14 age group. Between the ages of 14 and 16, pupils can choose from Standard Grade courses and Vocational Units, but every pupil will have to complete eight recognised curricular modules as part of their individual pupil programme. Flexibility is introduced both through the availability of subject choices and through a choice in exam levels. Spain (from 1990 to 1995) and the Netherlands (from 1993) combine a common curriculum with the availability of subject options. Between the ages of 12 and 14, pupils mostly take core subjects, with a combination of core and optional subjects for those aged 14-16. In Spain, flexibility is achieved through different subject levels (pupils can choose from extension or remedial credits for core subjects) or through subject types (pupils can choose different types of subject specialisation). The relative proportion of common and optional subjects is officially regulated, although the range of optional subjects offered differs from school to school.

In 1989, the Junior Certificate that replaced the existing Group Certificate (seen as a more vocational qualification) and the Intermediate Certificate (seen as more academic in nature) were introduced in Ireland. Curricular flexibility is brought about through a choice of subjects and a choice of subject levels for exams. For the mainstream Junior Certificate, pupils usually take nine exam subjects. The relative proportion of core and optional subjects and the type of optional subjects provided is heavily influenced by the school. The number of optional subjects is strongly related to school size, with larger schools providing a greater choice of subjects for pupils (Smyth, 1998). On average, second-level schools provide six to seven core subjects; pupils are allowed to choose two to three subjects. Within schools, the degree of choice open to pupils may differ from class to class. For example, pupils allocated to the 'bottom' class in a streamed school may have a different range of subject choices than those in the 'top' class. For the Junior Certificate, pupils may take Irish, English and mathematics at one of three levels: Foundation, Ordinary and Higher levels. Other subjects may be taken at one of two levels. The amount of choice pupils have in selecting an examination level varies from school to school and from class to class. A new feature of the Junior Certificate programme was the introduction of Foundation levels in Irish, English and mathematics, in an attempt to counter educational failure; this measure has achieved recognition by employers, for recruitment purposes.

Seven years after initiating curricular unification in Ireland, it was deemed necessary to introduce an alternative curriculum, the Junior Certificate School Programme, specifically targeted at schools with high concentrations of social and educational disadvantage, school failure, and early dropout. This measure occupies a more marginal position, since pupils have a different assessment and certification system. The vast majority of pupils take the mainstream Junior Certificate, with a small minority taking the Junior Certificate Schools Programme.

In the four countries, different types of qualifications have different consequences for access to higher education and employment. At the same time, there has been a tendency towards the integration of special education into mainstream education, with the Netherlands introducing these changes most recently (in 1994).

Flanders and Ireland have comprehensive schools as a 'third way'. Middle schools in Flanders form part of the heritage from 'Renewed Secondary Education' (a programme for the promotion of pedagogical innovation, established in 1990). These schools offer only the comprehensive stage (the first two years) of secondary education, and have a commitment to collaborate with all types of further education institutes and to offer a wide range of subjects so as to facilitate choice in the second cycle. In Ireland, community and comprehensive schools were established in an attempt to bridge the gap between secondary and vocational schools. However, all three types of school operate within the same curricular framework.

The development of flexible curricula has been evaluated in more detail than the partial unification measures described above. Schools which have adopted this approach seem to have obtained somewhat better outcomes in two respects: in keeping more young people within the school system (that is, the prevention of early school leaving), and in facilitating the transition to further education.

Among the participating countries, Scotland has the longest tradition (since 1981) of a comprehensive system. Comprehensive reorganisation of schools in Scotland was more thorough than comprehensivisation in England, and the Scottish state school sector reflects the principles of equality of access, with schools remaining non-selective in character. This process of comprehensivisation and curricular reform has been accompanied by a number of changes. First, post-compulsory educational participation has increased among young people in Scotland; in 1983 only 52% of students beyond age 16 stayed on in full-time education, but by 1994 the figure had risen to 70%. Second, social class inequalities in participation rates and attainment levels have declined somewhat (Paterson and Raffe, 1995). Paterson argues that: "Social class inequalities in school attainments as a whole narrowed in the early 1980s, as a result of comprehensive education, but have remained fairly constant ever since" (Paterson, 1997a). Gamoran (1996b) also found an increase in participation and attainment levels for Standard Grades among students from lower socioeconomic backgrounds, although they seldom achieved the pass threshold necessary for further study at Higher Grades. Third, there has been an expansion in the curriculum available to pupils in state schools. By the early 1990s, nearly all pupils were studying English, mathematics, a science, a technological subject and a social subject (Croxford 1994). Broad access to languages has also been developed. However, gender differentiation in subject uptake has persisted, especially among working–class pupils (Croxford 1994; Turner et al, 1995).

In the case of Ireland, the same period has seen an increase in participation in post–compulsory education, with a reduction in the proportion of pupils leaving school without qualifications since 1994 (source: ESRI, Annual School Leavers' Survey, 1980-1995).

It has been observed that students make better progress in systems aiming to reduce early segregation of students, such as the 'Autonomous Middle Schools' in Flanders, than they do in schools with only technical and vocational departments in their second and third cycles of secondary education; there is no significant difference in the rate of progress in schools with an academic option as part of their curriculum. However, streaming is not totally eliminated in these schools: improved progress in Autonomous Middle Schools is limited to pupils in the 'a' stream, but no such positive results are apparent among pupils in the 'b' stream (Bollens et al, 1998). The stigmatisation effects[2] of streaming within a school thus tend to restrict the impact of comprehensivisation on educational progress and mobility between curricular options. Nevertheless, from the perspective of the social objectives of compulsory education, the democratising impact of such an approach should not be underestimated (Osaer, 1984; OECD, 1995c).

Although the available data are fragmentary, improved outcomes seem to be achieved in comprehensive schools which are committed to maintaining a balance between subject options and which maximise the choices available to students by avoiding hidden curricula. These outcomes reflect the commitment to comprehensive education on the part of schools, teaching staff and even pupils' families. Such outcomes have been observed in the Experimental Compulsory Secondary Schools in Spain, which are an example of a more integrated schooling system. These schools have no internal streaming; general, vocational and technical education are not segregated; and special education has been integrated into the 'ordinary' schools since 1985. Evaluation studies indicate that these schools have the capacity to raise the 'graduation rates' (that is, the proportion of students who succeed in obtaining the accredited final certificate) by 15%. This was achieved with pupils who had already experienced educational failure (CIREM, 1997); these pupils had lower failure rates than in previous studies (CIREM, 1995). In both cases, the positive results can be partially explained by teachers' commitment levels, as teachers were trained for the attitudinal and practical changes required by the introduction of a more flexible curriculum.

However, the development of a comprehensive stage in all Spanish schools since 1995 does not ensure that similar positive results are obtained. Facilitating conditions include a balance between the subject choices offered, a personal guidance system to facilitate educational routes and to address family expectations, and the development of links between the subjects and their socioeconomic context. The introduction of such reforms involves not only additional material and/or human resources, but also conceptual innovation and a change in attitudes. Some studies highlight the fact that the persistence of traditional attitudes and practices is one of the most important reasons behind the failure or limited impact of such reforms. This factor was mentioned as a key element in the 1995 OECD report which stressed the need to allow time for transition on the part of teachers, as well as the need to provide additional training.

Two cases of curricular reform are presented as models of good practice; evaluations of these reforms indicate positive results, and they provide a good balance between diversity and equity.

Examples of good practice

Spanish comprehensive curriculum in compulsory secondary education (Educación Secundaria Obligatoria, 12-16 years)

A high proportion of the curriculum (60% in the first cycle, 50% in the second cycle) is standardised either by the state or by the autonomous authorities. There are three types of subject: compulsory, variable credits, and synthesis credit. The compulsory subjects include: native language (that is, the language of the autonomous region where it is not Castilian), Spanish language, a foreign language, mathematics, natural sciences, social sciences, physical education, design, and music. The so-called 'variable credits' are established by each school, but must be linked to a compulsory subject area, and may change every three months. Usually, variable credits involve a development of the contents and level of a particular subject, revision of a subject to raise standards, or the development of a subject in some specific direction or to incorporate new elements; for example, theatre (language or physical education), comics (language and design), radio and television, biosphere functioning and ecological problems, chemical change, automatic models, health education (including drugs), human rights and citizenship, study skills, and so on. The 'synthesis credit' is a final course credit that involves a cross-disciplinary applied project in which pupils must demonstrate their autonomy and teamwork skills; this is used as a complement to traditional examination assessment.

This curricular reform also stresses personal guidance for pupils; it includes specific tutorial time and a plan required from all educational centres along with educational strategies to address the diversity of pupils' backgrounds and educational needs. Pupils are assessed by the school using standard exam criteria, with results awarded at one of two levels, Secondary School Graduate or Schooling Certificate.

As mentioned earlier, the Experimental Compulsory Secondary Schools have proved very successful in raising the performance of pupils with a previous record of failure. However, it is uncertain to what extent this success will carry over after the generalisation of this curriculum.

Scottish comprehensive curriculum (12-16 years)

For the first two years of compulsory secondary schooling (S1-2), students continue with the broad 5-14 curriculum. For the second two years (S3-4), the curriculum is designed around Standard Grade assessment. Standard Grade courses are offered to students of all ability levels. The following curriculum modes should be reflected in individual pupils' programmes: language and communication, mathematics studies, technological activities and applications, creative and aesthetic activities, physical education, and religious and moral education. Pupils are assessed against performance standards related to three levels of award: Foundation, General and Credit. Students can also take vocational units, which can later lead to vocational certification.

Impact of the curricular measures on socially excluded pupils

The comprehensive systems have resulted in a higher general educational level without hindering progress among higher ability pupils. In addition to increasing the educational level, the pupils' success, progression and staying-on rates turned out to be significantly higher in the reformed schools, in contrast with those in which the old segregated structure persisted. The appraisal of the situation leads to the conclusion that option choice is a more motivating educational space for young people's education than the previously existing systems. The reforms have introduced teaching methods and contents more suited to pupils' interests, and have thus led to increased pupil retention and improved performance (Fernández Enguita, 1990). These results have been found in France (Prost, 1983), Spain (Fernández Enguita, 1987) and a larger number of countries by the International Association for the Evaluation of Educational Achievement (Husen, 1967; Comber and Keeves, 1973). Despite the achievements of comprehensive education, however, the reforms have not succeeded in breaking the strong association between social origins and school success (Fernández Enguita, 1990).

Three potential problems have been observed in the participating countries. The first of these is the 'ranking' of school types not on the basis of educational quality, but on the basis of the type of programmes offered. The second is the emergence of internal streaming (grouping by ability) because teachers have not absorbed the fundamental idea behind the 'treatment of diversity'.[3] Third, there is inadequate monitoring of flexible curricula, or there is an unwarranted choice of subjects and/ or levels.

When pupils are allowed to choose their subjects, their choices often reflect social expectations or a response to the school's limited supply or its internal streaming. This contributes to the emergence of different educational routes: academic education, vocational education and direct entry to the labour market. Thus, the segregation between options that the curricular reform aims to abolish may instead be reproduced. Many educational experts advocate a stricter control over subject choice in order to achieve greater social equality but without disregarding the diversity of pupils' interests. Furthermore, social differentiation may still take place through university (or other further) education, or by the transfer of resources and status to private schools or to occupational training.

From the data available, we can only speculate about the impact of such curricular reforms on pupils experiencing social exclusion. There is reason for scepticism since, only a few years after the introduction of more flexible curricula, all of the reforms have been supplemented with the introduction of alternative curricula[4] for pupils whose needs and capacities were not adequately addressed within comprehensive provision. Strategies for greater curricular unification and flexibility have promoted social integration and social mobility in facilitating the transition between options in secondary education; but to what extent have they met the needs of pupils who are at risk of achieving no qualifications whatsoever?

The transnational analysis indicates that almost all[5] of the countries have addressed the problems of 12- to 16-year-old pupils from socially excluded backgrounds by introducing alternative curricular measures. However, there have been differences in the implementation of such measures. Some countries have only adopted these measures on a partial basis, carrying out such measures in parallel to mainstream provision, or conflating those with special educational needs with those in special education. Other countries (such as Ireland) have introduced nationwide policies in a clear and direct manner although this has been limited by the need for voluntary participation on the part of the school; thus, the state has no control over the number of pupils who are excluded from such opportunities.

Measures of this type are targeted at (potential) early school leavers, truants, poor attenders, disruptive pupils and those who have experienced serious difficulties in primary schools; in other words, pupils who have the necessary intellectual capacity, but whose social conditions have not enabled them to succeed in mainstream education. They have been neglected by the school, 'sitting on a chair' for many years without learning much, if anything at all. Often these pupils have created conflict in the school, or joined alternative movements on the street. The impact of alternative curricula on such pupils is reported in Chapter 14.

One problem with alternative curricula is that most of these do not allow for access to other mainstream general education or vocational training (in the latter case, Ireland is an exception). These alternative curricula may thus become a marginal, residual form of education, since they do not result in specific qualifications or certification. Information from the participating countries indicates that it is only in post-compulsory education (after age 16) that more formal curricular measures are made available to this type of pupil. Still, in most cases, alternative curricula do not represent an equal treatment strategy, since pupils in these streams are not offered the same final certification as their schoolmates. It is a remedial or containment measure rather than an equal treatment measure, if we consider its social implications.

However, the positive results in terms of young people's learning mean that such measures deserve further consideration as a feasible alternative to a rigid education system which engages in selection, which underrates instrumental knowledge, which neglects those families who need their children to go out to work in order to survive; an education system which ignores the specific needs and priorities of this social group and their children. Some experts claim that in the future, educational systems will have to deliver high quality training in the 'multi-skilling' required by the information society. This means that young people's time at school will need to be more rewarding, as proposed by the European Commission White Paper on Education and Training (1995). However, the greatest challenge requires the development of measures which enable these pupils to take part in the standard educational routes which provide training in theoretical, technical and symbolic thought.

Conclusions

Over the past decade, all countries represented in this study have adapted their educational systems in the sense that they have created a more unified, comprehensive curriculum, particularly at the lower secondary level. In most cases, this evolution has been accompanied by some degree of flexibility in subjects, levels or pedagogy.

The available evaluations indicate that these reforms have heralded significant progress towards a more democratic, equitable, open and free school system. They have not turned out to be the promised panacea, however, and still contribute towards social inequalities in educational qualifications, which in turn produce a certain degree of inequality in social power (along with material wealth and political power).

From the perspective of this study, current educational structures and such curricular reforms do not convincingly prove adequate to meet the actual educational needs of pupils living in poverty. These pupils continue to experience social exclusion through their exclusion from the mainstream educational system. The information presented in this study suggests that strategies for unifying the curriculum and making it more flexible have had only a limited impact on pupils at risk of social exclusion. Hence, more recent approaches targeted at this risk group have involved the development of alternative curricula for pupils between the ages of 12 and 16. Unfortunately, these alternative strategies are not fully integrated into mainstream educational provision. They tend, again, to segregate the pupils from the lowest social backgrounds, and come into play only when young people have already experienced marginalisation within the schooling system.

A permanent tension appears to exist between the standardised training provisions in education systems and the social expectations and opportunities of those who experience social exclusion. Our society still expects the education system to select pupils according to given performance standards. The education system should, on the contrary, invent new strategies and certificates to realise all the opportunities of all its citizens satisfactorily.

It has been proposed that working-class culture and values should be incorporated into the school culture and curriculum content. However, this suggestion may also result in the reproduction of inequalities unless all pupils have guaranteed access to the knowledge and values of the standard culture. In order for equality in education to be realised, curricular measures (and other educational policy measures) should make it possible for *all* pupils to obtain standard educational qualifications. These measures must adequately support participation, accelerate the pace of learning, or otherwise motivate these 'invisible' pupils; pupils from socially excluded families whose background, expectations and objectives do not match those demanded for success in mainstream education. This is the greatest educational challenge for the future.

Notes

[1] Technical education in Flanders represents an intermediate stream between the vocational and academic options.

[2] The internalisation of social expectations on the part of pupils influences performance and curricular choices, as indicated in previous studies (Rogers, 1982; CIREM, 1994).

[3] 'Treatment of diversity' is a pedagogical concept that emphasises the need to take into account differences among pupils in ability levels, cultures and backgrounds in classroom management.

[4] Examples of alternative curricula in the participating countries include the Junior Certificate Schools Programme in Ireland, the Remedial Project in the Netherlands, Workshop classes and UAC in Spain, among others (see Chapter 14).

[5] With the exception of Portugal, which has focused its reforms on primary education and began a Petra initiative at the micro level; the Netherlands, which targets the Employment-Oriented Programme (or Practical School) at pupils with limited abilities who have been previously enrolled in special education; and Scotland, which uses different methods of filtering pupils into vocational training.

EIGHT

Social expectations, poverty and pedagogical innovations

Neus Roca-Cortés (CIREM)

In this chapter we deal with pedagogical aspects of the education of pupils from socially disadvantaged backgrounds. Our objective here is to analyse how pedagogical innovations have been used to improve the education of pupils from socially disadvantaged backgrounds, in schools and in educational measures described elsewhere in this book.

There are two important ways in which the education of pupils from socially excluded families may be improved. First, there may be an increase in the quality of education by, for example, extending the school day, reducing pupil–teacher ratios, employing classroom assistants to help teachers, or bringing other new professions into the educational scene. Second, improvement in the quality of education may be achieved through modification of lesson content and teaching methods. Qualitative improvements are the main focus of this chapter, in particular the underlying beliefs about the nature of education and how children learn.

Social expectations, social inequality and educational compensation

Compensatory policies and the pedagogy of diversity

School failure is dealt with in different ways depending on the type of school and its teaching methods. In the case of elite schools, which include some private schools receiving a state subsidy, pupils who have fallen behind may be sent to special schools or to other less prestigious institutions. The latter (often public schools, sometimes also subsidised private schools 'with a working-class vocation') apply traditional pedagogical methods in a segregated context. The pupils often remain deprived of the learning support that would help them overcome their supposed 'incapacity'. It is widely recognised that most underachieving pupils are from socially disadvantaged backgrounds.

During the past 20 years two strategies have been developed to counteract pupil failure, the **pedagogy of compensation** and the **pedagogy of diversity** (also referred to in different European countries as differentiated pedagogy, adapted pedagogy or individualised pedagogy). Compensatory education programmes have been based on the assumption that some children suffer from an educational deficit, which has to be compensated for. Therefore, special programmes are devised to give them the knowledge which, the school assumes, they should have already acquired. The teaching process is restarted at the level where the pupil's development halted. Hardly any changes are introduced in content or teaching methods, only in the pupil/teacher ratio. A great many pupils in these programmes end up by dropping out, and they are therefore unsuccessful in challenging school failure.

The criticisms against compensatory pedagogy are founded on the evidence that it has not enabled pupils from disadvantaged backgrounds to attain a standard level of education. Levin (1988), leader of the 'Accelerated Schools' movement, summarises the reasons why remedial or compensatory pedagogy may actually contribute to student failure. These are: (i) reduced expectations towards at-risk students and stigmatisation of such students as slow learners; (ii) the slower pace of instruction which makes at-risk students fall further behind; (iii) the emphasis on routine skills without providing substance and applications that will keep the students interested and motivated; (iv) the absence of mechanisms or incentives for closing the achievement gap between disadvantaged and middle-class students; (v) the promotion of strategies for at-risk students without adequate involvement of teachers and parents in their formulation. The contents, pace and knowledge characteristics of middle- and upper-class social groups remain equally alien to the interests and knowledge of socially disadvantaged pupils (Ayuste et al, 1994).

The various kinds of pedagogy of diversity include some forms of compensation, but the child remains in the mainstream class. These strategies are aimed at adjusting or adapting teaching to the pupils' different learning styles and levels of ability. Some of them emphasise that this differentiation must not be based on only one, two or three pupils who fall behind the foreseen school pace, but must be extended to the general curriculum to recognise the extent of pupil diversity with regard to level of attainment, culture, language, learning style, social background and interests.

The pedagogy of diversity represents a positive step towards the prevention of school failure among pupils from disadvantaged backgrounds. By adapting teaching methods to differences within the classroom, stigma is avoided and non-learning is prevented. However, the pedagogy of diversity involves a risk of resigning to differences, which may result in a perverse slowing down (Roca Cortés, 1995, 1998).

Neither compensatory education (more education) nor the pedagogy of diversity (more adequate pedagogy) can eliminate school failure[1] or the internalisation of school failure. In both cases, there is a shared assumption that pupils from working-class or socially deprived backgrounds are in a disadvantaged position, and it is therefore natural for their results to be inferior. By emphasising a deficit model, it creates and maintains low expectations, and above all, legitimates and hides from criticism a school system that only serves the interests of the middle and upper classes. Flecha states:

> If the objective is not to achieve homogeneous learning for all, but to respect the different processes, the fact of obviating the social inequality context leads to a positive vision of a range of curricular itineraries which imply very unequal educational levels. On following this dynamic, we are becoming already adapted from a very early age to the new type of inequality generated by the dual model of information society. (1994, p 74)

Bias effects of social expectations on individual school attainment

It is widely known today that social expectations and categorisations have an influence on academic attitudes and school attainment. If such expectations are positive, the level of attainment increases, whereas if they are negative, it decreases. From Rosenthal and Jacobson's experiments, which took place in the USA in the 1970s, this became known as the 'Pygmalion effect' or the self-fulfilling prophecy. To investigate the effects of streaming, a number of research studies were conducted in the social psychology of education which confirmed the effects of expectations on academic attainment, and the effects of academic attainment on teachers' expectations.

It has been shown from a number of observation studies that teachers direct a higher quality and amount of their teaching towards pupils categorised as good students, to the detriment of interactions with 'bad' students (Rist, 1970; Rubovits and Maehr, 1971, among others). For instance, teachers have a tendency to praise successful students and to criticise less successful ones (Brophy and Good, 1970). Positive or negative prejudice towards social groups of higher or lower status is also reproduced in the classroom, another aspect of the self-fulfilling prophecy (Bayton et al 1956; Aronson, 1972).

Learned helplessness is a strategy developed by pupils that maintains the biasing effect of expectations. Pupils assigned low expectations resist further development by refusing to take part in new learning activities at which they might succeed. Attribution theory suggests that after failing or succeeding in a task, we usually give explanations to ourselves about the reasons behind the outcomes. The causality attributions that we make will be the basis for subsequent motivation or confidence in our future activities. In this way, the successful student attributes failure to chance, whereas success is attributed to effort or capacity. The students who are not successful attribute their failure to themselves, and their success to the simplicity of the task or to chance (Rogers, 1982). Therefore, the strengthening of these attributions by parents and teachers are linked to children's academic achievements and attitudes.

The impact of expectations also has an effect on pupils' self-image. A negative self-image reduces the scope for expected attainment and vice versa (Rogers, 1982). Teachers' expectations are based on their perceptions of pupils' intellectual capacities, but also on motivation, level of participation, and the presence of culturally relevant characteristics (Crano and Mellon, 1978; Gilly, 1983). Pupils from disadvantaged backgrounds usually have few opportunities to reflect positive impressions because of the gap between their initial attitudes and social values and those of the traditional school. The deficit view of pupils from socially excluded settings places these pupils at a disadvantage. If people do not believe that the causes of their failure, such as their ability, are exogenous, then failure is not likely to continue in the future (Weiner, 1986; Manacero and Vázquez, 1993). The reduction, compensation or suppression of the undesirable effects of expectations is only possible through raising critical awareness, through a change in attitudes and, therefore, through a change in educational strategies.

Biased interpretation of school-related behaviour

There are still very few accounts of the relationship between schools and pupils from socially disadvantaged backgrounds. According to Nicaise (1999), weakness in school attainment is seen as intellectual weakness or lack of interest. Vocational guidance also reflects and reinforces existing social divisions (Verhoeven and Kochuyt, 1995). On the basis of in-depth interviews with teachers, parents and children, these writers suggest that the school careers of poor children are accompanied by an escalating conflict. Initially, parents expect a great deal from the school, precisely because of their own painful experience that failure at school contributed to their poverty. Nonetheless, they avoid direct contacts with the teacher because of shame regarding their poverty and educational ignorance. The absence of the parents from meetings is consistently interpreted as a lack of effort on their part in supporting their children's school career, and the school reacts by questioning the family situation. This, in turn, is perceived by the parents as a threat to the family integrity. All of this reinforces mutual prejudices, and the relationship between school and home becomes increasingly negative.

Pupils also experience this alienation from school (Nicaise, 1999). Kolvin et al (1990) also remind us that some behavioural problems of deprived children (weak concentration, lack of perseverance, hyperactivity) may simply be direct psychological consequences of deprivation, rather than consequences of relational or cultural problems. When behavioural problems are manifested by high status students, however, teachers are willing to interpret them as idiosyncratic. This is not so in the case of deprived children, and the teachers' low expectations lead to inadequate support.

Pedagogical innovations: the active and constructivist approaches

This section will consider pedagogical innovations versus traditional methods. Although it is well known that daily educational practice may have characteristics of both, traditional teaching pedagogy has a distinctive history and the major keys of this approach can be identified. The traditional approach sees teaching only as the transmission of school knowledge, which has to be acquired at a set pace. The person's holistic development is seen as additional or peripheral. Traditional educational practices often begin by imparting general concepts which have later to be applied to exercises; these exercises usually have a unique answer and are carried out by the pupil on their own. The traditional method is receptive rather than active; the teacher provides elaborate knowledge and the pupil must try to understand and reproduce it. In these practices, memorising and repetition have a predominant place as learning mechanisms, and any mistakes must be quickly corrected and replaced by the correct answer. The pupil's understanding of concepts is placed on a secondary level, as it is assumed that this will take place more or less 'automatically' within the pupil's mind. These teaching-learning strategies are not promoted, taught or spread; the teacher only provides direct answers to the pupils' questions (usually of those pupils who have thought carefully on their own) about aspects which they have not understood, or corrects mistakes in their exercises. Moreover, these methods reinforce the idea that only the teacher – and the books – know the answers, and that any explanations put forward by the pupils are copies, mere repetition acts with no effort involved; these are seen as not being useful for learning, as distracting attention or hindering correct assimilation. Traditional approaches allow little opportunity for pupils to choose either the themes to be studied or the activities to be carried out, and little attention is paid to themes and activities which could be of interest to pupils for social or personal reasons.

According to Leclerq (1993), it was necessary to resort to the so-called 'pedagogical revolution' in Europe in the middle of the century, in order to meet the evident diversity of the school when it was democratised. The changes proposed by the new educational approaches lay in the need for teaching to be adapted to the pupils, and not for the pupils to adapt to the teaching. Since the middle of the century, these methods have been largely applied in infant schools, in primary education, in the first cycle of secondary education (up to the age of 14) and, to a smaller extent, in the 15–18 age group (second cycle of secondary education).

In Europe, progressive or active methods were developed within the framework of the so-called 'new school' of the early 20th century, and were inspired by pedagogues such as Freinet, Ferrer i Guardia, Decroly, Dewey, and Claparède, among others (Ferrández and Sarramona, 1977). The many followers of the new school believed that change in teaching methods would help to create a pacific revolution that would reject the establishment and found a new social order (Legrand, 1971).

The major achievements of progressive education include the following: respect of children's nature, a new conceptualisation of the role of the teacher as a guidance and motivating figure, collaboration between school and family, education of children for democratic citizenship, and a revolution in teaching methods. Progressive methods must take into account the pupil's activity and interest, the individualisation of education, the child's social education, and the integrated curriculum (Ferrández and Sarramona, 1977). Progressive methods promote manual, practical and functional tasks as a means of motivating and fostering comprehension of abstract notions. They encourage pupils to select materials and texts and to plan their own work, since their personal effort will ensure their comprehension and will train their scientific and citizenship spirit (Gal, 1961).

Following criticism of its rather simplistic child–centred nature, progressive education was revised and consolidated in the 1960s and 1970s (Mialaret, 1966). New variations on progressive education developed, such as the pedagogy of autonomy (Leclerq, 1993), differentiated pedagogy (Quignard, 1972), the child–centred approach (Shield, 1966), and the pedagogy of self-management (Lapassade, 1971). This approach has also been called experiential education (Laevers, 1992). Nowadays, under the influence of the growing integration of pupils with disabilities, and increased awareness of multiculturalism, the pedagogy of diversity has developed.

Constructivist pedagogy (Sastre and Moreno, 1980; Moreno, 1983; Coll and Solé, 1989), inspired by the social and cognitive psychology of Piaget and Vigotsky, introduced new features to the broad field of progressive education. This latest development is characterised by the following elements: scientific knowledge about pupils' acquisition of a range of concepts[2] which makes it possible to adjust the teaching methods employed more precisely; the adoption of a thematic approach based on 'focuses of interest'; and the creation of teaching activities which lead to the comprehension of concepts by provoking a cognitive conflict. Memorisation and repetition are also used, but not as the main channel of learning.

On the basis of the brief background presented above, the major aspects of progressive education are as follows:

- education is focused on stimulating pupils' holistic development by taking their needs and interests into account;
- pupils take an active part in the construction of their knowledge and abilities and in their global development;
- activities are open[3] and related to problem–solving, often using a project approach;
- pupils play a major role in helping each other to learn. Group dynamics are used as a lever in teaching and learning: their positive impact has been verified in terms of attainment, attitudes towards the school and the social environment, motivation, and the reduction of prejudice in intercultural relations (Johnson et al, 1983; Slavin, 1990);
- pupils' out-of-school culture plays a central part in school and classroom activities;
- cultural, social and attainment diversity is accepted;

- parents and pupils take part in school and classroom management, creating a democratic school;
- school–community links are fostered;
- new forms of assessment are used; pupils are assessed in relation to group work and participation in classroom activities, as well as written work;
- teachers work in teams in order to provide curriculum coherence.

Active schools for pupils from socially disadvantaged backgrounds

Over the past 50 years, progressive or alternative schools have been introduced all over Europe. It is widely accepted that the social clientele of this type of school comes mainly from the new middle class (Bernstein, 1975; Varela, 1991), and that these schools have met the educational and socialisation needs of these families. It might therefore appear that pedagogical innovations are only valid for these social groups. There is little systematic applied research into the results of the progressive schools for pupils from disadvantaged backgrounds, although some have developed in the state sector.[4] Two case studies are presented below; their advantages and disadvantages are then considered.

Examples of good practice

Coves d'en Cimany: infant and primary public educational centre (Barcelona, Spain)

In the 1970s, Spain experienced a strong bottom-up movement of pedagogical renewal, which accompanied the return to democracy. It drew on the republican educational experience of progressive schools from the first decades of this century. Parents and teachers in cooperatives built up alternative schools on democratic principles using active pedagogy. Nowadays, most of these primary schools belong to the state sector, and the teachers' associations are integrated in a general movement of pedagogical renewal (MRP). Mostly, these parents and teachers are middle class, but some teachers are worried by the fast industrial development of the country, and have attempted to tackle educational disadvantage by applying progressive methods (Codina, 1988). This is the case in relation to Coves d'en Cimany.

Coves d'en Cimany is a small state school (250 pupils) located in the working-class district of El Carmel in Barcelona. The school population is made up of children aged 3 to 12-14 from socially excluded homes, some deprived gypsy families, low-income families, and immigrants from different countries (Maghreb, South America and Eastern European countries). It also has seven pupils with special educational needs, including emotional and behavioural difficulties and sensory impairments. Initiated by a group of teachers and the residents' association, the school was opened in a disused barracks. In 1983-84, already in the democratic period, the present school opened its buildings and sports facilities, which would be shared with the neighbourhood. The school was considered a special action school in the context of positive discrimination measures. Paradoxically, this priority status is now in danger, because the present educational authorities believe that the school is already achieving good results.

The teaching method centres on focuses of interest, including project work in infant and primary education, so as to favour the links between theory and practice and to foster a spirit of research among the pupils. The 3-6 group classes are arranged in corners, with curricular materials (not only paper and pencil) which make experimentation and representation possible. A strong emphasis is put on the sciences: the school has a lab, a pre-technology workshop, and a computer classroom operating at full capacity. All of these strategies facilitate a flexible approach to learning style and pace.

Relations with parents are fairly close. In addition to the institutional boards established by law, parents organise school finance, library, and school canteen committees. They collaborate in the reception of the youngest children, in the workshops, and in the organisation of cultural and academic events. Individual guidance meetings and parent-teacher meetings are seen as important, so that the parents will not feel distant from the school's educational goals. The headmistress commented: "We know that sometimes they feel out of place or ashamed when they think of or come to the school, but we keep an open, respectful and pedagogic attitude. If necessary, we go to their houses in order to win their confidence, which will have a positive repercussion on their children." Teachers work in teams and form a coherent unit that provides support to the school and the pupils as a whole and preserves the centre's identity so that it is respected and loved.

The situation as regards school results is also encouraging. From what teachers know about their former pupils, some have achieved a university degree, and a large number of them have engaged in a trade. Another significant result is the very low rate of dropout from school (one case every two years) and the nonexistence of truancy. In academic terms, 25% of pupils obtain the qualification of School Graduate, and 75% obtain the Schooling Certificate (eighth year). The overall rates of school failure in Catalonia are 40% (CIREM 1994). The school enjoys a high prestige compared with other state schools in the district.

Teachers do not have a feeling of inferiority because of working in a special school. According to the headmistress, they "are proud of being a special action school. Even if the pupils are pupils at risk, they leave the school with fairly acceptable levels of attainment. Our goal is that they leave as well-adjusted young people with a comprehensive education which enables them to interpret the world around them and to be happy. We are aware of the fact that the school is not omnipotent."

The school has a clear and public awareness of the district's poverty situation, and has developed a strategy to deal with it. Social deprivation is taken into account in its funding. All school materials are free, even pencils, erasers and textbooks. Diversity is also taken for granted:

> We reject an educational system which tends to homogenise and exclude any individual who differs from the common standard. This is why we believe that school has to be an integrating channel, with the capacity to respond to diversity ... no type of discrimination will be established because of differential traits, be these related to ethnic group, religion and family structure ... we shall attempt to eradicate authoritarianism from the classroom, but not authority.... (CEIP Coves d'en Gimany, 1995-98, pp 9-10)

The school educates its pupils in the values of solidarity, collaboration and critical participation, instead of competition.

De Buurt (Gent, Flanders) and the Innovative Project for Experiential Education (Leuven, Flanders)

De Buurt is a small school (under 100 pupils) in a popular district of Gent, with a concentration of immigrants and disadvantaged groups of native Flemish-speakers. The school was set up within a local network including (at different stages) a community action group, a children's club, a neighbourhood café, literacy courses for adults, evening classes for children, and an integration centre for migrants. The school gradually became an independent body, although it maintains close links with other initiatives and with the inhabitants of the neighbourhood. It deliberately chooses to run on a small scale, with children from the neighbourhood receiving priority in enrolments. The school population is fairly mixed, but includes a strong minority of migrant children (one in four) and a number of children from socially excluded homes.

The school promotes an emancipatory vision of education, and explicitly aims at minimising educational inequality. Using experienced-based projects in which, even more than in Freinet schools, the pupils' problem-solving capacities are actively stimulated, and pupils determine (directly or indirectly) the problems they want to consider. As projects exceed the separation between subjects, traditional textbooks have been replaced with worksheets developed by the school team. Project periods (usually lasting a week) are alternated with exercise weeks. There are no classes and no teachers; instead there are 'living groups' (aged 2½-3 years, 4-5 years, 6-8 years, and 9-11 years) and 'companions'. The system of living groups prevents individual children from always being the eldest or the youngest, the most or the least able pupil, and so on; it also avoids grade repetition to some extent. Each living group is accompanied by two companions, which also facilitates teamwork and differentiation, and prevents exclusive dependence on a single teacher.

Parent partnership is a cornerstone of the school's strategy. The heart of the school is a large kitchen where parents can have coffee when they bring their children to school in the morning; it is also the room where joint meetings are held monthly with parents and companions, by living group. Some parents are actively taking part in educational and other activities, which creates extra opportunities for differentiation. Others help with material work, but also with supervision, administration, and the development of the school's strategy. Even in-service training of the companions (teachers) is organised in mixed groups with parents. Parents who do not spontaneously participate in such meetings are visited at home. The school claims to offer something in return to parents; they acquire new skills such as assertiveness, speaking skills, organisation, democratic participation, and citizenship. From the early 1970s onwards, as a pilot project subsidised by the Department of Culture, De Buurt was a pioneer in educational community action.

This educational experience goes with a wider Flemish experience in progressive education, reflected in an innovative movement in Experiential Education. Twelve pre-school teachers, assisted by two educational consultants, wished to improve their teaching approach, and started a series of sessions with the intention of critically reflecting on their practice and discussing solutions to the problems they had encountered. Since 1976, under the guidance of the Research Centre for Early Childhood and Primary Education at the Katholieke Universiteit of Leuven (where the project started) and the Centre for Experiential Education (a foundation established by the pioneer group), this innovative project continues to grow through a fruitful process of research, development and dissemination.

There is a lack of evaluative research in this area. In fact, most progressive and constructivist schools have middle-class pupils, and there is little systematic knowledge of the ways in which progressive and constructivist pedagogical principles have been applied to schools in high social disadvantage settings. However, there is some evidence that such schools may avoid the permanent experience of school failure and contribute to increasing social integration, in as much as the educational system can have an impact on such a complex issue.

From the case studies presented, it can be inferred that the active and constructivist approach may be a realistic way of tackling the problems of pupils from deprived social backgrounds, allowing them to participate in the construction of knowledge. According to some experts (Codina, 1988), these children can only be retained and taught in the socialising framework of the school if the school gets nearer to the pupils' culture and promotes active participation. In dealing with the education of pupils at risk, the holistic personal development of each pupil is seen as a key objective. Practice suggests that the constructivist approach yields its earliest fruits in a burst of motivation and joy; pupils stop rejecting or avoiding school tasks, and a continuous progress in their attainment is observed (Roca Cortés, 1995).

According to Grignon (1990), the cultural relativism associated with progressive education (inspired by Rousseau) is a necessary condition for a less primitive, better adapted pedagogy, since it is better informed, more benevolent, more holistic, more developed, and fairer with regard to working-class children. It is, in addition, the only pedagogical method capable of making school a less alien and hostile environment. However, there are risks associated with progressive schools; for instance, the focus on self-esteem, basic literacy and numeracy, and popular culture may be at the expense of more traditional academic knowledge and formal qualifications. Schools with a majority of working-class pupils might become cultural ghettos. Approaching culture from a relative perspective may become an obstacle for working-class pupils in gaining access to knowledge and understanding of the dominant culture.

Another risk is that constructivist methods are applied only as a 'micro-teaching technique', with no prior social context analysis and no transformation of educational objectives.

Despite these recent and telling criticisms, it is widely recognised that progressive educational methods make a useful contribution to the education of pupils from socially disadvantaged backgrounds.

Recent pedagogical innovations: an open fight against low social expectations

Given the strong association between social background and school failure (see Chapter 1), it is radically defiant to think that this relationship can be broken. Whereas remedial pedagogy does not achieve its aims, and differentiated pedagogy seems to accept inequalities, the third way appears to be choosing diversity while not involving greater inequality. This rests on the assumption that disadvantaged pupils can reach standard levels of education within the same time span as other pupils. Their disadvantage is not attributed to lower ability levels, but to the fact that their interests, knowledge, expectations and so on are alien to the interests and expectations considered appropriate to the middle-class school (Ayuste et al, 1994).

Accelerated schools

In the USA, there have been some pilot projects involving accelerated rather than remedial teaching. Accelerated schools focus on pupil empowerment and aim to 'hothouse' socially disadvantaged pupils, helping them to develop advanced literacy and numeracy skills through intensive teaching. Accelerated programmes appear to have been more successful in counteracting educational disadvantage than remedial programmes that take a deficit model as their starting point (Levin 1988).

Example of good practice: Accelerated Schools (USA)

The Accelerated Schools Programme (ASP) was created at Stanford University under the inspiration and leadership of Henry Levin. Its origins date back to 1987, when Levin and his colleagues at Stanford University carried out, on an experimental basis, a transformation project in two schools. In both schools, which were particularly problematic, about 80% of the pupils lived in extremely poor areas. One of them, Daniel Webster Elementary School, located in Potrero Hill, achieved spectacular results. Discipline problems and school absenteeism rates were considerably reduced. In the California State standardised level tests, the school was second in mathematics and first in language among the 72 elementary schools existing in San Francisco, in the 1991-92 academic year. Before that time, the school had always ranked in the final positions. Systematic monitoring facilitated the programme development, and nowadays the programme is being used in 150 schools around the USA.

The programme is based on a different set of assumptions relating to effective strategies for helping at-risk students to achieve school success. At its heart is the notion of doing for at-risk students what has been done for many gifted and talented students; that is, striving to accelerate their progress, rather than lowering expectations for their advancement. The at-risk students prove able to close the achievement gap and perform at grade level by the time they leave sixth grade, when a strong sense of self-esteem and educational success is created; whereas previously they felt rejected by schools and frustrated about their own abilities.

Accelerated schools are characterised by high expectations on the part of teachers, parents, and students, target dates by which students are expected to meet particular educational requirements, stimulating instructional programmes planned by the educational staff, and the use of all available resources in the community, including parents, senior citizens, volunteers, employment services and social agencies (Levin, 1989a).

The organisational approach of accelerated schools (Levin, 1988) is based on three key principles: unity of purpose, empowerment and building on strengths. 'Unity of purpose' refers to agreement between parents, teachers, and students on a common set of goals for the school. 'Empowerment' involves expanding the ability of key participants to make important decisions at the school level, and in the home, to improve the education of students. 'Building on strengths' means utilising all of the learning resources that teachers, administrators, students, parents and communities can bring to the educational endeavour.

In addition to this, the programme includes other characteristics, such as: a transformation of the entire structure of a school, instead of simply grafting remedial classes onto a school with a conventional agenda; substantial parental involvement (parents are expected to sign a written agreement stating their obligations to their children); an emphasis on acceleration rather than remedying, intended to bring students up to grade level; and an extended-day programme with emphasis on language and problem solving (Finnan, 1996). Pedagogical techniques that were previously used for gifted pupils in selective schools (usually very expensive ones) are now being applied for the purpose of a more democratic education.

Perhaps the main innovation of this approach, compared with previous pedagogical innovations, is its explicit foundation on psychological and sociological analyses, which are linked to daily teaching practice. At the same time, many of its educational principles are inspired by the 'new school' approach.

Communities of learning and the communicative perspective

The communicative perspective (Ayuste et al, 1994) is rooted in practical educational approaches in adult literacy and in successful schooling experiences of at-risk students. Thus, this perspective deals directly with the dialectic of inclusion/exclusion of socially disadvantaged groups in the education system, and with its underlying educational conceptions. Its pedagogy is based on a sociological analysis of the information society (Castells et al, 1994) and on other authors such as Paulo Freire, Vigotsky, Scribner, Habermas, and so on. Learning is regarded as a dialogical process in which all participants should have the same power. The communicative perspective will not promote an idealistic vision of the world; its specificity rests in stating explicitly the rules of social functioning and in raising awareness of everyone's position. Hidden curricula are made visible and subject to critical analysis. The final objective is to provide the learners with the technological instruments, knowledge and capacity which will enable them to find and use resources for their full sociocultural participation and integration (Ayuste et al, 1994).

The 'Community of Learning Project' (*Proyecto de transformación en Communidades de Aprendizaje*) was initiated by the Research Centre in Adult Education (CREA) of Barcelona University. The Centre supports public education establishments that aim to transform their practice, to improve their quality, to introduce innovations and experimentation in the classroom, and to make families take part in their children's comprehensive education (CREA, 1995). This is achieved through an open dialogue (and a decision making process) about the different perspectives on education, society, and educational objectives. The project was inspired by the theory of communicative education and by several educational innovations such as active and constructivist schools in disadvantaged areas, the Accelerated Schools scheme, and other special programmes developed in the USA.

In addition to the key characteristics of Accelerated Schools, the Community of Learning Project rests on the following principles:

- all theoretical and practical resources that can foster learning will be used, unless they exclude certain groups of pupils or slow down learning as a result of compensatory conceptions;
- cooperation and solidarity (not charity) should help facilitate the access of all learners to the skills required by today's information society;
- teachers commit themselves to collaborate within the classroom whenever it is considered necessary by their leaders.

The Community of Learning project proposes five experimental phases (to be permanently revised – CREA, 1995, 1998): raising awareness; decision making; 'dreaming' about the school and education desired; context analysis and selection of priorities; and development of an action plan. Some Spanish schools have joined the project on the initiative of teachers and parents; others have obtained support from the Basque autonomous government (Gumuzio, 1998). They are still in the early phases of the project. This is the case of the Ramón Bajo and Karmengo Ama public schools (C.P.Virgen del Carmen, 1998), among others.

Example of good practice: the Ramón Bajo Public School (Vitoria-Gasteiz, Arava)

The Ramón Bajo Public School is currently serving 75 pupils, a third of whom are autochthonous inhabitants, a third from Maghreban or other African countries and a third of low-income gypsy origin. The school was formerly a prestigious public school, deeply involved in the city's life, but it lost much of its fame and became a marginal school. The teachers reacted with many partial experiments but there was a persistent feeling of dissatisfaction which led the school to search for a more comprehensive answer to the new circumstances.

The transformation process was started in the school year 1995-96. One year later, after the initial information sessions, the 'dream' phase brought a lot of suggestions, even from the school inspectors. In the next phase, four priorities were selected for immediate action:

- creating a school canteen, run by the teachers, with educational objectives relating to eating habits, recreational activities, and so on;
- creating a computer classroom, also accessible for parents and the neighbourhood;
- changing the school's methodology and educational organisation;
- strengthening parents' participation.

Three school committees were also created.

The educational organisation and teaching methods were radically changed. Pupils are no longer grouped by levels but in workshops, cycles, project work, and subject areas. The teachers have specialised in subjects and are responsible for teaching them throughout the school years. According to the teachers, rather surprisingly, the redistribution of work has been highly satisfactory and is now accepted enthusiastically. The classroom has become an inclusive space: special education support is now given within the classroom, and the teaching of students at different educational levels is not considered a major problem as teachers work two by two in the classes.

Some school materials have been 'socialised', while the rest are being administered by the parents' association (Luna and Jaussi, 1998).

The transformation is still ongoing. Although there has been no systematic evaluation, the teachers have openly expressed their satisfaction with the reform. There have been remarkable improvements in the participation of parents, the organisation of teaching, and the use of resources. The pupils

---

are said to be more motivated, and truancy and dropout have been reduced at all ages. According to the teachers, the pupils learn more and their level of attainment has risen.

Pedagogical innovations incorporated in other educational measures for disadvantaged pupils

This section will briefly point to the innovative pedagogical aspects of educational measures described elsewhere in this book. Four common threads can be observed in these measures:

- some of their structural (rather than didactic) characteristics are derived from innovative pedagogical principles;
- some of them imply partnerships with families;
- on the other hand, it seems that few of these measures explicitly assign power to the parents, as regards the remit, contents and stimulation patterns of education;
- all of them are partial, and include neither an overt change in expectations from the deficit model towards an empowerment model, nor a change of the school itself.

In the early childhood intervention programmes (see Chapter 6), the number of hours devoted to school activities (particularly to literacy and numeracy courses) is increased, while at the same time, all these programmes are subject to continuous pedagogical innovations. They do not implicitly assume low expectations towards pupils, as a high potential for development is attributed to small children who have hardly been moulded in their families' expectations and values. The programme evaluations reveal improved outcomes that are related to the strengthened links between children and their parents. Sometimes these effects are achieved through intervention at home, which affects educational styles within families. Other programmes link the children's education with the families' social promotion; for example, by providing training and guidance to women returning to the labour market, or by promoting structures for social participation and cultural initiatives.

Some curricular reforms (see Chapter 7) do not involve structural changes – rather, they are based on modifications in educational concepts; increasing the value of the whole learning process, and catering for the previous educational levels of the pupils as well as their social and cultural diversity (for example, the 1992 reform in Portugal, LOGSE in Spain, and the 5-14 Programme in Scotland). Special attention has also been paid to linking instrumental with theoretical learning, as in the Flemish workshop-classes or the Flemish and Dutch part-time vocational education, for example. Elements of active learning methods can also be found in the alternative curricula described in Chapter 14, and in the pedagogical dimension of educational priority policies (Chapter 12).

The first parent-school-community initiatives (Chapter 10) were promoted simultaneously with the consolidation of the 'new school' (the 1960s and 1970s). They have resulted in increased levels of attainment as well as closer involvement of parents with the school. However, these initiatives have been criticised for being too 'partial'. The parents most in need of support, those who were facing economic difficulties or who had literacy problems themselves, were less likely to get involved in the projects. Other criticisms relate to the fact that disadvantaged families are expected to adapt to a dominant form of literacy, which may reinforce feelings of inferiority rather than empowering them. These criticisms highlight the value of the more balanced parent-school-community relations in accelerated schools and communities of learning.

Conclusions

Compensatory education and remedial strategies do not actually manage to equalise the attainment of pupils from socially disadvantaged backgrounds with the attainment of their more privileged peers. The major criticism of compensatory pedagogy is that it ignores the social context of inequalities and upholds a biased interpretation of the behaviour of pupils and families from socially disadvantaged backgrounds. On seeing their behaviour as deficient, compensatory pedagogy creates and maintains low expectations and, above all, legitimates the pupils' exclusion from school and society. The pedagogy of diversity (also called differentiated pedagogy or adapted pedagogy) represents an improvement on remedial strategies.

The heritage of European educational culture, recent cognitive research and new developments in critical social thinking could bring about innovative pedagogical approaches that include pupils living in poverty. The wider use of active and constructivist methods for socially disadvantaged pupils could improve social inclusion considerably, but unfortunately there is no systematic evaluation of their potential to raise the school achievement of poor pupils. However, recent attempts to implement progressive educational principles suggest that they may yield positive results in terms of considerably increasing the proportion of at-risk pupils obtaining educational qualifications.[5] This certainly applies to accelerated schools in the USA. In Europe, the 'Community of Learning' project is still in its infancy.

Whereas active and constructivist schools do address social disadvantage, the accelerated and community-of-learning schools introduce this commitment more explicitly from the perspective of emancipation, based on a critical analysis of social inequality. Both the accelerated schools and the community-of-learning approach cover most of the key elements of active education. However, they add to this an awareness of the negative effects of low social expectations, as well as specific measures to counter them. Compared to traditional schools, the accelerated schools meet the challenge of achieving equal outcomes rather than equal treatment.

To conclude, we must underline the urgent need for more systematic evaluation of these educational experiences, in terms of both process and outcomes.

Notes

[1] Perhaps school failure cannot be avoided, because all educational centres are more or less successful, since they always have a percentage of student failure and conflict (CIREM 1994).

[2] This research has been developed in several subjects, mainly in Spain, France, Switzerland and some Latin American countries.

[3] 'Open' means that more than one correct answer or suitable procedure of response is admitted. This type of instruction, also called authentic tasks or contextual learning (winter issue of the *Review of Educational Research*) involves the pupils in thinking and acting at higher levels of complexity by providing them with relevant, motivating and challenging experiences and materials in different subjects.

[4] The author is grateful to Ms. Teresa Codina (teacher consultant) for her kind contribution in time and experience on schools coping with social exclusion in Barcelona. We would also like to thank Mr. Julian Lavado (pedagogic consultant, COP de Renteria), the head teacher of CEIP Coves d'En Cimany, Mrs Hilde Struyvelt from De Buurt school, and C.P. Virgen del Carmen-Karmengo Ama, as well as their respective school teams, for their willingness to appear in this document.

[5] Given this success, it is ironic that progressive teaching methods have been so heavily criticised within the UK, and have been blamed for school failure, rather than being given credit for widening the horizons of many disadvantaged children for whom education might otherwise represent a destructive experience.

NINE

Teacher training

Nelson Matias (IESE)

The information concerning the training of teachers gathered in the context of this research was very limited. In fact, this information appears to be unavailable for most of the countries or regions involved in this study, which in itself is a relevant finding. In the case of countries or regions for which it was possible to obtain some information, that which was gathered cannot be considered sufficient, particularly in relation to pertinent subjects such as teacher training policies, programmes and/or initiatives aimed specifically at addressing the problems analysed in this study.

Therefore, this chapter is intended to help reflect upon the main European trends in the area of teacher training, and in particular on the measures and initiatives aimed at preventing educational exclusion and promoting equal opportunity for socially underprivileged groups.

Concurrently, there will be an outline of some of the measures, projects and/or initiatives that the team was able to identify from the information gathered for the countries covered by this study. In addition, the reasons why there are so many difficulties in coming to grips with the problems we are faced with within the current context of this project will also be discussed.

Development of educational systems and new teaching skills

The changes that have occurred in contemporary systems of education, namely those of the European Union, have inevitably and significantly affected teachers.

Among these changes, the most important has been the systematic increase in the duration of compulsory schooling; this has been associated with, and even preceded by, a large increase in school enrolment, which thus reflects the growing social demand for education that characterises post-war societies. The second most important change has involved the measures of democratisation associated with the increasing development of schools with a single curriculum – or at the very least, with a common core syllabus – which have also contributed to the heterogeneous social and cultural nature of the 'single school system'. In this system we now have students of various ethnic, social, and cultural origins carrying with them different aspirations and academic and professional expectations. These students possess varied abilities and have varying attitudes towards education, school and teachers. These differences are becoming quite obvious in the classroom and are making the job of teaching increasingly difficult. Teachers are, therefore, becoming progressively obliged to diversify their methodologies and individualise their teaching. They must get to know each of their students better in order to adapt teaching (and learning) methods to each student's different abilities. This involves establishing and applying the most appropriate strategies for each case and/or situation.

The third most important change that should be pointed out is the fact that the process of diversification of methodology and individualisation is in line with other measures of democratisation. This is especially true regarding underprivileged groups of students or cases of evident academic disadvantage, ethnic or linguistic minorities and the immigrant population, and, in particular, groups of children who are traditionally grouped in 'special education'.

In fact, current educational thinking tends to go beyond the traditional distinction between extrinsic obstacles (due to sociological, economic, psychological or cultural factors) and intrinsic obstacles (such as physical, psychological, sensorial or mental disadvantages). This has resulted in the creation of different departments organised by category or social group, with the responsibility of developing appropriate policies and specific programmes of action.

This situation is currently undergoing profound change, with the emergence of the concept that some students have special educational needs that need to be addressed according to the quantity and quality of additional educational support that they require (see Chapter 11).

The implementation of numerous programmes promoting equal opportunity and the prevention of educational and social exclusion has also taken the growing multiculturalism of European societies into account. Processes of decolonisation and sustained economic development through migration and immigration have created an increasing potential for diversity and conflict in European societies that has contributed to the expansion of social and political democracy.

As multiculturalism establishes itself and becomes socially recognised, therefore, teachers are confronted with cultural, ethnic, linguistic, and national diversity, all within the same classroom. Schools adapt their programmes to students with special educational needs, a concept which tends to favour the educational integration of students that were once 'forced' to follow a single programme, and which has replaced the traditional view of deficiency and handicap.

Policies aimed at eliminating educational inequalities attempt, on the one hand, to integrate students into normal schools, whatever their individual or group abilities may be; on the other hand, they endeavour to guarantee the human, material and financial resources required for the educational development of the students in question and the schools they attend, as discussed in other chapters of this study.

The fourth change that has occurred involves the fact that education today tends to be viewed as more than just a transfer of knowledge, particularly with regard to the levels of compulsory schooling. It has come to be viewed as a means of achieving a holistic education. This fact has resulted in greater complexity and flexibility in the teaching profession. Schools are required to go beyond teaching a certain curriculum and/or developing specific technical skills. They are expected to provide a civic education, while teachers are expected to support and promote a student's psychological and emotional development.[1]

Last of all, it should be pointed out that a qualitative change coupled with a significant increase in management tasks, both institutional and educational, has become apparent. This has occurred within the context of schools that are open to their environment, and has involved an increasing participation of the educational community in every aspect of education. Teachers are 'obliged' to acquire new skills and develop new attitudes regarding social relations, in order to be able to negotiate with parents and, with their support, resolve educational problems that affect children and young people.

In addition to measures of positive discrimination and compensatory education, there are programmes aimed either at integrating typical special education students or at intercultural education. There is also a new educational work ethic for schools and teachers that encourages the educational community – especially the parents – to participate in school activities and in the development of new educational integration practices. These new practices are based on a new concept of inclusion (and inclusive schools), and on practices of diagnosing educational needs and implementing educational projects within the classroom and within the educational establishment in general.

Main lines of development in initial teacher training

Taking into account the significant efforts that have been made in this century, particularly in the post-war period, to promote the democratisation of education and to increase its quality in European countries, it is clear that these efforts have also affected the development of initial teacher training at various levels, whether because of the increasing demand for teachers or because of the increasing attention that has been focused on their training.

The traditional model of initial teacher training which was predominant in the first half of the century implied a shorter, more practical, and less academic approach to training primary school teachers, as opposed to a less practical and more academic approach – generally at the post-secondary level and based on educational science – to training secondary school teachers. This is the model of initial teacher training that has been brought into question by the development of the educational systems mentioned above. The changes that have taken place since this time have occurred in two tiers. The first contributed to an increase in the value attributed to the training of primary school teachers and resulted in an increase in their academic and vocational training level. The second resulted in a more vocational and practical approach to the training of secondary school teachers that progressively became linked to theoretical training, more focused on the curriculum that was to be taught – which was, until then, the only form of training. There has been a convergence in the training levels of all teachers which, in the European Union, is invariably conducted at the post-secondary – generally university – level; this has been accompanied by a convergence in training models, which now include professional, theoretical, and practical pedagogical training within a real work environment for teachers on all levels, except the post-secondary level.

In effect, there has been an almost global restructuring of initial teacher training, in which some countries have established new training systems and even new institutions specifically dedicated to this type of training, such as the ESEs[2] in Portugal and IUFM[3] in France. Other countries have standardised their teacher training programmes and/or teaching careers, thereby integrating the two into a single process which can be internally differentiated, and which includes all educators and teachers from pre-school through to secondary education.

Upon analysing each aspect of these changes, it becomes apparent that the amount of training for primary school teachers has increased along with the value attributed to it. This has been expressed in the following forms: (i) an increase in the number of years and level of preliminary academic qualification required in order to take part in vocational training; (ii) an increase in length of the period of training, which currently ranges from three to five years; (iii) a generalised[4] upgrading of the level of qualification to the post-secondary level; (iv) the status of specialised training has been maintained, having always been conducted in specialised vocational schools – initially secondary or post-secondary institutions; today, specialised departments in universities or other post-secondary institutions.

This evolution has allowed the standards of initial training for primary school teachers to become similar, and in some cases equivalent, to those of secondary school teachers, even in the various areas of scientific training. It has also placed an increased value on the pedagogical, theoretical and practical training of primary school teachers. Thus, the evolution of initial training of primary school teachers has taken into account the fact that these teachers need post-secondary training in the educational, social and human sciences, in order to teach young people and ensure that they get a solid basic education.

With regard to secondary school teachers, it is widely accepted that initial training based solely on learning the curriculum to be taught is not sufficient to guarantee a high level of success in democratic educational systems that are open to students with varying capabilities and sociocultural backgrounds. The increasing heterogeneity of the student body that teachers must deal with largely explains why the acquisition and development of pedagogical skills should take place at the university level. These skills include teaching methods, the ability to create and apply learning tools and materials along with the ability to create evaluation methods, and a training programme geared to achieving a better understanding of the sociocultural, community, and family contexts of a student's daily life and the evaluation of their educational potential. These skills also include the ability to critically analyse the operational methods of educational organisations, and the ability to overcome the constantly re-emerging obstacles that stand in the way of the educational success of students.

Thus, in Portugal, programme requirements for the initial training of all teachers – including secondary school teachers – has begun to include theoretical training in educational sciences, namely in psychology, sociology and anthropology. It is now common to encounter courses entitled 'Educational Contexts', 'Sociology of Education', 'Anthropology of Education', 'Psychology of Development and Learning', 'Educational

Organisations', and 'School Management' in the curriculum of teacher training courses for both primary and secondary schools, particularly those given at ESEs and, at least partially, in universities. The University of Barcelona also includes some of these subjects and/or study fields in its study plans, and the same is happening at several universities in Ireland, whether in the formation of teachers – of the primary school and of the secondary school – or in the formation of school directors.

The curriculum of initial teacher training courses includes a range of other disciplines and/or areas of training considered relevant to this study: for example, Special Educational Needs, in the case of Portugal, or Individual Differences and Educational Integration in the case of Catalonia. These types of subjects are to be found in the teacher training curricula in Ireland as well, though they always appear as 'elective courses'; that is, subjects which teachers can choose from a list of ten options. However, this list may differ every year, and therefore it is not certain that all subjects will be taught every academic year, or that all students will have a chance to attend them. Nevertheless, it is possible for instance to find 'Approaches to Education in Disadvantaged Communities', an annual subject for intensive study,[5] or 'Remedial and Special Education in the Post-Primary Schools',[6] which is offered as a half-yearly optional subject.

In all of these countries or regions, courses in these subject areas are to be found in the initial, complementary or postgraduate training programmes. Generally, these are specialisation courses, or courses in special education or educational administration. For instance, in Ireland the Higher Diploma in Educational Administration (University of Cork) may include in its curriculum the subject of educational policy, which for example includes themes such as 'cultural education', 'traveller education' and 'disadvantaged pupil's special needs education'. It should be noted, however, that:

- this concerns the training of specialists rather than ordinary teachers; that is, professionals who assist teachers or schools and whose contribution depends on the different ways of organising special education, as well as on the level of investment in educational support in each country, region or school;
- it is not known whether the orientation of these courses has a stigmatising effect or not, nor whether the specialists and teachers who take these courses receive training only with regard to sensory, motor or mental deficiency.[7]

Concurrently, the growing research in the fields of psychology and education has prompted justifiable changes in initial teacher training, including practical (and not just theoretical) training. The result has been that teaching practice in the classroom has gradually come to be considered an essential part of training in most countries of the European Union. This is one of the most significant changes that have occurred in the curriculum structure.

In effect, all the new programmes require that teachers (particularly non–primary teachers) be specialised in a particular field, and that they know the curriculum that is to be taught. They must also be able to test new teaching strategies adapted to various educational contexts, types of students, and learning difficulties. This is why initial teacher training programmes require all teachers to participate in a period of supervised teaching or a probationary practice.

The vocational and practical training that has been systematically introduced in all the EU countries has followed one of two models: (i) an *integrated training* model, in which pedagogical and practical training is conducted together with basic theoretical training (training taking place in a real work environment coupled with periods of supervised teaching), with an alternation between theory and practice starting in the first year of study; (ii) a *sequential* model, where a new professional, practical training cycle is preceded by academic training and ends with a probationary supervised practice.

In summary, the development of educational systems and of the social and cultural heterogeneity of school classes has led to the creation of new teaching functions, and thus to new requirements for training. These requirements have been met by altering the initial teacher training systems as follows:

- increase in the overall number of years that the training takes;
- higher level training for all teachers, including primary and kindergarten teachers;
- specific theoretical and practical vocational training, rather than just academic training, in the subjects taught, especially for secondary school teachers;
- practical training, including situations in which the trainees come into contact with real teaching of their courses and, at least during the final phase, supervised teaching experience;
- teachers' initial training organised in accordance with an alternating methodology; that is, a methodology seeking to coordinate three main areas: an in-depth technical knowledge of the subjects to be

taught (demonstrated by the possession of a higher education degree); theoretical pedagogical knowledge; and hands-on teaching experience.

At the same time, a succinct analysis of the curricular structure of the initial training courses[8] would seem to indicate that the problems involved in school exclusion and the promotion of equal opportunities for underprivileged groups are being taken into account in the subjects included in the educational science curriculum. However, the limited weight given to these issues in the various curricula and the tendency to pay more attention to theoretical content and to the general problems of the subjects in question seem to indicate that the only ways in which adequate teacher training in this matter can actually be developed are through subsequent reflection on first-hand and/or observed experience, and in the practical parts of the supervised pedagogical sessions. It should be remembered that some countries and regions are currently moving toward a position where supervised pedagogical experience – including observing and commenting on real-life situations – constitutes around 20-30% of the total curriculum.[9] An alternating training methodology can be said to be a suitable strategy for achieving aims of this kind.

Continuing training and the promotion of social equality in education

Most European Union countries have been paying increasing attention to the continuing training they provide for teachers. Consequently, the authorities responsible for educational activities in the various countries and regions have been implementing a wide range of measures aimed at promoting continuing training amongst their teachers. In some cases they practically make it obligatory, in as much as career advancement is subject to participation in training programmes or activities.[10] In other cases they seek to involve occupational organisations and schools, as well as the teachers themselves, in promoting and/or organising this type of training.[11] In most cases, they decentralise either the training demand initiative (teachers can apply in the schools where they work, and this is implemented via school educational projects in which the training component must be present) or the training offer initiative (which may be provided by the teachers' initial training institutions, and in which an attempt is made to promote the coordination of continuing and initial training).[12]

In this context, the state plays the role of the supervisory body, which simultaneously finances and accredits both the entities that provide training and the training itself – and also, consequently, their expected end products.[13]

A number of factors which explain the phenomenon of the growing attention that has been paid to continuing teacher training are to be found within the context of the development of the educational systems described above. On the one hand, the demands on the teaching profession are growing, while at the same time, the average age of teachers as a whole is increasing. Due to the fall in the birth rate, the teaching profession has ceased to renew itself with the intensity that had characterised the last period in which the number of children at school boomed. On the other hand, teachers' skills and knowledge are becoming out of date much more quickly, while educational reforms are becoming more frequent and/or are tending to remain in an unstable 'experimental' phase involving programmes, teaching methodologies and projects which include extracurricular activities and the involvement of parents, or partnerships with other actors within the education community.

In this way, a relatively large demand for continuing training arises from the teachers who are involved in educational reform processes (reforms of the curricula, the school management, teaching careers, and so on) or in 'educational projects' which are either centrally initiated or locally encouraged, as a result of the new partnership relationships that have been built up in the mean time. The uncertainty caused by these reform processes and/or innovations leads to a demand for training. At the same time, it requires a training response from both the educational administration and the schools. This response must contribute to finding answers to the problems raised by the education policy measures themselves, or to problems regarding the commitment of those taking part, or to any emotional and professional instability that may occur.

However, it must be admitted that it is still quite difficult to 'make' teachers attend continuing training courses. The best way to achieve this objective – as has been recognised by the education authorities of the various countries in the European Union – is still via income-based motivation and the use of continuing training as a criterion to determining career advancement.

We know that it is essentially via continuing training (particularly when that training is associated with concrete educational projects or measures) that a positive relationship can be created between teacher training and the promotion of equal opportunities for socially or academically disadvantaged social groups. However, it is difficult to gain access to basic information about this training because it is only produced within the framework of evaluation reports on the projects themselves – and such reports are rare when it comes to micro-level projects – or in the form of papers/reports about particular experiments, which are presented at seminars or congresses. Such presentations are often only given orally, and are either not published or do not highlight adequately the teacher training component within a project's overall framework, or the contribution that training has made to the project's results.

It is possible to report the existence of continuing training in areas that are pertinent to the issues raised in this study. Thus, the 'multicultural education' area is often encountered within the framework of the continuing training programmes promoted by education authorities and contained in their activity reports, as is the case in Flanders, Catalonia, the Netherlands, and Portugal, for example. There are also subjects such as 'diagnoses of learning difficulties' and 'differentiation of educational methods' in Portugal, Spain, and in the Flemish region of Belgium where, according to the information gathered, these subjects are being considered for integration into the curriculum of in-service teacher training, along with disciplines dealing with multicultural education and educational reform and innovation. And in the case of Flanders, there are new subjects such as 'behavioural problems amongst children with learning disabilities in special education'.

Two examples of innovative continuing training projects related to educational reform at the micro level are given below.

Examples of good practice

Intercultural nursery nurses in Flanders

This scheme initially took the form of a training programme for women teachers from ethnic minorities in Flanders. The women were engaged in a combined employment and training project, working part-time as 'intercultural mediators' for a better integration of migrant children in nursery schools, and being trained the other half of the time as nursery teachers, using a curriculum that was designed especially for them in adult education. The first cohort of intercultural mediators graduated in 1997, and are now employed on a full-time basis (not without some difficulties). This first experiment opened the way for the subsequent implementation of other training projects for immigrant women aimed at ensuring their acquisition and development of professional skills for use in the nursery education sector. Both the curricular and methodological flexibility employed in each of these cases and the coordination of learning with work during the course were considered to have contributed to the project's success. Designing a specific, alternative curriculum spread over a longer period (five years) and providing the chance to combine work and study made it possible to bring training closer to its recipients, and to turn what could, at first sight, have been seen as obstacles to training on the part of these social groups into real training opportunities (Vandevoort, 1997).

Setúbal Teacher Training College and the 'Inclusive Schools' project

The second example is a continuing training programme for primary school teachers, developed within the framework of the 'Inclusive Schools' project in the region of Setúbal (Portugal). It was financed by the national continuing teacher training programme, and came about thanks to the initiative taken by the Setúbal Teacher Training College, which was looking for a real-world response to the problems raised by a given education policy measure. The type of training chosen – the Study Circle – proved to be particularly well suited to the nature of the training, to its objectives and to the activities included in the programme. The training was based on an analysis of the teachers' perception of the educational needs of the classroom, and it attempted to provide adequate responses to given contexts. It sought to analyse integration techniques and to reinforce them by creating an 'inclusion' concept, by drawing up educational projects at individual classroom and school level, and by involving parents and other partners in the education community.

Conclusion

Several studies have shown that teachers experience difficulties with the relationship between school and a socially and culturally heterogeneous population in their day-to-day practice. This relationship creates 'victims' through discrimination and exclusion of the most disadvantaged – the 'most different' social groups – from the educational process.

In this context, the teachers are aware of the existence of a specific field of possible intervention which is 'reserved' to them – that of the teaching methodology and particularly of the strategies of pedagogic differentiation. Nonetheless, the operational difficulties of this teaching intervention are also generally recognised. These difficulties have been diverse.

First, traditional theoretical perspectives had focused too exclusively on individual deficiencies and/or on 'individualised support' by the teachers or educators, rather than on the group and its social organisation of learning (the class and/or the school). This approach obviously involved the risk of leaving the school unchanged.

Second, there has been a perpetuation of the conditions of operation of the educational organisations; these are based on a 'Taylor-type school' rather than a 'flexible school' (as reflected in the curricula, in the constitution of student groups, in the spaces and times of learning, and so on). This has been a permanent obstacle to the transformation of the teaching and learning methods associated with pedagogic differentiation, and to the individualisation of teaching and educational answers.

Third, this type of problem has seldom been given much weight in the daily practice of teacher training – either initial or in-service.

In fact, pedagogic differentiation as a strategy of inclusion of the most discriminated social groups can only be adequately taught in the context of a training programme based on teaching practices and in real schools. But, as we have seen, this it is not a widespread organisational model of teacher training. Neither can it be observed as a common practice in the institutions or in the respective teacher training curricula of the countries or regions where this model has been adopted.

In the context of initial training, when the students themselves go looking for practice teaching positions – as, for instance, in Ireland – they naturally do not go looking in schools or classes with major problems, nor would they be encouraged to take on such positions where the intervention of the teacher-trainer and of the training institution would be much more necessary and pertinent. Similarly, when training institutions assume the task of finding positions – for instance, in Portugal – it is not common to go looking for problematic schools and/or classes, as trainers try to avoid the risks that may cause a reduction either in the teacher-trainer's control over the process of training or in the student's performance, because their future job opportunities depend on their marks.

On the other hand, an intervention developed within the context of in-service training struggles with other kinds of problems, namely:

- The teachers' mobility: 'disadvantaged schools' typically display high turnover rates among their teachers. There are, indeed, always possibilities for teachers to escape from their problems if they feel unable to change their teaching practices, the working conditions or the social context and recruitment policy of the school. In any case, this 'flight' of teachers tends to reduce the impact of specific training programmes geared towards problematic teaching situations.
- The voluntary character of the continuous training: when this has a

compulsory character (as in Portugal), the option is to choose another less demanding and more rewarding training subject.
- Last but not least, the limitations of any intervention based exclusively on training, ignoring the other dimensions of anti-exclusion strategies and, particularly, the difficulties of changing the conditions of operation of the schools and of cooperation between the teachers.

Hence, it is only within the context of a concrete educational project (that is, a teacher training institution cooperating with a certain school or a group of schools) – and (almost) always within the context of a more comprehensive educational strategy[14] – that one can expect to find the prerequisites for effective teacher training. In such a context, another type of in-service teacher training emerges, which is much less frequent but also more 'invisible' in activity plans and reports divulged by the training institutions. Sometimes it involves methods of research-training or training-action. The cooperation between institutions then occurs through a cooperation between the teacher-trainer and the 'mentor', a teacher from the elementary or secondary school. Hence, the ideal training has the following characteristics: (i) it is embedded within the school(s) and the project(s) under development; (ii) it is 'practice-oriented' in a way that tries to relate directly to 'practical tasks and problems in the home schools of participants'; (iii) it is modular and flexible – in its contents and timing – so as to respond to the changing needs of the work context, of the teacher-student and of the pupils; (iv) it produces material and immaterial products – new teaching materials, alternative curricular structures and, particularly, tests of pedagogical strategies and models of learning organisation – that contribute, together, to the development of alternative paths of learning.

In short, although teachers frequently express the need for specific training relating to social exclusion and ways to cope with it, references to specific subjects dealing with these issues seem to be scarce in the curricula of the teachers' initial training. Therefore, though it is difficult to measure the extent to which educational disadvantage constitutes a preoccupation in the teachers' training programme, the available data suggest that this matter has been neglected and its inclusion in the training programme varies widely, depending on: (i) the familiarity of university departments or teams with projects in this area; (ii) the personal commitment of someone in the university to transpose this knowledge into the initial or continuous training programme, thus creating opportunities for the students/future teachers; (iii) the interest and sensitivity of the latter to take advantage of these opportunities in a field which is still neglected in curricular plans and continuous training offers.

Again, it should be emphasised that teacher training to combat social exclusion needs to be anchored in a more comprehensive educational strategy that the authorities should seek to implement, and for which they should mobilise all relevant partners, ranging from schools to universities, from teachers to trainers of teachers.

Notes

[1] Take, for example, the three main objectives listed for compulsory schooling in (French-speaking) Belgium as part of the latest educational reforms: (i) education should promote the development of each student's personality; (ii) education should help young people develop independent thought and should enable them to become active participants in the economy; (iii) education should encourage young people to become responsible citizens in a free society.

[2] *Escola Superior de Educação.*

[3] *Institut(s) Universitaire(s) de Formation des Maitres.*

[4] The exception in the European Union is Italy where, in spite of the mentioned law having been approved years ago, its implementation started only in 1998-99.

[5] It is one of the optional subjects of the curriculum 'Higher Diploma in Curriculum Studies' in the University College of Cork, and it is taught every year.

[6] It is one of the optional subjects of the curriculum 'Higher Diploma in Education' in the University College of Dublin.

[7] The collected information provides details regarding the objectives of some of the courses taught in Portugal and Catalonia. In both countries, the syllabuses contained a general study of Educational Sciences and Psychology of Development and Learning. More than 50% of the course descriptions contained subjects related to 'psychoeducational aspects', sensory, motor or mental deficiencies, and special teaching methods geared towards children with deficiencies.

[8] It must be remembered that this analysis has been extremely limited due to the superficial nature of the information to which the authors have had access during the course of this study.

[9] In Belgium, the weight given to this aspect of primary school teachers' training increases gradually from the first year of the curriculum onwards, and may reach as much as 50% in the final year. The situation in Portugal is quite similar when it comes to the training given to teachers covering pupils in the 6-15 year age range.

[10] This route has been taken by countries such as Portugal, Spain and the Netherlands.

[11] For example, this is the case in the Spanish Teacher Centres and in the Training Centres belonging to Portuguese schools' associations and professional or union organisations.

[12] These measures normally arise from reforms in the management of educational establishments. Such reforms promote the schools' autonomy and partnership and tend to involve both a greater responsibility for a school's results on the part of the teaching staff and the institution as a whole, and the need for planning and educational management instruments, of which educational projects and activity plans are the best examples.

[13] In some cases – for example, in Portugal – entities have been created specifically to coordinate the continuous training programmes. They enjoy a considerable amount of autonomy from the central educational administration and have the authority to approve training entities and programmes/initiatives.

[14] That is, a strategy including financial support, alternative curricula, learning support, the reinforcement of teaching staff, and so on, as discussed in other chapters of this book; but also a strategy that includes new patterns of organisation, management and administration of schools, strengthening their autonomy and responsibility towards their 'public' and providing them with adequate instruments, as in the case of 'schools' educational projects'.

TEN

Parent-school-community relationships

Alastair Wilson, Sheila Riddell and Kay Tisdall (SCDR, CCS)

This chapter looks at the nature of cooperation between home, school and the community in the six member countries. It begins by focusing on the theoretical debate concerning the nature of choice as self-determination, collective action or consumerism. It examines educational reforms to increase parental participation in education which have occurred across Europe since the early 1970s, and develops a particular focus on how such cooperation affects the education of socially excluded children. On the basis of this theoretical analysis, it examines those initiatives, mostly at a school-based level, which have developed home-school-community relationships and increased the educational attainment of socially excluded children. In developing a thematic analysis of these initiatives, this chapter will address the discourses reflected in these initiatives, asking whether these schemes may be judged effective and whether they can contribute to the development of positive home-school-community relationships in other countries.

Current trends and issues in parent-school-community partnerships in the member countries

Parental involvement in education

There has been a plethora of legislation and educational reform in favour of parental participation in education across Europe since the early 1970s. The 1990s have continued this trend, with both legislation and educational reform providing a statutory basis for parental participation in the educational systems of all the member countries (European Commission, 1997). However, the nature and extent of parental participation established by such reforms varies greatly between the countries involved in this study. In general, parental participation in education and schools across the project countries can be viewed in terms of:

Mandatory rights, consisting of:

(i) representation in school-level management and, in some countries, meso- and national-level decision making;
(ii) 'choice' of school;

Non-mandatory rights, consisting of:

(i) groups: parent-teacher associations, parent advisory groups, parent councils and various parent fund-raising groups;
(ii) involvement in children's education; for example, reading programmes and homework.

Perhaps the first point to be made in relation to both mandatory and non-mandatory parental rights is that parents are not a homogeneous group. Each will bring an unique experience and agenda to the forum of parental involvement. Parents may, for example, object to particular aspects of education, or alternatively be in favour of various forms of school segregation as a consequence of their differing social class, religious stance or ethnicity. Hence, strategies to involve parents in education are likely to require different approaches depending on the group targeted. It is also evident that some strategies for involving parents in their child's education are intended to utilise parental choice as a means of promoting market forces, whilst other strategies are intended to nurture the parental 'voice', as is compatible with a social democratic agenda.

Parental involvement in school governance

A major development across Europe was the increasing encouragement of parental involvement in the management of schools, again with the view that this would act as a spur to schools to improve their performance. In the countries involved in this study, there was considerable activity in the form of legislative and educational reform to give parents a formal voice in their children's education throughout the 1980s. The 1990s have continued this trend, with educational reform providing a statutory basis for parental participation in the educational systems of all these countries (European Commission, 1997). Central to these developments has been the issue of the extent of parental participation in the management of increasingly autonomous schools, although the historical and political context of such reforms varies greatly between the different countries.

In practice, the establishment of school boards worked out very differently in advantaged and disadvantaged schools, and there was evidence that the longer they were established, the less popular they became. In March 1990 (SOEID, 1995), 19.3% of schools in Scotland had no school board, but by May 1994, this proportion had risen to 25%. In May 1994, 53.5% of special schools, with their concentration of socially disadvantaged pupils, lacked a school board. Apparently, such classical models of participation are based on cultural assumptions that converge with middle-class culture rather than with the interests of socially excluded groups. This development will, therefore, be largely ignored in this chapter.

Parental partnership in education

Recent developments in parent–school relations in the member countries can perhaps be charted as moving from a compensatory model of parental involvement in education towards one based more on partnership. The compensatory approach, which was prevalent in the 1970s, was based on the idea that children from disadvantaged backgrounds/families were at a distinct educational disadvantage. Schools and teachers were expected to make up the deficit caused by poor parental input. More recent recognition of the positive role that parents can play in the individual education of their children has resulted in schools developing communication with parents, particularly with regard to addressing behavioural and truancy problems. The concept of partnership with parents has, to a large extent, replaced the idea that the establishment of good home–school communications was sufficient. The model of partnership with parents goes further and recognises parents as the primary educators of their children. It seeks to establish cooperation between parents and the school, with each party making an essential contribution to the child's learning. The definition of partnership put forward by Pugh and De'Ath has been widely quoted in this area and establishes partnership as "a working relationship that is characterised by a shared sense of purpose, mutual respect and the willingness to negotiate. This implies a sharing of information, responsibility, skills, decision-making and accountability" (Pugh and De'Ath, 1989, as quoted in Bastiani and Wolfendale, 1996, p 50).

This concept of parental partnership has become an increasingly key feature of the literature on education in Europe in the past 10 years.

However, it has been difficult to fully realise in practice, and has aroused considerable debate. Central to the debate has been the argument that parental participation, whether expressed through mandatory or non-mandatory rights, is encouraged by schools under the rhetoric of 'partnership'. In this context, however, the model of 'partnership' actually advocated by the school is often reduced to specific parent-teacher interactions that serve to co-opt parents into supporting teachers in their fulfilment of the school agenda. The power in such a relationship is still firmly in the hands of the professionals, with parents playing a supportive but relatively passive role.

The argument can be illustrated by certain types of home-based literacy programmes for socially disadvantaged pupils. The Scottish Office has argued that, between birth and age 16, children spend only 15% of their waking time in school, compared to the 85% of the time for which they are in the direct care of their parents. Hence, it follows that parents play a key role in the education of their children, and that the home is a crucial site of learning (Macbeth, 1998). On the basis of such thinking, there has been considerable interest since the mid-1980s in developing family literacy programmes which, rather than focusing on either the child or the adult, identify the whole family as a site for educational intervention. Tett and Crowther (1998), however, found that although family literacy programmes may support the parents' attempts to help their children in school, they may also exert a controlling influence, promoting a middle-class model of the family which may be inappropriate for socially disadvantaged parents to emulate.

Parent-school-community educational initiatives have indeed attracted considerable criticism for their inability, especially in socially disadvantaged areas, to encourage and enable effective parent and/or community participation. In an examination of the 'rhetoric of community education', Baron has argued that community education initiatives in the UK have often "been imposed on areas with little understanding of the problems and less connection with the lives of local people" (Baron, 1989, p 98). This has occurred at the expense of nurturing the expression of the needs and desires of the local people towards whom the initiatives have been targeted. Hence it seems that educational initiatives, especially when targeted at disadvantaged families, may often appear to engage parents and the community on an equal footing, when in fact it is the culture and interests of schools and professionals which dominate.

Parental power, participation and school choice: voice versus exit

As has been discussed above, much educational literature across Europe has centred on developing partnerships between parents, schools and local communities. This has largely been based on the widespread recognition that involving parents and, to a lesser extent, communities in children's education enhances the child's chances of educational success. Robinson (1997), referring to the National Child Development Study, has argued that the variable of parents' interest in their child's education tended to reduce the effect of other variables such as social class and parental education. Furthermore, schools are now increasingly accepting the need to acknowledge and respond to pupils' varying cultural home environments (Smit and van Esch, 1993) to realise those pupils' potential.

The term 'partnership', however, implies that parents, schools and communities should have equal levels of participation, commitment and mutual responsibility in the educational process. However, in parallel with this rhetoric, and perhaps in direct opposition to it, has been the advance of the 'new Right' agenda which establishes parental power in consumerist terms. As has been established by the previous Conservative government in Scotland and the UK, parental power in education is exercised through the parent's individual role as a consumer. The 1980 Education (Scotland) Act (as amended) gave parents the right to request places in schools outside their designated catchment area. The publishing of school examination results and school rates of absenteeism and exclusions was intended to assist parents in making the choice as to which school they could request their child be admitted. Schools and the education system as a whole were expected to respond to the simple withdrawal of custom by parents, as these parents chose to withdraw their children from less attractive schools and send them instead to more favoured ones. The customer demand for the more attractive features of one school should then encourage other schools to satisfy this demand.

It has been argued that power delegated to parents as consumers may hinder rather than enable their participation in the education process (Vincent, 1996). As consumers, parental power and participation is limited to withdrawing their child from the school – 'exit' – rather than collectively participating in and challenging the processes of school management – 'voice' (Hirschmann, as quoted in Vincent, 1996, p 12). The ability of all parents to exercise equally their 'voice' in such a system is discussed below.

The cultural gap between home and school

An aspiration towards true partnership and communication between the school and socially disadvantaged parents and their communities underpins many parent-school-community initiatives. The extent to which this ethos can be realised in practice, however, is often limited, as it requires at least some transfer of power from professionals in the school to parents and the community.[1] Such an ethos is intended to bridge the cultural gap between the school and the home, which is often a source of tension. For example, there is now some evidence to suggest that children from families of low socioeconomic status may experience a series of mutual prejudices between the school and their parents. This then has a negative effect on the pupil's self-confidence and general interest in schoolwork, resulting, in some cases, in underachievement and dropout (Verhaeghe et al, 1998). Therefore, enhancing the participation of parents of low socioeconomic status in their children's education becomes a key factor in tackling social exclusion.

Parents as consumers – increasing disadvantage?

It may be argued that an underlying feature of policies that are in favour of legislative and educational reform which seeks to increase parental involvement – and particularly parental choice of school – is the vision of the parent as an individual and responsible consumer, who makes informed choices as to their child's education and future. This assumption raises several complicating issues. First, there is the debate surrounding the extent to which parents should have the right to exercise absolute control over their children's education, and the potential conflict of this policy with children's rights.

Moreover, the application of 'quasi-market' principles (so termed because in the school-parent market no real cash is exchanged, and 'choice' is often severely limited) to education has attracted considerable criticism. There is now evidence that the establishment of the concept of parents as consumers and schools as producers in the educational marketplace has served to widen social class inequalities at the expense of working-class and poor parents.

Findings from different parts of the UK present a fairly complex picture of the way in which the policy of parental choice has worked out in practice. In London, Ball et al (1996) found that middle-class parents were much more active at making choices than lower-class parents, and in many cases were deciding between the independent and state sectors. In Scotland, the picture looked slightly different (Willms, 1996; Adler, 1997). Overall, there was less use of the independent sector, with the exception of Edinburgh, where a third of children of secondary school age are in independent schools. In the cities, middle-class parents tended to live in socially advantaged areas in which the higher-performing, formerly selective schools were located. Educationally ambitious working-class parents tended to seek places for their children in these higher-performing schools, and were thus rather more likely to exercise choice than their middle-class counterparts, who were already living within the catchment area. In the remote rural areas of Scotland, few parents exercised choice because there was often no other school in the area. All commentators, however, agree on the consequences for the poorest schools in inner city areas and peripheral housing estates. As upwardly mobile parents took their children out of these schools, they suffered the consequences of declining resources and reduced teacher and pupil morale. Far more likely to be defined as failing than their more privileged neighbours, education authorities wrestled with the dilemma of whether to close such schools down, thus reducing community resources even further, or seek to turn them into more effective institutions. A clear consequence of the introduction of market principles into education has been the creation of a rump sector within the school system, which fails to conveniently disappear as market theory would wish.

In Scotland, Willms (1996), Echols et al (1990) and Adler (1997) have argued that the application of free market principles to educational policy has not significantly increased pupils' educational attainment and, furthermore, has widened the gap between socially advantaged and disadvantaged schools. The exercising of 'parental choice' has meant that schools in socially disadvantaged areas are left with declining numbers of pupils and a rump of pupils from the most disadvantaged families. In a study of more than 600 parents in Scotland, Adler (1997, referring to a 1980s study) established that parental choice of schools was driven more by a desire to avoid particular designated schools in the locality, rather than to actively seek high-performing schools. Scottish Office statistics (SOEID, 1998) show a steady increase in the placing of requests.[2] In 1986/87, just over 10% of parents of children entering primary one made a placing request. By 1996/97, this figure had risen to just over 20%. Over this period, the percentage of placing requests met has fallen from 97.1% to 92.2%. Overall, 40% more placing requests were received in 1996/97 than in 1986/87.

The growing influence of parental choice in the Netherlands has meant that parents are becoming increasingly interested in assessing school effectiveness. Even in a system which provides equal funding for state and private schools, educational inequality may develop, as it has been shown that parents' knowledge of school effectiveness and their ability to act upon it correlates with their own educational levels (Dronkers, 1995, p 237). Currently, schools are required to produce details of performance, such as examination results. These publications are likely to aid parents who are themselves better-educated to choose schools for their children.

Furthermore, there is evidence to suggest that the long-established system of school choice in the Netherlands may be increasing ethnic and socioeconomic segregation. Karsten (1994) has argued that, while its society is becoming increasingly multicultural, the Dutch education system, by encouraging freedom of parental choice of school, is effectively increasing the segregation of pupils along ethnic lines. The law in the Netherlands permits state funding for a viable number of parents to establish their own school, and this has recently been utilised by Muslim parents to found new schools for those sharing their faith.

There is a growing population of ethnic groups in the Netherlands; this is increasingly evident in Amsterdam and Rotterdam, where numbers of Moroccan and Turkish children have become increasingly concentrated. In some urban areas, this has resulted in segregation between state schools and religious schools (Walford, 1995, p 254). Religious schools (approximately 65% of all Dutch schools) cannot refuse pupils on the grounds of their ethnic origin, but can refuse them on religious grounds. Research reported by Karsten (1994) has indicated that ethnic pupils are unevenly distributed amongst the various schools, with lower proportions in private religious schools than public authority schools. Since there is a link between ethnic origin and low socioeconomic status in the Netherlands, it would appear that the system of free school choice can act as a double-edged sword, enshrining freedom of choice while at the same time increasing segregation along ethnic and socioeconomic lines.

There would appear to be a considerable amount of active selection of schools by parents in Ireland. The National Survey on Co-education reported that only half of the pupils surveyed attended their nearest or most accessible school. Furthermore, since 10% of those surveyed stated that they had no alternative school to that which they were attending, the real figure of those actually choosing their nearest school is likely to be even lower (Hannan et al, 1996b). One of the main features of parental choice in Ireland is the active selection of single-sex schools;

58% of those surveyed attending single-sex schools were not attending their local school.

It is interesting that in Ireland the tendency of parents to actively choose schools for their children seems irrespective of their socioeconomic status, and that the distribution across social classes is fairly close to overall proportions (Hannan et al, 1996a). The only exception to this is the case of upper middle-class parents, where 60% did not attend their nearest school. This could perhaps be attributed to the fact that such parents may opt to send their children to boarding schools.

It would appear that parental choice of school in Spain is particularly determined by socioeconomic status. The Spanish education system incorporates three different types of school:

- private schools in which parents pay all the costs associated with their children's attendance: these are generally very expensive and constitute only a small percentage of schools;
- private schools with public financing: in these schools, parents do not pay for their child's educational expenses but are required to pay for any additional costs such as extracurricular activities, transport, uniforms and other material resources. These schools are usually associated with religious orders or middle-class high schools in urban areas;
- public system schools: education in these schools is free, although parents are expected to pay for books and are invited to contribute to the school's parents' association.

Thus, parental choice of school may be largely determined by the socioeconomic status of the parents. This is complicated by the fact that, in some areas, middle-class parents wishing to send their children to public schools, perhaps because they are non-religious or innovative in some way, may have their application refused on the grounds that there are other families living on lower incomes in the same geographical area.

Parent-school-community initiatives for socially excluded children

In the post-war period it was believed that children from disadvantaged backgrounds were at a distinct educational disadvantage. Under such circumstances, teachers were expected to make up the deficit caused by poor parental input. Since parents were deemed deficient, they were not encouraged to participate in their child's education. During the 1960s and 1970s, a belief developed that there was a direct link between effective education and national economic prosperity. Research showed that the most effective schools were those characterised by positive home-school relations; efforts were therefore made to involve all parents as partners in the education process. A number of parent-school-community initiatives aiming to raise the educational attainment of children from disadvantaged areas have adopted the language of partnership, and some of these, from a number of EU countries, are discussed below.

Early literacy programmes: parents as a lever

Chapter 6 of this volume reviewed a series of early intervention programmes in Europe, and presented an assessment of their evaluation. What follows is just a reminder of the most striking experiences, with an emphasis on the role of parents. A key feature of these initiatives has been the recognition of the valuable role to be played by children's parents, carers and the wider family in encouraging and fostering children's educational progress. Parents especially have been recognised as the primary educators of their children; as such, they are a resource with whom schools are expected to form partnerships.

Increasing parental involvement has therefore been a strong feature of early intervention initiatives, especially with regard to pre-school programmes. In Ireland, the Rutland Street Project, which was established in 1969 to prevent school failure in disadvantaged areas, introduced pre-school children to an innovative curriculum designed to prepare them for primary school. A further important aspect of the project was a strong emphasis on strengthening school-family relationships and encouraging parents to see themselves as educators. The overall impact of the project in combating educational disadvantage was unambiguously positive. The project has influenced the more recent (1994) and comprehensive Early Start programme, which is also targeted at disadvantaged areas. The Early Start programme is primarily intended to improve children's numeracy and language skills. To assist in this process, the project seeks to involve parents at three levels:

* the day-to-day running of the centre;
* taking part with their children in the centre's activities;
* participation in an advisory group at the centre.

Specific pre-school programmes in Scotland have been part of the wider early intervention programme and have been linked to urban funding initiatives for the disadvantaged. Projects such as the 'Learning is Child's Play' initiative in a disadvantaged area of Paisley have concentrated almost exclusively on developing parents, grandparents and carers as the primary educators of their children. The emphasis in such programmes has largely been to develop parent/grandparent/carer confidence in nurturing their children's exposure to literacy, and to provide essential support enabling parents/grandparents/carers to increase their children's interest and awareness of sounds in the spoken language – especially rhyme – and concepts of print. The Scottish early intervention programmes for pre-school children have, as yet, not been fully evaluated. However, there is some research evidence (see, for example, SOEID, 1998), to suggest that phonological training in rhyme awareness for nursery stage children may not be as effective as intensive individual and specialised support.

This intervention strategy, led by the Scottish Office, is still in the early stages of implementation. However, early intervention programmes have already been piloted in Scotland with some success. The Pilton Early Intervention Project is one of the most outstanding examples. It involved the assignment of home-school link teachers whose role was to support parents in the education of their own children. These teachers organised workshops for parents on early literacy in both pre-school and early primary years; they developed resources to enable parents to stimulate literacy, and provided opportunities for children and parents to work together.

With the exception of the Rutland Street project in Ireland, the early intervention initiatives referred to above are relatively new and, as such, their long-term effectiveness is yet to be explored. Evaluations to date, which have largely measured children's levels of literacy and numeracy in their early years at school, have been encouraging. American research would indicate that working with parents rather than solely within in-school programmes is essential, and that such early intervention has significant long-term effects.

On the other hand, some critical comments have been made about the narrow focus of family literacy programmes in disadvantaged areas. The phrases 'partnership with parents' and 'empowerment' are particularly common in the literature surrounding this approach. However, the extent to which such rhetoric is fulfilled is often unclear. In general, family literacy programmes have been designed to develop parents as the primary educators of their children, and increase the educational attainment of both parents and their children. In exploring such programmes in disadvantaged areas, Tett and Crowther (1998) have argued that family literacy projects, rather than being empowering, may in fact locate the family as the source of educational failure. Tett and Crowther argue that education cannot be a neutral process, and that middle-class culture and literacy is favoured over those of the working class.

Such an argument has particular consequences for parent-school-community relationships in disadvantaged areas. If families in such communities are expected to adjust to a dominant form of literacy, it may well serve to undermine and devalue their own vernacular form of literacy. Rather than being empowered, such parents may well be made to feel inferior, with the result that their sense of social exclusion is increased.

Liaising with parents to transform the school?

The Home-School-Community Liaison (HSCL) Scheme was introduced by the Irish Department of Education in 1990 as an initiative to counteract disadvantage by increasing cooperation between schools, parents and community agencies in the education of young people. At present, some 184 schools and 68,137 pupils are involved in the scheme, representing a total expenditure of 4.2 million ECU per annum. The main aims of the programme have been:

- to maximise the active participation of pupils in the learning process, especially among those at risk of educational failure;
- to promote active cooperation between the home, school and relevant community agencies in promoting the educational interests of children;
- to raise awareness among parents of their own capacities, and to assist in developing skills related to the educational process;
- to enhance the uptake of education, pupil retention within the system, and progress to further education;
- to disseminate the positive outcomes of the scheme throughout the school system (Ryan, 1994; ESF Programme Evaluation Unit, 1997).

The scheme involves the provision of a school-based coordinator to liaise with parents and the community. It has a national steering committee (which includes representatives from the Department of Education, teachers' unions, parents' associations, and relevant experts in the area), a national coordinator, local coordinators, local committees, and a team of evaluators. The scheme involves a number of features, including financial assistance to the school, home visits, the provision of additional school facilities, the education of parents through courses, and teacher education in relation to the process of partnership. The scheme is supported through regular in-service courses and cluster meetings of coordinators within a local area. While the HSCL coordinators' brief includes liaising with school teachers and community groups, an analysis of actual workloads indicates that their work with parents takes up at least two thirds of their time. The parents' main area of involvement amounts to attendance at courses and activities, in particular those related to self-development, parenting, home management, and their child's education. At primary level, there has been greater parental involvement in paired-reading programmes and classroom activity than within second-level schools (Ryan, 1994).

Evaluation was built into the programme from the outset, and an initial evaluation has indicated some positive effects. First, HSCL coordinators and teachers have reported improved personal development among parents, with a greater awareness of, and involvement with, the school. This pattern is somewhat less evident at post-primary than at primary level. Secondly, most schools reported increased contact between parents and teachers. Coordinators reported greater understanding of parents among teachers, and parents found it easier to approach teachers. These effects were apparent in both primary and second-level schools. Thirdly, coordinators perceived the effects on 'some' pupils in terms of improved behaviour, attendance, achievement, and more positive attitudes to school and teachers. However, few teachers perceived any immediate effects on pupil performance. Fourthly, the scheme triggered the development of useful links between the primary and post-primary schools involved in the scheme, especially in relation to the transition of students (Ryan, 1994).

However, a number of cautionary points should be noted. The positive effects of the programme were generally confined to parents who were actively involved in activities, and who were often regarded by teachers as being least in need of the scheme. A survey of uninvolved mothers indicates that they experience greater socioeconomic disadvantages, being more likely to come from unemployed households, to be single parents, and/or to have more children. While home visits were considered an effective strategy for reaching parents who had no other contact with the school, the issue of self-selection in parental involvement needs to be addressed. Furthermore, very few parents had taken a leading role in parental activities; there was a tendency to adopt a more passive role. In particular, fathers were much less likely to get involved in school-related activities than mothers. It is too early to assess whether the scheme has had an impact on pupil attainment. However, baseline information on pupil achievement has been collected, and this issue will be examined in the future (Ryan, 1994).

In Flanders, one action research project, funded by the King Baudouin Foundation, has been established with the specific intention of designing effective strategies for enhancing poor parents' involvement with their children's school life, by bridging the gap between the pupil's social environment at home, and that of the school. In fact, this project builds upon an earlier scheme sponsored by the Foundation, where several activities were set up to promote the involvement of parents at school (see Chapter 5). Teachers were encouraged to visit all pupils at home twice a year, while an open-door policy in nurseries and primary schools sought to bring parents into the schools. Parents could take part in language courses, received guidance on how to support their children's homework, and were involved in organising sociocultural activities. The home visits were seen by parents, young people and teachers as extremely useful, although teachers found the visits time-consuming. Since the home environment makes contacts less formal, the conversations were also perceived as less threatening by parents, and a wider range of issues (often not related to school) could be covered. These visits reached parents who were not otherwise involved in nurseries or schools through such formal means as parents' committees (Vettenburg and Thys, 1996).

The present project, entitled 'Poverty and Primary Education' goes a step further. It was established in October 1997 and involves 11 primary schools. It has four main aims:

- to design and try out effective strategies and activities for enhancing poor parents' involvement with their children's school life;
- to design strategies to enable primary schools to assess and evaluate the effects of the activities undertaken on students, parents, and the school team;
- to design strategies to enable primary schools to set their own goals and to design their own activities, and strategies for enhancing poor children's educational opportunities;
- to create case studies in which the activities and strategies mentioned above are described; these could provide a source of inspiration for other primary schools and school advisory agencies (Verhaeghe et al 1998, p 2).

Although still in its initial stages, the project has established that two strategies should be followed simultaneously by the participating schools: bringing school life closer to home, and bringing home life closer to school. In adopting these strategies, the project aims to develop activities which focus not just on parents but equally on children and their teachers. In summary, the key aspects of the project are that teachers and schools in general increase their understanding of the pupil's social environment, that children are encouraged to express their views and feelings, and that parents are encouraged through positive means and informal contacts to be more involved in their children's education.

Still in Flanders, 'School Community Action' is developing as a new type of service. It concentrates on the empowerment of disadvantaged groups (students, parents and neighbourhoods) as well as intensifying the dialogue between these groups and the school, with the aim of combating prejudices and discrimination. Community action workers engage in a wide range of activities such as counselling parents, setting up parents' groups, accompanying parents on school visits and teachers on home visits, training educational staff concerning social exclusion, disseminating information about innovative approaches, and so on. The projects are mainly funded from the Social Impulsion Fund, an urban renewal and local anti-poverty programme. Negotiations concerning a more solid legal framework are ongoing, although School Community Action is officially recognised as an indispensable partner in educational priority policy programmes (see Chapter 13).

It is too early for a clear-cut evaluation of the impact of School Community Action. Field workers claim to observe stronger commitment of parents to school problems, increased participation in parents' groups within and outside the schools (in some schools), increased awareness of problems related to social exclusion and greater commitment to solving these problems on the part of teachers (some teachers even engaging in sociocultural activities in inner city districts during holidays and after school), and better counselling and decreased failure risk on the part of pupils.

One of the difficulties appears to be excessively close involvement of some community workers in traditional homework classes and student guidance; these activities are extremely time-consuming, and are being increasingly criticised for replacing parents and teachers rather than supporting them. In some cases, homework classes have been organised even without any collaboration with schools, which of course has created some mistrust on the part of schools.

A second problem relates to the imbalance between immigrant

children and disadvantaged indigenous children within School Community Action, the latter having fewer social networks on which to build. There are also some tensions between both target groups.

Lastly, the precarious financial situation of the projects themselves leads to high turnover among their staff, weighs on the continuity of relations with all parties, and hampers the professional development of workers (Uit de Marge, 1994).

Partnership with local communities

Another line of action in Flanders relates to 'magnet schools'. The 'Flags and Banners' project has been initiated in 12 primary schools by a cooperative network between the Department of Education, the King Baudouin Foundation, the Centre for Intercultural Education (*Steunpunt Intercultureel Onderwijs*) and the 'Centre for Amateur Arts'. The project has been extended to 20 schools in the academic year 1998-99.

Its aim is to strengthen the links between schools, parents and the local community by means of arts projects carried out with pupils within the schools. Art expression is seen as a means, not as an end; for example, mime and theatre appear to develop the pupils' social skills in a way that would not be achieved through verbal communication. Teachers allegedly observe an improvement in the school climate (less aggression, better expression of emotions, and so on). Non-verbal communication (in painting, for example) can also be a lever for the participation of non-native pupils and, more generally, for pupils who perform less well in verbal communication.

The art projects in the schools are supposed to act as 'magnets' on the community. Local organisations have started collaborating with the schools, parents visit exhibitions and performances, and so on.

According to the initiators, monitoring the social dimension of the projects is of crucial importance. Without particular emphasis on that aspect, the projects may become islands in the local environment (as has frequently happened in the US, where the idea of magnet schools originated).

Scottish Office funding through the Urban Programme has financed a number of individual initiatives aimed at improving the educational attainment of children living in disadvantaged communities. The Home-School-Employment Project (HSEP) based in Paisley is the longest running of these initiatives, and has been evaluated continuously throughout its existence. This project was established in 1991, but ended in 1998 due to a lack of resources. Its was set up with the aim of enhancing the educational achievement of young people living within the Ferguslie Park and Shortroods area of Paisley. This is a socially disadvantaged area with a population of approximately 6,000 (one third of whom are aged under 16), to the south west of the city of Glasgow. It was recognised that poor educational attainment was a major contributory factor to the unemployment rate of the area, which was estimated at 40% in 1988. Ferguslie Park now has the status of a Priority Partnership Area (PPA).

The Home-School-Employment Project (HSEP) was set up with the clear intention of raising the educational attainment of children in the area by developing closer liaison and communication between the school and the home. In partnership with other groups and agencies[3] as well as schools and parents, HSEP supports young people (and their families) throughout their schooling and into the early stages of (un)employment.

A team of 16 people consisting of a principal project officer, three area officers, eight project officers and four clerical staff work on the project. They are divided between three secondary schools serving the area, and their caseload consists of children of families in the area who attend either one of the secondary schools or their associated primary schools. The project staff have no teaching responsibilities and work entirely on developing parent-school relationships. They divide their time between direct educational help for young people (homework clubs, for example), monitoring of school attendance, workshops for parents, promoting effective communication between school and home, the training of professionals, and the promotion of work experience and transition to further education.

The key findings of the mid-term evaluation (Robertson, 1995) were as follows:

- the strategy of home visiting and support for parents in their contact with the school has been productive in both raising parents' awareness of their children's educational progress and increasing school-parent liaison. Home visits were recognised as a valuable tool in making parents aware of specific issues affecting their child's progress;
- the strategy of providing extra support to pupils and their parents at times of transition – from nursery to primary or primary to secondary school – was particularly effective in maintaining parent contact with the school and in helping children and young people adjust;
- whereas rates of attendance at Strathclyde Regional schools remained static over the period, rates of attendance at the three secondary

schools associated with the project generally increased. There was a particular increase in secondary years 1-2;

- HSEP staff and some school staff expressed the need to work more closely on specific educational issues such as developing the curriculum to meet the educational, personal and social needs of the young people;
- the higher levels of pupil satisfaction with the activities of the project expressed in secondary classes 1-2 declined in secondary classes 3-6. HSEP advocated closer cooperation with other agencies such as the Careers Service and Employers Groups as essential to rectifying this.

It is apparent that this evaluation of the HSEP stresses the importance of making parents aware of their children's educational progress, increasing home-school liaison, and reducing rates of absenteeism. However, the extent to which 'partnership with parents' (implying a sense of real involvement and responsibility) is either sought or established remains unclear. The evaluation makes reference to the fact that HSEP staff and teachers expressed a mutual need for closer cooperation on educational matters in order to make the curriculum more relevant to young people. There is, perhaps, a conspicuous absence of parental input in this process. On the other hand, the embeddedness of the project within a 'holistic' development strategy for the area, as evidenced by the attention devoted to transitions from school to work and the collaboration with various partners from outside the education system, can be seen as a trump card in the fight against social exclusion.

Example of good practice: the Family Clubs of S. João de Deus School (Oporto)

The latter feature mentioned above undoubtedly characterises a pilot project in Oporto, Portugal. The population of the Areosa district of Oporto is marked by wide ethnic diversity, social inequality and poverty. Those in employment are faced with low-paid and insecure jobs. Drug abuse, prostitution and crime are common experiences in the lives of both adults and some children living in the area. The area is designated for priority educational treatment (or TEIP as it is known) and consists of a primary school, a year 5 to year 9 school, and a year 1 to year 9 school. The TEIP aims to develop a common educational policy with the following goals:

- improving the school-family relationship;
- fighting dropout;
- fighting social exclusion;
- building a school open to the community.

The S. João de Deus School, which is part of this TEIP, has developed an educational project aiming to change the school to "the students' social, cultural and emotional benefit", with the ultimate goal of "changing mentalities, values, rules and behavioural standards which affect students ... and trying to transform society" (Amaro et al, 1998, p 50). The cultural gap between the school, its pupils, their families and communities is evident, with many parents (for example immigrants without papers and former prisoners) fearful of developing a formal relationship with the school. For this reason, the prospect of forming a parents' association remains distant.

However, Amaro et al, in rehearsing the positive aspects of parent-school relationships, argue that initiatives such as the 'family clubs', which seek to establish an informal meeting place for parents, teachers and pupils, have had a considerable impact on improving the relationships between the school, parents and the community. Pupil behaviour has also improved. The main point made by Amaro et al is that the central focus of fostering parent-school relationships has been to provide information and training "on health and hygiene, socialisation, family relationships and drug addiction", fields which do not, at least immediately, translate into improved educational achievement. The question in such circumstances is whether the school should be seeking to improve the educational achievement of pupils when basic human needs have not yet been met (Amaro et al, 1998, p 58).

Conclusion

Over the past two decades, widespread attempts have been made across Europe to increase parents' involvement in the education of their children. However, the nature of this involvement varied according to the parents' social status, and was driven by different policy agendas which, at times, were in conflict with one another. Broadly, we outlined the following three policy thrusts, and the type of parental involvement which each of these promoted.

Parents as the engine of the market

All six European countries allow parents some degree of choice of school. In Scotland in the 1980s, the parents' Charter explicitly identified parental choice of school, fuelled by information about schools' performance across a range of indicators, as the means by which the effectiveness and efficiency of schooling were to be raised. The theory was that poorly performing schools would lose pupils, and would eventually wither on the vine. What happened in practice, not only in Scotland but also in North America (Willms, 1997), was that schools were judged on the sole criterion of raw examination results and, as a result, schools in socially disadvantaged areas lost pupils. Such schools, however, proved extremely difficult to close, partly due to parents' demand for local education and, in the West of Scotland, strong opposition from the Catholic Church to the closure of any of its schools. Falling rolls, declining resource base, teacher redundancies, and a concentration of children with learning and behavioural difficulties in socially disadvantaged schools meant that morale plummeted, contrasting markedly with the buoyancy of schools operating at full capacity. School effectiveness research (Robinson, 1997) demonstrated that the proportion of a primary school's intake with a middle-class background had a significant positive impact for all pupils. Conversely, the proportion of intake with a working-class background had a negative effect for all pupils. The increase in social segregation, which turned out to be the main effect of parental choice, thus had a depressing effect on the effectiveness and efficiency of the system as a whole, although it may have had particular benefits for individual pupils.

Parents and communities as pathogenic

Attempts to involve parents in their children's education are generally fuelled by the belief that this will improve school effectiveness and the quality of individual children's education. Another clearly detectable strand of thought, however, is that if parents and communities are not inculcated with the school's values, they may act as a profoundly destructive force, undermining the school's goals. This serves to remind us that the function of education in Western society is not simply to provide people with skills and knowledge so that they may contribute to the economy and sustain the social fabric, but also to exercise social control by diffusing potential threats to social stability.

In the preceding discussion, we highlighted the way in which community literacy projects tend to target socially disadvantaged areas, as if it were the people within them that were in need of remediation, rather than the conditions in which they live. Whilst early intervention may yield spectacular short-term results in terms of accelerating children's progress in literacy and numeracy, the extent to which these benefits are sustained in the long term are uncertain if the surrounding conditions remain unchanged. As we saw in Chapter 3, there is a strong positive association in Scotland between receiving free school meals (used as a proxy measure of poverty) and being absent or excluded from school. The question therefore arises as to whether early intervention measures are sufficient to counteract the negative long-term and cumulative effects of poverty. The evidence from Glasgow's Priority Partnership Areas is that even though schools located within them have, for many years, received economic subsidies under a range of anti-poverty programmes, only a very small number of pupils actually qualify for higher education.

A true partnership model

Parents are clearly more than simply an extension of the school. In addition to their indisputable role as partners in early stimulation and literacy programmes, parents also represent the cultural environment in which children develop. If schools are not able to become positively involved this (sub)culture, they will continue to fail and to provoke conflict. If they are not aware of the obstacles which children encounter in the learning process, they will underestimate and even look down upon and discriminate against pupils. For this reason, investing specific human and financial resources to strengthen the parental sounding board should not be regarded as a superfluous luxury. Measures such as the Home-School-Community Liaison in Ireland and School Community Action in Flanders rate this as a top priority.

Projects and programmes geared towards integrating the school into the social fabric of the area are broader still. As well as the family, cooperation in social life with employers and government departments, is also targeted. In this sense, perhaps the most typical examples are the 'magnet schools' in Flanders and the Home-School-Employment Partnership in Paisley, Scotland. The S. João de Deus School in Oporto again illustrates how a school can develop to become a lynchpin in combating the social deterioration of an entire neighbourhood.

Notes

[1] Arnstein's ladder of participation may be a useful framework for analysing parent-school-community relationships in this context. The bottom rungs of participation – manipulation and therapy – reveal decision-makers' intentions to educate and cure rather than involve and consult and could be perhaps representative of the deficit model of some family literacy programmes. As we move up the ladder the rungs represent the lessening of professional control and the establishment of partnerships with citizen control being the top rung.

[2] Requests by parents to their local education authority to have their child attend a school other than that designated for their catchment area.

[3] For example: employers' groups, psychological services, the Careers Service, parent groups, social work and further/higher education bodies.

ELEVEN

Provision, integration and inclusion for children with special educational needs

Alastair Wilson, Sheila Riddell and Kay Tisdall (SCDR , CCS)

Separate special education developed across Europe in the 19th century, to ensure that all children had access to education. Pupils who could not keep pace and failed in the ordinary classroom situation were largely viewed as having learning difficulties which were best remedied by the expertise of certain teachers working outside of the mainstream classroom, either in a separate school or a special unit attached to the mainstream school. More recently, such a deficit view of these pupils has given way to the arguably more positive concept of pupils having 'special educational needs'. How these needs are met, however, has been the source of continued debate. Separate special education establishments/units may have better resources, and may be more capable of providing an adequate and individualised education for children with disabilities and particular learning difficulties, than could be provided within mainstream. However, these establishments have increasingly been viewed by parents, educators and policy makers as a means of segregation and stigmatisation.

As a result, the governments of the member countries have become committed to developing educational policies that serve to promote and encourage the integration/inclusion into mainstream education of pupils who would formerly have attended special schools. However, in those countries with an established structure of segregated special education, conversion to mainstream education for all pupils remains problematic. Hence, despite a range of official policies on integration/ inclusion across the member states, there is a strong emphasis, for a variety of reasons, on the early categorisation of special needs pupils, and their placement in special schooling.

The nature of impairments of pupils categorised as having special educational needs

The Netherlands has perhaps the most extensive and differentiated system of special education of all the member countries. After a process of professional evaluation, pupils may be referred to one of 15 separate categories of special school. There are segregated special schools for:

1. deaf children;
2. children with impaired hearing;
3. children with severe speech disorders (not in groups 1 or 2);
4. blind children;
5. partially sighted children;
6. physically handicapped children;
7. children in hospitals;
8. chronically sick children;
9. mentally handicapped children;
10. infants with development difficulties;
11. severely maladjusted children;
12. children with learning and behaviour problems;
13. children in schools attached to pedagogical institutes;
14. children with multiple handicaps;
15. severely mentally handicapped children.

Belgium has also developed a considerably differentiated system of special education in order to meet student needs. Special education in Belgium is organised on the three levels of pre-primary, primary and secondary. Currently, special segregated education is divided into eight categories:

1. for children and adolescents with slight mental retardation (not at nursery level);
2. for children and adolescents with moderate and/or severe mental retardation;
3. for children and adolescents with emotional disturbances;
4. for children and adolescents with physical deficiencies;
5. for children and adolescents with learning difficulties;
6. for children and adolescents with visual deficiencies;
7. for children and adolescents with auditory deficiencies;
8. for children and adolescents with disorders of speech or language and/or serious learning difficulties (O'Hanlon, 1993).

Provision for special needs students in Ireland is also categorised according to disability/learning difficulty. Special schools in Ireland address 11 categories of children:

1. mildly mentally handicapped pupils;
2. moderately mentally handicapped pupils;
3. young offenders and the disadvantaged;
4. emotionally disturbed pupils;
5. hospital schools for physically handicapped pupils;
6. physically handicapped pupils;
7. hearing impaired pupils;
8. travellers;
9. multiply handicapped pupils;
10. blind/partially sighted pupils;
11. children with reading disability.

Differentiation of learning difficulties is largely based on IQ tests, with those children functioning below an IQ of 70 being considered 'mentally handicapped'. These students are then further divided, with those of an IQ of 50-70 being categorised as mild, 35-50 as moderate, 20-35 as severe, and 0-20 as profound. Children with a mental handicap are generally placed in a special school or in a special class within mainstream schooling; however, over a 1,000 children with severe and profound levels of ability are in special care units of the Department of Health (Lynch, 1995). Since 1986, projects have been piloted to teach children in this group within the Department of Education, and the Review Committee on Special Education (1993) recommended that such provision be extended to all children with severe and profound mental handicap. Special classes within mainstream schooling in Ireland exist for:

1. mildly mentally handicapped children;
2. moderately mentally handicapped children;
3. hearing impaired children;
4. language impaired children;
5. traveller children.

Prior to the mid-1970s, special and separate schooling existed in Scotland for pupils categorised as blind, partially sighted, deaf, partially deaf, educationally subnormal, epileptic, maladjusted, physically handicapped, or with speech defects (Closs, 1997, p 82). The Warnock Report (DES,

1978) challenged this categorisation of pupils according to their disability and, instead, advocated the identification of the needs of individual pupils in relation to the curriculum, and the development of educational programmes to ensure that these needs could be met. As a result, specific special schools for pupils with specific difficulties have largely been replaced (schools for the deaf and the blind notwithstanding) by more generic schools that provide education for pupils with a range of different impairments. Nevertheless, certain categories of description have persisted, and pupils in special schools or with a record of needs in mainstream schools are divided into the following categories (Scottish Office, 1997):

1. hearing impairment;
2. visual impairment;
3. physical or motor impairments;
4. language and communication disorder;
5. social and emotional difficulties;
6. moderate learning difficulties;
7. severe learning difficulties;
8. profound learning difficulties;
9. specific learning difficulties;
10. complex or multiple impairments;
11. dual sensory impairment;
12. moderate learning difficulties plus other;
13. severe learning difficulties plus other;
14. profound learning difficulties plus other;
15. other.

The British concept of special educational needs has been influential in educational policy making in Spain. In 1989, the Ministry of Education White Book for Educational System Reform moved the focus of special education in Spain from a deficit and segregating view of individuals to one that explored the possibilities of providing an educational experience that met the needs of all pupils. However, despite such a philosophical shift, the Royal Decree (1995) has signalled a return to the categorisation of pupils according to their disability/learning difficulty. In this sense, the move towards integration and inclusion in education in Spain has suffered a setback.

In general, it would appear that professionals across the member countries categorise certain pupils as being unable to succeed in mainstream education and, as a result, in need of some form of specialist intervention. The education of pupils with special educational needs occurs largely in special schools, or at least within special units in mainstream schooling. As a result, special education and the pupils it serves seem to exist as a separate system of education apart from mainstream schooling, rather than being incorporated within it. In some cases, the categorisation and special treatment applied to such groups as those with 'social and emotional difficulties', 'the disadvantaged' and 'travellers' reveals that the problems encountered or diagnosed by professionals are part of much wider social issues than can be resolved by education and schooling alone.

The links between impairment and social and economic disadvantage

The indications are that there is a strong link between special educational needs and economic and social disadvantage. In Scotland, secondary schools that serve Priority Partnership Areas[1] in Glasgow represent approximately 18% of the city's education authority secondary school population, but constitute approximately 42% of the population of pupils with a record of needs.[2] Special schools do not appear to dramatically improve young people's employment prospects.

Only 5% of pupils leaving special schools in Glasgow in 1997 entered employment, compared with 23% of those in mainstream schooling. Dyson (1997, p 115) has argued that special needs education policy in the UK as a whole has largely ignored the "relationship between children's difficulties in school and wider patterns of socioeconomic disadvantage and inequality".

Disadvantaged children in Belgium are similarly overrepresented in special education. This is illustrated strikingly by two small samples (Nicaise and De Wilde, 1995; ATD-Fourth World et al, 1995) of children from Belgian families living in persistent poverty.[3] These studies revealed that 22% of these children had ended up in special education.[4] More recent samples drawn by the Belgian division of the Movement ATD-Fourth World[5] show proportions of a quarter to one third of such children attending special schools. Furthermore, roughly half the children from persistently poor families spend part of their youth in an institution or with a foster family (Nicaise and De Wilde, 1995). Care institutions are often linked to a particular school for special education, in which the children are then enrolled more or less automatically. It is estimated that 40% of young people in Flemish special youth care institutions are placed in special education (Hellinckx and De Munter, 1990). Looking at the same phenomenon from a different angle, Goffinet and Van Damme (1990) found that 77% of the pupils in special education are children of working-class families and marginal workers.

Little information is available, as yet, as to the type of special education attended, but casual observation indicates that most poor children are referred to type 8 education (serious learning difficulties), as well as type 1 (slight mental retardation) and type 3 (emotional disturbances).

In general, there are four factors which may help explain the overrepresentation of children from socially excluded families in special schools in Flanders (although again, very little systematic research is available on this issue – see Nicaise, 1998):

- poor health (perhaps as the result of a high incidence of chronic diseases, accidents, malnutrition, stress, polluted environment, and so on);
- misinterpretation of low IQ scores (70% of the variance in IQ at age 12 in Flanders can be explained by social background variables, although this is obviously no indication of genetic ability);
- financial aspects: special education is relatively well subsidised and, hence, can offer educational as well as material services to pupils (speech therapy, physiotherapy, remedial teaching, but also transport to school, hot meals, and so on) at a much lower cost than mainstream schools. Casual information collected by ATD-Fourth World reveals that this advantage tends to sway poor parents in their school choice;
- the links between state care and special education.

The concepts of integration and inclusion

The integration of pupils with special needs into ordinary or mainstream schools has been a prominent feature of educational policy in the member countries for the past two decades. The Warnock Report recognised this in the UK, with the strong endorsement of the principle of integration. Referring to it as "the central contemporary issue in special education", Warnock argued:

> The principle of educating handicapped and non-handicapped children together, which is described as 'integration' in this country and 'mainstreaming' in the United States of America, and is recognised as a much wider movement of 'normalisation' in Scandinavia and Canada, is the particular expression of a widely held and still growing conviction that, as far as is humanly possible, handicapped people

should share the opportunities for self-fulfilment enjoyed by other people. (DES, 1978, p 99)

The current trend in the member countries and the European Union as a whole is towards the integration of pupils with special educational needs into mainstream schooling. However, the extent to which this occurs varies greatly, as does the interpretation of the term 'integration'. Integration can vary across the member countries, from pupils attending segregated special classes in ordinary schools to, in some cases, learning with other pupils in mainstream classes. The extent to which 'integration' varies within these limits in the member countries is largely governed by arguments concerned with the extent to which schools have the resources to meet the needs of such pupils, and to what extent such pupils will affect the education of other pupils in the class.

More recently, however, and especially in the UK, policy making in special education has been increasingly influenced by the disability movement. The social model of disability emphasises the structures and barriers in society which prevent disabled people's full participation in society, and maintains that legislative and broader societal change is required to remove these barriers. In the field of special educational needs, the disability movement has argued powerfully for abolishing separate provision for children with special educational needs. There has been a resulting philosophical shift away from a focus on the barriers facing the accommodation of pupils with special educational needs into mainstream schooling, towards a restructuring of mainstream education itself to make it more easily accessible to all pupils.

Such an approach has been strengthened by more recent international policy statements. The 1989 UN Convention on the Rights of the Child, which was ratified by all member countries, establishes the right of disabled children to "active participation in the community" and maintains that their education should lead to the "fullest possible social integration and individual development" (Article 23). The Salamanca Statement and Framework for Action on Special Needs Education (UNESCO, 1994) went even further; part 2 of the Statement established that:

- every child has a fundamental right to education, and must be given the opportunity to achieve and maintain an acceptable level of learning;
- every child has unique characteristics, interests, abilities and learning needs;

- education systems should be designed and educational programmes implemented to take into account the wide diversity of these characteristics and needs;
- those with special educational needs must have access to regular schools which should accommodate them within a child–centred pedagogy capable of meeting these needs;
- regular schools with this inclusive orientation are the most effective means of combating discriminatory attitudes, creating welcoming communities, building an inclusive society, and achieving education for all; moreover, they provide an effective education to the majority of children and improve the efficiency, and ultimately the cost-effectiveness, of the entire educational system.

Statements such as these have been instrumental in providing official sanction for the 'inclusion' movement. In this context, inclusive education is a much broader concept than integration. It is a process that extends beyond the boundaries of the school and addresses the pupil's position in their community and society as a whole. Sebba and Ainscow (1996) provided the following definition:

> Inclusive education describes the process by which the school attempts to respond to all pupils as individuals by reconsidering and restructuring its curricular organisation and provision and allocating resources to enhance equality of opportunity. Through this process, the school builds its capacity to accept all pupils from the local community who wish to attend and, in so doing, reduces the need to exclude all pupils.

In the UK, critics of integration have used the term 'inclusion' to shift the responsibility for change away from the individual child towards the school and society as a whole.

Official policy on integration/inclusion in the member states

As stated above, special needs education across the member states is currently moving from special, separate schooling towards integration/inclusion. This takes a variety of forms across the member countries, ranging from special classes within mainstream schooling to fully integrated schooling, in which children with special needs are educated with other pupils in a mainstream class. Hence, the degree to which integration/inclusion of special needs pupils occurs varies greatly across the various educational systems of the member states. Each country has its own political, social and cultural influences; these have contributed to very different approaches to integration/inclusion.

Scotland

Building upon the Warnock Report (DES, 1978), special educational needs provision in Scotland was also influenced by the Scottish HMI[6] (Scottish Education Department, 1978) which argued for a much stronger commitment to the integration of children with learning difficulties into mainstream classes. Indeed, in the view of HMI, withdrawing children into segregated remedial classes tended to accentuate rather than alleviate their difficulties and distract attention away from the central source of problems; that is, the curriculum in mainstream schools. In this document, the principle of integration is seen as more important than the individual parent's right to a say in the location of their child's education. By the 1990s, after more than a decade of Conservative government, the market and individual choice, rather than collective welfare, had become the established policy framework, evident in documents such as *The Parents' Charter for Scotland* (1991). The language of equity and social justice was conspicuously absent from such documents. In their place was a conceptualisation of citizenship as consumption, producing competition between providers which would raise standards and lead to greater value for money in the public sector (see Chapter 10).

In the early 1990s, endorsement of the principle of integration as well as choice was evident (see SOED, 1993, 1994). Decisions on placement tended to be framed in terms of meeting the needs of individual children; for instance, in the document *A parents' guide to special educational needs* (SOED, 1993), integration is presented not as a governing principle but as a possible option which might be selected by individual parents on their children's behalf, almost as a life-style choice. The document *Effective provision for special educational needs* (SOED, 1994) stated that placement in mainstream education would be considered as the first option for a child with learning difficulties, but there was no consideration of the possible tension this could create with the principle of parental choice of schooling for their children. Confusion was reflected in local authority policy statements, as Labour-controlled authorities attempted to support integration whilst simultaneously endorsing the principle of choice.

As New Labour seeks to establish a distinctively different political philosophy from that of Old Labour and the Conservatives, such tensions are still in evidence. The wave of policy documents that has accompanied Labour's first year in office is reviewed below.

The Labour government, which came to power in May 1997, has attempted to pursue a middle way between a commitment to the market as the ultimate arbiter of public service provision, and social democratic principles, which are seen as placing too much emphasis on rights and not enough on responsibilities. As a result, the policy documents of the Labour government represent a significant break with the Conservative agenda by asserting that inclusive education reflects a moral imperative, rather than simply being a response to the wishes of parents as consumers. However, acknowledging the paramount importance of the needs of individual children might be seen as a 'get-out clause' to ensure the survival of special schools:

> Where pupils do have special educational needs there are strong educational, social and moral grounds for their education in mainstream schools. Our policy for schools will be consistent with our commitment to rights for disabled people more generally. But we must always put the needs of the child first, and for some children specialist, and perhaps residential, provision will be required, at least for a time. That is compatible with the principle of inclusive education. (DfEE, 1997, p 34)

A discussion paper, *Parents as partners: Enhancing the role of parents in school education* (SOEID, 1998), readopts the language of partnership rather than consumerism, and emphasises influence through 'voice' rather than 'exit' (Hirschman, 1970). Ways are sought to encourage parents to play a more active role in running schools, through school boards for example, rather than seeking to influence schools indirectly by taking their custom elsewhere if dissatisfied with the service on offer. The power to challenge and effect fundamental change in education policy and schools, however, remains out of reach for parents.

A Green Paper on special educational needs in Scotland, published in May 1998, outlined the future direction for special educational needs provision in Scotland. "Selecting an appropriate placement" is listed as one of the ways in which parents may be involved in the education of their child. Other ways include: participating in assessment and review; suggesting effective approaches to teaching and learning; passing on to teachers relevant information from doctors and other professionals; offering advice to other parents and pupils in the school; supporting school activities and reinforcing new skills; and learning at home and in the community. The general emphasis on 'working together' is much more in line with Warnock's idea of partnership than with the notion of parents exerting consumer power.

To summarise, the policy documents of the late 1970s supported integration – rather cautiously in the case of Warnock, and more firmly in the case of the 1978 Progress Report of the Scottish HMI. Scottish legislation, on the other hand, contained no promotion of integration, but affirmed parental choice (with a range of caveats) as the overriding principle, with an underlying assumption that many parents would favour integrated provision. By the early 1990s, government documents consistently reiterated the centrality of parental choice, although financial concerns introduced a number of constraints which meant that in practice, parents of children with special educational needs had less freedom of choice than others.

Spain

The special education reform movement in Spain effectively dates from 1978 when, following the death of Franco, Spain entered a more democratic era. Within the resulting educational reform movement came a commitment to integrating, and improving services for, people with special needs. In March 1985, the Department of Education introduced national guidelines (Royal Decree) to facilitate the integration into mainstream schooling of pupils who were previously assigned to special schools. The 1990 Education Act (LOGSE) built upon this theme and introduced the concept of one education system that "provides necessary resources for students with temporary or permanent special needs; they can attain the same general aims in the same system established for all students" (Chapter 5, Articles 36 and 37, 1990 Education Act, quoted in Pastor, 1998, p 51).

Although these reforms were part of a national programme, each autonomous community within Spain was responsible for developing its own processes of integration. The Basque Government, in particular, made advances in integration, with the Basque Plan in 1982; this advocated the position of the ordinary school as a focus point for the transformation of education for pupils with special educational needs. This was furthered in 1987 with the formation of the Committee on Special Education, whose recommendations were founded on five basic principles:

- the aims for education are the same for all students;
- a policy of positive discrimination should be used for students with greatest disadvantages and needs;
- students' special needs should be seen as relative, temporary, interactive and linked to curricular adjustments;
- integration should be an essential part of the education system and should engage all who are involved in the system, not only the teachers of students with special educational needs;
- a change of attitudes, aims and practice in schools and in the community must be developed; this includes early intervention from birth, collaboration between parents and teachers, involving the student in taking decisions on educational action, the development of resources within the school system, and collaboration between schools on provision.

According to Pastor (1998), despite these enthusiastic proclamations, the reform of special education in Spain has been stunted by 'fiscal (budgetary) realities' (Pastor, 1998, p 53). The result, Pastor argues, has been that the 1995 Royal Decree entitled 'Organisation of special needs students' actually serves to re-establish the categorisation of students. This signals a return to a deficit view of disability, in which the term 'special educational needs', and with it a perspective that sees special needs as interactive and relative, is sacrificed for one which sees special educational needs as dependent on:

- social and cultural context;
- the students' antecedents prior to entering school;
- the students' individual characteristics, such as giftedness, mental disability, sensorial or physical handicaps, and severe behavioural problems.

Official policy on integration in Spain appears to be subject to financial restrictions, with the result that the processes leading towards integration and inclusion of special needs students have been slowed considerably. In Catalonia, such fiscal realities have meant the introduction of special classes for pupils with special educational needs within mainstream schooling which may even, on occasion, be situated outside of the main school campus.

Such policy has affected parental choice for parents of children with special education needs. The 1995 Royal Decree in Spain (Article 9) makes reference to the rights of parents in the educational process;

however, the wording of the Article makes it clear that integration is possible only in certain circumstances:

> In any case, in compulsory education, parents or tutors will be entitled to choose the school in which they want to enrol their children with special educational needs among those schools which have the personal resources and suitable materials to guarantee educational attention of quality, according to the report resulting from the psychopedagogical assessment and within the framework of the general criteria established for pupils' admission. (Royal Decree 696/1995, 28 April 1995)

In this way, parental choice of school in Spain is effectively limited by professional opinion and school resources. Parents do not participate in the decision making process and have only a right to be informed. Their opinion, however, is valued by those professionals involved, and in this way often informs the process.

Portugal

Policy concerned with the integration of special needs pupils in Portugal has also been significantly influenced by developments in the UK, and the Warnock Report in particular. Developments in legislation in Portugal from the late 1980s to the early 1990s have established the basic right of all children with disabilities to be educated, to be included within compulsory education, and to have priority given to their education in normal/mainstream schools. A further decree, in 1991, established a variety of different measures that were required to be in place in mainstream schooling in order for it to meet the special educational needs of particular students. It seems, however, that these reforms are still very much under development in Portugal.

Ireland

Legislation promoting integration in the Republic of Ireland has, so far, been limited. In 1990, the Minister for Education proposed a resolution on the integration of children with special educational needs which was adopted by the EC Council of Ministers of Education. In Ireland, this was followed with the Green Paper on Education (*Education for a changing world*, 1992), in which the Government pledged to accommodate children with special educational needs as far as was possible within mainstream education. It was, however, stated that provision within mainstream schooling would remain inappropriate for some pupils. The 1995 White Paper, *Charting our education future*, further addressed the problems of pupils with special educational needs; it proposed that a database should be created containing information on every pupil with a disability, and that each of the proposed education boards should have a statutory responsibility for all disabled students in its region (Booth and Ainscow, 1998). It is still the case in Ireland that children with 'severe mental handicaps' are not the responsibility of the education system. The Special Education Review Committee (SERC, 1993) established the need for a wider range of provision within mainstream schooling but nevertheless endorsed the need for special schools and classes within ordinary schools (Booth and Ainscow, 1998, p 150).

It is unclear to what extent parents of special needs pupils can exercise choice in terms of schooling in Ireland. Referral to a special school seems subject to professional assessment and parental consent. However, parent organisations have been active in campaigning for the right of children with Down's syndrome to attend mainstream schooling. In some instances, this pressure has resulted in the Department of Education providing support for teachers to enable a child with Down's syndrome to attend mainstream schooling. There are, however, similar tensions in parental attitudes in Ireland, as in Scotland and the Netherlands, between some parents calling for more integration and others resenting the closing of special schools.

Belgium

Integration of special needs students has taken a very different form in Belgium than it has other countries. Special school education was established in the early 1970s to overcome the problem of what was seen as poor quality education for special needs pupils, provided in special classes within mainstream schooling. There are now some initiatives within the French community to establish special schools within mainstream schooling, but these have been treated cautiously (OECD, 1995a, p 94). Within the Flemish community in Belgium, there has been a more significant move towards promoting integration. The 1986 Special and Integrated Education Act preserved the status of special separate schooling, but advocated integration within mainstream schooling for some students. Integration in this sense meant that certain pupils (those with motor, visual and hearing impairment) could attend mainstream schooling, provided they had the ongoing support of special school staff. However, the opportunity of integrated education is limited to those pupils with motor, visual or hearing impairment who are able to satisfy the following criteria:

- the pupil's general intellectual ability should be at the same level as that of the average of the group into which he or she is to be integrated;
- the school attainment level should increase; at the very least, to the average level of the group;
- the disabled child must have strong and sound motives for attending regular class;
- he or she must show enough emotional stamina to cope in an ordinary school;
- the home environment should provide sufficient and adequate support;
- the ordinary school should have a positive general attitude towards the integration of the handicapped; the whole school team must be prepared to take special and appropriate measures;
- the reception group should show sufficient openness; some appropriate preparation might be needed. (O'Hanlon, 1993, p 21)

Despite these apparently strict and exclusive regulations, the number of children entering this form of integrated education in Belgium more than doubled in the period 1983-91 (O'Hanlon, 1993, p 19). Admission to integrated education appears to be influenced by social class; working-class children are three or four times less likely to receive integrated education than they are to receive special education provision (O'Hanlon, 1993, p 20). The attendance level of upper middle-class children in integrated education is three or four times higher than it is for such children in special education.

As in other countries, the wider debate on inclusive education in Flanders was developed following the 1994 UNESCO conference in Salamanca. In 1998, the Flemish Educational Council pledged to gradually (and partially) dismantle schools for special education, and to integrate pupils as far as possible, with the help of professionals from special education, into ordinary classes (with or without extra staff) or into separate classes within mainstream schools. A few schools have already begun this process despite the lack of a statutory framework; however, Ghesquière et al (1996) and the Flemish Education Council (Vlaamse Onderwijsraad, 1998) do describe a number of conditions for this process, most of which can only be met in the long term:

- strengthening the teaching skills of teachers, as relating to pupils with special needs;
- developing a wide range of facilities within mainstream education. Outside the context of integrated education, just a few well-off parents can currently afford extra support; this is increasingly being purchased on the free market at high cost, and there is still a great shortage;
- bringing about a change of mentality among all parents and teachers, especially those of pupils without special educational needs (they are afraid that non-disabled pupils will lose attention or resources);
- a thorough organisational reform (upscaling, new consultative structures);
- an overhaul of the entire curriculum, with a view to differentiation and 'treatment of diversity';
- a new method of funding based on the principle of case management, rather than the present lump-sum subsidies granted per pupil and per type of handicap;
- finally, respect for the freedom of choice of every pupil and their parents, who may have psychological or social reasons for choosing segregated education in the company of pupils with similar needs.

Netherlands

The number of pupils attending special schools in the Netherlands has grown in recent years, and as a result, government policy has been to move tentatively towards encouraging increased integration. To achieve this, the Dutch government has sanctioned developments to try and make the special school system less dominated by categories (as referred to above) of handicap (1985 Interim Act). The Advisory Council for Primary and Special Education proposed the following categories for special education:

- **category 1 schools** for children with delayed development, children with learning disabilities, children with learning and behaviour problems;
- **category 2 schools** for children with very specific educational needs; for example, physically handicapped children;
- **category 3 schools** for children who need support during their whole life; for example, severely mentally retarded children.

Furthermore, the 'Going to School Together' Act, which went into effect in 1994 and is specifically targeted at mainstreaming education for category 1 children (those with learning and behavioural problems), heralded a new start in special education. The Act is designed to mainstream education for children with learning and behavioural problems by bringing such schools together and transforming their role to regional support centres. Furthermore, teachers from schools for special education offer extra help for pupils who might otherwise be referred to (secondary) special education, enabling students to attend schools for mainstream education. This help is aimed not only at pupils, but also at supporting teachers of mainstream schools (Ministry of Education, Culture and Science, 1998).

In general, however, such policies have made slow progress, perhaps because integration in the Netherlands does not have the uniform support of regular or special schools, or of parents. Indeed, it is a particular feature of special education in the Netherlands that parents have not been a driving force in promoting integration. In the Netherlands, parents make the decision whether to refer their child to special education after consultation with teachers, school principals and school support. The admission board of the special school concerned then carries out an assessment of the pupil to see if they require special provision. Parents rarely object to the decision of the school teacher and principal concerned, and 90% of such referrals are placed in special schools (Booth and Ainscow, 1998, p 124).

Although supportive of integration in principle, parents in the Netherlands seem to hold the view that adequate education for special needs pupils is difficult in regular schooling due to the large differences in pupil ability in the same class. It is argued that this situation is too difficult for an ordinary teacher to manage; hence, parents feel their children's needs can be better met in segregated education (Pijl and Pijl, 1998, p 17). As a result, 95% of children with special educational needs in the age group 4–12 still attend special schools, despite the fact that the Dutch Constitution establishes the principle of free school choice.

An exception to this has been children with Down's syndrome, whose numbers in regular schools have increased in recent years (Pijl and Scheepstra, 1996, p 312). Parent organisations have been particularly active in this process, and have received assistance from the Dutch government in the form of regulations permitting extra staff support for such children. Schools have also been instrumental in accommodating such pupils, even though they have no legal obligation to do so.

A further and possibly inhibiting factor has been raised by Booth and Ainscow (1998, p 124), who point out that integration in the Netherlands is complicated by the organisation of the education system into state, Protestant and Roman Catholic regular and special schools. This, they argue, means that integration can be seen as a threat to the current religious divisions of the system. Separate funding structures further complicate the issue, as the funding mechanism allows more money to be made available to meet pupils' needs in special education than in mainstream education. Hence, it is often economically expedient for mainstream schools to refer a pupil to special education, and for special schools to keep such pupils once they enrol.

With the exception of the integration of some children with Down's syndrome, integration for other categories of special needs children, though on the official policy agenda, seems severely hindered by the existence of the Netherlands' differentiated system of special schooling (Den Boer, 1995).

In summary, it would appear that all the member countries have established policies aimed at increasing integration into mainstream schooling for pupils with special educational needs. However, such policies seem largely dominated by an emphasis on, and examination of, the pupils' ability to adapt to mainstream schooling – this is particularly apparent in Belgium and the Netherlands. Within these policies, then, integration is seen largely in the physical sense of placing pupils together in a classroom. The existing school structure remains, for the most part, unchanged, and pupils with special educational needs are required to adapt.

Sample statistics on integration/inclusion of special needs pupils

Scotland

Given the commitment of most education authorities in Scotland to educate children with special educational needs in the least restrictive environment or in integrated settings, one would have expected to see a gradual rise in the rate of integration. Across Scotland as a whole, however, the number of pupils with Records of Needs has increased, and is currently about 2% of the school population (compared with 3% of pupils with Statements of Special Educational Needs in England and Wales). Admittedly, between 1983 and 1993, there was a big increase (from 6% to 42%) in the proportion of pupils with Records of Needs in mainstream education. Although these figures suggest an increased use of mainstream education, it is not clear whether children who might once have been placed in special schools are now being placed in mainstream schools, or whether the increased use of mainstream placements is due to children with less severe difficulties, who previously would have been supported in mainstream without a Record of Needs, now being recorded.

It appears that, although numbers of children in special schools have fluctuated, the proportion has remained approximately the same. Since special departments may make it easier for a child with special educational needs to spend part of their day in mainstream schooling, one might argue that the shift from special school to special unit suggests that more integration is taking place. However, a recent study of mainstream and special school provision (Allan et al, 1995) indicates a wide variety of practice in relation to the amount of integration taking place in special units. Placement in a special unit does not in itself guarantee a greater degree of integration than education in a special school.

Overall, then, although the figures point to a significant increase in the number of children with Records of Needs in mainstream classes, a significant decrease is not evident in the overall proportion of children placed in the special sector.

Belgium

In the period 1977-89, the number of children in segregated special education in Flanders fluctuated at around 3%. Since then, however, this figure has increased steadily (Ghesquière et al, 1996), reaching 3.6% in the 1995/96 school year. In particular, the number of children of 'type 8' (children with serious learning difficulties) has undergone explosive growth (more than quadrupling) in the past 20 years. These figures raise serious issues for the education system in Flanders, not least regarding the ability of the mainstream education system to cope with children with learning difficulties.

Spain

Spain has a remarkable record as regards integrated education. In the country as a whole in 1994/95, 2.1% of all pupils aged 4-14 were identified as having special educational needs. Three quarters of these SEN pupils were integrated into ordinary classes in mainstream schooling, while 3% were being taught in special units within mainstream schooling and 22% were being educated in separate special schools. The situation was similar for Catalonia, where 71% of pupils with special needs were being educated in mainstream schools, and 29% were being educated in special schools; there are no figures recorded for Catalonia for pupils in special units within mainstream schooling.

Ireland

In Ireland, Department of Education statistics (1996/7) indicate that the number of special schools has been fairly stable since the mid–1980s (119). However, in the context of overall declining numbers at primary level, the number of pupils in special schools has declined (but only by 12% compared with 18% for ordinary schools). The number in special classes within ordinary schools has more than doubled. However, we do not know what percentage of the population with special needs are covered, or how many are 'fully integrated' within ordinary schools.

Examples of good practice

El Margalló (Spain)

The *El Margalló* school is located in the Garraf region of Catalonia, which is situated close to Barcelona and has a population of about 150,000; it is both a rural and industrial area, and is easily accessible. The region as a whole was selected and given resources to provide integrated schooling for special needs pupils. The El Margalló school was established as a pilot integration school in 1983. The school itself is located in a borough of the main town, a region which is mostly inhabited by working-class and disadvantaged families. As a public school, it does not select its pupils, and those resident in the borough are given priority. With respect to pupils with special educational needs, these come from any part of the region, since no other specialised resources in the area are capable of meeting the needs of those with severe disabilities. However, the school is very strict in ensuring that the proportion of pupils with special educational needs does not exceed the percentages established when it was created. At the moment, the school enjoys high prestige because of the quality of the teaching provided. The attention to pupil diversity and the educational and moral values emerging from this constitute an important part of the school's educational project.

The school has the following staff: 11 tutors of ordinary classes, six tutors of special education classes, two assistants/supports, four speech therapists/supports, four educators, two physiotherapists, and one physical education teacher (a specialist in psychomotor physical exercise).

The number of pupils in specific special education classes ranges from a minimum of three pupils to a maximum of eight per classroom, depending on their characteristics. All staff members share the same educational project and take part in the outings, residential camps and parties. In the academic year 1996/97, the school had a total of 286 pupils, 45 of which had special educational needs (making 16% of the school roll). Of these 45, 26 pupils with special educational needs were in special educational classes, and 19 were integrated into mainstream class settings. This gave an average of two special needs pupils per mainstream class. The children with special needs were categorised by the school as having a variety of different disabilities including cerebral palsy, psychosis, autism, Down's syndrome, mental retardation, severely disturbed personality and Prader Billi's syndrome.

There are a number of activities which go beyond the classroom framework and which contribute to and support integration. The fact that pupils share transport, the playground and the tables in the dining hall, that they participate in the same parties and go out together on excursions and/or residential camps and so on, fosters sociable behavioural and relationship patterns among special education pupils, and helps ordinary education pupils learn to accept and respect pupil diversity.

In addition, all of these activities help establish ties of relationship and friendship among the pupils, as well as teaching them how to live together.

As regards teaching, there is complete integration in mainstream classes for some pupils with special educational needs. For some pupils with more complex needs, the school has specific educational units ('reduced groups', in the Margalló School's own terms) which specialise in a particular type of disability, or bring together pupils who share an acute need for curricular adaptation. Of these special needs pupils not in fully integrated programmes, there is almost total integration in the ordinary classroom for those pupils in learning groups 1 and 2, which are for 5- and 6-year-olds in their final year of infant school and their first year in primary school. Pupils with special educational needs in their second and third years of primary education, and who are not on the fully integrated programme, are partially integrated with mainstream classes for up to half of the school day.

De Rank (Belgium)[7]

De Rank is a primary school in Wezemaal, near the Flemish city of Leuven. The large sign at the school gate immediately catches the attention: "Take courage, children. Especially those of you who find it difficult at school ... There's a place for you here, too." The school head was formerly a remedial teacher. He kept the remedial class at his school going while those in other schools gradually disappeared. Furthermore, he was able to convince his teachers to relinquish the convenience of smaller classes in order to free up resources for the remedial class. He has stated: "The school isn't there only for the most able. And what can give a teacher greater satisfaction than a problem child that he manages to put on the right track?" In addition to the remedial class, three female teachers also provide Extended Care.[8] The pupil monitoring system starts as early as the infant class and ensures that the children's progress is tested regularly. If problems occur, the remedial teacher and class teacher act together to remedy the situation as quickly as possible.

De Rank does its best to take advantage of educational innovations. In the first and second school years, the classes are divided up into play-learning groups, in which pupils are able to work independently. In the third year, a start is made on contract work. Lessons generally start with the class together as a group, but thereafter, pupils with difficulties can also approach the teacher separately. At the same time, the most able carry out advanced exercises. From the fourth year on, a good deal of attention is focused on learning to learn: planning work, self-evaluation, establishing priorities, and applying *aides-memoire*. A form of 'peer tutoring' is also being tried out, between first-year pupils and infants.

Such a differentiated approach demands a great deal of flexibility and dedication from the teaching staff. "That is only possible with a motivated team. The people who work here aren't afraid to work a few hours extra", says the school head. "The pupil monitoring system also forces them to enter into dialogue and cooperation. This gives rise to the growth of a new culture. The classroom is no longer an island."

No systematic evaluation has been carried out as regards the effectiveness of the educational approach of De Rank. The head teacher claims that the number of referrals to special education has fallen dramatically over the past 10 years, while grade retention has also diminished. However, it must also be said that the school does not seem to be faced with genuine social exclusion among its pupils.

Conclusion

In a study of social exclusion in education, children with special educational needs occupy a particular place; after all, they often have to cope simultaneously with two types of exclusion. First, children with any form of handicap still found it difficult to gain access to education until a few decades ago. Their access to ordinary schools is still a major area of conflict today. Moreover, the few studies performed reveal the strength of the link between social background and special educational needs; children from socially excluded families are far more likely to suffer from serious learning difficulties, and are heavily overrepresented in special education.

It is evident that opportunities across the member countries for integration/inclusion of pupils with special educational needs are predominantly structured by the nature of the pupil's impairment. A professional opinion as to the ability of the pupil to adapt to mainstream schooling is often the means of determining whether a pupil enters special segregated schooling or special classes within mainstream education. A number of further factors can be detected across the member countries, such as social class and policies promoting parental choice of schooling, which also influence the degree of integration/inclusion experienced by pupils with special educational needs.

What seems to remain constant throughout the member countries is an adherence to the vision that pupils with special educational needs must be able to adapt to mainstream schooling, which itself remains largely unchanged. Where this status quo has been challenged, as in Spain, it seems that financial constraints have led to a return to the model of categorisation of pupil's impairments and segregation. Thus, integration for pupils with special educational needs in the member countries seems limited to the physical integration of certain groups of 'special' children. The broader rhetoric of 'inclusion', implying structural and societal change, is rarely realised, and is perhaps in danger of being associated with more conservative integration policies.

Despite the widespread adoption of the rhetoric of integration or inclusion, very little is known about the quality of experiences of children with special educational needs within mainstream schools and classes. If a policy of total inclusion is pursued, there is a danger of ignoring the needs of children with the most significant impairments, such as behavioural problems, autism, or little or no speech. The number of such children is likely to be very small (less than 0.5% of the population), but in order to make progress they are likely to need extremely intensive one-to-one contact with a specially trained teacher. Both the training of teachers and the tuition of pupils are likely to be very expensive and cannot be justified in human capital terms, since these pupils are unlikely ever to make a significant contribution to the economy. Given the growing focus on accountability throughout the European education system, it is almost inevitably the case that teachers in mainstream classes will have neither the time nor the energy to devote to such pupils. Indeed, while it may be appropriate for a child with moderate learning difficulties to attend a physics class and follow a differentiated learning programme, children who are struggling to develop basic social and communication skills are unlikely to gain much benefit from a physics class. There is a clear danger that a total inclusion policy could make life worse rather than better for such children.

Finally, there is much evidence that disabled people experience disadvantage because of the social, economic and attitudinal barriers they face. The challenge for education in the future is to minimise, rather than amplify, these disadvantages. While the disability movement has successfully focused attention on the negative features of segregated education, there is a danger that an over-enthusiastic adoption of integration/inclusion policies could make matters worse rather than better for children with the most significant impairments.

Nonetheless, a great many socially disadvantaged children, as well as other children with special needs, are wrongly referred to special education, often out of a lack of commitment on the part of educators. No matter how well these schools are equipped to cope with special needs, the very nature of their segregated approach leads to further social exclusion. A more inclusive form of education is imperative for these children. It is clear that this imposes fairly radical requirements on the education system, as well as on all the parties involved; these requirements include a change in mentality among teachers, parents and fellow pupils, an expansion in schools' resources, better teacher training, and so on. However, this is the only correct way to eliminate the present unequal treatment of pupils with special needs.

Notes

[1] Priority Partnership Areas are designated by the Scottish Office and represent Scotland's most deprived urban areas. They normally have a population of 5,000-30,000.

[2] A Record of Special Educational Needs is an official assessment and plan for a pupil as having special educational needs within mainstream schooling, based on data supplied by the Scottish Office Education Statistics division.

[3] The first sample was part of a study of contacts with the special youth care services (Nicaise and De Wilde, 1995); the second was part of the General Report on Poverty (ATD-Fourth World et al, 1995). Together these data cover around 102 children in primary and secondary education.

[4] The share of special education in the overall school population in Flanders is between 3.5% and 5%.

[5] ATD-Fourth World (Belgium), unpublished data.

[6] Her Majesty's Inspectors of Schools.

[7] Based on Roox (1998).

[8] See Chapter 12 for a fuller description of Extended Care.

Part Four:
Equal outcomes strategies

TWELVE

Educational priority policies

Joaquim Bernardo (IESE) and Ides Nicaise (HIVA)

The adoption of specific priorities in the educational policies associated with additional funding arises as a kind of measure for promoting the school success of socially excluded children. In fact, as we will notice further on, the definition of priorities in the distribution or allocation of funds to schools is usually dependent on criteria connected with the proportion of pupils in the school population that are particularly at risk of being excluded from the education system.

Educational priority policies (EPP) can be regarded as a lever for the development of positive discrimination processes designed to support schools or educational areas that are undergoing problems that have a special importance in the regional or national context. These positive discrimination processes can be achieved in practice through actions such as remedial teaching, extra language courses for migrant children, differentiation within the classroom, and so on.

The content of the actions conducted under educational priority policies will not be described in this chapter, because these types of actions are discussed in detail in other chapters (see, for example, Chapters 5, 6, 10 and 13). As far as possible, we will present a typology of measures and actions that are usually associated with the financing mechanisms of educational priority policies.

It must also be stressed that educational priority policies are part of the regular or mainstream education system, and are not related to the alternative routes in education, such as special education.

To summarise, the delimitation of the subject of this chapter – educational priority policy – is based upon three crucial criteria:

- it is mainly about additional financing mechanisms that allow special support to be provided in specific areas or to specific groups of students with more serious problems of integration in the education system;
- it implies positive discrimination over other educational areas and

groups of students where the school exclusion problems are less serious;

• finally, the application of this policy takes place in the mainstream education system.

The objectives of educational priority policies

Generally speaking, educational priority policies are based on objectives that are very similar throughout the different countries. In fact, the adoption of special financing mechanisms is usually justified by the needs of schools or educational areas where the incidence of students with serious learning and developmental difficulties is more pronounced, due to factors of a cultural, economic and social nature.

In this way, educational priority policies indirectly provide a response to the needs of students coming from poorer social and cultural environments, because these are the people who traditionally exhibit more learning and developmental difficulties in the education system. Although this population is usually not explicitly mentioned in the general objectives as the target group of this type of measure (leaving the matter open to interpretation by mentioning only students with learning difficulties, as in the case of the Educational Priority Policy in Flanders), the targeting is much more explicit when we get to the level of the eligibility criteria of schools or areas that should receive extra financing (see below), given that most of the students with learning difficulties come from disadvantaged backgrounds.

The differences between countries in the adoption of this kind of measure relate mainly to the specific objectives, target groups, actions and priorities that are defined by each national, regional, or even local administration. These parameters vary according to the specific problems, and cultural and economic backgrounds, that schools are confronted with. There are also important differences between the countries in the management and follow-up measures that are created to deal with these financing systems.

Table 12.1 summarises the specific objectives of each type of registered intervention under the educational priority policies.

A comparison of the specific objectives related to the type and level of intervention under the educational priority policies reveals a wide and varied range of objectives, mainly due to the specific characteristics of the education systems in the different countries analysed. In broad terms, however, five general types of specific objectives emerge in relation to the extra financing of schools or groups of schools:

Table 12.1: Specific objectives of Educational Priority Policies, by country and type of measure

Country/ region	Measure	Specific objectives
Flanders	Educational Priority Policy (EPP)	- Acquisition of language skills in Dutch (the local language) by migrant children - Preventing or attenuating the learning and development problems of the pupils - Encouraging the involvement of parents and teachers in the school career of the students - Promoting intercultural education
	Educational Priority Areas	- Similar to the EPP
	Extended Care	- Broadening the range of materials and activities available to pupils and developing multidisciplinary consultation - Differentiation and individualisation in teaching methods - Gradual introduction of pupil monitoring systems - Developing support for developmentally endangered children and children with socio-emotional problems
Ireland	Programme of Special Measures for Primary Schools (Dublin, Cork and Limerick)	- Encouraging the acquisition of books and other school material - Development of home-school liaison
	Scheme of Assistance to Schools in Designated Areas of Disadvantage	- Recruitment of additional teachers - Strengthening of school management - Acquisition of books and other school material - Development of home-school liaison
	Breaking the Cycle (the earlier schemes are now all integrated into Breaking the Cycle)	- Recruitment of extra teachers - Acquisition of books, equipment and other school material - Professional development of teachers (continuous vocational training)
	Additional capitation grants for Special Schools and Junior Training Centres for Traveller Children	- Reducing student-teacher ratios - Supporting school transport for the traveller children

Table 12.1: Specific objectives of Educational Priority Policies, by country and type of measure (continued)

Country/region	Measure	Specific objectives
Ireland (contd)	Demonstration Programme on Educational Disadvantage	- Establishment and support of locally based networks whose role is to develop an integrated response to the problem of educational disadvantage in a given area
Netherlands	Educational Priority Policy – OVB (Weighting rule)	- Improving educational attainment in language and arithmetic in primary education - Improving language skills in Dutch for children with a different mother tongue - Equalising the shares of disadvantaged students across study fields - Improving the initial reception of newcomers - Reducing truancy - Reducing the numbers of children leaving secondary school without qualifications
	Educational Priority Areas	- Combating educational disadvantages in areas where the typical disadvantage features are concentrated high unemployment, poor educational levels, limited cultural participation, high percentage of immigrants - Promoting cooperation between schools, as well as between schools and other actors such as welfare institutions
	Educational Priority Policy – Projects	- General objectives of the OVB - Specific objectives relating to each type of project
Portugal	Educational Priority Territories (TEIP)	- Promoting an integrated strategy between different schools in territories with a high concentration of disadvantaged children - Diversification of the training on offer in these areas (for example, alternative curricula) - Promoting the training of the staff involved (teachers, non-teaching personnel and even actors within the community – continuous vocational training) - Promoting an integrated management of the resources and development of extracurricular activities - Promoting cooperation/integrated action between public services and other local agents

Table 12.1: Specific objectives of Educational Priority Policies, by country and type of measure (continued)

Country/region	Measure	Specific objectives
Spain	Compensatory Education Actions/Programmes	- Promoting curricular adaptation and diversification in order to meet the interests, motivations and needs of disadvantaged children - Improving school management and making it more flexible - Promoting activities to welcome/integrate disadvantaged children into the education system, and combating school failure among those children - Promoting experiences to enrich the socialisation process of students - Development of forms of home-school liaison, namely between education centres and families - Promoting familiar orientation and formation - Development of programmes for scholarship, and for the follow-up and reduction of school absenteeism - Promoting activities of non-formal education
Scotland	Partnership in Education Project[1]	- Creation of a cohesive and supportive educational environment favourable to young children's growth and learning, and activating local resources to achieve this goal - Confirmation of the parents' status as the child's prime educators, encouraging them to understand their own role in that context - Development of networks between all statutory services and voluntary groups in the intervention area - Raising the educational level of local children within an area
	Early Intervention Programme	- Promoting extra support in schools through the employment of learning support teachers, educational psychologists, classroom assistants and home-school link personnel - Development of a baseline assessment of children's skills and abilities as soon as they enter primary school (5–6 years old)
	Urban Programme Funding – Funding for Priority Partnership Areas; Funding for Regeneration Strategies	- Supporting educational projects in deprived urban areas that improve the school careers of the most deprived children - Supporting educational projects in deprived areas that involve the schools and the local community

[1]This project had three phases of extra financing. Initially, it was based in a specific area in the south west of Glasgow and funded for a three-year period (1983-86), but it was extended for two similar periods (1986-89 and 1989-92) with differences in the structure of objectives. For that reason, the objectives of the first phase of the project are presented here, because those of the other two phases pointed basically to similar final goals. The big difference that can be found is in the fact that they are more centred in the consolidation, development and dissemination of the work done throughout the duration of the project.

- to promote the learning of certain basic skills that children from disadvantaged backgrounds traditionally have more difficulty in acquiring: learning the official language of the country (or even region), and mathematics;
- to facilitate the improvement of support mechanisms for teachers and schools (for example, acquisition of books and other teaching materials, rental or purchase of equipment, improvement of school infrastructure, creation or enlargement of areas for extracurricular activities, financial support for school management, teacher training, and so on);
- to enable the development of educational activities, integrated with or separate from the school curricula, which promote school success, particularly of disadvantaged students. It may, for example, be necessary to engage more human resources to support these activities, thus reducing the student/teacher ratio or the ratio of students to non-teaching personnel;
- to foster the development of partnership between the school, families and other local bodies (such as businesses, local associations, public services in other sectors such as health or welfare, local government, and so on). In this way, it is possible to contribute in an effective way to the promotion of more integrated forms of intervention that may provide an effective response to the specific needs of disadvantaged children;
- to tackle the specific and more pressing needs of schools/areas where the problems of school exclusion are more acute due to the higher number of disadvantaged students.

In some countries (such as Ireland) the specific objectives are mainly focused on the development of the instruments that are required to achieve the final purpose of the measures; in other countries (such as the Netherlands) they are instead focused on the expected outcomes of these measures. This might imply more positive evaluations in the former group of countries, as such intermediate objectives are more easily achieved. However, the effects produced in terms of improved educational outcomes or social integration may be less rosy, given that the allocation of extra resources and support to schools does not always produce the expected results.

The funding criteria of the educational priority policies

The funding criteria of educational priority policies vary between the countries studied, and even according to the type of measure considered within countries. In the following analysis, a distinction is made between criteria relating to needs and those relating to the utilisation of funds.

Target groups and areas selected within the context of educational priority policies

The conditions of access to additional financing tend to depend mainly on the proportion of students from disadvantaged environments within a school. In some cases, the amounts of funding (also) vary according to the relative proportion of such students in a certain area or region. An overview of the precise criteria in the main EPP measures from the six study countries is given in Table 12.2.

We can identify the following three main types of target groups:

- children whose parents have low levels of education and professional qualifications, usually with one of the parents in an unemployment situation, especially those in long-term unemployment, living in run-down neighbourhoods or poor housing, and with scarce access to other services (such as healthcare and welfare benefits);
- children from immigrant families who often suffer from a tension between the specific culture of their families and the school culture, in addition to the characteristics mentioned above, and language barriers;
- children from travelling or itinerant families.

It is obvious that the three main types of target groups often face a cumulative series of obstacles to integration and educational success. For example, many children from immigrant or travelling families have parents with low levels of education and professional qualifications, and live in poor areas or neighbourhoods.

We must also draw attention to the fact that some of the national measures of the various countries are restricted to pupils in certain levels of primary or compulsory education; for example, Extended Care in Flanders is targeted exclusively at 4- to 7-year-old children in the transition period between the nursery and primary school,[1] while the Early Intervention Programme in Scotland is specifically aimed at

Table 12.2: Overview of operational criteria relating to needs

Country/measure	Territorial or target group approach	Parameters used to establish eligibility
Flanders: Educational Priority Policy	Target group	- Ethnic origin of mother/grandmother + low educational level of mother - Regressive funding when share of target group exceeds 50% (in order to discourage over-concentration)
Flanders: Educational Priority Areas	Target group + area	- See Educational Priority Policy - 10 parameters at municipal level measuring % young and long-term unemployed, minimum income recipients and other low income groups, single parent families, children in state care, housing problems
Flanders: Extended Care	Target group	- Single-parent families or low education of mother or both parents inactive
Ireland: Breaking the Cycle	Target group	- Long-term unemployment of parents or low educational level of parents or living in public housing
The Netherlands: EPP weighting system	Target group	- Parents have low educational level or are bargees or travellers or foreigners with low level of education
Portugal: TEIP	Area	- Mainly ethnic minorities or travellers or other factors related to high school failure rates (flexible criteria)
Spain: Compensatory Education Programme	Target group + area	- Decentralised and flexible criteria – with priority given to pupils from ethnic and cultural minorities, travellers, children in hospitals, isolated rural areas
Catalonia:	Target group + area	- Target groups: % pupils from ethnic and cultural minorities, pupils who have entered the school very late, truants - Areas: % unemployment, low income, illiteracy, ethnic minorities
Scotland: Urban Programme Funding	Area	- Nature and level of unemployment, family income, education, crime, housing conditions etc
Scotland: Early Intervention Programme	Target group	- No restriction but priority to schools with high proportion of children receiving free meals or clothing grants

Note: only programmes that are still in effect are included in the table.

improving literacy and numeracy standards among 5- to 6-year-old children.

As regards the areas on which EPP is focused, we can again point to three major types.

- Urban areas with a high concentration of economic activity and, consequently, a high population density, and where, in certain neighbourhoods, we can observe a higher presence of the more disadvantaged population. Usually these are degenerated areas of the large urban agglomerations where, for example, the immigrant populations have settled.

- Areas located in urban surroundings or, to a lesser extent, in rural or intermediate surroundings suffering from economic restructuring. This is reflected in the unemployment of large sections of the labour force who, due to their characteristics (age, gender, qualification level), face strong obstacles to occupational reintegration, which in turn affects the living conditions of their children.
- Finally, backward rural areas where, especially in some countries, poverty continues to persist, at least in relative terms, due to specific regional development problems.

A debate has arisen in the literature about the relative effectiveness of the 'territorial-based' versus 'target-group-based' funding mechanisms. One major advantage of the former is the possibility of combining educational with other local or regional development strategies. Thus, for example, an educational priority area can (and probably should) be both an employment priority area and an area where there is an integrated development programme, because in this manner there may be relevant synergy effects between different policies.

The Irish 'Priority Partnership Areas' and, linked with this programme, the Demonstration Programme on Educational Disadvantage, launched in 1996, illustrate how educational priority policies can be integrated with other territorial policies aimed at combating the spatial inequalities or social exclusion problems inside each country or region. The aim of this programme is the creation and development of locally based networks that support the conception and implementation of integrated strategies designed to tackle the problems of educational disadvantage and social exclusion within each of the four areas involved.

Nevertheless, the territorial approach of EPP has been criticised for its limited target efficiency; it overlooks disadvantaged pupils living outside the priority areas, while at the same time, part of the resources are being allocated to schools or pupils that are less disadvantaged. This issue has been studied and brought into discussion in Flanders, with a view to the integration of EPP with the Extended Care programme; simulations on databases have demonstrated that there may be significant variations in the diagnosis of schools' needs, depending on the criteria adopted (Bollens et al, 1998). Due to administrative problems in direct data collection from pupils and their parents, and related control problems (including a debate about the protection of pupils' privacy), one of the hypotheses of the research was that it would be possible to identify the eligible schools on the basis of indirect, territorial indicators. Most of these indicators are available on the level of districts within municipalities from public databases (Census data, fiscal statistics, unemployment statistics, and so on). Linking these data with the addresses of the pupils can provide an approximate picture of the socioeconomic profile of the pupils. These data were then used in a regression analysis to study the impact of socioeconomic background on school performance, using survey data on 6,000 secondary school pupils. In parallel, the same analysis was carried out using direct survey information on pupils' family backgrounds. The predictive power of the latter approach exceeded by far that of the indirect, territorial approach. One possible explanation is the segregation of pupils between schools within a given district; another is the fact that 'territorial' variables yield, at best, 'average' information about pupils, while micro-data tend to reflect the individual problems more accurately. Hence, the option of using territorial indicators of needs was rejected. This conclusion is consistent with earlier research developed in the US by Kennedy et al (1986) and Riddel (1992). This may mean that the policy adopted, for example, by the Priority Educational Territories in Portugal may not be the most adequate one, unless it guarantees that these areas have a homogeneous school profile based on the students' characteristics.

In Ireland, where the scheme of Assistance to Schools in Designated Areas of Disadvantage started in 1989, Kellaghan et al (1995) have also drawn attention to the need for using more adequate targeting in the selection of areas or schools supported by that programme. The programme was criticised for placing excessive emphasis on urban areas, whereas the majority of educationally disadvantaged pupils (that is, those with low reading scores and from families with low income) live in rural areas.

Another problem highlighted in this evaluation was the fact that intervention was focused primarily on the schools and less directly on the disadvantaged students themselves, which meant that many of these students were not actually reached. The study concluded that these students should be more directly targeted.

The conclusion that the 'needs' criteria are measured more accurately when using individual rather than territorial or indirect indicators suggests not only that EPPs could be much more efficient when funds are allocated to individual schools on the basis of the profile of their students' populations, rather than on the characteristics of the area in which the schools are situated, but also that actual utilisation of the funds to assist the most disadvantaged pupils within the eligible schools should, in some way, be guaranteed.

However, excessive selectivity or positive discrimination in the way the funding mechanism is implemented can also raise some questions. Focusing on the entire school, rather than only on particular groups of disadvantaged students, can have a more structural impact on the learning process, mainly because all of the educational agents can be involved in this way.

Criteria relating to the implementation of educational priority policies

We have seen that, in general terms, the type of groups or areas covered by EPPs in the six European countries are fairly similar. By contrast, there are major differences between these countries regarding the conditions of implementation of these policies.

For example, in the Flemish Extended Care policy, schools have to submit a plan of activities in which they state where they want to invest the extra resources that might be granted to them. The extra funding depends on the approval of this plan by the competent authorities. Multidisciplinary consultation must take place between the headmaster, teachers and other members of staff, and, if possible, external experts, at least three times per year (interim progress evaluations). Similar conditions apply in the Flemish Educational Priority Policy; besides the submission of a 'utilisation plan', schools have to accept external educational consulting and specific in-service training of teachers. Moreover, they have to collaborate with a social or sociocultural organisation working with migrants, with a view to developing 'school community action' (see Chapter 10). Conversely, the Dutch Educational Priority Policy has been criticised for failing to impose such conditions (see below).

Generally speaking, however, some conditions are imposed in most of the recorded measures of this type. Applicants for funding must prove that the additional amounts they may receive will support activities that will allow them to serve the relevant people more effectively, promoting the integration of these individuals into the education system. As illustrated in Figure 12.1, the basic scheme of intervention consists of four steps: the first step (A) is a diagnosis of the problems in a specific area or school; next, the eligible projects or schools with special needs

Figure 12.1: Operational scheme of the educational priority policies

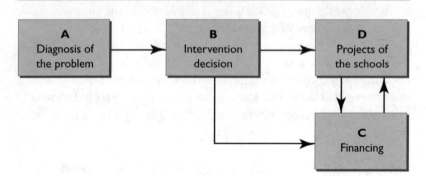

are selected (step B). However, we can find two major types of different financing procedures as regards steps C and D:

- in the 'voluntaristic approach', schools are supposed to carry out more or less 'automatically' the operational actions that meet the general and specific objectives defined by the national authorities in the funding criteria (A–B–C–D sequence). The decision on funding is taken accordingly;
- the alternative approach is more 'conditional' upon a set of implementation or output criteria; schools first have to submit projects according to the main purposes of the EPP, while funding depends on the successful implementation of these projects (A–B–D–C sequence).

In both cases, the target schools are obviously subject to monitoring of their activities by those who coordinate those measures, in order to ascertain whether the envisaged objectives are being achieved.

Types of actions developed within the context of educational priority policies

The types of measures and actions that can be developed under educational priority policies are obviously very heterogeneous, and depend on the projects that are presented for funding within that context. As stated earlier, these actions are often the same as those supported in other areas, such as activities to prevent early dropout, integration of specific at-risk groups, teacher training, extra support within schools or classes, and so on.

On the other hand, the fact that schools have to submit educational projects to justify the allocation of extra funds appears to lead to a much wider scope of actions.

In fact, EPP regulations often set priorities as regards the fields of intervention that the projects should focus on. These fields are often reflected in the specific objectives defined for the measures, as depicted in the first part of this chapter.

For example, the specific objectives of the Educational Priority Policy in Flanders focus on three intervention areas:

• learning the official language of the country or region (for example, by means of extra courses or extra support in that subject for students with difficulties);
• prevention and remedying of learning and developmental problems, either through adaptation of the curricula to the specific needs of the students, or through extracurricular activities;
• promoting the involvement of other agents in the school life of the students.

In the case of Extended Care, the specific objectives actually restrict the range of appropriations; for example, to the acquisition of school material, to the introduction of methodologies of differentiation or individualisation inside the classroom, and to the development of special services to children with socioemotional problems (through the presence of a psychologist, for example).

In Ireland, the Breaking the Cycle programme also promotes a restricted set of standard actions: for example, the allocation of more human resources (mainly teachers) to guarantee that no class contains more than 15 students, the purchase or rental of school material and equipment, and the professional development/training of teachers. However, an enhanced per capita grant of £75 per pupil (compared with a standard grant of £45) is also granted under this programme, which can be used in a very flexible way to help meet the needs of the schools or intervention areas.

In the Netherlands, while the priorities of the Educational Priority Policy are focused on mastery of the official language and the development of numeracy skills, the specific objectives refer to a wide set of actions that can be supported under this measure, such as:

• the promotion of vocational guidance services to stimulate the orientation of disadvantaged children to study fields in which they are traditionally underrepresented;

- the development of services to welcome and integrate new pupils at different levels of the education system;
- implementation of pedagogical methodologies and organisational models that may contribute to the decrease of school dropout;
- the creation or consolidation of cooperative networks between schools, parents and other local actors.

In Portugal, the regulations on Educational Priority Territories also focus on standard actions related to:

- experimentation and dissemination of alternative educational methodologies;
- the vocational training of the staff involved in the projects;
- development of forms of integrated school management, mainly involving local agents;
- extracurricular activities that promote the integration of students from disadvantaged backgrounds into the education system.

The eligibility criteria of the Compensatory Education Programmes in Spain refer to a profile of actions that is very similar to that of the other European countries. Some of these actions are centred on the internal functioning of schools – curricular diversification and adaptation, flexibility in school organisation, and so on – while others are more external – for example, programmes to improve the relationships between families and educational centres.

In Scotland, the general structuring of the type of activities to be developed under the Urban Programme Funding is left to each council's area-wide partnership, which applies for funding under this programme. The task of these councils is to take into account the characteristics of that area in drawing up an adequate local regeneration strategy. Some advice is given to potential candidates regarding the elaboration of the intervention strategy, pointing out a range of factors to be taken into account in that process. These recommendations focus on a set of intervention areas for the actions to be promoted, rather than on particular kinds of activities. Many of these areas are related to the socioeconomic context of the intervention area of the partnership, which in turn has an impact on the schools (for example, the level and nature of unemployment, household income levels, health of the population and their levels of education, and so on). In practice – in projects such as the North Ayrshire PPA and the Home-School Partnerships, for example – the funds are used for the acquisition of pedagogical materials, the development of home-school-community relationships, the reinforcement of the school's staff, and so on.

In the same region, The Early Intervention Programme and the Partnership in Education Project have already associated a range of specific activities to these special financing mechanisms. In the first case, the Programme was directed to support, for example, the enlargement of the staff in schools that receive children between 5 and 6 years old. In the second case, the project focused on fostering parent/professional and interprofessional partnerships, namely in the first phase, with the general objective of creating and developing local networks between different actors that should support children's educational careers.

To sum up, the additional financing made available through the educational priority policies in the countries studied are used for action on three main levels:

- the improvement of conditions related to the learning processes of the students, conditions which often reach beyond the responsibility of the school itself (equal opportunity strategies);
- the promotion of educational activities and methods which are more adapted to the needs of disadvantaged children;
- the promotion of partnership between schools and other local stakeholders – not only the teachers and parents, but also local institutions, social partners, associations, and so on.

For each of these areas of intervention, a set of actions that can be undertaken with the additional funding granted within the scope of EPP can be identified (see Table 12.3).

It should be borne in mind while reading this table that the examples given do not occur in all the measures or registered programmes in the countries studied. The degree to which they occur also varies widely, depending on the type and level of intervention of these programmes.

Finally, we must also stress that in many cases it is impossible to know exactly which activities are being developed at the micro level in each educational project financed under the educational priority policies. This would require a specific survey at that level in each country.

Table 12.3: Examples of types of actions in the different intervention areas

Intervention areas	Types of actions
Conditions related to the learning process	- Purchase or rental of school materials and equipment - Contracting of more human resources (teaching and non-teaching staff) - Training of teaching staff and non-teaching staff - Development of specific services to students and families (eg, psychological support, vocational guidance, school transport, catering, home visits, etc) - Economic assistance to students and families
Pedagogical activities and methods adapted to the needs of disadvantaged children	- Adaptation of curricula - Development of innovative pedagogical strategies - Development of extra-curricular activities that promote the integration of students into the school (eg, study visits, improvement of the school surroundings, parties, etc) - Catch-up courses for students with learning difficulties - Extra courses or subjects for specific groups of disadvantaged students (eg, extra language courses for immigrant children)
Partnership between local stakeholders	- Formal and effective participation of the various local actors in the projects supported under the educational priority policies (eg, in advisory committees or even administration of the project) - Liaison between the school and families

The effectiveness of the educational priority policies

The evaluation of educational priority policies registered in the six EU countries under study must take into account the fact that in some cases, these programmes have been in effect for just a short period of time (for example, in Portugal[2] and Spain). For these countries, few conclusions can be drawn from the available results. Nevertheless, there are already various thoroughgoing studies of the adopted measures in some countries (such as Flanders and the Netherlands), whose results are worth mentioning.

The evaluation obviously depends on the characteristics of these measures, especially the way in which they are structured and their levels of intervention within the scope of their respective education systems. In Flanders, the first evaluation (Vanhoren et al, 1995) began after two years of application of EPP. Its conclusions can be summarised in three main points.

- Positive effects were felt only after a rather long period of access to the funds. In fact, the implementation of the innovative actions was evaluated positively only during the third year of operation of this policy. This was explained by the need for consolidation of some basic conditions for the development of these actions (for example, the acquisition of didactic material), as well as the greater experience of working with the target group in question – in this case, children from immigrant families.

- The existence of a consulting or support network for these schools plays a strategic role in the development of innovative activities, especially when this work is well received and integrated into the management dynamics of these schools.

- The presence of a dynamic and united team of teachers leading these processes also plays a crucial role in the efficacy of the actions. Moreover, efficacy tends to be higher when the teaching team manage to engage the rest of the teaching and non-teaching staff in the promoted activities, as well as the families and other educational agents in the area.

The first results of these actions in terms of the students' performance are not very significant, at least in the first years after the start of EPP. In primary education, no systematic differences could be observed in the results achieved in language and arithmetic tests by students of the schools involved in EPPs, and those outside them.

Despite these disappointing findings, it is considered premature to conclude that the instruments used are not effective. On the one hand, the period of application of these measures in the schools was rather short; and on the other hand, other evaluation processes will have to be completed before it is possible to check the validity of this preliminary conclusion.

The evaluation cannot be confined to the impact of the promoted activities on the school performance of students, because other evaluation criteria need to be taken into account; for example, the effects on the relationship between schools and the local community or on the promotion of multicultural educational projects.

The evaluation of the priority areas in the province of Belgian Limburg, after five years of implementation, comes to similar conclusions (De Winter et al, 1997). In this case, however, the effects on students' school performance seem to have been more positive, with a slight improvement noted in educational performance in a number of learning areas. Admittedly, the target group – migrant children – continues to score significantly lower than those whose native language is Dutch, due to their initial handicap.

As regards the evaluation of the Extended Care programme

(Verhaeghe, 1994), again in Flanders, one of the conclusions concerns the strategic role played by teachers in the application of the actions financed by the programme; the results turned out weaker in those schools where teachers had a less positive view of their pupils' potential.

The teachers' training plays a crucial role in the creation of better conditions for the implementation of EPP actions. This training should not only involve the learning of pedagogical strategies that are more suited to the needs of disadvantaged pupils, but it should also contribute to changes in the attitudes and personal motivations of the teaching staff.

Concerning the impact of Extended Care on the pupils' school performance, Bollens et al (1998) found that the number of teacher hours spent on extended care proved to have a significant positive effect on the pupils' progress.

The evaluation of the Irish scheme, Assistance to Schools in Designated Areas of Disadvantage (Kellaghan et al, 1995), has already been discussed in this chapter. The authors have questioned the adequacy of territorial criteria in allocating funds among target schools. Another weakness pointed out in this study was the inadequate structure of the actions developed under this scheme. This weakness was mainly a consequence of a lack of incentives or obligation for schools to adopt types of action more directly related to the problems of disadvantaged children. This highlights the need to allocate the extra funds only to actions that aim clearly to respond to the needs of the target group.

This evaluation led to a profound reconfiguration of this educational priority policy, leading to the Breaking the Cycle programme in 1996; this was directed at schools in urban and rural areas with a higher concentration of disadvantaged populations. Since this is a recent programme, its impact cannot yet be evaluated, but the reduced number of selected schools up to this point (25 out of 190 candidates) raises some questions regarding the conditions of access to this programme. Perhaps there is a need for more caution in the regulation of access criteria to the EPPs, so as not to make them either too flexible, or too rigid and demanding. Excessive flexibility may lead to less accurate targeting and poorer effectiveness; however, if the rules are too restrictive and demanding, this may exclude or discourage schools that would otherwise respond perfectly to the spirit of the policy.

In the Netherlands, evaluation of the educational priority policy (OVB) depends greatly on the level of intervention. The weighting rule at macro level deserves a negative evaluation because of the relatively scarce resources available to each school and the absence of rules and (social) control. Mainly for these reasons, in many schools, the OVB exists only on paper, for all intents and purposes (Mulder, 1996).

According to Jungbluth (1997), OVB's poor results at the macro level[3] may be attributable, at least in part, to the fact that this policy is too weak to outweigh the negative influences of social segregation in schools. Indeed, social segregation between schools is visible not only in terms of the average social and cultural background of the pupils, but also in terms of quality of the teaching staff. In 'disadvantaged schools', the teaching staff appears to be less experienced, younger, to have lower qualifications, and to switch as soon as possible to middle-class schools or to another professional career. As a consequence, disadvantaged schools are facing poorer conditions for an optimal utilisation of the extra funds in coping with poverty and social exclusion.

This may also indicate that EPPs can produce better results when faced with a bottom-up approach, where the schools or educational areas have to apply for funds on a project basis. An approach like OVB (weighting rule) at the macro level implies a top-down strategy, which may be less motivating for the educational agents, especially if the additional financing is modest.

The poor impact of OVB in the Netherlands, however, has been attributed mainly to the poor relationship between the attribution of extra money and the fulfilment of performance criteria (for example, a reduction in school dropout or an increase in the school results of disadvantaged students). The present mechanism tends to be an administrative redistribution rule, rather than a means to promote specific actions targeted at students with special needs.

At the meso level, the evaluation in selected OVB areas has been more positive (Mulder, 1996), mainly because intervention at this level requires the participation of local agents in the application of the measure. In fact, the greater quantity of extra facilities and the collective (and thus less noncommittal) approach have meant that both the formation and components have worked substantially better in schools in OVB areas.

Finally, at the micro level, the evaluation of the projects developed under the scope of the educational priority policy varies substantially from project to project, as might be expected (Jacobs et al, 1995). The type, content and intensity of the projects varies a great deal, and there are substantial differences between the regions; consequently, the quality of the projects is relatively heterogeneous.

Furthermore, it was verified that only a restricted number of projects were based in secondary schools, and that in many cases there was evidence of ineffective internal articulation or coordination between the activities promoted in that context.

Despite those problems, the overall quality of the analysed projects was very good: a set of actions had been developed whose results seemed to be quite positive, given their restricted framework. For this reason, one of the recommendations points out the need to disseminate some of the best experiences supported under the auspices of the OVB.

The projects supported by the Urban Programme Funding in Scotland also produced very different results, because they depended mainly on the initiative and capacity of implementation of each school. There are a great variety of projects supported throughout Scotland,[4] though many of them are of too recent origin to have been subject to serious evaluation (for example, the North Ayrshire Priority Partnership Area).

We should note, however, that the decision of the Scottish Office to create the new Priority Partnership Areas was made on the basis of the relative success (according to them) of four piloted partnerships that were set up in 1988. These pilot partnerships established the principle of building a comprehensive and coordinated approach between members of the private, voluntary and community sectors, together with local authorities and national government agencies for urban regeneration, and this was considered by the Scottish Office to be a good result.

The Home-School-Employment Partnership, financed by the Urban Programme in the past seven years, was evaluated continuously throughout the experience. The conclusions of the mid-term evaluation produced by the Quality in Education Centre at the University of Strathclyde in Glasgow (Robertson, 1995) relate to three basic areas.

- The intervention had good results as regards the involvement of parents in the school life of their children. Strategies such as home visiting and support for parents in their contacts with school, and the extra support given to them and their children at times of transition between educational stages, proved to be very effective in achieving this objective.
- The rates of attendance in the schools involved in this measure were raised, whereas the rates in the other schools of the region remained stable over the same period. This reflects the high levels of student satisfaction concerning the activities developed within the context of this policy, despite the fact that in the upper levels of the secondary school, these levels of satisfaction declined; this was mainly because

of the difficulties of 'articulation' between the schools and employment agencies.

- The continuous vocational training of the schools' staff, and even of the staff involved in implementing this policy, in order to be able to work more closely on specific educational issues (such as developing the curriculum to meet the educational, personal and social needs of the young people) was a necessity expressed by those actors.

In Scotland, the Partnership in Education Project was also continuously evaluated throughout its three phases. Again, one of the major conclusions was that parental involvement in the school life of their children greatly contributes to good results, helping mainly to prevent low literacy scores in children's early stages.

The evaluation process also revealed that the project had a great impact on the involvement of the school staff members who took part in the activities developed. However, nearly two thirds of professionals involved or associated with the project raised concerns about the time, flexibility and resources required by the type of activities promoted. This was mainly due to a lack of effective managerial support that many field workers felt.

The extra funding allocated by the Early Intervention Programme to a pilot project involving four schools in the Edinburgh District produced very good results for the children involved. Prior to the programme, 85% of primary four children were at least a year behind in their reading. This figure dropped to 45% in the course of the project (1994-97). In level 3 of primary school, the percentage of pupils spelling at or above average levels has also shown a large increase, from 9.5% to 33.5% (Paterson, 1997a – see also Chapter 6 of this book).

To sum up, the good results produced by some EPP measures can be attributed to a number of factors, most of them related to the capacity and initiative of the schools themselves in promoting effective actions. The presence of good management at the local level, the reasonable level of human and material resources allocated, and the methodology that they were able to promote, are among the key factors.

Potentialities and problems of educational priority policies: main conclusions

The evaluations carried out in some of the study countries allow some critical issues to be identified in the implementation of educational priority policies. The main issues that have to be taken into account in assessing the value of this kind of strategy can be summarised as follows.

- To begin with, a clear definition of the criteria for the allocation of funds and the effective control of their application in the selected schools or educational areas involves a strategic decision on the targeting of the actions. This means that the main criteria for the distribution of the funds should be (i) the relative weight of well-defined target groups in the school population, and (ii) the existence of an action plan targeted at those groups. The use of geographic criteria should be confined to territories where there is a major concentration of the target groups of the educational priority policies.
- As a consequence of the first conclusion, the support given to these schools or areas should be based not only on the diagnosis that the share of children from disadvantaged backgrounds in their catchment area is high, but also on the presentation of plans with principles of usage that justify from the start the allocation of these funds.
- The functioning of the programmes of this type must be sufficiently flexible, guaranteeing in advance the extra funds allocated, and providing in its structures for technical assistance to the schools or areas involved, possibly facilitating a better development of the planned actions.
- This flexibility and technical support to EPP schools should be regulated in order to promote a better usage of the extra funds by conditioning the funding upon the fulfilment of certain basic requirements (see above) and the results produced by schools.
- The quality of the teaching staff in the schools plays a strategic role. For example, the presence of a dynamic and committed core group of teachers, encouraging the other teachers to participate more actively in that process, is a crucial factor in the results obtained. In-service training and coaching of teachers has an important role to play, including training in relation to the specific needs of the target groups, more encouraging teacher attitudes and effective methods of intervention.
- EPP should cover all relevant areas or schools where the proportion of disadvantaged children is high; not only urban areas with large concentrations of the target population, but also rural areas.
- The capacity to mobilise all educational agents is another critical success factor in this type of policy.
- Last but not least, programmes of this type should be allocated adequate financial resources to prevent frustration of the expectations

created among the various educational agents (mainly the teaching and non-teaching staff); otherwise, the impact of these programmes is so restricted that the results become tenuous.

At the micro or local level, there seems to be a consensus that the success of EPP actions depends on the commitment and leadership of the teaching and executive staff of the schools, as well as their capacity to engage the different local actors. At the macro and even the meso levels, the success of EPP measures depends on the capacity of the administration to define clear and measurable objectives that the schools must achieve and, at the same time, it depends on the provision of effective technical support to schools.

Notes

[1] Integration of this measure with the Educational Priority Policy is now being studied in Flanders. In this context, the extra funds will be available for use throughout nursery, primary and secondary education, for disadvantaged Belgian children as well as pupils from ethnic minorities.

[2] The Priority Educational Territories in Portugal will be evaluated year after year by the Institute of Educational Innovation, but the results for the first year of operation have not been made available yet.

[3] This limited impact of EPP was also found in the Flemish case, where no effect on learning progress was found in the short term (Vanhoren et al., 1995).

[4] For example, the Education Department of the Edinburgh City Council approved 48 projects across the city.

THIRTEEN

Learning support

Renze Portengen and Ben Hövels, ITS

The provision of learning support, targeted at marginalised groups or individual students at risk, can be seen as a form of positive discrimination. Learning support aims to enhance literacy in order to improve a child's chances of selection for specific types of secondary or tertiary education, or to improve attainment in external examinations.

We can assume that the most common form of learning support is that provided by teachers in their day-to-day practices. An example of their learning support activities in the Netherlands is provided by a study into the pedagogical-didactical measures that teachers in primary schools take when dealing with students at risk (Derriks et al, 1997). Teachers were asked to choose from a list of measures. These were:

- remedial activities: extra explication of material, individual practice with pupils, repeating material, giving special remedial material, giving extra exercises, controlling work more often;
- motivating activities: strengthening emotional ties, giving positive feedback, avoiding criticism, asking questions that pupils can answer, loosening criteria;
- disciplinary activities: discussing behaviour, punishment, setting individual goals, giving extra homework, putting a pupil in front of the class.

Classroom teachers in mainstream primary schools were found to use remedial measures more often than motivating activities and disciplinary activities.

However, teachers often call in the assistance of specialists; educational, psychological and other professionals contribute to various forms of 'learning support', which is more specific than the 'integrated services' discussed in Chapter 5.

We assume that every teacher will face a class in which pupils differ in their capabilities. To what extent do these differences translate into extra support targeted at those performing poorly? The answer to this question can show cross-national variation. For example, it is not impossible that the provision of learning support is an ad-hoc phenomenon in some countries or schools. It is also possible that the provision of support is structured. Using a term from the Belgian and Dutch Extended Care policies (see previous chapter), a school's care structure consists of the procedures and activities used to aid those who are in need of learning support. Policies with regard to care structures can be formulated by (national) governments, regional and local authorities, or schools themselves. Some of the six EU-countries in this study have articulated policies at the macro level (see below), yet often the provision of learning support is structured by schools operating in a regional context.

We will also try to pinpoint the way these policies reflect important concepts, namely remediation, compensation, prevention and differentiation. Remediation is in order when learning difficulties are at hand; compensatory educational programmes are constructed to organise remedial activities. Many claim that remediation is ineffective in promoting equal chances, as habits, once acquired, are difficult to break; therefore, they claim, prevention of learning difficulties is much more effective. Yet prevention of future (therefore not yet identifiable) difficulties requires that all pupils receive support. To achieve this, the concept of differentiation is introduced: a teaching style in which every child receives the education that best suits their needs. Not only students at risk receive extra support, but also the most successful students.

Several questions are dealt with in the following paragraphs:

- What are the most common forms of learning support provided in the six EU countries; what methods and range of activities are chosen in general?
- What learning outcomes are supported, and how are those in need of care identified?
- Are there striking differences or similarities between the six EU countries in the organisation of learning support?
- To what extent do evaluative studies show effects of learning support?

Finally, we will draw conclusions based on the material presented.

Forms of learning support

In the United States, stimulated by the federal compensatory programme TITLE I, the large majority of schools offer support via the **pull-out** or **withdrawal** model. Students are 'pulled out' during regular class hours. Individual pupils or small groups receive support in reading, writing and mathematics outside the mainstream class (Vermeulen et al, 1987; Stringfield, 1991). This model has been criticised, by the federal government among others, because the additional time-on-task for students at risk remains limited (LeTendre, 1991). Alternative support forms are sought outside regular school hours, including Saturday and summer programmes. US schools with a high concentration of disadvantaged students can use targeted resources for school-wide projects to increase the quality of education for all students.

The example of the US demonstrates that there are actually three broad ways in which learning support may be delivered:

- in remedial classes (either in separate classes where pupils spend almost all of their time, or through occasional withdrawal of individuals or small groups from mainstream classes for additional support when required);
- by increasing the pupils' time-on-task (lengthened school days, Saturday classes, summer courses, and so on);[1]
- by enhancing resources per pupil and per time unit (for example, through additional support in the class, a learning support teacher or extra material for differentiated learning).

These three strategies are discussed below.

Remedial teaching

In the six countries, the pull-out model, known in the UK as withdrawal, is still probably the most common form of remedial teaching (and indeed of learning support) for disadvantaged students. There are exceptions, however (such as the UK), where support is normally given in the mainstream class by the learning support teacher, who works alongside the class teacher.

In Ireland, remedial teaching is common. Special remedial groups are formed, and pupils are withdrawn during ordinary classes, or small group tuition for a fixed period each week takes place. The use of remedial teachers dates back to 1963. Remedial educational services are designed to assist pupils who have difficulties in attaining basic skills in literacy and numeracy, or difficulties of a more general nature. The emphasis is placed on early identification and prevention. Smyth (1998) reports a school with an intensive approach to remedial support, allowing for 14-15 class periods per week. Another school uses a withdrawal system for mathematics, but provides a second classroom teacher for remedial English classes. In 1995, one small-scale initiative involved the installation of teacher counsellor posts, aimed at retaining disruptive students in school. Another example is the Basin Street Project in Dublin; in this scheme, six children with special needs are grouped together twice each week, for a period of 90 minutes.

In Portugal, there is a project based in primary schools in run-down areas of Lisbon (OECD, 1995a). Its objectives include developing pupils' oral and written communication skills. Interesting features are the division into four preliminary stages, designed to tap the knowledge and secure the interest and commitment of those teachers who intend to participate. The programme does not rely on modifications of existing materials, but uses the child's own experience as the basis for developing individualised teaching materials. In regular teacher meetings, led by counsellors, important decisions are made concerning the programme.

In Scotland, withdrawal for individual tuition is used particularly at primary level, but there is anxiety that it will increase some children's feelings of being stigmatised by receiving extra attention. In addition, in schools in socially disadvantaged areas, withdrawal for individual tuition is not regarded as a practical option because such a large proportion of children have learning difficulties. Separate remedial classes were condemned by a report of the Scottish HMI in 1978, since they engaged children in rather boring and repetitive exercises and isolated them from their peers, thus demotivating them. Mainstream support with occasional withdrawal was regarded as a preferable option and, at least at secondary level, remedial provision outside the mainstream class on a long-term basis virtually disappeared. Recently, a very small number of schools in socially disadvantaged areas have reintroduced remedial classes on the grounds that this is the only way to concentrate resources effectively on those children in the greatest need. However, these moves have been regarded by many teachers as a return to an old-fashioned and discredited model.

Increasing time-on-task and/or resources per time unit

Alternative approaches to (pull–out) remedial teaching include the provision of extra inputs and/or the lengthening of the time pupils spend on school or on homework. In England, for example, 'education action zones' have been developed in schools with large numbers of students at risk. This is seen as a way of allowing the government to concentrate resources on the most deprived areas, improving the teacher-pupil ratio. Additional provision includes the establishment of literacy summer schools and lengthened school days. In Scotland, the establishment of new community schools also involves the targeting of resources on the most socially disadvantaged areas. The additional resources not only provide for additional classroom support, sometimes provided by classroom assistants rather than teachers, but also for the appointment of social work and health personnel to work in schools, thus eliminating bureaucratic delay in addressing pupils' problems, and preventing unnecessary exclusion. These forms of learning support seem highly popular in all six EU countries studied, and receive much attention from national and local policy makers and pedagogical professionals. However, the approach still seems to be in an experimental phase and awaits thorough evaluation.

The Pilton Early Intervention programme, described in detail in Chapter 6, is another example of an innovative learning support project in Scotland. Within this project, four primary schools in very poor areas were granted extra funding. A key aspect of the project was to improve staffing. For example, nursery assistants were employed to help pupils acquire literacy skills at a very early age. Reading scores in the schools improved so dramatically that it was decided to extend the scheme much more widely in Scotland. This of course raises the problem that if additional teaching becomes standard for all, it no longer redresses the imbalance experienced by the most disadvantaged, and could even further enhance the position of the most advantaged groups. Evaluation of the early intervention scheme in Scotland is still underway.

In Flanders, the King Baudouin Foundation (see Chapter 5) has financed pilot projects focused on complementary services. Projects focused on language development are targeted at ghetto schools with a high concentration of migrant children. Conversation circles in the classroom take place, together with activities aimed at extending learning time. Other activities include language holidays, sports and cultural activities after school (Saturday and Wednesday afternoon), and homework guidance (involving parents, and with home support for the most disadvantaged children).

The Learning Support programme in Flanders, a joint project between 40 Psychological-Medical-Social centres (PMS[2]) and 132 primary schools, is based on individual action plans, as opposed to measures such as referral to special education, grade repetition or grouping of disadvantaged students (remedial groups). Maximum remediation within the classroom is attempted.

In the Netherlands, a typical example of attempting to lengthen time-on-task is homework supervision outside school. An example is a local programme run by the Social Services Department of the city of Utrecht. On average, 80% of the participants are immigrants. Participants are supervised individually or in small groups while they do their homework. Participation is voluntary. In a study from 1995, four of these projects were evaluated. In general, the projects seemed to reach the target groups well. The value of these schemes seems to lie particularly in supporting the motivation to learn, and in helping pupils to deal with school as an institution.

Also in the Netherlands, experiments with extended school days are underway (see Chapter 5). A number of primary schools, and some secondary schools with high concentrations of students at risk, are implementing these projects. The basic assumption is that extracurricular activities help children to acquire skills that may be of importance to their social development and career. In 1992, these projects started as an experiment, the concept being borrowed from the US. During the extra time pupils spend in school, they participate in activities in the field of artistic education, sport and play, science and technology, and nature and environmental studies. As the projects are usually associated with high numbers of migrant pupils, the working assumption is that these young people do not come into contact with such activities in their spare time or at home.

In Portugal, unemployed people were trained and then engaged in educational support activities in schools in socially underprivileged areas, in periods not taken up by the curriculum. The programme was launched in 1996/97 in schools included in the national priority policy: it involves 200 schools and 400 animators.

Outcomes supported

What outcomes of learning are supported by the programmes? Clearly, not all programmes will have distinct goals. General goals are often used without specification of (short-term) objectives.

Literacy and numeracy

Compensatory programmes for disadvantaged children have a strong tendency toward remedying problems with reading and numerical skills. In the GOALS 2000: Educate America Act, outcomes such as improved student achievement in primary and secondary education, a reduction of dropout in high school, and more students taking courses in mathematics, science and engineering are mentioned. Also, in the English White Paper *Excellence in schools* (1997), national goals are formulated with respect to the literacy and numeracy of 11-year-olds (Van Langen and Portengen, 1998).

The formulation of national goals on literacy and numeracy is not specific to Anglo-Saxon countries, but seems common in all developed countries, including those studied here. For example, the Dutch Educational Priority Policy stresses the importance of language and numeracy skills, as well as the reduction of referrals to special schools and unequal outcomes in terms of educational level, both in the type of qualification as well as the percentage of dropout. To combat the difficulties that some children face when they enter primary education, work is being done to tackle the problem through a pre-school intervention programme. Much attention is also being devoted to teaching Dutch as a second language for ethnic minority children, particularly during the first years of primary education. Furthermore, education in one's own language and culture (OETC) will be approached differently in primary education. It will be offered outside the regular curriculum.

In Flanders, it is noted that 15% of students in primary schools experience some learning difficulties relating to literacy and numeracy, and 6% experience serious problems (Ghesquière et al, 1995). Intervention strategies are therefore focused on literacy and numeracy. In Ireland, remedial teaching focuses on skills in literacy and numeracy, or difficulties of a more general nature.

Social skills, learning skills, behaviour, and qualifications

The provision of learning support can also be directed toward other psychological traits and social and behavioural aspects. In the Irish Basin Street Project, a Dublin programme, self-respect and the ability to cope with the school system are critical variables. Also, in a small-scale provision involving 31 schools in the Dublin area, teacher counsellor posts have been established to combat truancy and dropout. In Scotland, attempts have been made to improve external examination results, and also to measure and improve dropout rates, absenteeism, stress levels and self-esteem.

In the Netherlands, the reading promotion programme aims at enhancing children's motivation to read, rather than boosting reading attainment as such (OECD, 1995a). The activities also involve the local library and the community centre. This small-scale example of goals related to the process of learning itself, rather than to direct outcomes, is also visible at the macro level. The Dutch government wants to attain the following goals in education, as described in the memorandum entitled *The school as a learning organisation* (1995). Schools should help pupils to increase self-study skills. Establishing 'study houses' in secondary education in the Netherlands is also a way of promoting independent study attitudes.[3] Attempts are also made to prepare students for democratic citizenship using self-advocacy techniques. Schools have been given the task of counselling pupils on study and career choices, ensuring that as many pupils as possible obtain either vocational qualifications, at least at a basic level, or a transfer qualification to higher education. This could involve new educational routes geared towards the labour market.

Organisational aspects of support provision

Several organisational aspects are interesting to consider, such as the level of decision making, other organisations involved, and the way students in need of support are identified. In the introduction to this chapter, it has already been mentioned that the provision of support can be an activity left entirely up to schools or even individual teachers (the micro level), or that regional or national actors can try to structure such support provision (the meso or macro level).

It seems that learning support in the form of particular policies and programmes is most developed at the primary level. Programmes also exist in some secondary schools, but such instances seem rare. In Scotland, a case study of six schools (Smyth, 1998) found that provision of remedial teaching in mathematics and the native language tended to be targeted at those in the junior cycle, particularly first-years, in all of the schools studied. In Ireland, remedial teaching initially only happened in primary education, but was later extended to include secondary education; in 1995, 2,256 schools at primary level and 330 at secondary level offered remedial teaching. In Flanders, the Learning Support project was concentrated in the third and fourth year of primary school.

The macro level: national policies

In the Netherlands and Flanders, official government policies exist in which schools are guided in their organisation of learning support (see Chapter 12, Extended Care). These policies aim to structure schools' actions, especially the broadening of the provision of care in primary schools. Under certain conditions, schools can obtain extra staff and resources to develop an educational approach which is better geared to backgrounds and developmental needs of individual children with learning problems. The activities are confined to the transition from nursery to primary school. Schools have to formulate an action plan and broaden the range of materials, work on differentiation, introduce a monitoring system, and develop extra support for children in need. However, there are questions as to whether these policies are in fact implemented at lower levels of decision making. For example, in the Netherlands, the impact of the Educational Priority Policy (1986-98) depended upon implementation by schools. As the use of additional resources was not supervised by the government, decisions on supportive measures were taken by the school heads (Mulder, 1996).

In Portugal, pedagogical support comprises a set of activities aimed at helping to prevent dropout and promoting better school results. It was set up in 1993, and the measures can include all sorts of goals, ranging from subject matter to remedial teaching, differentiation or orientation activities. All activities are entirely organised by the schools; they also define the modalities and decide upon the form and evaluation of concrete support.

The meso level: regional and local actors

Until now, the Flemish centres for psychological, medical and social counselling (PMS – see Chapter 5) have been concerned mainly with a systematic screening of children at the end of each educational stage in order to assess their readiness for transition to the next level. Another task is to assist pupils and their parents in their choice of study field. These centres are currently being merged with the teams for medical inspection in schools and transformed into 'pupil guidance centres' (*centra voor leerlingenbegeleiding* – CLB) with a broader mission. At the same time, they are being reoriented towards pupils at risk, and play an increasing role in advising schools on how to adapt their teaching and assessment methods to these pupils. This reform has been partly inspired by the Learning Support project, which was in effect between 1991 and 1993. In this project, a strong accent was placed on collaboration between class teachers, remedial teachers, parents and PMS officers. The latter intervened mainly as system counsellors, and did not usually provide individual support. Decisions were reached through consensus, where regional PMS officers took part in school teams and could intervene if necessary.

In Scotland, extra formation is allocated to disadvantaged schools under the Learning Support programme. Teaching support is provided by a team of teachers that work throughout each education authority. Classroom teachers also receive training or cooperative teaching methods. Time allocation of educational psychologists is closely linked to this programme. A case study of a Local Education Authority showed that seven psychologists manage 36 primary and nine secondary schools; the time allocated varies and the maximum is two days per school.

In the Netherlands, supervisors of Educational Priority Areas support schools in a regional network of disadvantaged schools. Cooperation between disadvantaged schools was stimulated by the priority policy. Now that this policy has been decentralised to municipalities, these networks no longer have a legal basis and can no longer decide upon the distribution of finances. Instead, schools with high concentrations of at-risk pupils have to cooperate with local government, as well as all other local schools, to decide upon the content of the local educational priority policies. These local schools also participate in a platform dealing with the school advisory services. Primary schools in the Netherlands usually also cooperate in other networks. An example is the network introduced by the policy to integrate students with special educational needs, Going To School Together. In secondary education, cooperation is usually extended to include welfare organisations and businesses.

In the Dutch study on the provision of support by teachers in primary schools, seven types of professionals were identified: remedial teachers, internal assistants (*interne begeleiders*), school assistants (*schoolbegeleider*), speech therapists, school physicians, social workers, and ambulatory coaches (*ambulante begeleider*). Some of these are school staff, but most of the professionals mentioned are staff linked to regional educational or medical organisations, or special schools. Within secondary schools, pupil counsellors aim to prevent and identify problems at an early stage. Pupil counselling has developed over the last decades from a subject-related task to an independent discipline. The development of this profession has led to various methodologies and systems, including support and advice with regard to learning activities of individual pupils, referrals to specialised pedagogical-didactic support, school or career guidance, and improving relations between teachers and pupils. In secondary schools, other facilities have arisen that can help schools with children who, for various reasons, cannot follow the normal programme, such as those with reading problems (dyslexia), fear of failure, difficulties in study and career choice, behavioural problems, demotivation, and so on. Most of the facilities are not exclusively related to one school. Teachers do not act on their own, but often call in the assistance of specialists.

The micro level: schools

Even in national or regional policies targeting resources to schools with high concentrations of students at risk, those schools are frequently at liberty to decide upon the internal allocation of support. Identification of students at risk in schools, however, is no easy topic. It is interesting to note that taking tests at regular times seems to be beneficial to students at risk (Clayton, 1991).

In the Netherlands, primary schools use different tests, but teachers also use their daily experiences as a tool for identification of students in need; only when first attempts fail do they call in help. At the end of primary schooling, instead of certificates or diplomas, pupils receive a school report showing their progress at school and their learning potential. In determining the latter, over 60% of primary schools use the CITO test (final basic education test from the National Institute for Educational Measurement). Records of Progress are becoming more and more popular in primary schools. Each child's progress is systematically registered, and approximately half of all schools work with such a system. The Inspectorate, however, criticised secondary schools for not introducing these systems into their organisation.

In Scotland, the Local Education Authorities (LEAs) have to establish if a child has special educational needs (SEN). Such children, who make up 1.4% of the pupils in primary education, get a Record which entitles the school where they are registered to additional funding. Apparently, these assessments have not proven completely reliable, as many children with special needs are not recorded (see Chapter Eleven). Assessment in the 5-14 curriculum is not by means of a national test, as in England and Wales. The Scottish Office agreed to a system whereby teachers use formative and summative assessment within a classroom context to decide when a child has achieved a certain level.

Evaluation

Large-scale longitudinal surveys or quasi-experimental studies of programmes and their effects are an important source of information. In the US in 1975, the Sustaining Effects Study started (Carter, 1984; Kennedy et al, 1986). Important findings were that TITLE I students showed more progress at reading, writing and mathematics tests than students from comparable backgrounds without such learning support. Yet such progress is not enough to catch up with the average student. It is interesting to observe that positive effects were absent for the weakest TITLE I students. These findings seem to indicate that remedial teaching in the form of pull-out programmes, the most common form of learning support under TITLE I, is not very effective. However, research into the effects of summer programmes shows that the impact of such schemes upon literacy and numeracy are also limited or even absent. This is not surprising, as such forms of support are not directed at these learning outcomes, but focus more on personal and social outcomes which were not measured. (See Chapter 12 for discussion of the effectiveness of educational priority areas.)

In the Netherlands, as part of the national evaluation of their educational priority policy, teachers and directors of 700 primary schools were interviewed in 1992 (Mulder 1996). Only those who were participating in the regional networks of disadvantaged schools were well informed. These schools used the additional funds for targeted support in the form of remedial teaching, new materials, closer contact with parents from ethnic minorities, or specific activities for non-Dutch children, such as purchasing a new method for teaching Dutch as a second language (NT2). Almost 60% of schools that received additional resources for hiring teachers but were not in the networks were not even aware of these possibilities. Nor did they realise that these resources were targeted at pupils from weak social milieus, so the additional formation was used to reduce the overall pupil-teacher ratio.

In Flanders, in the context of the Extended Care programme in primary schools, a study was initiated to determine current practice relating to detecting, preventing and remedying developmental and learning problems in children (Verhaeghe, 1994). It showed that teachers are quite attached to their autonomy. They have the greatest confidence in their personal information, and they first try to remedy problems themselves. Teachers also tend to restrict themselves to subject material intended for one school year. They prefer measures with less drastic organisational consequences. More recently, Bollens et al (1998) have analysed the effects of Extended Care on pupils' learning progress in the first year of primary school, after controlling for other pupil and class management characteristics. The number of extra teacher hours spent on Extended Care appeared to have a significant positive effect (see also Chapter 12).

Similarly, positive effects have been registered in the Learning Support project carried out by the PMS (CLB) centres in Flanders in the period 1991-93. Ghesquière et al (1995) found that learning problems could, to a large extent, be solved by the learning support provided; often this was more effective than grade repetition, referrals to special education and even remedial classes. The latter appeared to have a positive impact only on children with serious difficulties.

The evaluation also confirmed the need for a shift in the role of PMS centres from mere diagnostic screening and individual counselling of pupils and parents to more system-oriented support. The PMS workers indeed focused their intervention mainly on coordination and counselling of teachers and school teams.

It is interesting to see that the 'education field' itself also seeks to measure student progress and educational output (Van Langen and Portengen, 1998). In the US, federal legislation states that schools should be held accountable for the progress of their (disadvantaged) students. In 1990, more than 5,000 US schools were deemed ineffective. A similar approach to schools and their outcomes is visible in England and Wales. Since 1994, approximately 10% of all schools for primary or secondary education have been criticised for serious weaknesses; 2% underwent special measures from the Local Education Authority. In extreme cases, schools have been closed. In Scotland, about 20% of all primary and secondary schools have been found to have some weaknesses by the Scottish HMI.

It should be noted that most studies on changing the way schools support children and youth at risk are not controlled experiments, but evolutionary activities. Control groups and experimental-group comparisons are usually absent, and evaluations are descriptive and characterised by personal judgements (OECD, 1995a). It is also very difficult to measure the results of prevention strategies, as is noted with respect to Dutch pupil counsellors in secondary schools (Eimers and Hövels, 1997). The relationship between preventive measures and outcomes is hard to establish. In Ireland, neither remedial education, nor the teacher counsellor posts, nor the Basin Street project have been evaluated thus far, although intentions to do so have been mentioned.

Conclusions

Learning support is generally provided in the six EU countries studied, though it is mostly limited to primary education and especially the earliest grades. It is associated with the large compensatory programmes in the United States and the United Kingdom, following political developments in the 1960s, as typified by President Johnson's War on Poverty and the English Plowden Report. In the traditional form of support, the pull-out or withdrawal model, students are pulled out during regular class hours. Individual pupils or small groups receive support in reading, writing and mathematics. The outcomes supported are thus largely cognitive in nature; that is, literacy and numeracy. This model has been criticised due to limited additional time-on-task for students at risk. Thorough evaluation in the US shows that those pupils with the poorest performance show no improvement.

Another form of learning support is to provide for extra hands in the classroom. In an increasing number of schools, it is common for the learning support teacher to work alongside the mainstream classroom teacher in assisting individual pupils and groups. One outstanding example is the Pilton Early Intervention Programme in Scotland. Support time for all early-years pupils was increased. In the Flemish Learning Support programme, remediation within the classroom was also successfully implemented. In Portugal, in 1996, unemployed people were trained and then engaged in educational animation activities in schools in socially underprivileged areas, during periods not taken up by the curriculum.

Other forms of support are sought outside regular school hours, including Saturday and summer programmes. In general, these forms do not aim to enhance cognitive outcomes directly, but focus more on social and behavioural outcomes. The Belgian King Baudouin Foundation has financed pilot projects where language holidays, sports and cultural activities after school (Saturday and Wednesday afternoon), and homework guidance take place in schools in poor areas. In the

Netherlands, extended school day projects started in 1992 as an experiment. During the extra time pupils spend in school, they participate in activities in the fields of artistic education, sport and play, science and technology, and nature and environmental studies.

Are there striking differences or similarities between the six EU countries in the way the provision of learning support is organised? First of all, the provision of learning support in all countries predominantly takes place in primary schools. Lately, the organisation of support in secondary schools has become more of a policy concern.

A strikingly similar national policy exists in two countries, namely the Netherlands and Flanders. These national governments try to guide schools in their provision of learning support. Schools are stimulated to integrate and organise the activities of several internal and external actors. They are encouraged to formulate an action plan, broaden their range of teaching materials, work on differentiation within the classroom, introduce a system to monitor each pupils' progression, and develop new forms of learning support. However, an evaluation of the somewhat similar Dutch Educational Priority Policy has shown that schools do not always implement such national policies to the full (Mulder, 1996). In the other countries, such national policies seem absent.

At the meso level, all countries seem to have important regional actors aiding individual schools and teachers in their daily dealings with children who need care. Educational psychologists and school social workers are usually part of regional organisations, such as the Flemish PMS (now CLB) and the Dutch school advisory services. Nevertheless, in all six countries, it seems that actual changes enjoyed by students at risk depend to a large extent upon decisions by individual schools and teachers; that is, decisions made at the micro level. To identify educational needs, teachers in classes rely upon their own assessments, as is shown in the Belgian study intended to evaluate the national policy on schools' structuring of care (Verhaeghe, 1994). Teachers, however, may hold unrealistic or low expectations with respect to pupils, especially those with disadvantaged backgrounds.

More and more, therefore, the use of pupil monitoring systems has become a topic with respect to the organisation of learning support in schools. As the pedagogical concept of differentiation is used more and more in policy statements, and remedial activities outside regular classes are being replaced by forms of learning support provided by teachers inside classes, the attempt to identify learning needs more objectively seems worthwhile. National governments or regional actors can and should cooperate with schools, as one cannot expect school boards and heads to have the time and background which are necessary for the implementation of a well-developed care structure.

Notes

[1] Grade repetition will not be treated below as a form of learning support, although it is seen by some as remedial action, the argument being that learning time is increased (OECD, 1995a). Yet this claim only holds if the particular student does not stop before getting his certificate and if decisions to proceed with education are not influenced by his earlier prolonged stay. In fact, repeating a grade can even be detrimental to further educational outcomes. Given its contentious nature, the authors choose to leave this measure out of the picture.

[2] PMS centres have recently been transformed into 'pupil guidance *centres*' (*centra voor leerlingenbegeleiding* – CLB).

[3] The study houses are a new provision in Dutch upper secondary schools aimed at increasing the students' learnings skills (learning to learn). Classes are split up into small groups for several hours a week, and students sometimes work individually in order to 'acquire' knowledge rather than receiving it from the teacher.

FOURTEEN

Alternative curricula, transition systems and second-chance provisions

Sjaak van den Berg and Ben Hövels, ITS

Despite all efforts and strategies described in the previous chapters, educational underachievement remains problematic at all levels of educational systems, with many young people leaving full-time education with little or no formal qualifications. Children from socially excluded backgrounds tend to be overrepresented among this category of pupils. There are provisions for young people and adults in most countries that, in principle, can be taken advantage of to obtain educational qualifications at a later stage. Although these provisions have been developed with different goals in mind and for different groups, many of them are intended to provide a 'second chance' for people who did not achieve the necessary qualifications during full-time education. However, a discussion of all forms of second-chance provision is beyond the scope of the current study. Instead, we focus specifically on provisions for young people 'at risk'; that is, young people who did not achieve the necessary qualifications during compulsory education and/or in the transition from school to work. In the Dutch context, this group is referred to as those who lack a 'starting qualification' to achieve integration into the labour market. This term is used throughout the remainder of the chapter.

Research has shown that the general economic situation and associated labour market conditions have very important consequences for young people at the stage of transition to the labour market. This can be illustrated by recent developments in the debate concerning 'over-education'. Due to the surplus of school leavers with academic qualifications, many low- or semi-skilled youngsters have been having considerable problems entering the labour market. During this period, youth unemployment has become an important issue for labour market policy. At the present time, however, huge labour shortages are being experienced in various sectors of the economy and at different levels of qualification. The labour market has demonstrated its flexibility and capacity to absorb young school leavers with low levels of qualifications. In such a situation, formal educational qualifications appear less influential than more general characteristics such as 'social capital'. In the present situation (at least in the Netherlands), there is less a problem of mass youth unemployment than a problem for certain categories of young people that are not seen as 'adapted' for a position in the formal labour market. In many cases, this 'adaptation' problem has also played an important role in their previous educational failure. Their social, cultural and socioeconomic backgrounds and characteristics are too different from that which is accepted as 'normal' to bridge the gap by means of the educational system.

In summary, it should be noted that educational level is not the only explanatory factor in determining labour market opportunities or one's general position in society. In addition to variations in economic and labour market conditions, 'non-adaptation' features, both of young people themselves and of the educational system, are clearly important. In relation to the labour market, formal educational qualifications often appear to function more as a screening device for employers.

In any event, research from all countries involved in this research indicates that – despite the positive results of some recent reforms – a certain proportion of young people still leave initial education without formal qualifications, and that this pattern is only partially related to their intellectual abilities.

In order to improve educational outcomes for these young people, it is vital for the mainstream education system to invest in innovation, financial and human resources, expertise, research, and so on. Meanwhile, the limitations of the opportunity structure within the educational system should be noted, and it should be recognised that equal opportunities, and particularly equal outcomes, may not be fully attainable by the education system, or at least not in isolation from wider societal influences.

This chapter will focus on the nature and effectiveness of educational provisions for those young people who have not been successful in mainstream education. The individual schemes or programmes in each of the countries under study will not be described in detail; instead, the chapter will focus on the main forms of provision in this area.

A descriptive model of measures to combat early school leaving

Following earlier research, Eimers (1995) developed a generic model that classifies measures to combat early school leaving. In a somewhat adapted form, this model can be presented as in Figure 14.1, below.

The first line in the model shows 'intermediate activities' which involve the interaction between education and relevant actors in other areas who are involved in the problem of preventing and/or remedying 'early school leaving'. These agencies include community-school networks, regional-local-school cooperation concerning compulsory education, tracking of and provision for truants, and so on. The second line indicates different general, preventive and remedial measures. These measures are explained below. The third line indicates the relationship between these measures and the educational system: general and preventive measures take place fully within the educational system, while transition measures (reorientation to school and the transition to work) take place in the border region between education and the labour market. Most of these measures are based on 'alternating' models of education; that is, alternation of courses with work experience as a more powerful and motivating learning method. 'Safety-net' provisions are targeted at dropouts without (starting) qualifications who have serious problems and are in need of specific help. This type of provision is usually located outside the mainstream education system. The fourth line shows the goals towards which the different measures are directed: prevention measures are aimed at providing a standard level of qualification; transition

Figure 14.1: Measures taken against early school leaving: a descriptive model

Intermediate activities

Accessibility/ quality of education	General prevention	Selective prevention	Reorientation to education	Transition to work	Safety-net measures

Fully within education		On borders of education		Parallel to education	Fully outside education

Goal is a 'starting qualification'			Goal is a limited 'starting qualification'		Not primarily directed to a 'starting qualification'

programmes are aimed at achieving a minimum 'starting' qualification; while the safety net is primarily directed towards the achievement of a minimum level of social functioning, and is less concerned with the attainment of qualifications.

In order to locate alternative curricula, transition and second-chance provisions within the overall structure of the project, the following paragraphs elaborate on the nature of these measures.

Access to education

Improvement in access to education is important for the transition from one phase of (secondary) education to another. Measures such as the provision of advice, information, and guidance for later school, vocational, and labour market choices are of relevance to all pupils. However, measures such as orientation and bridging opportunities are of particular importance for pupils who are uncertain about their future (school and/or work) career; for example, after a break in their education.

Quality of education

In principle, improvement of the quality of education in general is relevant for all pupils, but some specific measures can have particularly positive effects for the educational career of pupils at risk. Examples of such measures include better organisation of the educational process (breaks in the scheduling of lessons, mixing theoretical and practical lessons), the provision of 'dual' learning routes (more and/or longer practical working/learning), specific programmes for practically oriented pupils, and the modernisation of teaching methods.

General and selective prevention measures

Preventive measures take different forms, ranging from general measures to those adapted for specific categories of pupils.

General prevention is directed towards all pupils, or a significant proportion of them. This type of measure is directly aimed at the prevention of truancy and dropout. General measures include, for example, the registration of absenteeism (to combat truancy) and measures for groups facing particular risks, such as lengthening of the school day, provision of homework facilities in school, day-release courses in vocational education, and so on.

Selective prevention is directed towards the problems of individual pupils who are likely to drop out of school or otherwise experience educational failure. These interventions are focused on individual problems and, due to the severity of these problems, external agents (such as social workers, youth workers, and so on) are often involved in such measures.

'Reorientation to education' measures are directed at pupils who have left a certain school, but still fall within the parameters of compulsory schooling. The goal of 'reorientation to education' measures is to help early school leavers return to (another) school through special provisions. These involve out-of-school measures with a 'shelter' function, such as truancy projects. Different actors are involved in these measures, and there tends to be close cooperation with educational actors.

Remedial measures: reorientation to education, transition to work and safety-net provision

For young people who have left the educational system early or without adequate qualifications, provisions could be made available for facilitating the transition to work; these include targeted education/training, career guidance, social skills development, and support in finding and keeping a job. Employment agencies often play an important role in guiding young people towards work (or sheltered employment).

When reorientation to education or the transition to work seem unfeasible in the short run (for the most problematic category of school leavers without qualifications), then safety-net projects and programmes such as immediate assistance and shelter are given priority, with education/training only possible after a period of time. Often, there is a shortage of places in these programmes for the most problematic cases.

One example of this approach is the 'second-chance school', which was developed under an EC pilot scheme. In 1998, 13 of these projects were being carried out in different EC countries. The aim of these 'schools' is not to create a new qualification structure; rather, they aim to organise a personalised pathway of educational and work activities focused on the needs of young people and the local labour market.

This descriptive model indicates that alternative curricula, transition and second-chance provisions can, in theory, be located at different stages:

- alternative curricula are mostly offered within the educational system during the stage of compulsory school attendance;

- transition programmes are set up in the transition period between school and work;
- second-chance provision is generally situated beyond the compulsory stage of education.

There is another typology of policy measures which is very similar to the general model presented here. This typology distinguishes between four types of policy measures: prevention; recovery, or 'leading back'; transition; and integrative/compensatory training (Hannan et al, 1995). The main difference in comparison to the typology described above relates to the last type of provision, which is 'narrower' in Hannan's model.

In the next section, an overview of measures taken in the various countries participating in this project will be presented. The discussion focuses on provision related to equal outcomes strategies. However, it should be noted that it is not always easy to distinguish measures focused on achieving equal opportunities from those focused on equal outcomes. In addition, many of the measures discussed are located in a 'grey area' between the mainstream educational system and other institutional structures.

Second-chance provision, alternative curricula, and transition measures in the six countries

To a certain extent, various EC countries face the same problem of a certain proportion of young people leaving the educational system without adequate qualifications. In spite of this similarity, however, the different educational systems in these countries respond to this problem in ways that are shaped by their specific institutional characteristics.

Based on the countries' information concerning second-chance provision, these measures can be classified as in Table 14.1.

This overview indicates that three main categories of second-chance provision are currently available or in the process of development in the participating countries:

1. Alternative curricula within the mainstream (vocational) education system. In most cases, these involve a practical curriculum for pupils who have not succeeded for various reasons in the mainstream learning pathways. In most cases, these learning routes have been introduced very recently. Examples include the JCEP and LCAP

Table 14.1: Overview of measures in participating countries

County	Measures within full-time education	Measures outside full-time education
Flanders		- Apprenticeship for self-employment - Job corps programme *(deeltijdse vorming)* - Part-time vocational education (PTVE)
Ireland	- Junior Certificate Elementary Programme (JCEP) - Leaving Certificate Applied Programme (LCAP)	- Youthreach
Netherlands	- KMBO - Assistant Training - Practical Education - 'watertight approach'	- Apprenticeship
Portugal	- 'Alternative Curricula'	- Apprenticeship
Scotland		- Skillseekers
Spain		- Occupational training programme - Workshop schools - Social guarantee programme

programmes in Ireland, Assistant Training and Practical Education in the Netherlands, and the 'alternative curricula' in Portugal.

2. Forms of alternating/dual learning for young people in the transition phase from school to the labour market. Examples include part-time vocational education (PTVE) in Belgium, workshop schools in Spain, and the apprenticeship system in Portugal. The Belgian PTVE and the Spanish workshop schools are discussed below.

3. Programmes outside the initial education system. These programmes, aimed at young people who have left the educational system without qualifications, are sometimes directed towards qualifications, sometimes towards labour market integration, and sometimes involve a combination of the two. Typical examples include the 'job corps' (*Projecten Deeltijdse Vorming*) in Flanders and the Irish 'Youthreach' programme.

Alternative curricula

Practical learning routes

In almost all of the countries, there are examples of the development of alternative curricula for pupils who are 'at risk' during compulsory education. This has involved the development, often at the school level, of a specific curriculum for pupils who have difficulties with the mainstream educational system.

In the Netherlands, Practical Education (*praktijk onderwijs*) will be made available as part of the restructuring of vocational education. In Ireland, the Junior Certificate Schools Programme and the Leaving Certificate Applied Programme have been introduced in recent years, while workshop classes have existed in Spain since 1987 (although these are currently under threat).

These programmes are intended for pupils who would not normally succeed in mainstream learning routes (for example, pupils who have failed in primary school and pupils with problems in secondary education, including early leavers, truants, and so on).

These different types of curricula have some characteristics in common:

- they are vocational or job-oriented in nature, specially directed to the acquisition of operational, practical knowledge;
- there is less of a clear-cut division between theory and practice in the learning methods adopted than there is in mainstream curricula;
- much attention is paid to personal and social development, to self-esteem, social skills, and so on.

For most countries, these new forms of education involve important innovations in methodology, pedagogy, didactic methods and curriculum content. However, relatively little is known to date about the nature and impact of these innovations. A systematic evaluation of these reforms is still premature, because in most cases these innovations have only recently been initiated and need time to develop further. However, many of the actors involved report positive results; in particular, they expect that this reform will lead to the retention within the education system of a problematic group of pupils, with consequent positive effects on their development and subsequent labour market chances.

One potential problem with the introduction of alternative curricula may be its labelling as marginal or residual education. Most of these 'practical' routes are intended as final education, often without any form of certification (except in Ireland) and without giving access to other educational opportunities. This is a particularly serious problem, and these reforms should be evaluated carefully in this respect in the future. The implications for labour market integration among young people who have taken 'practical' routes will have significant consequences for the evaluation of this new form of education.

Example of good practice: KMBO[1] in the Netherlands

At the end of the 1970s and the beginning of the 1980s, the Netherlands was confronted with a serious economic recession. This recession resulted in mass youth unemployment and a lack of trainee positions in the apprenticeship system (one of the well-known weaknesses of the apprenticeship system is its sensitivity to cyclical fluctuations). To counter this rise in youth unemployment, experiments were initiated to prevent early school leaving and to offer alternative learning pathways. These experiments took place in the context of a new form of vocational education positioned between the apprenticeship system and regular full-time vocational education. This new form was called 'Short Vocational Education' (in Dutch, KMBO). The courses in KMBO are characterised by several features:

- young people achieve the same level of education as those on primary apprenticeships;
- there are no entry requirements;
- it involves school-based courses with some periods of practical application or work experience;
- curricular innovations in terms of modularisation have taken place;
- new pedagogical approaches are used;
- the courses qualify young people directly for the labour market (level 2 functions) and give access to the second year of the 'long MBO', as well as to continued education through apprenticeship.

Participation in KMBO grew spectacularly from 2,900 pupils in 1980 to 30,000 at the beginning of the 1990s, and has subsequently stabilised at this level.

Pupils in KMBO have different origins:

- a large majority do not have any certificate. Some of them enter KMBO via so-called orientation and bridging programmes (O&S);
- another group enter from VBO (Preparatory Vocational Education) with a certificate;
- a third group (approximately 10%) are made up of pupils who dropped out from (long) MBO.

This pattern of KMBO entry clearly indicates the second-chance character of an important proportion of KMBO pupils. Prior to the existence of this new provision, a significant proportion of these unqualified school leavers would have disappeared from the educational system.

In addition to this second-chance function, KMBO plays an important role in tackling the cyclical sensitivity of the apprenticeship system. At times when trainee positions for apprenticeships are in short supply, the 'school-based variant' of the apprenticeship system (KMBO) can absorb these young people.

The composition of the population in the two educational forms – school-based and 'dual' – is fairly similar, although the 'dual' apprenticeship system is increasingly involving second-chance education for adults (with a growth in the average age of participants).

Thus, KMBO and the apprenticeship system represent an important route to formal starting qualifications for many low-achieving pupils in the Netherlands. However, statistics on the internal effectiveness of these systems (that is, the number of pupils leaving these forms of education with a qualification) indicates that a significant number of these pupils are not successful. Average effectiveness in the apprenticeship system is about 50% (with variation between 30% and 70% in the different sectors), and the estimated effectiveness of KMBO is about 60%. Thus, 40%-50% of these pupils do not achieve success through second-chance education.

Until recently, KMBO has occupied a stable position in the Dutch vocational education system; it has even been integrated into the new Education and Vocational Training Act (WEB). However, the existence of KMBO currently seems to be in danger for financial reasons. Schools have achieved increasing autonomy in their overall financing, and research indicates that the additional costs involved in KMBO programmes may represent a reason to phase out this form of vocational education.

The 'watertight approach' in the Netherlands

In recent years, a very important shift in educational policy has taken place in the Netherlands, with increasing priority being given to preventive measures. This policy has resulted in a shift of position, role, and tasks among different institutions within the restructured education system. The new configuration includes not only traditional prevention measures, such as educational priority policies for schools with a high proportion of disadvantaged pupils, but also the integration of other measures (such as O&S, day release courses, truancy projects, and so on). Intermediate actors in various networks also play an important role in the prevention of early leaving, and in facilitating a reorientation to education for those who have temporarily left school (truants). The target of this policy is that no pupil will leave education with inadequate qualifications; this is the so-called 'watertight approach'. The reader is referred to Chapter 3 for a further description and comments on this strategy.

Until recently, different remedial measures were available for school leavers who lack adequate qualifications for employment. Many intermediate organisations at both the local and regional level are active within education, as well as on the borderline between education and the labour market. They utilise different measures (including shelter, training, and career guidance) for different target groups. The future of these intermediate organisations is uncertain, however, due to the recent policy focus on the development of preventive activities within education, rather than on remedial measures outside the education system.

This restructuring of the educational system to achieve a starting qualification for every pupil is very ambitious. A number of problems have arisen during the implementation process. Preliminary evaluations of the effects on pupils from cultural minorities question the feasibility of the 'watertight approach'. Tesser and Veenman (1997) formulate their critical remarks as follows:

> The availability of a policy measure for each risk factor does not mean that this policy is also effective. Evaluation of the different measures indicates that this is so only to a limited degree. This does not mean that the policy makes no sense.... In this context one has to realise that 'watertight approaches' can only be realised in exceptional cases given the social context. So, if you want to tackle a risk factor with a watertight approach, you expect a negative evaluation of the results beforehand. It is almost always the case that part of the group will not be reached, that another part will drop out and that for yet another part the goals will not be realised.... In order to prevent frustration, it seems sensible to formulate more moderate goals based on realistic assumptions about the possibilities, constraints and motivations of the target group, on the one hand, and the needs of society, on the other hand (Tesser and Veenman, 1997).

Another risk associated with the implementation of an unrealistic watertight approach is that existing measures will be abolished before the new approach has proved itself. A more incremental approach does not carry the same risks.

Transition through alternating training

In many countries, transition programmes are available for pupils who are still attending part-time compulsory education as well as (unemployed) youth with or without vocational qualifications. Alternating learning methods are used in most of these programmes, in addition to the normal apprenticeship system.

Specific transition programmes include, for example, 'Skillseekers' in

Scotland, the apprentice system in Portugal, PTVE in Belgium, and various programmes in Spain.

In the Scottish Skillseekers programme, each 'skillseeker' receives a training credit which can be used to purchase their own training. Training is provided either directly by the employer or by a training provider, and must lead to a nationally recognised vocational qualification. Although no evaluation of this measure has taken place to date, one problem appears to be that many skillseekers with special training needs are trained not in an employer-based environment, but within a college or workshop. This non-employer-based training environment is likely to have a less positive effect on the subsequent employability of the skillseeker. It is relevant to study the background of this problem: is the problem due merely to a lack of training positions in general, or is it related to the characteristics of the skillseekers themselves?

The apprenticeship system in Portugal fulfils different functions for different participants. It represents normal educational provision for young people endeavouring to obtain a starting qualification at level 1 or 2, it has a second-chance function for pupils who did not succeed in other vocational education, and for others it can be seen as a transition system from school to work. Apprentices have thus followed very different transition paths from school (or from (un)employment) to apprenticeships. Two thirds of young apprentices in this system with lower educational levels had already experienced unemployment or had some work experience. Participants in this system are often from disadvantaged backgrounds, children of manual workers or farmers, and so on.

The problem of the Portuguese apprenticeship system, which is broadly similar to the German dual system, is the availability of trainee positions in companies and the content of the practical training provided. Although this problem also exists in countries where the apprenticeship system has a long history (such as Germany, Denmark, and the Netherlands), the lack of training positions in Portugal could be related to the lack of familiarity with this system among Portuguese firms.

In Spain, various transition programmes have developed in recent years, primarily in response to high levels of youth unemployment. Most of the programmes aim to provide young school leavers and unemployed young people with improved access to the labour market through (minimal) vocational qualifications. Three examples can be mentioned here:

- Social Guarantee Programmes (SGP): training in these programmes is partly organised in alternating form, with participants qualifying at occupational level 1;
- youth transition programmes, made up of apprenticeship contracts (recently abolished), workshop school programmes, and occupational training (OT) programmes for the unemployed;
- return to education for unqualified youth through entry examinations to the new Vocational Training programme and a programme of adult education for young participants.

This mix of programmes does not always function to achieve its stated goals. This is primarily related to the poor employment prospects for young people in general, a situation that hinders the development and availability of practical training positions in companies.

In this context, the Workshop Schools represent an interesting programme because of the heterogeneous partnership of private and public bodies, enterprises and local trade unions. There are almost 3,300 workshop schools across the country, employing 25,000 workers. This programme operates quite well, with a high percentage (62%) of participating students integrated into employment. Little is known about the effects of other programmes (for example, in terms of the numbers of pupils acquiring a formal qualification and/or a regular job), but in some cases (such as the occupational training programme) the results have proven to be very poor.

The Flemish Part-Time Vocational Education (PTVE) programme illustrates a different approach to alternating learning systems. For this reason, a short description of the PTVE system is presented here.

The part-time education system was created in 1984 with the following objectives:

- Part-time education is a necessity for a particular group of young people who can be characterised as the 'school-fatigued'. As a result, there are no selection or eligibility requirements for entry. The part-time education system is intended to meet the specific needs of its pupils by means of alternative structures, different objectives, new course content and methods which are better geared to the particular characteristics of this group of young people.
- The part-time education system is based on the principle of part-time study and part-time work. With this concept, it is intended to provide a meaningful initial vocational qualification for young people

for whom the full-time education system does not provide an appropriate response.

- The part-time education system is also intended to promote the pupils' subsequent employment chances, their active participation in society, and their personal development.

Pupils who want to follow a part-time educational programme in Flanders can register in one of the 48 PTVECs. These centres are more or less independent, though they work closely together with one or more technical and/or vocational schools.

The young people receive a minimum of 15 hours per week of training, including a minimum of six hours of general social and personal skills training, along with a minimum of six hours of vocationally oriented training. The PTVE pupil chooses for themselves a vocational training programme from among the programmes offered at the centre, such as construction, metalwork, office sales, materials handling, and so on.

In addition to the 15 hours of in-school training, priority is given to related work experience. This work experience can take four different forms:

- some pupils combine their part-time training with a part-time job in a company;
- 'alternating training' programmes, based on the concept that the job and training should be closely linked and that both the centre and the company should be responsible for supervision of the young person (supported by the ESF);
- 'bridge projects' for young people who are not considered 'mature' enough for employment (also supported by ESF);
- those working at home or in a family business are called 'home helpers'.

Not all young people are able (or willing) to combine part-time training with part-time work. Roughly half of them remain unemployed or dependent on their parents.

In practice, the PTVE programme has the following outcomes:

- participation has shown a rapid growth from 500 to 4,000 pupils over a five-year period, but has since stabilised;
- the training programmes on offer in PTVE have been adapted to enhance the labour market chances of pupils;

- ESF funding is important in effecting a job or trainee position in a company;
- pupils who have had a (part-time) job in their PTVE period have a substantially better chance of employment after finishing PTVE (64% after 12 months, compared with 43% for a comparison group with no work experience during PTVE);
- the 'pure' alternating education variant of PTVE (subsidised by ESF, in which a tutor is available in the company, part-time working pupils are paid normal wages, and their training is monitored) is very successful; 67% are in employment 12 months after leaving school, and this figure rises to 100% after four years (Nijsmans and Nicaise, 1993).

The alternating learning system, then, demonstrates that educational, social and economic objectives need not necessarily be in conflict; young people from deprived backgrounds receive thorough training and a reasonable wage, while companies are able to pursue a rational personnel policy. In the medium term, this substantially increases the chances of labour market integration among the young people concerned. Unfortunately, the recession in Belgium at the beginning of the 1990s, possibly compounded by lack of promotion on the part of the Education Department, has meant that the system has remained limited in scale.

On the basis of different research projects, the following policy recommendations have been formulated for the PTVE:

- There is a need for a better referral mechanism to the part-time education system. There is a potential PTVE target group which, at present, continues in full-time education with potentially poor probabilities of success.
- For most of the pupils, PTVE constitutes their last chance to obtain a vocational qualification. As a result, there has been a call to turn this form of education into vocationally qualifying education.
- Due to the high unemployment level within the PTVE system, the proposed concept of part-time study combined with part-time work can be realised for only a minority of participants. In order to enlarge the group of those in part-time employment, the introduction of an employment guarantee for all PTVE pupils who want work has been advocated.
- Finally, the need for good guidance and counselling of pupils from the time they enter the PTVE system until they have found a job in

the regular labour market has been emphasised (Douterlungne et al, 1997).

Example of good practice: alternating education in Flanders

The 'pure' alternating education variant of PTVE deserves some further attention. In this framework, employers receive a subsidy each time they recruit a young person for a part-time job which matches the orientation of their study, on the condition that a tutor is appointed within the company and complementary practical training is given. The young people concerned (1,200 every year) are paid normal wages; their training is monitored periodically by officials from the Education Department.

Admittedly, the 'stronger' candidates are selected among the participants in PTVE: students in alternating education are somewhat older and have experienced a slightly better school career (nearly half of them have a certificate of lower secondary education); moreover, those with weaker profiles tend to drop out more frequently.

On the other hand, the employment results after leaving school are particularly encouraging for these projects; a follow-up survey of the first 'graduates', carried out four years after they left school, shows that all of the participants had found employment – significantly more than in the control group, even after other features were controlled for when measuring the employment advantage.[2] Also, the jobs found by ex-alternating students concurred more with the content of their training than those found by other PTVE graduates (Nijsmans and Nicaise, 1993).

Since the founders of the experiment were concerned about the possible exploitation of the participating young people as cheap labour, the employers were interviewed about their cost/benefit considerations (Nicaise and Douterlungne, 1990). Do employers see the contract as an investment for the longer term, or merely as a means of obtaining temporary cheap labour? The survey showed, first of all, that the wages paid to the young people were above the minimum wage, largely negating the exploitation concerns. During the first year of the training (which generally lasts two years), the costs of wages and training are higher for the companies than the benefits (estimated output plus wage subsidies), indicating that employers really do see the training as an investment in human capital and do not particularly abuse these cheap employees. During the second year, the young people's productivity increases, and the investment begins to produce a return.

The risk associated with the investment – mainly that young people will move to a different company after the first year of training – was pooled by employers at sectoral level; all employers in a particular sector contribute to a training fund, which reimburses part of the wage costs. Similar mechanisms in the Dutch apprenticeship system are described by De Vries and Heere (1993).

Employers do admit that they use this subsidised company training as a screening instrument; the dedication and productivity of young people can be extensively tested during the training contract before they are taken on definitively. However, this screening motive is secondary to the investment motive. It is possible that this form of subsidised screening helps to overcome some of the prejudices felt by employers towards deprived young people, although this hypothesis was not tested in this study.

A parallel study of the learning effects of alternating education (Deceulaer et al, 1995) revealed that, generally speaking, participants had achieved as much progress as young people in full-time vocational education. Their increased self-confidence was particularly striking, and could clearly be attributed to the fact that they had work.

The alternating learning system, then, demonstrates that educational, social and economic objectives need not necessarily be in conflict; young people from deprived backgrounds receive thorough training and a reasonable wage, while companies are able to pursue a rational personnel policy. In the medium term, this substantially increases the chance of the young people concerned being integrated into the labour market. Unfortunately, the recession in Belgium at the start of the 1990s, possibly compounded by the lack of promotion by the Education Department, have meant that the system has remained limited in scale.

Second-chance provision for young people in the labour market

It is possible to develop policies to assist young people who have left the educational system without qualifications in their efforts to enter the labour market. Such programmes usually involve training. Examples of such programmes are found in Spain, where they are intended to combat youth unemployment.

Although the operation and effectiveness of these programmes have not been systematically evaluated, the results in terms of qualifications achieved and access to employment are not considered very positive. This must be seen in the context of the extremely difficult socioeconomic conditions within which such programmes are provided.

In Ireland, the Youthreach programme has been developed for this category of young labour market entrants, and the programme is relatively well documented. There are remarkable similarities to the Belgian PTVE, but clear differences are also evident.

Youthreach was introduced in 1989 under the government's 'Social

Guarantee' programme. The objective of the programme is "to equip early school-leavers with the skills needed for employment or further training and to provide integrated education, training and work experience over a two year period and thereby to enhance their job prospects and life chances" (Department of Education, 1995). The programme is targeted at young people who leave school without formal educational qualifications, and who have been unemployed for six months or more.

Youthreach is a joint response by the Department of Education and the Department of Enterprise and Employment. The Department of Education provides access through Youthreach Centres run by local Vocational Education Committees, while access is also provided through Community Training Workshops by FÁS, the state training agency. The programme is divided into a foundation year and a progression year for those who have successfully completed the first-year phase. The foundation phase is designed as a 46-week programme of 35 hours per week. The course content is person-centred, with an emphasis on the development of basic literacy and numeracy skills, along with vocational training and work experience. The bulk of the provisions are focused on basic training in woodwork, metalwork, catering, hairdressing, computer skills, basic welding, personal development, social skills, and literacy/numeracy. Standardisation of the curriculum has only taken place since 1995. While they attend the Youthreach programme, participants receive a trainee allowance. In 1995/96, 2,900 foundation positions were provided in 110 centres throughout the country. In addition, 625 progression positions were provided for those who successfully completed the first year phase. Expenditure on the programme totalled 52.2 million ECU between FÁS and the Department of Education in 1993 (ESF Programme Evaluation Unit, 1996).

Evaluation of Youth Reach indicates that the level of satisfaction among programme participants appears to be relatively high (ESF Programme Evaluation Unit, 1996). However, a number of problems with the adequacy of this programme in addressing the needs of the educationally disadvantaged have been identified. First, there is a relatively high level of dropout from the programme; it has been estimated that up to one third of participants fail to complete the foundation phase of the programme (ESF Programme Evaluation Unit, 1996). It has been recommended that the programme should therefore be refocused in order to make it more attractive and relevant to those who are alienated from the formal educational system (NESF, 1997). Second, there is very little movement from the foundation to progression phases of the programme; only about one fifth of those completing the foundation course go on to the second year of the programme (ESF Programme Evaluation Unit, 1996; Sexton and O'Connell, 1996). Furthermore, there is no nationally agreed curriculum or certification for the progression phase of the programme. Without a further progression phase, these young people are unlikely to have the required skills and capacities to compete in the labour market (Hannan, 1996). Third, the number of positions provided is inadequate in relation to the existing stock and flow of early school leavers (Hannan, 1996). It has been estimated that there is a shortfall in training positions of 3,180 for those with no formal educational qualifications (NESF, 1997). The existing system fails to adequately 'track' those who leave school without qualifications, in order to encourage them to participate in such programmes (Hannan, 1996).

In relation to the project's aims "to enhance ... job prospects", follow-up surveys indicate a high proportion of post-programme unemployment among young people who have taken part in Youthreach (ESF Programme Evaluation Unit, 1996). However, given the relatively low initial level of educational qualifications among participants, it is difficult to assess the net impact of the programme. Other research has indicated that general training of this type is in itself unlikely to improve the job prospects of participants, unless it is followed by progression to training or employment programmes which have strong linkages to the open labour market (Sexton and O'Connell, 1996).

Apart from Youthreach, unqualified young people make up a relatively small proportion of participants in other FÁS-delivered training programmes (ESF Programme Evaluation Unit, 1996). It has been recommended that barriers to accessing mainstream training programmes (such as age limits and educational criteria) should be removed, and that progression routes and extra positions for unqualified leavers should be provided in specific skills training programmes that are more likely to enhance job prospects for participants (NESF, 1997).

Summary and conclusions: second chance or different chances?

In this chapter, the authors have attempted to present an overview of provisions for young people who do not succeed during their 'first chance' in education. In the past decade, this issue has received increasing attention in all of the countries considered. In different countries, however, different emphases have been laid on the way in which, and the stage at which, such provision takes place. Programmes can be offered before these young people leave the educational system, in the transition period between education and the labour market, and (shortly) after they have entered the labour market.

Within the education system as such, three types of measures to deal with the dropout problem can be identified in the countries studied:

- 'general prevention': this involves the organisation of the educational system in such a way that – ideally – no pupil leaves this system without the desired level of qualifications (the 'watertight approach' in the Netherlands, for example);
- setting up more practice-based, vocational learning routes for pupils who fail in the academic track: this takes on different forms in different countries;
- specific alternative curricula for 'at-risk' pupils: for example, KMBO in the Netherlands.

These measures are not, in fact, genuine second-chance provisions, since they are of a preventive nature. However, it is clear that alternative learning routes and alternative curricula are also required for pupils who need a second chance after earlier educational failure, disruption in their school career, or other problems.

Sometimes there are 'reorientation to education' programmes (mostly on a micro, school level) which are not themselves 'second-chance' in nature, but which prepare pupils to take advantage of 'second-chance' provisions.

Actual second-chance programmes consist of:

- some type of apprenticeship. Whereas the apprenticeship system in some countries is primarily part of the mainstream educational system (as in Germany or the Netherlands), it is mainly used in other countries (such as Portugal) as a second-chance provision;
- alternating training during the transition to the labour market (for example, Workshop Schools in Spain, PTVE in Belgium);
- alternating training provisions for young people who have left the educational system and/or who are unemployed: examples are Youth Reach in Ireland and the Social Guarantee Programme in Spain.

Some second-chance measures have proved to be fairly successful in terms of participation and in terms of the proportion of pupils leaving with a qualification. But at the same time, there is always a proportion of the participants (sometimes a sizeable group) who do not succeed in obtaining a qualification, and suffer the consequent negative effects on their labour market position. Despite huge efforts in financing, innovation, expertise, and so on, results to date have been limited.

For this reason, the development of alternative learning routes through the various forms of 'practical education' must be accepted as an inevitable development. This approach recognises the fact that offering 'failing' pupils new (second or even third) opportunities in the same educational system is not an appropriate solution for all pupils.

This new learning route has only very recently been introduced in most countries. At present, therefore, we know little about the implementation or effects of this alternative approach. In all of the countries studied, access to 'practical education' tends to be limited to pupils who are less suited to academic, theoretical ways of learning in the regular education system. Another common feature in these schools is that they do not award recognised qualifications. The question is whether this reinforces their marginal position. These characteristics could further isolate second-chance schools from the educational system, an outcome that should be avoided.

Perhaps a less academic and more practical curriculum should be accessible for larger numbers of young people at upper secondary level. Most likely, a proportion of those participating but not succeeding in regular education would be more successful if they could be transferred to this alternative route. On the other hand, this form of education should be accorded a more equal position in education and should unquestionably be linked to other learning trajectories such as different forms of alternating learning.

The development of a specific curriculum for 'at-risk' pupils in regular education can be successful, as is demonstrated by the KMBO in the Netherlands. Its attractiveness resulted in a strong growth in participation, and it has become fully integrated into mainstream education. At present it is still attractive, but less so for the original category of disadvantaged pupils.

Nevertheless, KMBO remains important as a school-based alternative to the apprenticeship system, since the latter is under continuous pressure from the shortage of trainee positions, even in spite of very healthy economic conditions in the Netherlands. The continuity of KMBO is also very important as a specific first chance for disadvantaged pupils, and as a second chance for pupils who have failed in another educational programme or who have temporarily interrupted their education. The success of KMBO indicates that success is always relative; about one third of pupils leave these courses without adequate qualifications, and the labour market position of the KMBO-qualified is, in any case, fairly weak.

The apprenticeship system and different varieties of alternating learning will remain important as second-chance provisions. All provisions in the transition phase are used for young unqualified (and often unemployed) people in the labour market involve forms of alternation: Skillseekers in Scotland, workshop schools in Spain, apprenticeship in Portugal, the PTVE schools in Belgium, and the Youthreach programme in Ireland. It is evident that alternating learning methods are considered highly suitable for this purpose in all these countries. The 'genuine' alternation within the Flemish alternating system (within PTVE) is very successful, although the number of participants is limited, while the Spanish workshop schools also seem successful, given the large number of participants. In both cases, the relationship between the different partners involved is well organised and highly coordinated. However, the commitment of participating companies seems to be decisive in its success. In Belgium, the availability of extra subsidies for firms has certainly played a role in promoting firm participation (both in the availability of trainee positions and the tutoring of pupils).

The participation of companies has proven to be a weak point in most of the other programmes. In most countries, the functioning of the alternating programmes may be problematic due to the lack of trainee positions in firms; this includes Scotland, Ireland, Portugal and Spain. The current general operating mode in firms seems to be less and less suited to the combination of working and learning; this is also evidenced by ongoing developments in Germany, Denmark and the Netherlands. It is crucial for all forms of alternating learning – which is a real alternative to regular education in the school system – that conditions for adequate learning possibilities should be created within the firms.

This will be a real challenge for all parties involved. If, at the same time, alternating education could be linked to 'practical education' in the mainstream educational system, then children with less academic capacities would have their own appropriate and valued learning route. Their failure rate would diminish and second-chance provision would become less necessary for them. The educational system should therefore promote the parallel development of second-chance provision and alternative curricula within mainstream upper secondary education.

Notes

[1] With the introduction of the new Education and Vocational Training Act (WEB), KMBO and MBO have been integrated into a Vocational Training Route (*Beroeps Opleidende Leerweg*); the labels KMBO and MBO are bound to disappear, although their syllabi will remain in effect.

[2] Nonetheless, some reserve is called for in connection with possible non-observed heterogeneity.

Conclusions and recommendations

Ides Nicaise (HIVA)

Reality and ideology

The debate about the democratisation of education has dwindled over the past 20 years, giving way to an increased emphasis on efficiency and output. As a result, the vision of the education system presented has become more narrowly focused on preparation for the labour market, in the hope that more efficient education will solve the problem of youth unemployment and improve national competitiveness.

Very recently, the issue of democratisation has been rediscovered, partly thanks to the surprising results of transnational research. While the general level of education has increased, it has been demonstrated that in most countries inequality in education is passed on unrelentingly from generation to generation (Shavit and Blossfeld, 1993; Erikson and Jonsson, 1996; OECD, 1997b). The attention devoted to social exclusion brings this inequality sharply into focus, although the empirical evidence in this respect is scarce and fragmented. The poorest children often fail, and large numbers of them end up in special education or in 'second-rate streams' of secondary education. Halfway through their school careers, they still score extremely poorly in terms of literacy and numeracy. They leave school – if not before the end of compulsory education, then without qualifications – with a damaged self-image, and disillusioned about what society has to offer them. The vicious circle of exclusion is thus perpetuated, because uneducated young people become the first victims of unemployment and poverty, more frequently have to deal with illness, are more likely to become delinquent and, in this age of 'lifelong learning', benefit much less from every form of adult education.

Recommendation I

Information about the position of the most disadvantaged groups in education is extremely scarce and fragmented. Genuine comparative research in this respect at EU level is currently impossible because the basic information is not available. The European Commission should play a proactive role in the collection and harmonisation of information (both quantitative and qualitative). Existing data sources, such as the European Community Household Panel Survey and Eurostat's Labour Force Surveys, could be developed to take account of these issues.

The education system thus filters, segregates and reproduces social inequality. This reality is in stark contrast to the expectations of a democratic education system – the dream of equal opportunities and unhindered social mobility.

Upon closer inspection, our education system is still far removed from that ideal. It is even unclear whether the political will exists to achieve a genuinely 'democratic' education system, where everyone is entitled to benefit to a reasonable extent from their education. Whether consciously or subconsciously, many harbour a meritocratic view of education; it is assumed that everyone has equal opportunities, but equal profit (or equal outcomes) is certainly not an aim because, according to the theory, the unequal nature of the benefits gained from education merely reflects the efforts and talents of each individual. As Goldthorpe (1996b) demonstrates, the meritocratic ideology explicitly (and somewhat naively) perceives unequal educational outcomes as 'fair'; in so doing, it hastily passes over the issue of the fundamentally unequal society in which education is rooted.

A priori opportunities are not equal and, hence, unequal outcomes are not 'fair'. If it is true, as most experts – including 'meritocrats' – assume, that the genetic aptitude of individuals is equally distributed across all social groups, then this initial equality is already seriously distorted by the beginning of the school career. In one group, talents are carefully nurtured and further developed in a protected, prosperous environment with well-educated parents; in another group, these talents are crippled by deprivation, stress, illness and disdain from the rest of society. Schools may well try to remain neutral and guarantee that every child receives equal input, but all too often they are dragged down into subtle mechanisms of discrimination and social exclusion (Nicaise, 1999).

Some educationalists do recognise the socially unequal distribution of opportunities upon entry into education, but accept it as an unalterable fact. Children from socially excluded families are regarded as less favoured by nature. This is then apparently confirmed by 'objective' criteria such as test scores and IQ tests. In this way, stigmatisation, prejudice and discrimination are simply reinforced.

Nonetheless, research and practice do show that the higher the expectations held for them, the better pupils (and deprived pupils in particular) perform. An effective approach, therefore, starts with the ambition of using education as the main driving force to combat social exclusion.

Equal opportunities, equal treatment, equal outcomes

So how far do we want to go towards ironing out social inequalities in education?

In this research, a distinction has been made between three different approaches: equal opportunities, equal treatment, and equal outcomes (see Chapter 2). The first angle of approach concerns the preconditions for enabling children from underprivileged backgrounds to enjoy a normal school career. The second is geared towards eliminating (negative) discrimination within education, and the third approach is aimed at promoting 'positive discrimination'.

Equal opportunity strategies

Equal opportunity strategies operate 'upstream' against the pernicious context of the unequal society within which education is rooted: inequalities in terms of income, health, family background, access to culture, and so on. It is clear that the school cannot eliminate these inequalities on its own. An integrated approach to poverty, inequality and social exclusion in all these fields is the only way to eradicate the problem at its roots. Nor, however, is it any use waiting for the 'great reform of society' before making a start. Chapters 4 and 5 discussed the ways in which an integrated approach is particularly possible at the local level. In several Irish programmes, financial and cultural stimuli are combined in order to encourage pupils to continue on to further education. In the Dutch 'Extended School Day' experiment, the school offers many different types of extracurricular activities to children who do not have such resources at home: sport, culture, nature exploration, and so on. At the same time, the children's inquisitiveness is stimulated, which in turn means that they find school 'more interesting'. Moreover, activities such as sport and drama contribute directly to the development of basic abilities such as assertiveness, team spirit and fair play, and to a reduction in aggression at school.

Recommendation 2

A number of local experiments, together with partial moves towards an integrated service for underprivileged pupils at the national level, do exist at present. However, none of the countries examined has a fully developed system which meets the following five basic criteria: (i) systematic detection and follow-up of the specific needs of underprivileged (groups of) pupils (pupil monitoring system); (ii) effective provision of integrated services (education for parents, language development, homework supervision, healthcare, cultural activities, and so on); (iii) a 'longitudinal' integration of supportive activities throughout the entire school career; (iv) a network of all the relevant partners (after all, the school must not repeat the work done elsewhere); and (v) a local body which can develop and coordinate all of the above. Further steps in this direction should be taken, taking each country's possibilities and resources into account.

Recommendation 3

At the material and financial level, it is first of all necessary to make sure that all provisions within nursery and compulsory education are effectively free of charge. In addition, study grants will still be necessary to make up at least in part for the indirect costs of education (the income forgone by young people at school), if the dropout rate within compulsory education (particularly in southern European countries) and in further education (in all countries) is to be reduced. Suggestions relating to improved targeting of the grants, administrative control, and links with other types of intervention have been made in Chapter 4.

In various countries, it has been found that this type of integrated approach is more effective the earlier it is implemented. The Rutland Street Project in a deprived area of Dublin produced the same spectacular long-term results as the most renowned projects in the US Head Start programme. It contributed to the development of the national 'Early Start' programme. In Scotland too, the measured effects of the Pilton Early Intervention Project were so encouraging that a national programme has been developed. Similar projects are underway in various other countries. American research in this field seems to demonstrate that this type of preventive approach to social exclusion is the most effective and even the most financially profitable investment, not only because of the spectacular learning effects achieved, but also as a result of the reduced number of failures and referrals to special education, the increased number of successful educational careers, the decline in socially maladjusted behaviour, and so on.

In Scotland, however, critics point to the danger that early childhood intervention programmes are overshooting their mark if they are generalised into a 'recipe for success' for all children within the context of (exaggerated) international competition in education. This would set the standard higher for everyone, and the most underprivileged children would become even less likely to be able to keep up with their contemporaries.

Recommendation 4

Early intervention programmes for deprived children deserve an added boost in all EU member states. The results of various pilot projects in Ireland, Scotland, the Netherlands and elsewhere are convincing. Decades of experience have already been gained from the Head Start programme in America. Important deciding factors for the success of this strategy include selective targeting of the most underprivileged children, close involvement of the parents, an integrated approach (see above), and the extent to which the efforts are subsequently sustained within lower and secondary education. In the long term, the investment required for this type of project is more than justified.

The EU can play an important stimulating role in this context by contributing to the dissemination of national experiences, by subsidising pilot projects and studies, and by promoting a more preventive approach in addition to the existing 'second-chance' approach.

Within the equal opportunity approach, legal measures that are intended to ensure that all young people achieve a minimum qualification must also be mentioned. This study has shown that, in all countries, legal school leaving ages are being systematically raised. This is not without its problems; control measures and sanctions are increasingly being taken in order to actively impose compulsory schooling. True, the compulsory measures are sometimes accompanied by educational and curriculum reforms, so as to make the school more attractive by providing qualitatively better education and offering more comprehensive care for pupils. Nevertheless, most underprivileged young people still leave school (during or after the end of compulsory schooling) frustrated and without qualifications. For this reason, unemployment legislation sometimes forces them, even after leaving school, to continue in education.

The scientific evaluations of extending compulsory schooling, however, indicate mixed results. On the one hand, the percentage of unqualified school leavers is falling. On the other hand, young people from vulnerable backgrounds often seem to fail during their extended stay at school, and to benefit less from their qualifications. Moreover, other groups attempt to maintain their advantage by studying for even longer.

Recommendation 5

Experience shows that an extension of compulsory schooling can never stand alone as a strategy. It is best combined with educational and curriculum reforms in order to increase school success, and increased concern for the wellbeing of the young people in question. In addition, learning rights must be reinforced; these include the right of admission to a school of one's choice, a reduction in expulsion or exclusion from school, the right to free and appropriate learning assistance for special needs pupils, and the expansion of second-chance programmes for young people who have failed in ordinary education.

Equal treatment strategies

In contrast to 'equal opportunity strategies', the 'equal treatment' approach places the emphasis on a more 'fair' treatment within the school; in other words, the removal of discrimination against socially excluded groups. After all, it is clear that the school makes as much of a contribution (whether consciously or subconsciously) to social exclusion as do other sections of society. Some of the many expressions of this include prejudices about the 'natural weakness' of deprived children, socially and culturally biased curricula, conflicts with deprived parents and young people and, in particular, the unjustified separation of young people into 'side tracks' such as special education or dead-end curricula.

The curriculum structure in Europe is highly diverse. Nonetheless, consensus in academic and policy circles is growing that social inequality in education can be combated; for instance, by offering a joint, broad curriculum up to the age of 16, possibly including a limited number of optional subjects which are not binding in terms of subsequent course choices. In addition to the 'commonality' of this curriculum, a broad, experience-oriented content is important, as is the commitment of teachers to providing equal education for all young people. The 'Experimental Compulsory Secondary Schools' in Spain have recently demonstrated the success of this approach; the success figures were 15% higher than those for the old system (see Chapter 7).

Nonetheless, success in a comprehensive curriculum is by no means guaranteed for the most deprived pupils. This is highlighted by the fact that, after its introduction, all the countries studied reintroduced alternative curricula for the weakest groups in the 12-16 age range. These curricula cannot be termed 'equal treatment', given that they do not usually allow for a return to mainstream education, even after completion.[1] Nor do they provide equivalent certificates. Their primary aims are to provide a few years of meaningful education for young people and to prevent further failures and dropouts. Perhaps, at the educational level, they could even serve as a model for ordinary education. At the same time, these alternative curricula are also an indicator of the lack of radical thinking that characterises the implementation of the comprehensive curricula.

The most serious injustice done to deprived children by education is perhaps their frequent referral to special education. Special education itself is not to blame for this; rather, it is caused by the lack of commitment on the part of ordinary education in pushing to one side learning difficulties with a social cause. Children may be better served by special education (research that might provide an answer to this question is scarce), but they are also segregated and stigmatised, which reduces rather than improves their chances of integration in the longer term.

Nonetheless, Europe is rich in scientific understanding of education, which can be usefully applied not only to the most excluded pupils, but also to other groups. In some places, 'active' (experience-based), 'constructivist', or 'communicative' educational theory is applied in schools in deprived areas. Coves d'en Cimany (Barcelona), De Buurt (Ghent) and Ramón Bajo School (Vitoria-Gasteiz) are just a few examples which stand out as a result of their carefully considered approach (Chapter 8). As regards 'inclusive education' for pupils with special educational needs (see Chapter 11), there were also good examples in Catalonia (El Margalló) and Flanders (De Rank). Although striking signs of success are evident in each case, thorough evaluation has yet to be performed. In the US, academic evaluation is more inherent to each experiment. For example, the added value of the Accelerated Schools in the US has been clearly proven; these offer an accelerated programme based on high expectations, emphasis on 'core skills' and close cooperation with parents and other actors (see Chapter 8).

Recommendation 6

Within the six countries studied, the target of comprehensive education up to the age of 16 has not yet been achieved in Flanders or Portugal. In the other countries too, the comprehensive curriculum still requires some work to make 'side tracks' superfluous up to the age of 15-16.

This type of curriculum is probably not entirely feasible if it is not associated with further-reaching educational reforms. Experiments of this type deserve much more attention and thorough academic evaluation. The EU can also play a pioneering role in this respect.

Recommendation 7

'Inclusive education for pupils with special needs' also deserves special attention. Close cooperation between ordinary and special education can mean that at least half of pupils with special needs can continue their school careers in mainstream education. In this respect, Spain and Scotland are much further ahead than the other countries studied.

Teacher training plays an essential role in these education reforms. Even without reforms, however, teachers must be made aware of the specific difficulties facing socially excluded children. Simply by interpreting signals more accurately, a lot of prejudice, discrimination and conflict can be avoided.

The analysis in Chapter 9 shows that, in most countries, the initial training of teachers lags behind the social developments in education (extension of compulsory learning, democratisation, multiculturalism, the decline of the family as an educational environment, and so on). Teacher training is still targeted, in a way which is far too one-sided, at subject knowledge, and deals only fleetingly with the sociological and socioeducational analyses of deprivation, learning difficulties, social inequality or cultural differences, let alone appropriate strategies for dealing with these matters. Portugal is currently making major advances in this respect. In other countries, these matters are at most dealt with in optional subjects or in further training courses, such as those for special education, or in a noncommittal way, as part of in-service training.

Recommendation 8

It is imperative that the sociological, sociopsychological and socioeducational dimensions of teacher training be reinforced. This must take place both in their initial training and as part of in-service training.

- In initial training, so that in the future, no single teacher has to deal with this problem in ignorance;

- In further education, so that not only new generations but also older teachers are informed; because understanding develops and because in-service training is better placed to take advantage of teachers' own experiences in the field.

The EU can contribute to this by explicitly placing emphasis on this topic within the context of exchange programmes (for teachers, teacher trainers and experts) as well as teacher training programmes in Objective 1 regions co-financed by the ESF.

Ideally, the training modules in this respect are offered as part of a sandwich course, and are linked to social education reforms. They may not be confined to an analysis of problems, but must also involve critical consideration of the teachers' own performances and information about all kinds of successful innovations at European and world levels.

Given that discrimination is often rooted in sociocultural prejudices, it must be combated through better mutual understanding between the school and deprived families/parents. The analysis in Chapter 10 shows that some trends in recent policy regarding parental participation have done more harm than good. In some countries, the government is attempting to improve the quality of education by organising a public battle between schools to 'win the favour of the parents/consumers'. This strategy leads to more rather than less social discrimination; middle-class families withdraw from schools with a deprived target public, where average scores are lower. Educational sociological literature demonstrates that this type of segregation causes more harm among weak pupils than benefit among the 'strong' groups.

Some schools understand that parents can be important partners in combating school failure. By involving parents in educational activities and by supporting them in their educational role at home, very encouraging progress can be made, particularly among young children.

Above all, however, it is important that parents are also involved in transforming the educational process itself; in order to narrow the gap between socially underprivileged children and the school, the children involved must not only receive more support (deficit approach), but the school must also be able to take advantage of their culture, experiences, expectations and strengths more effectively (pedagogy-of-diversity approach). Parents are important mediators in this adjustment process, as are other local players (associations, employers, social services, and so on).

The policy discourse also tends to see parents as 'consumers' or 'partners' within education; this is not, however, how children are percieved. Yet children are the most direct 'consumers' of education. The UN Convention on the Rights of the Child requires that children's welfare, views and educational rights be central to education. Such consideration could create a more 'democratic' educational system, which promotes children's sense of responsibility, self-esteem and ownership of their education.

Recommendation 9

Socially excluded parents are not 'obstacles' to a good school career. On the contrary, they are essential partners in a more effective education. It is therefore worth recommending that there be more investment in these parents than is currently the case. The classic channels (parents' committees, parents' evenings) are not necessarily the most appropriate for this group. It is probably better to work via home visits, school community action, specific projects for parents and, more generally, through a climate where the school sees its role as the lynchpin in the development of the entire environment (as illustrated by the Family Clubs in Areosa [Oporto]).

True, the statement made above must not allow us to forget that, in extreme cases, parents may not be able to act as partners; for example, when children are in residential care, if parents are so weighed down by exclusion that they cannot take on any responsibilities with respect to schooling, or in cases of conflict within the family. These children risk being even more excluded unless policies promoting parent–school partnerships acknowledge and address their situations.

Equal outcomes strategies

Based on the understanding that equal treatment of underprivileged young people is not enough within the context of a fundamentally unequal society, the idea of 'positive discrimination' has been in circulation since the Plowden Report (1967). Such positive discrimination can be translated into 'educational priority policies', which are additional financing mechanisms for schools with a high concentration of socially excluded young people. Within the schools, these resources can be used for additional staff training, innovative projects, differentiation, teaching assistance, and so on.

Such policy aims face significant questions in implementation. What criteria are used to distinguish target group schools? What types of activities are the subject of additional financing? How strong should positive discrimination be? How are perverse effects to be avoided? The comparative analysis in Chapters 12 and 13 enables us to formulate some specific recommendations.

Recommendation 10

The selection of schools within the context of educational priority policies generally takes place more effectively if needs can be determined on the basis of the profile of the pupil population of every school, rather than on subregional indicators of disadvantage. It is also advisable to impose implementation criteria to force schools to develop a clear strategy in favour of the target group(s). External coaching and continuing education of teachers are essential ingredients of this strategy. Pupil monitoring systems must, on the one hand, lead to improved knowledge of the pupils' backgrounds and, on the other hand, enable their learning progress to be evaluated (and possibly for learning plans to be adjusted).

Educational priority policies also seem to be effective only if the financing is sufficient to provide a counterbalance to the deprivation factors faced not only by underprivileged pupils, but by the school as a whole.

Only if it is obvious that all the aforementioned strategies have failed can alternative curricula and 'second-chance schools' be used to boost the qualifications of the weakest pupils at the end of their school careers. These provisions are not aimed at 'equal outcomes' but represent a last-ditch attempt to reduce inequality. In Chapter 14, a distinction was made between three types of provision: alternative curricula within compulsory education, transition systems from school to work, and pure second-chance schools for pupils who have already turned their backs on school for some time. Short secondary vocational education (KMBO) in the Netherlands, and alternating education in Flanders, show that such provisions can actually be successful in terms of learning effects, preventing dropout, and employment opportunities upon completion.

The most important conclusion drawn from the analysis of alternative curricula, transition systems and second-chance schools seems to be – somewhat paradoxically – that these ought to be 'mainstreamed' within higher secondary education. Their carefully considered (usually alternating) educational approach is, after all, suitable for a great many at-risk pupils who now continue to languish in mainstream education. Moreover, mainstreaming also implies that the training courses in question result in recognised qualifications (but without becoming less accessible to the most deprived pupils).

In addition, the authors advocate more active involvement by employers, particularly by making jobs available in the apprenticeship system or in part-time work, but also through participation in curriculum development, methods, and materials, and by recognising qualifications.

Final remarks

To round off this summary of findings and conclusions, we would like to make a few general comments.

First, let it be clear that the three types of approach complement rather than compete with one another. The authors believe that ideological differences about what is actually the most 'structural' or 'progressive' approach do not serve the interests of the socially excluded children themselves. In so far as it can be observed that they are saddled with a 'deficit', compensation for this must be made. Observing a deficit should not at all be regarded as a stigmatising or less structural interpretation. After all, it is a consequence of the deprivation of the children and their families at other levels of social life. On the other hand, it is pointless to take compensating action if the pupils simultaneously (or subsequently) have to battle against a form of education which alienates, degrades and, again, side-tracks them. Action must be taken simultaneously on all fronts.

Second, it must be observed that the evaluation literature about educational policies addressing social exclusion in Europe is far from well developed. Impressive records of experiments and innovative measures notwithstanding, very little is known about their effectiveness and efficiency; this is in contrast to the situation in the US, where innovative measures are generally accompanied by a legal obligation to evaluate. The existing evaluation studies in Europe are not only few and far between, but are also often limited in their intention and methodologically debatable because of their limited financing.

> **Recommendation 12**
>
> More far-reaching and longitudinal research is needed into the effectiveness and efficiency of educational reforms from the point of view of the battle against social exclusion. In the first instance, this is a national responsibility, but the EU can encourage transnational research through the Framework Programmes for Research and Technological Development.

The same applies to the transfer of research results, not only within the academic world (which has its own dissemination channels), but also, particularly, to policy makers, educationalists, social services and associations in the field. It is hoped that this research may contribute to this transfer.

Finally, this research has devoted little attention to the costs of the various strategies. This would require separate, far-reaching research. Nonetheless, recent literature concerning the economics of education has demonstrated repeatedly that equity and efficiency make good partners in educational strategies for socially deprived target groups. Prevention programmes among young children are the most striking example of this. Cost-benefit evaluations of such programmes, mainly in the US literature, have shown rates of return exceeding those of the best financial investments. This is perhaps the strongest argument in favour of such policies. Expenditure on educational measures for disadvantaged groups can thus be an extremely rewarding investment in Europe's human capital.

Note

[1] There are some exceptions, such as the altenative curricula in Portugal and KMBO in the Netherlands.

Bibliography

AA.VV (1987) *Comparative Education Review*, vol XXI, no 1 (special number to second study of IEA).

AA.VV (1994) 'La formación profesional reglada y ocupacional: el reto ante el mundo del trabajo', in *España 1993: Una interpretación de su realidad social*, Madrid: Fundación Encuentro.

AA.VV (1994) *L'évaluation des Zones d'Éducation Prioritaires – description, typologie, fonctionnement, résultats*, Paris: Mínistère de l'Éducation Nationale et de la Culture, Direction de l'evaluation et de la prospective.

AA.VV (1994) *Temes d'Infància. Educar de 0 a 6 anys*, vols I and II, Barcelona: Rosa Sensat.

AA.VV (1995) *Capital humano*, Valencia: Fundación Bancaixa.

AA.VV (1996) 'Educación y desarrollo', in *España, 1995: Una interpretación de su realidad social*, Madrid: Fundación Encuentro.

AA.VV (1996) *Verslagboek 10 jaar leerplichtverlenging*, Brussels: Stichting Daniel Coens.

Abbring, I.M., Meijer, C.J.W., and Rispens, J. (eds) (1989) *Landenstudies. Het onderwijs aan leerlingen met problemen in internationaal perspectief* ('Country studies. Education of pupils with problems in international perspective), First report of the CASE project, Groningen: RION.

Abreu, I. and Roldão, M. do Céu (1989) 'A evolução da escolaridade obrigatória em Portugal nos ultimos 20 anos', in AAVV, *O ensino básico em Portugal*, Rio Tinto: Asa, pp 41-94.

Adler, M. (1997) 'Looking Backwards to the Future: parental choice and education policy', *British Educational Research Journal*, vol 23, no 3.

Adler, M., Petch, A., and Tweedie, J. (1989) *Parental choice and educational policy*, Edinburgh: Edinburgh University Press.

Aldgate, J. and Tunstill, J. (1995) *Making sense of section 17*, London: HMSO.

Allan, J., Brown, S., and Riddell, S. (1995) *Special educational needs provision in mainstream and special schools in Scotland*, Final report to the Scottish Office, Stirling: University of Stirling.

Alves Pinto, C. (1988) *Disparidades regionais dos níveis de instrução dos jovens. Medidas que promovam o sucesso escolar*, Lisbon: Comissão de Reforma do Sistema Educativo.

Amaro, R. et al (1998) *Parental participation in schools: An overview of the Portuguese context*, A contribution for Action III, 3.1 of the Socrates Programme: 'Parental participation in schools', Lisbon: Ministerio da Educação, Instituto de Inovação Educacional.

Andersen, J., Bruto da Costa, A., Chigot, C., Duffy, K., Mancho, S., and Mernagh, M. (1995) 'Contribution of Poverty 3 to the understanding of poverty, exclusion and integration', in P. Conroy (ed) *The lessons of the Poverty 3 programme*, Brussels: European Commission DG V/E/2.

Angus, L. (1993) 'The sociology of school effectiveness', *British Journal of Sociology of Education*, vol 14, no 3, pp 333-45.

Antunes, J.J. (1989) 'Os Abandonos Escolares no Ensino Básico', in AAVV, *O ensino básico em Portugal*, Rio Tinto: Asa, pp 95-132.

Antunes, M. da Conceição (1991) 'Implicações da dinâmica escolar na motivação para a aprendizagem e no sucesso escolar: o cenário da aula', *Sociologia – Problemas e Práticas*, no 10, pp 91-113.

Apple, M.W. (1982) *Education and power*, London: Routledge and Kegan Paul.

Archer, P. and Kellaghan, T. (1975) 'A home intervention project for pre-school disadvantaged children', *Irish Journal of Education*, no 9, pp 28-43.

Armstrong, D.K., Galloway, D., and Tomlinson, S. (1993) 'Assessing special educational needs: The child's contribution', *British Educational Research Journal*, vol 19, no 2, pp 121-31.

Aronson, E. (1972) *The social animal*, San Francisco: Freeman W.H. and Company.

Arroteia, J. (1991) 'A democratização do ensino e a reforma do sistema educativo português: Algumas reflexões, in Sociedade Portuguesa de Ciências da Educação', *Ciências da educação em Portugal – situação actual e perspectivas*, Porto, pp 185-90.

Ashworth, K., Hill, M., and Walker R. (1994) 'Patterns of childhood poverty: new challenges for policy', *Journal of Policy Analysis and Management*, vol 13, no 4, pp 658-80.

Ashworth, P. D. and Saxton, J. (1990) 'On competence', *Journal of Further and Higher Education*, vol 14, no 2, pp 3-25.

ATD-Fourth World, Fondation Roi Bandouin, Union des Villes et des Communes Belges (1995) *Rapport Général sur la Pauvreté*, Bruxelles: Fondation Roi Bandouin.

ATD-Fourth World (1999) 'L'enseignement obligatoire n'est pas gratuit!', mimeo, Brussels.

Atkinson, A.B., Maynard, A.K., and Trinder, C.G. (1993) *Children and parents: Incomes in two generations*, Aldershot: Avebury.

Audit Commission (1994) *Seen but not heard*, London: HMSO.

Australian Conference of Directors General of Education and Commonwealth Youth Bureau (1991) *Children and youth at risk. Effective programs and practices*, OECD/CERI.

Ausubel, D.P. (1968) *Educational psychology: A cognitive point of view*, New York: Holt.

Ayuste, A., Flecha, R., López Palma, F., and Lleras, J. (1994) *Planteamientos de la pedagogia crítica. Comunicar y transformar*, Barcelona: Gra Editorial.

Azevedo, J. (1994) *Avenidas de Liberdade – Reflexões sobre política educativa*, Rio Tinto: Asa.

Bairrão, J. et al. (1989) 'Care and education for children under age 6 in Portugal', in P.P. Olmsted and D.P. Weikart (eds) *How nations serve young children*, Ypsilanti, Michigan: High/Scope Press.

Ball, S., Bowe, R., and Gerwitz, S. (1996) 'School choice, social class and distinction: The realization of social advantage in education', *Journal of Educational Policy*, vol 11, no 1, pp 89-112.

Banks, J. (1994) *Strategies to improve young people's access to, and their progression within, initial vocational training*, Brussels.

Barnett, W.S. (1995) 'Long-term effects of early childhood programs on cognitive and school outcomes', *The Future of Children*, vol 5, no 3, pp 25-50.

Baron, S. (1989) 'Community education: from the Cam to the Rea', in S. Walker and L. Barton (eds) *Politics and the progresses of schooling*, Milton Keynes: Open University Press.

Barr, N. and Falkingham, J. (1993) *Paying for learning*, London: BP/ Suntory-Toyota International Centre for Economic and Related Disciplines, Welfare State Programme discussion paper 94.

Bartlett, W., Propper, C., Wilson, D., and Le Grand, J. (1994) *Quasi Markets in the Welfare State*, Bristol: SAUS.

Bastiani, J. (1993) *UK Directory of home–school initiatives*, Cambridge: Black Bear Press.

Bastiani, J. and Wolfendale, S. (eds) (1996) *Home–school work in Britain*, London: David Fulton.

Baudelot, C. and Establet, R. (1976) *La escuela capitalista en Francia*, Madrid: Siglo XXI.

Bayton, J.A, McAlister, C.B., and Hamer J. (1956) 'Race–class stereotypes', *Journal of Negro Education* (winter), pp 75-8.

Benavente, A. (1990a) *Escola, professoras e processos de mudança*, Lisbon: Livros Horizonte.

Benavente, A. (1990b) 'O insucesso escolar no contexto português – abordagens, concepções e políticas', *Análise Social*, vol 108-109, pp 715-33.

Benavente, A. (ed) (1994) 'Democratização e qualidade do ensino', Report no 3/93 of the National Education Council, Diário da república, series II, 15 February.

Benavente, A., da Costa, A.F., and Machado, F.L. (1990) 'Práticas de mudança e de investigação – conhecimento e intervenção na escola primária', *Revista Crítica de Ciências Sociais*, no 29, pp 55-80.

Bernstein, B. (1975) *Poder, educación y sociedad*, Barcelona: Roure.

Bernstein B.B. (1974) 'A critique of the concept of "compensatory education"', in D. Wedderburn (ed) *Poverty, inequality and class structure*, Cambridge: Cambridge University Press.

Berrueta-Clement, J.R. (ed) (1984) *Changed lives: The effects of the Perry Preschool Program*, Ypsilanti, Michigan: High/Scope Press.

Best, F. (1996) *La politique des zones d'éducation prioritaire, une réponse au problème des enfants à risques. Un exemple: la ZEP d'Alençon-Perseigne*, International Conference on Youth at Risk, Noordwijkerhout: Stichting Jeugdinformatie Nederland and Dutch Ministry of Education.

Blaug, M., Dougherty, C. and Psacharopoulos, G. (1982) 'The distribution of schooling and the distribution of earnings: Raising the school leaving age in 1972', *Manchester Sch. Econ. Soc. Stud.*, vol 50, no 1 (March), pp 24-40.

Boavida, J. and Barreira, C. (1993) 'Nova avaliação, novas exigências, *Inovação*', vol VI, pp 97-105.

Bollens, J., van de Velde, V., Cnudde, V., van Obbergen, B., Vansieleghem, N., Douterlungne, M., Nicaise, I., and Verhaeghe, J.P. (1998) *Zorgverbreding in het basis- en secundair onderwijs: Een zoektocht naar financieringscriteria*, Leuven/Ghent: Hoger Instituut voor de Arbeid/ Vakgroep Onderwijskunde.

Booth, T. and Ainscow, M. (1998) *From them to us: An international study of inclusion in education*, London: Routledge.

Borus, M.E., Brennan, J.P., and Rosen, S. (1970) 'A benefit-cost analysis of the Neighbourhood Youth Corps: The out-of-school program in Indiana', *Journal of Human Resources*, vol 5, no 2, pp 139-59.

Bosl, M. (1996) *Immigrant children and adolescents in Germany, school-related problems*, International Conference on Youth at Risk, Noordwijkerhout: Stichting Jeugdinformatie Nederland and Flemish Ministry of Education.

Boudon, R. (1974) *Education, opportunity and social inequality*, New York: Wiley.

Bourdieu, P. (1973) 'Cultural reproduction and social reproduction', in R. Brown (ed) *Knowledge, education and cultural change*, London: Tavistock.

Bourdieu, P. and Passeron, J.C. (1970) *La reproduction: Éléments pour une théorie du système d'enseignement*, Paris: Ed. de Minuit.

Bourdieu, P. and Passeron, J.C. (1977) *Reproduction in education, society and culture*, Beverly Hills, CA: California: Sage Publications.

Bowles, S. and Gintis, H. (1976) *Schooling in capitalist America*, New York: Basic Books.

Breen, R. (1984) *Education and the labour market: Work and unemployment among recent cohorts of Irish school leavers*, Dublin: ESRI.

Breen, R. and Whelan, C.T. (1996) *Social mobility and social class in Ireland*, Dublin: Gill and Macmillan.

Breen, R., Hannan, D.F., and O'Leary R. (1995) 'Returns to education: Taking account of employers' perceptions and use of educational credentials', *European Sociological Review*, no 11, pp 59-75.

Brophy, J. and Good, T. (1970) 'Teachers' communication of differential expectations for children's classroom performance: Some behavioural data', *Journal of Educational Psychology*, no 61, pp 365-74.

Bruijn, E. (1995) *Changing pathways and participation in vocational and technical education and training in the Netherlands*, Amsterdam: SCO.

Bruijn, E. (1995) *Het (initieel) beroepsonderwijs in Nederland: Gids Beroepsonderwijs en Volwasseneneducatie*, The Hague: VUGA.

Bruto da Costa, A. (1988) *Reformulacao de politica de accao social escolar*, Lisboa: Ministerio de Educacao.

Bryant, D. and Maxwell, K. (1996) 'The effectiveness of early intervention for disadvantaged children', in M.J. Guralnick (ed) *The effectiveness of early intervention*, Baltimore: Paul Brookes.

Bryk, A.S., Lee, V.E., and Holland, P.B. (1993) *Catholic schools and the common good*, Cambridge, Massachusetts: Harvard University Press.

Burgess, R., Hughes, C. and Moxon, S. (1989) *Educating the under five in Salford*, CEDAR (Centre for Educational Development, Appraisal and Research), Coventry: University of Warwick.

C.E.I.P. *Coves d'en Cimanyö: Projecte Educatiu del Centre (PEC) (1995-98)*, Internal document, Barcelona.

C.P. Ramón Bajo (1998) 'Comunidad de aprendizaje Ramón Bajo', *Aula de Innovación educativa*, no 72, p 58.

C.P. Virgen del Carmen (1996–97) 'Proyecto de Transformación del C.P. Virgen del Carmen en Comunidad de Aprendizaje', Internal document. Pasaia (Guipuzcoa).

C.P. Virgen del Carmen (1998) 'Las comisiones de trabajo en una comunidad de aprendizaje', *Aula de Innovación educativa*, no 72, pp 58-9.

Cabitsis, S., Fusulier, B., Stegen, P., Vanheerswynghels, A., and Stegen, P. (1994) *Prolongation de la scolarité obligatoire: dix ans après*, Brussels: YKB/UCL/UELG.

Campos, B.P. (1989) *Questões de política educativa*, Rio Tinto: Asa.

Carabaña,J. (1993) 'Sistema de enseñanza y clases sociales' in M.A. Garcia de Leon (ed), *Sociología de la educación*, Barcelona: Barcavona.

Caria, T. (1990) 'As classes populares perante o fim da escolaridade obrigatória em meios sociais do interior do distrito de Vila Real', in *A Sociologia e a sociedade portuguesana viragem do século*, Actas do 1º congresso português de Sociologia, Lisboa, Fragmentos, pp 91-100.

Caria, T. (1994) 'A reforma da avaliação dos alunos no ensino básico analisada no contexto das culturas dos professores', *Sociedade e Culturas*, 1, Educação, pp 159-72.

Carney, C., Fitzgerald, E., Kiely, G., and Quinn, P. (1994) *The cost of a child*, Dublin: Combat Poverty Agency.

Carter, L.F. (1984) 'Sustaining effects of compensatory and elementary education', *Educational Researcher*, vol 13, pp 4-13.

Castanheira, C. and São, P., Emília (1987) *Que população escolar? A origem socioeconómica do aluno e o sucesso escolar*, Lisbon: GEP-ME.

Castells, M., Flecha, R., freine, P., Giroluv, H., Macedo, D. and Willis, P. (1994) *Nuvas perspectivas críticas en educación*, Barcelona: Paí dos Hérica.

Castro, Rui Vieira de, and Lima, Licínio C. (1987) 'Insucesso e selecção social na disciplina de Português: O(s) discurso(s) do professores – uma abordagem interdisciplinar', *Psicologia*, no 3, pp 299-310.

Centre for Educational Research and Innovation (CERI) (1980) *School and community*, vol II, Paris: OECD.

CES (1995) *Memoria sobre la situación socioeconómica y laboral. España 1994*, Madrid: Consejo Económico y Social.

CIREM (1995) *Exit i fracàs escolar a Catalunya*, Barcelona: Fundació Jaume Bofill.

CIREM (1997) *Desigualtats d'èxit i fracàs a l'educació secundària obligatòria*, Barcelona: Departament d'Ensenyament de la Generalitat de Catalunya.

Clancy, P. (1995) *Access to college: Patterns of continuity and change*, Dublin: Higher Education Authority.

Clayton, C. (1991) 'Chapter 1 evaluation: Progress, problems, and possibilities', in *Evaluation and Policy Analysis*, no 13, pp 345-52.

Closs, A. (1997) 'Special Education Provision' in M. Clark and P. Munn (eds) *Education in Scotland*, London: Routledge.

CMRS (1992) *Education and Poverty*, Dublin: Conference of Major Religious Superiors.

Codina, T. (1988) 'El dret a ser diferent sense quedar al marge: projecte duna educació en la diversitat. Estudi i propostes de l'educació de l'infant procedent de la pobresa a la ciutat de Barcelona', Document submitted to the competitive examinations for obtaining a permanent post as a teacher in a public school, Barcelona.

Coleman, J.S., Campbell, E., Holson, C., McPartland, J., Mood, A., Weinfeld, F. and York, R. (1996) *Equality of educational opportunity*, Washington, DC: Government Printing Office.

Coll, C. and Soler, I. (1989) 'Aprendizaje significativo y ayuda pedagógica', *Cuadernos de Pedagogía*, no 168, Barcelona.

Collins, M. (1991) *Adult education as vocation*, London: Routledge.

Comber, L.C. and Keeves, J.P. (1973) *Science education in nineteen countries: An empirical study*, New York: Wiley.

Connell, R.W. (1994) 'Poverty and education', *Harvard Educational Review*, vol 2, no 64, pp 125-49.

Consejo Economico y Social (1996) *La pobreza y la exclusión social en España*, Informe no 8, Madrid: CES.

Conway, S. (1997) 'The reproduction of exclusion and disadvantages: Symbolic violence and social class inequalities', in *'Parental choice' of secondary education, Sociological Research Online*, vol 2, no 4.

http://www.socresonline.org.uk/socresonline/2/4/4.html

Coolahan, J. (1981) *Irish education: History and structure*, Dublin: Institute of Public Administration.

Correia, J.A., Stollerof, A., and Stoer, S.R. (1993) 'A ideologia da modernização no sistema educativo em Portugal', *Cadernos de Ciências Sociais*, no 12/13, pp 25-51.

Cortesão, L. (1991) 'O conceito de educação intercultural', *Inovação*, vol IV, no 2–3, pp 33-44.

Corwin, R.G. and Dianda, M.R. (1993) 'What can we really expect from large-scale voucher programs?', *Phi Delta Kappa*, vol 1, no 75, pp 68-74.

Cosin, B. and Hales, M. (eds) (1997) *Families, education and social differences*, London and NewYork: Routledge and Open University.

Cossey, H., Hedebouw, G. and Ringoot, M. (1983) *Studiekosten in het secundair onderwijs*, Leuven: Hiva.

Costa, A. F. and Machado, Fernando L. (1987) 'Meios populares e escola primária – pesquisa sociológica num processo interdisciplinar de investigação-acção', *Sociologia, Problemas e Práticas*, no 2, pp 69-89.

Crano, W.D. and Mellon, D.M. (1978) 'Casual influence of teachers' expectations on children's academic perfomance: A cross-lagged panel analysis', *Journal of Educational Psychology*, no 70, pp 39-49.

CREA (1995) 'Proyecto de transformación de centros educativos en Comunidades de Aprendizaje', Internal document of the Centre de Recerca en Educació d'Adults, Divisió Ciéncies de l'Educació, Universitat de Barcelona.

CREA (1998) 'Comunidades de Aprendizaje: propuesta educativa igualitaria en la sociedad de la información', *Aula de Innovación educativa*, no 72, pp 49-51.

Croxford, L. (1994) 'Equal opportunities in the secondary school curriculum in Scotland, 1977-91', *British Educational Research Journal*, vol 20, no 4.

Croxford, L. and McPherson, A. (1992) *School leavers in Glasgow and its areas of regeneration*, A report to the Glasgow Development Agency by the Centre for Educational Sociology at the University of Edinburgh, Edinburgh.

Crozier, G. (1997) 'Empowering the powerful: A discussion of the interrelation of government policies and consumerism with social class factors and the impact of this upon parent interventions in their children's schooling', *British Journal of Sociology of Education*, vol 18, no 2.

Cullingford, C. (1996) (ed) *Parents, education and the state*, Cambridge: Cambridge University Press.

Day, C., van Veen, D., and Walraven, G. (1997) *Children and youth at risk and urban education, research, policy and practice*, Leuven: EERA and Garant.

Deceulaer, M., van Leeuwen, K. and Verhofstadt-Denève, L. (1995) *Onderzoek naar leereffecten, leerling-en centrumkenmerken in het deeltijels, beroepssecundair onderwijs*, Gent:Vakgroep ontwikkelingspychologie R.U. Gent.

De Graaf, P.M. and Ganzeboom, H.B.G. (1993) 'Family background and educational attainment in the Netherlands for the 1891–1960 birth cohorts', in Y. Shavit and H.P. Blossfeld (eds) *Persistent inequality: Changing educational attainment in thirteen countries*, Boulder: Westview Press.

De Winter, L., Dierynck, R., Gommers, E., Meeusen, S., van de Velde, J., Verhesschen, P., van den Berghe, R., and Smeyers, P. (1997) *OVGB: een uniek samenspel met vele partners. Evaluatie van het onderwijsvoorrangsgebiedenbeleid in Limburg*, Leuven: Centrum voor Onderwijsbeleid en Vernieuwing.

De Wit, W. and Dekkers, H. (1996) *(G)een goed voorbereide start?*, Nijmegen: ITS.

Deem, R (1988) 'The Great Education Reform Bill – some issues and implications', *Journal of Education Policy*, vol 2, no 3, pp 181-9.

Delhaxhe, A. (1989) 'Early childhood care and education in Belgium', in Olmsted, P.P. and Weikart, D.P. (eds) *How nations serve young children*, Ypsilanti, Michigan: High/Scope Press.

Den Boer, K. (1995) "Weer Samen Naar School" – a national programme for primary and special schools' in C. O'Hanlon (ed) *Inclusive education in Europe*, London: David Fulton.

Denys, J. (1987) *Studiekosten in het secundair onderwijs*, Leuven: HIVA.

Department of Education (1966) *Investment in education*, Dublin: Stationery Office.

Department of Education (1992) *Education for a changing world: Green Paper on Education*, Dublin: Stationery Office.

Department of Education (1994) *School attendance/truancy report*, Dublin: Department of Education.

Department of Education (1995) *Charting our education future*, White Paper on Education, Dublin: Stationery Office.

Department of Education (1996a) *Tuarascáil staitistiúil 1994/95*, Dublin: Stationery Office.

Department of Education (1996b) *Junior certificate elementary programme: Guidelines for schools*, Dublin: Department of Education.

Department of Education (1998) *Compulsory education monitoring instrument*, Brussels: Flemish Community, Department of Education.

Department of Education and Science (1978) *Special education needs*, The Warnock Report, London: HMSO.

Department of Education and Science (1991) 'Children and Youth at Risk', *Seminar on Children and Youth at Risk*, OECD/CERI.

Department of Health (1995) *Child protection: Messages from research*, London: HMSO.

Derriks, M., Jungbluth, P., de Kat, E., and van Langen, A. (1997) *Risicoleerlingen in het basisonderwijs*, De Lien: Academisch Boeken Centrum.

de Vries, I.E.M. and Heere, F.A.P.M. (1993) *Kosten en baten van het leerlingwezen bij bedrivjen*, Den Haag: OSA.

Dias, E.L. (1989) *Em busca do sucesso escolar – uma perspectiva, um estudo, uma proposta*, Lisbon: Livros Horizonte.

Ditch J., Barnes, H., Bradshaw, J., and Kilkey, M. (1998) *A synthesis of national family policies 1996*, Brussels: European Commission.

Domingos, A.M. (1989) 'Influence of the social context of the school on the teacher's pedagogic practice', *British Journal of Sociology of Education*, vol 3, no 10, pp 351-66.

Douterlungne, M. (1994) *Dag school! Een onderzoek naar het voortijdig schoolverlaten in de tweede graad van het beroepssecundair onderwijs*, Leuven: Hoger Instituut voor de Arbeid.

Douterlungne, M., Nijsmans I., van de Velde, V. (eds) (1997) *Toekomstgerichte reflectie over de deeltijdse leerplicht*, Leuven and Apeldoorn: Garant.

Downes, T.A. and Pogue, T.F. (1994) 'Adjusting school aid formulas for the higher cost of educating disadvantaged students', *National Tax Journal*, vol 1, no 47, pp 89-110.

Dronkers, J. (1992) 'Komt de afname van het belang van het sociaal milieu in het onderwijs door vergroting van onderwijsdeelname of door meritoscratisering?', *Mens en Maatschappij*, no 67, pp 56-69.

Dronkers, J. (1995) 'The existence of parental choice in the Netherlands', *Educational Policy*, vol 9, no 3 (September), pp 227-43.

Dronkers, J., and Kerckhoff, A. (1990) 'Sociaal milieu, taalvaardigheid en schoolsuccess bij allochtonen, dialect en standaardtaalsprekers', *Sociologische Gids*, vol 37, no 5, pp 304-19.

Dronkers, J. and Schijf, H. (1984) *Neighbourhoods, schools and individual attainment*, International Sociological Association.

Dronkers, J. and Schijf, H. (1986) 'Neighbourhoods, schools and individual attainment', in A.C. Kerckhoff (ed) *Research in sociology of education and socialisation*, Greenwich, CT: JAI Press.

DSW-Deutsches Studentenwerk (1997) *Current developments in the educational assistance systems in Western Europe in connection with the family burden equalisation systems*, May, p 235, Bonn.

Duncan, G.J., Brooks-Gunn, J., and Klebanov, P.K. (1994) 'Economic deprivation and early childhood development', *Child Development*, no 65, pp 296-318.

Dyson, A. (1997) 'Social and educational disadvantage: Reconnecting special needs education', *British Journal of Special Education*, vol 24, no 4 (December).

Echols, F.H. and Willms, J.D. (1995) 'Reasons for school choice in Scotland', *Journal of Educational Policy*, vol 10, no 2, pp 143-56.

Echols, F., McPherson, A., and Willms, J. (1990) 'Choice among state and private schools in Scotland', *Journal of Educational Policy*, no 5, pp 207-22.

Edwards, D. and Mercer, N. (1987) *Common knowledge. The development of understanding in the classroom*, London: Methuen.

Egan, O. and Hegarty, M. (1984) *An evaluation of the Youth Encounter Project*, Dublin: Educational Research Centre.

Ehrenberg, R.G. and Sherman, D.R. (1987) 'Employment while in college, academic achievement and post-college outcomes: A summary of results', *Journal of Human Resources*, vol 1, no 22, pp 1-23.

Eimers, T. (1992) 'Ondersteuning bij het schoolgaan. De verlengde schooldag tegen voortijdig schoolverlaten', *Vernieuwing: Tijdschrift voor onderwijs en opvoeding*, vol 5, no 51.

Eimers, T. (1995) *Een vangnet van strohalmen. Opvang- en preventieprojecten voor voortijdig schoolverlaters in regionaal perspectief*, Nijmegen: ITS.

Eimers, T. and Moor, G. (1995) *Armoedebestrijding in Nederland*, Nijmegen: ITS.

Eimers, T. and Hövels, B. (1997) *Cursus sociale wetenschappen: vroegtijdig schoolverlaten, hoofdstuk 1*, Heerlen: Open Universiteit.

Entreculturas (1992) *Escola e sociedade multicultural*, Lisbon: Ministério da Educação.

Erikson, R. (1996) 'Explaining change in educational inequality – economic security and school reforms', in R. Erikson and J.O. Jonson (eds) *Can education be equalised? The Swedish case in comparative perspective*, Boulder: Westview Press.

Erikson, R. and Jonsson, J.O. (1996) *Can education be equalised? The Swedish case in comparative perspective*, Boulder: Westview Press.

ESF Programme Evaluation Unit (1996) *Early school leavers provision*, Dublin: ESF Evaluation Unit.

ESF Programme Evaluation Unit (1997) *Preventive actions in education*, Dublin: ESF Evaluation Unit.

ESRI (various years) Annual School Leavers' Survey, Dublin: ESRI.

Essen, J., Lambert, L., and Head, J. (1976) *School attainment of children who have been in care*, The National Child Development Study.

Esteves, A.J. (1993) 'Família, fratria e escolarização', in *Estruturas sociais e desenvolvimento, Actas do 2° Congresso Português de Sociologia, Fragmentos*, Lisbon: pp 275-95.

Esteves, M.J.B. (1993) 'Jovens sem a escolaridade obrigatória – que formação?' in *Estruturas sociais e desenvolvimento, Actas do 2° Congresso Português de Sociologia, Fragmentos*, Lisbon: pp 317-35.

European Commission (1995a) *Kerncijfers op onderwijsgebied in Europese Unie*, Luxembourg: Office for Official Publications of the European Communities.

European Commission (1995b) *Teaching and learning – towards the learning society*, White Paper on education and training, Luxembourg: Office for Official Publications of the European Communities.

European Commission (1996a) *Employment in Europe 1996*, Luxembourg: Office for Official Publications of the European Communities.

European Commission, DG V, MISSOC (1996b) *Social protection in the member states of the European Union: Situation on the 1st of July 1995 and evolution*, Luxembourg: Office for Official Publications of the European Communities.

European Commission (1999) *Joint Employment Report 1999*, Brussels: Directorate General Employment and Social Affairs.

European Commission (1997) *Eurydice Unit, The role of parents in the education systems of the European Union*, Luxembourg: Office for Official Publications of the European Communities.

European Commission, DG XXII (1997) *Getting on with training*, Strategical dossier, Brussels.

European Social Fund Programme Evaluation Unit (1996) *Evaluation report on early school leavers provision*, Dublin.

Eurostat (1996) *Europe in figures*, Luxembourg: Office for Official Publications of the European Communities.

Eurostat (1997a) 'Poverty and income distribution in the Europe of 12 in 1993', *Statistics in focus: Populations and social conditions*, no 6, Luxembourg: EUROSTAT/Directorate of Social Statistics.

Eurostat (1997b) *Youth in the European Union. From education to working life*, Luxembourg: Office for Official Publications of the European Communities.

Eurydice (1994a) *Measures to combat failure at school: A challenge for the construction of Europe*, Luxembourg: Office for Official Publications of the European Communities.

Eurydice (1994b) *Pre-school and primary education in the EC*, Luxembourg: Office for Official Publications of the European Communities.

Eurydice (1997) *A decade of reforms at compulsory education level in the European Union*, Luxembourg: Office for Official Publications of the European Communities.

Eurydice, Cedefop (1995) *Structures of the education and initial training systems in the European Union*, Luxembourg: Office for Official Publications of the European Communities.

Eurydice Eurybase (1996a) *The education system in Spain*, http://www.eurydice.org/eurybase/files/SPEN/SPEN78-81htm

Eurydice Eurybase (1996b) *The education system in France*, http://www.eurydice.org/eurybase/files/FREN/FREN105-114.htm

Eurydice Eurybase (1996c) *The education system in Italy*, http://www.eurydice.org/eurybase/files/ITEN/ITEN72-77.htm

Eurydice Eurybase (1996d) *The education system in Finland*, http://www.eurydice.org/eurybase/files/FIEN/FIEN73-79.htm

Eurydice Eurybase (1996e) *The education system in the Netherlands*, http//www.eurydice.org/eurybase/files/NLVO/NLVO40.htm

Felix, C. (1991) *Waardering van het OPSTAP-programma*, Amsterdam: SCO.

Fernández Enguita, M. (1987) *Reforma educativa, desigualdad social e inercia institucional*, Barcelona: Laia.

Fernández Enguita, M. (1990) *Juntos pero no revueltos. Ensayos en torno a la reforma de la educación*, Madrid: De. Aprendizaje Visor.

Ferrández, A. and Sarramona, J. (1977) *La educación. Constantes y problemática actual*, Barcelona: Ediciones Ceac.

Ferrão, J. and das Neves, A.O. (1992) *Caracterização regional dos factores de abandono escolar nos 2º e 3º ciclos do ensino básico*, Lisbon: Ministério da Educação.

Ferreiro, E. and Teberosky, A. (1979) *Los sistemas de escritura en el desarrollo del nido*, Mexico: Siglo XXI.

Field, J. (1991) 'Competency and the pedagogy of labour', *Studies in the Education of Adults*, vol 1, no 23.

Finnan, C. (1996) *Accelerated schools in action. Lessons from the field*, Newbury Park, California: Corwin Press.

Flecha, R. (1994) 'Las nuevas desigualdades educativas', in M. Castells, R. Flecha, P. Freire, H. Giroux, D. Macedo, and P. Willis, *Nuevas perspectivas críticas en educación*, Barcelona: Paidos Educador.

Fleming, M., Figueiredo, E., Maia, Â., and Sousa, A. (1987) 'Insucesso escolar e auto-avaliação na adolescência', *Psicologia*, no 3, pp 289-97.

Fontes, P.J. and Kellaghan, T. (1977) 'Incidence and correlates of illiteracy in Irish primary schools', *Irish Journal of Education*, no 11, pp 5-20.

Formosinho, J. and Alves Pinto, C. (1987) 'A atribuição causal do insucesso – o posicionamento de uma amostra d eprofessores', *Psicologia*, no 3, pp 259-64.

Förster, M.F. (1994) *The effects of transfers on low incomes among non-elderly families*, France: OECD.

Foucault, M. (1977) *Discipline and punishment*, London: Penguin.

Freinet C. and Salengros, R. (1960) *Moderniser l'école*, Cannes: Éditions de l'École Moderne.

Fulcher, G. (1989) *Disabling policies? A comparative approach to education policy and disability*, London: Falmer Press.

Fuller, W.C., Manski, C.F., and Wise, D.A. (1983) 'The impact of the basic educational grant program on college enrolment', in E. Helpman (ed) *Social policy evaluation. An economic perspective*, pp 123-42.

Funes, J. (1997) *Les aules-taller. Experiències educatives amb joves adolescents exclosos*, Barcelona: Edt Ice-Horsori – Fundació de Serveis de Cultura Popular.

Gal, R. (1961) 'Où en est la pédagogie' (Paris: Buchet-Chastel, pp 71-8), reprinted in P. Juif and L. Legrand (1980) *Textes de pédagogie pour l'école d'aujourd'hui. Les grands orientations de la pédagogie contemporaine*, Paris: F. Nathan.

Gamoran, A. (1996a) 'Curriculum standardization and equality of opportunity in Scottish secondary education', *Sociology of Education*, no 69, pp 1-21.

Gamoran, A. (1996b) *Improving opportunities for disadvantaged student: Changes in S4 examination results, 1984-1990*, Edinburgh: Centre for Educational Sociology, University of Edinburgh.

García, C. (1998) 'Integration in Spain: A critical view', *European Journal of Special Needs Education*, vol 13, no 1.

Garner, C.L. and Raudenbush, S.W. (1991) 'Neighbourhood effects on educational attainment. A multilevel analysis', *Sociology of Education*, vol 64 (October).

Garner, R. (1990) 'When children and adults do not use learning strategies: Toward a theory of settings', *Review of Educational Research*, no 60, pp 517-30.

Garrett, P., Ng'andu, N., and Ferron, J. (1994) 'Poverty experiences of young children and the quality of their home environments', *Child Development*, no 65, pp 331-45.

Geelen, H., van Unen, A., and Walraven, G. (1994) *Services integration for children and youth at risk in the Netherlands*, The Hague: Sardes.

Gentile, M. (1991) 'Subjects at risk of "dropping out": Definition, detection, problems', in *Seminar: Project Children and Youth at Risk*, Palermo: OECD/CERI.

GEP/ME (1992) *Análise Conjuntural 90*, Lisbon: Ministério da Educação.

Ghesquière, P., de Fever, F., and van Hove, G. (1996) *Op weg naar inclusief onderwijs!? Elementen voor de discussie rond de hervorming van het buitengewoon onderwijs in Vlaanderen in functie van de internationale tendens tot integratie*, Brussels: Flemish Education Council.

Ghesquière, P., Ruijssenaars, W., Hellinckx, W., Grietens, H., and Luyckx, E. (1995) *Leerproblemen in het gewoon lager onderwijs: onderkenning en opvang van leerlingen met leerproblemen in de eigen school*, Leuven: Afdeling Orthopedagogiek.

Gillborn, D., Nixon, J., and Rudduck, J. (1991) *Teaching children at risk of educational failure. The challenge for secondary schools*, England: Qualitative and Quantitative Studies in Education Research Group, University of Sheffield.

Gilly, M. (1983) 'Psychologie social de l'education', in S. Moscovici (ed) *Introduction a la Psychologie Social*, Paris: F. Nathan.

Goffinet, S. and Van Damme, D. (1990) *Functional anel-fabetisme in Belgie*, Brussels: Koning Boudewijn-stichting.

Goldthorpe, J.H. (1996a) 'Class analysis and the reorientation of class theory: The case of persisting differentials in educational attainment', *British Journal of Sociology*, vol 3, no 47, pp 481-512.

Goldthorpe, J.H. (1996b) 'Problems of meritocracy', in R. Erikson and J.O. Jonsson (eds) *Can education be equalised?*, Boulder: Westview Press, pp 255-87.

Gomby, D.S. et al (1995) 'Long-term outcomes of early childhood programs: analysis and recommendations', *The Future of Children*, vol 3, no 5, pp 6-24.

Gonzalez, G., Gol, T., and Nogueras, A. (1991) 'La historia personal. Escola Pública Coves d'en Cimany', *Cuadernos de Pedagogia*, no 174, pp 51-3.

Gordon, J. (1990) *Summary report on compulsory education and vocational training qualifications*, European Education and Social Policy Institute.

Goulder, J., Simpson, M., and Tuson, J. (1994) 'The 5-14 Development Programme in Scottish secondary schools – the first phase', *Curriculum Journal*, vol 1, no 5, pp 69-81.

Grácio, R. (1986) 'A educação, dez anos depois – que transformações, que reforma, que continuidades?', *Revista Crítica de Ciências Sociais*, no 18-20, pp 153-82.

Grácio, S. (1986) *Política educativa como tecnologia social - as reformas do ensino técnico de 1948 e 1983*, Lisbon: Livros Horizonte.

Grácio, S. (1987) 'Variáveis escolares e aproveitamento escolar no primário', *Cadernos de Ciências Sociais*, no 5, pp 51-64.

Grignon, C. (1990) 'La escuela y las culturas populares', *Archipiúlago* (Madrid), no 6, pp 15-19.

Gumuzio, E. (1998) 'El papel de la administraciõn en las comunidades de aprendizaje', *Aula de Innovación Educativa*, no 72, pp 52-3.

Guo, G., Brooks-Gunn, J., and Mullan-Harris, K. (1996) 'Parents' labor force attachment and grade retention among urban black children', *Sociology of Education*, no 69, pp 217-36.

Hagenaars, A.J.M., de Vos, K., and Zaidi, M.A. (1994) *Poverty statistics in the late 1980s. Research based on micro-data*, in *Series 3C*, Eurostat, Luxembourg: Office for Official Publications of the European Communities.

Hall, S., Kay, I., and Struthers, S. (1992) *The experience of partnership in education*, Stanley Publisher.

Hallett, C. and Murray, C., with Jamieson, J. and Veith, B. (1998) 'Deciding in children's interests', Social Work Research Findings no 25, Edinburgh: The Scottish Office.

Hallinan, M. (1987) 'Ability grouping and student learning', in M. Hallinan (ed) *The social organization of schools*, New York: Plenum Press.

Halsey, A., Heath, A. and Ridge, J. (1980) *Origins and destinations*, Oxford: Clarendon Press.

Hannan, D., Hövels, B., van den Berg, S., and White, M. (1995) '"Early leavers" from education and training in Ireland, the Netherlands and the United Kingdom', *European Journal of Education*, vol 30, no 3 (September).

Hannan, D.F. (1996) *Adapt/Emploi Report on Youthstart in Ireland*, Dublin: ESRI.

Hannan, D.F. and Boyle, M. (1987) *Schooling decisions*, Dublin: ESRI.

Hannan, D.F., Raffe, D., and Smyth, E. (1996a) 'Cross-national research on school to work transitions: An analytical framework', in R. Breen Werquin and J. Planes (eds) *Youth transitions in Europe: Theories and evidence*, Marseille: Céreq.

Hannan, D.F., Smyth, E., McCullagh, J., O'Leary, R., and McMahon, D. (1996b) *Co-education and gender equality: Exam performance, stress and personal development*, Dublin: ESRI/Oak Tree Press.

Harlen, W. (1996) *Four years of change in education 5-14*, Edinburgh: Scottish Council for Research in Education.

Harlen, W., and Malcolm, H. (1994) 'Putting the curriculum and assessment guidelines in place in Scottish primary schools', *Curriculum Journal*, vol 1, no 5, pp 55-67.

Harmon, C. and Walker, I. (1993) 'Schooling and earnings in the UK: Evidence from the ROSLA experiment', *Economic and Social Review*, vol 1, no 25, pp 77-93.

Haveman, R., Wolfe, B., and Spaulding, J. (1991) 'Childhood events and circumstances influencing high school completion', *Demography*, no 28, pp 133-57.

Hayes, N., O'Flaherty, J., and Kernan, M. (1997) *A window on early education in Ireland*, Dublin: DIT.

Hedebouw, G. (1997) *Uit de schoolse boot. Schoolverzuim en voortijdige uitval in het secundair onderwijs*, Leuven: HIVA/Comité voor Bijzondere Jeugdzorg.

Heginbotham, C. (1993) 'User empowerment in welfare services' in N. Thomas, N. Deakin, and J. Doling (eds) *Learning from innovation: Housing and social welfare in the 1990s*, Birmingham: Birmingham University Press.

Heid, C. (1991) 'The dilemma of Chapter 1 program improvement', *Educational Evaluation and Policy Analysis*, no 13, pp 394-8.

Hellinckx, W. and de Munter, A. (1990) *Voorzieningen voor jongeren met psychosociale problemen. Onderzoek naar residentiële voorzieningen, diensten voor begeleid zelfstandig wonen en dagcentra*, Leuven and Amersfoort: ACCO.

Hernandez, F. and Ventura, M. (1992) *La organización del curriculum por proyectos de trabajo. El conocimiento es un calidoscopio*, Colección Materiales de Innovación Educativa, Barcelona: Edt Gra–ICE de la Universitat de Barcelona.

Hirsch, D. (OECD) (1997a) (CERI) Centre for Educational Research and Innovation, *Parents as partners in schooling*, Paris: OECD.

Hirschman, A. (1970) *Exit, voice and loyalty*, Cambridge, Massachusetts: Harvard University Press.

Hirst, M. and Baldwin, S. (1994) *Unequal opportunities: Growing up disabled*, London: HMSO.

HMI (1996) *Attendance and absence in Scottish schools 1995-96*, Edinburgh: Scottish Office Education Audit.

Holland, S. (1979) *Rutland Street*, Oxford: Pergamon Press.

Hövels, B. (1993) *Startkwalificatie tussen individu en arbeidsmarkt*, Bunnik: A&O.

Hövels, B. (1996) 'Early school leaving: The perspective of qualification and the labour market', *School-Related Problems, International Conference on Youth at Risk*, Noordwijkerhout: Stichting Jeugdinformatie Nederland.

Hövels, B., van Kuijk, J. and Teerling, L. (1996) *Strategies to improve young people's access to and progress within initial vocational training*, Amsterdam: Max Goote Kenniscentrum.

Hover, C. (1995) *Risicodoelgroepen in de eerste fase VO. Achtergrondstudie ten behoeve van de beleidsreactie op het advies 'Recht doen aan verscheidenheid'*, Zoetemeer: Ministrie van Onderwijs, Cultuur & Wetenschappen.

Hubbard, M.M. (1992) 'School leavers with multiple disabilities: An exploratory story of the issues and problems relating to the planning and provision of formal post-school services', Unpublished PhD thesis, Stirling: Stirling University.

Hurell, P. and Evans, J. (1996) 'Strategic, operational and field levels: The theoretical and practical dimensions of integrated services', *Successful Services for our Children and Families at Risk*, Paris: OECD, pp 87-98.

Husen, T. (ed) (1967) *International study of achievement in mathematics: A comparison of twelve countries*, New York: Wiley.

IARD (1998) *Dropping out and secondary education*, Milan: IARD.

Ikastola Publikaren Karmengo Ama (1995) 'Ikastetxearen Hezkuntz – Proiektua', Proyecto Educativo de Centro, Internal document, Pasaia (Guipuzcoa).

INEM (1995) *Información sobre Mercado de Trabajo: 1994*, Madrid: Instituto Nacional de Empleo, Servicio de Publicaciones.

Inspectie van het Onderwijs (1997) *Onderwijs over het jaar 1996*, The Hague: SDU.

International Educational Association (IEA) (1991) *Reading literacy study*.

INTO (1994) *Poverty and educational disadvantage*, Dublin: Irish National Teachers' Organisation.

Ishida, H., Müller, W., and Ridge, J.M. (1995) 'Class origin, class destination and education: A cross-national study of ten industrial nations', *American Journal of Sociology*, no 101, pp 145-93.

Iturra, R. (1990a) *Fugirás da escola para trabalhar a terra*, Lisbon: Escher.

Iturra, R. (1990b) *A construção social do insucesso escolar – memória e aprendizagem social em Vila Ruiva*, Lisbon: Escher.

Jacobs, van der Vegt, J. van der Grinten, M. and Appelhof (1995) *Achterstandbestrijding met perspectief*, Utrecht: ISOR.

Jencks, C., Smith, M., Bane, M., Cohen, D., Gintis, H., Keynes, B. and Michelson, S. (1972) *Inequality: A reassessment of the effects of family and schooling in America*, New York, NY: Basic Books.

Jessup, G. (1991) *Outcomes: NVQs and the emerging model of education and training*, London: Falmer Press.

Johnson, D.W., Johnson, R.T., and Maruyama, G. (1983) 'Interdependence and interpersonal attraction among heterogeneous and homogeneous individuals: A theoretical formulation and a meta-analysis of the research', *Review of Educational Research*, vol 1, no 53, pp 5-54.

Jones, J.D., Vanfossen, B.E., and Ensminger, M.E. (1995) 'Individual and organizational predictors of high school track placement', *Sociology of Education*, no 68, pp 287-300.

Jonsson, J.O. (1993) 'Persisting inequalities in Sweden', in Y. Shavit and H.P. Blossfeld (eds) *Persistent inequality: Changing educational attainment in thirteen countries*, Boulder: Westview Press.

Juif, P. and Legrand, L. (1980) *Textes de pédagogie pour l'école d'aujourd'hui. Les grands orientations de la pédagogie contemporaine*, Paris: F. Nathan.

Jungbluth, P. (1997) *Verzeiling, segregatie en schoolprestaties*, Ubbergen: Uitg Tandem Felix.

Justel, M. and Martinez Lazero, U. (1981) 'Sobre el caracter selectivo de las pruebas de acceso a la Universidad', *Revista Espanola de Investigaciones Sociologicas*, no 15, pp 115-32.

Karsten, S. (1994) 'Policy on ethnic segregation in a system of choice: The case of the Netherlands', *Journal of Educational Policy*, vol 9, no 3, pp 211-25.

Kellaghan, T. (1977) *The evaluation of an intervention programme for disadvantaged children*, Slough: NFER.

Kellaghan, T. and Brugha, D. (1972) 'The scholastic performance of children in a disadvantaged area', *Irish Journal of Education*, no 6, pp 133-43.

Kellaghan, T. and Greaney, B.J. (1993) *The educational development of students following participation in a preschool programme in a disadvantaged area*, Dublin: Educational Research Centre.

Kellaghan, T., Weir, S., Óh Uallacháin, S., and Morgan, M. (1995) *Educational disadvantage in Ireland*, Dublin: Department of Education/Combat Poverty Agency.

Kennedy, M.M., Jung, R.K. and Orland, M. E. (1986) *Poverty, achievement and the distinction of compulsory education services*, Washington, DC: Office of Educational Research and Improvement, US Department of Education.

Kerckhoff, A.C. (1993) *Diverging pathways: Social structure and career deflections*, Cambridge: Cambridge University Press.

Kerckhoff, A.C., Fogelman, K., and Manlove, J. (1997) 'Staying ahead: The middle class and school reform in England and Wales', *Sociology of Education*, no 70, pp 19-35.

Kirp, D. (1982) 'Professionalisation as policy choice: British special education in comparative perspective', *World Politics XXXIV*, no 2, pp 137-74.

Kloas, P.W. (1996) 'New approaches to youth training and employment', *Youth Unemployment, International Conference on Youth at Risk*, Noordwijkerhout: Stichting Jeugdinformatie Nederland and Flemish Ministry.

Kloprogge, J. (1991) *Reducing educational disadvantages. Developments in the educational priority policy program in the Netherlands*, The Hague: Institute for Educational Research.

Kolvin, I., Miller, F.J.W., Scott, D.M., Gatzanis, S.R.M., and Fleeting, M. (1990) *Continuities of deprivation? The Newcastle 1,000 family study*, Aldershot: Avebury, p 416.

Laevers, F. (1992) *Ervaringsgericht werken in de basisschool*, Leuven: Centrum voor Ervaringsgericht Onderwijs.

Landelijk Platform voor scholing en opvang (1997) *Wachters aan de poort*, Zevenbergen: LPS.

Lang, K. and Kropp, D. (1986) 'Human capital versus sorting: Effects of compulsory attendance laws', *Quarterly Journal of Economics*, vol 3, no 101, pp 524-609.

Lapassade, G. (1971) 'L'auto-gestion pedagogique', in P. Juif and L. Legrand (1980), *Textes de pédagogie pour l'école d'aujourd'hui. Les grands orientations de la pédagogie contemporaine*, Paris: F. Nathan.

Lauder, H. (1988) 'Traditions of socialism and educational policy', in H. Lauder and P. Brown (eds) *Education in search of a future*, London: Falmer Press.

Lavado, J., Morgado, M.J., and Audicana, J.C. (1998) 'Función del asesor en los proyectos de formación: Transformación del centro en comunidades de aprendizaje', *Aula de Innovación educativa*, no 72, pp 54-5.

Leclerq, J.M. (1993) *L'enseignement secondaire obligatoire en Europe*, Paris: Edt La Documentation Française.

Legrand, L. (1971) 'Une méthode active pour l'école d'aujourd'hui' (Neuchâtel: Delachaus et Niestlés, , pp 15-18 and 21-2) in P. Juif and L. Legrand (1980) *Textes de pédagogie pour l'école d'aujourd'hui. Les grands orientations de la pédagogie contemporaine*, Paris: F. Nathan.

LeTendre, M.J. (1991) 'The continuing evolution of a federal role in compensatory education', *Educational Evaluation and Policy Analysis*, vol 4, no 13, pp 328-34.

Levin, H. (1987) 'New schools for the disadvantaged', *Teacher Education Quarterly*, vol 14, no 4, pp 60-83.

Levin, H. (1988) *School success for students at risk. Analysis and recommendations of the Council of Chief State School Officers*, San Francisco: Harcourt Brace Jovanovich.

Levin, H. (1989) *Accelerated schools: A new strategy for at-risk students*, Accelerated School Project, California: CERAS, School of Education, Stanford University.

Levin, H.M. (1989) 'Economics of investment in educationally disadvantaged students', *American Economic Review*, vol 2, no 79, pp 52-6.

Levin, H.M. (1989) 'Financing the education of at-risk students', *Educational Evaluation and Policy Analysis*, vol 2, no 79, pp 47-60.

Levin, H.M. and Kelley, C. (1994) 'Can education do it alone?', *Economics of Education Review*, vol 2, no 13, pp 97-108.

Litt, J. (1980) *Origine sociale et scolarité*, Louvain-La-Neuve: UCL.

Lothian Regional Council (1995; 1996; 1997) *Deprivation, early intervention and the prevention of reading difficulties*, Lothian: Lothian Regional Council, Department of Education.

Lubeck, S. (1995) 'Nation as context: Comparing childcare systems across nations', *Teachers College Record*, vol 3, no 96, pp 467-91.

Luna, F. and Jaussi, M.J. (1998) 'C.P. Ramón Bajo de Vitoria-Gasteiz. Una comunidad de aprendizaje', *Cuadernos de Pedagogia*, no 270, pp 36-44.

Lynch, K. (1989) *The hidden curriculum*, London: Falmer Press.

Lynch, K. and O'Riordan, C. (1996) *Social class, inequality and higher education*, Dublin: Equality Studies Centre, University College Dublin.

Lynch, P. (1995) 'Integration in Ireland: Policy and practice' in C. O'Hanlon (ed) *Inclusive education in Europe*, London: David Fulton.

Macbeth, A. (1998) 'Home + school = learning', *Times Educational Supplement*, 27 February 1998.

MacLean, C. (1994) 'The theory and practice of equal opportunities in Scotland', *Scottish Affairs*, no 6, pp 36-51.

Malcolm, H. and Thorpe, G. (1994) *Attending school: How much does it matter?*, Edinburgh: SCRE.

Manasero, M.A. and Vázques, A. (1993) 'La atrilrición causal lomo deermiinante de las expectativas', *Psicothema*, vol 7, pp 361-76.

Mare, R.D. (1980) 'Social background and school continuation decisions', *Journal of the American Statistical Association*, vol 75, no 370, pp 295-305.

Martínez, R., Marques, R., and Souta, L. (1994) 'Expectations about parents in education in Portugal and Spain', in A. Macbeth and B. Ravn (eds) *Expectations about parents in education – European perspectives*.

Martínez, R., Mora, J.G., and Vila, L. (1993) 'Educación, actividad y empleo en las comunidades autónomas españolas', *Revista de Estudios Regionales*, no 36, pp 299-334.

Mayer, R. (1996) 'Facilities for the assistance of socially disadvantaged pupils', *School-related problems, International Conference on Youth at Risk*, Noordwijkerhout: Stichting Jeugdinformatie Nederland and Dutch Ministry.

McCoy, S. and Hannan, D.F. (1995) *Early school leavers: Reform of the Junior Certificate, educational achievement and employment chances*, Dublin: ESRI Working Paper no 67.

McCoy, S. and Whelan, B.J. (1996) *The economic status of school leavers 1993–1995*, Dublin: ESRI/Department of Enterprise and Employment/Department of Education.

McDonough, J.T. and Jordan, K.F. (1992) 'State funding for at-risk programmes and services: Opinions and practices', in P. Anthony and S.L. Jacobsen (eds) *Helping at-risk students. What are the educational and financial costs?*, Newbury Park, California: Corwin Press, pp 93-135.

McKenna, A. (1988) *Childcare and equal opportunities*, Dublin: Employment Equality Agency.

McPherson, A. (1973) 'A sociology of ancient Scottish universities' in R. Brown (ed) *Knowledge, education and cultural change*, Papers in the sociology of education (contributed to the Annual Conference of the British Sociological Association held at the University of Durham, 7-10 April 1970), London: Tavistock Publications.

MEC (1992) *Las desigualdades en la educación en España*, Madrid: CIDE-MEC.

MEC (1996) *Estadística de la Enseñanza en España. 1993/94*, Madrid: MEC.

MEC (1996) *Catálogo de investigaciones educativas del CIDE: 1983-1994*, Madrid: MEC.

Meijnen, G.W. (1987) 'From six to twelve: Different school careers in primary education', *Zeitschrift für Sozialisationsforschung und Erziehungssoziologie*, vol 7, no 3, pp 209-25.

Merino, R. and Planas, J. (1996) 'Els itineraris post-obligatoris dels joves i la reforma educativa', *Temps d'Educacio*, no 6.

Mialaret, G. (1966) 'Education nouvelle et monde moderne' (Paris: PUF, pp 7-15), in P. Juif and L. Legrand (1980), *Textes de pédagogie pour l'école d'aujourd'hui. Les grands orientations de la pédagogie contemporaine*, Paris: F. Nathan.

Ministerie van de Vlaamse Gemeenschap (1991) *Education in Belgium: The diverging paths*, Brussels: OECD.

Ministry of Education, Culture and Science (1994) 'Regional reporting and coordination function in the fight against early school leaving', in *Explanation of OCW rules*, Zoetermeer: OCW, no 18, pp 32-3.

Ministry of Education, Culture and Science (1996a) *Discussion memorandum, RMC Policy Debate held on 26 April 1996*, Zoetermeer: Ministerie van Onderwijs, Cultuur & Wetenschappen.

Ministry of Education, Culture and Science (1996b) *Secondary education in figures*, Zoetermeer: Ministerie van Onderwijs, Cultuur & Wetenschappen.

Ministry of Education, Culture and Science (1998) *Kansen voor kinderen. Overzicht beleid fundemende educatie*, Zoetermeer: Ministerie van Onderwijs, Cultuur & Wetenschappen.

Mora, J.G. (1996) 'The demand for higher education in Spain', *European Journal of Education*, vol 3, no 31, pp 341-53.

Morais, A.M. (1992) *Socialização primária e prática pedagógica*, vol I, Lisbon: Calouste Gulbenkian Foundation.

Morais, A.M., Neves, I., Pestana Medeiros, A., Peneda, D., Fontinhas, F., and Antunes, H. (1993) *Socialização primária e prática pedagógica*, vol II, Lisbon: Calouste Gulbenkian Foundation.

Morais, A.M., Peneneda, D., and Medeiros, A. (1992) 'Discursos instrucional e regulador no ensino das ciências: influência de práticas pedagógicas no aproveitamento dos alunos,' *Revista de Educação*, vol II, no 2, pp 73-93.

Morais, A., Fontinhas, F., and Neves, I. (1992) 'Recognition and realisation rules in acquiring school science', *British Journal of Sociology of Education*, vol 13, no 2, pp 247-70.

Moreno, M. (1983) *La pedagogia operatoria. Un enfoque constructivista de la educación*, Cuadernos de Pedagogia, Barcelona: Laia.

Moreno, M. and Sastre, G. (1980) *Aprendizaje y desarrollo intelectual*, Barcelona: Gedisa.

Moss, P. (1990) 'Childcare in the European Communities 1985-1990', *Women of Europe Supplements*, Brussels: European Commission.

Mulder, L. (1996) *Meer voorrang, minder achterstand? Het onderwijsvoorrangsbeleid getoetst*, Nijmegen: ITS.

Müller, W. (1996) 'Class inequalities in educational outcomes: Sweden in comparative perspective', in R. Erikson and J.O. Jonsson (eds) *Can education be equalized?*, Boulder: Westview Press.

Munn, P. (1993) *Parents and schools*, London and New York: Routledge.

Munn, P. (1997) 'Devolved management of schools in practice', *SCRE Newsletter*, no 60, Spring.

Munn, P., Cullen, M.A., Johnstone, M. and Lloyd, G. (1997) *Exclusions and in-school alternatives*, Interchange No 47, Edinburgh: The Scottish Office, Education and Industry Department.

Munn, P. and Johnstone, M. (1992) *Truancy and attendance in Scottish secondary schools*, Edinburgh: Scottish Council for Research in Education.

Murphy, J. (1974) 'Teacher expectations and working-class underachievement', *British Journal of Sociology*, no 25, pp 326-44.

Murphy-Lawless, J. (1992) *The adequacy of income and family expenditure*, Dublin: Combat Poverty Agency.

NESF (1997) *Early school leavers and youth unemployment*, Dublin: National Economic and Social Forum.

Neves, I. (1992) 'Posicionamento da criança no contexto da socialização primária: Influência no aproveitamento escolar', *Revista de Educação*, vol II, no 2, pp 35-54.

Neves, I. and Morais, A.M. (1993) 'A orientação de codificação no contexto de socialização primária – implicações no (in)sucesso escolar', *Análise Social*, no 121, pp 267-307.

Neves, I. and Morais, A.M. (1996) 'Teorias de instrução na família e aproveitamento escolar', *Sociologia – Problemas e Práticas*, no 19, pp 127-64.

Nicaise, I. (1998) 'Actief arbeidsmarktbeleid: Plichten genoeg, tijd voor garanties', in *Nieuwsbrief Werkgelegenheid Arbeid Vorming*, no 1-2, pp 51-5.

Nicaise, I. (1999) *Poverty and human capital*, Aldershot: Ashgate.

Nicaise, I. et al (1995a) *Groupes faibles face au marché du travail: point de mire du Fonds Social Européen. Evaluation finale du Cadre communautaire d'appui belge (1990–1992) relatif aux objectifs 3 et 4*, Leuven: Hoger Instituut voor de Arbeid.

Nicaise, I., Bollens, J., Dawes, L., Laghaci, S., Thaulow, I., Vendié, M. and Wagner, A. (1995b) *Labour market programmes for the poor in Europe: Pitfalls and dilemmas – and how to avoid them*, Aldershot: Avebury.

Nicaise, I. and de Wilde, C. (1995) *Het zuraand van Damocles. Ohne gezinnen over de byzondene jengdzong*, Leuven/Apeldoorun: Garant, p 159.

Nicaise, I. and Douterlungne, M. (1990) *Alternating education: Its impact on the labour market entry of disadvantaged youth in Flanders (Belgium)*, Leuven: Hoger Instituut voor de Arbeid.

Nicaise, I. and Winters S. (1995) 'Studietoelagen en/of studieleningen?', *De Gids op Maatschappelijk Gebied*, vol 79, no 5, pp 415-26.

Nijsmans, I. and Nicaise, I. (1993) *De effectiviteit van de ESF-projecten in het Vlaams deeltijds onderwijs: Altenerend leren en brugprojecten. Ex-post evaluatie van de Vlaamse operationele programma's 1990-1992 met betrekking tot doelstelling 3-4*, Deelrapport 2, Leuven: HIVA.

Nisolle, N. and Vandenbosch, V. (1991) *Réussir contre toute attente ... Une étude exploratoire menée auprès d'élèves de 6ième année primaire, dont les familles émargeant au CPAS*, Mons: CERIS.

Nolan, B. and Whelan, C.T. (1996) *Resources, Deprivation and Poverty*, Oxford: Clarendon.

O'Hanlon, C. (1993) *Special integration in Europe*, London: David Fulton.

O'Hanlon C. (1995) *Inclusive education in Europe*, London: David Fulton.

OECD (1980) Centre for Educational Research and Innovation (CERI) *School and community, volume II*, Paris: OECD.

OECD (1983) *Compulsory schooling in a changing world*, Paris: OECD.

OECD (1994) Centre for Educational Research and Innovation (CERI) *School: A matter of choice*, Paris: OECD.

OECD (1995a) *Integrating students with special needs into mainstream schools*, Paris: OECD.

OECD (1995b) *Our children at risk*, Paris: OECD.

OECD (1996a) *Integrating services for children at risk, Denmark, France, Netherlands, Sweden, United Kingdom (England and Wales)*, Paris: OECD.

OECD (1996b) *Successful services for our children and families at risk*, Paris: OECD.

OECD (1997a) *Literacy skills for the knowledge society*, Paris: OECD.

OECD (1997b) *Education and equity in OECD, Education et Equité dans les Pays de L'OCDE*, Paris: OECD.

OECD (2000) *Education at a glance*, Paris: OECD.

Office for Standards in Education (1996) *The education of travelling children. A survey of educational provision for travelling children*, London: Her Majesty's Chief Inspector for Schools.

OFSTED (1997) *Standards and quality in education 1996/1997*, http://www/official-documents.co.uk/document/ofsted/ciar

Osaer, L. (1984) *Externe VSO-evaluaties*, Brussels: Licap, p 97.

Osborne, A. and Saint Claire, L. (1987) 'The ability and behaviour of children who have been in care or separated from their parents', *Early Child Development and Care*, vol 3, no 28.

Oyen E.S., Miller, M. and Syed, A. (1996) *Poverty: A global review. Handbook on international research*, Oslo: Scandinavian University Press.

Pais, I.S. (1993) 'Crianças de imigrantes em Portugal – oportunidades', *Estruturas sociais e desenvolvimento*, Lisbon: Actas do 2° Congresso Português de Sociologia, Fragmentos, pp 296-316.

Palacios, J. (1989) 'Childcare and early education in Spain', in P.P. Olmsted and D.P. Weikart (eds) *How nations serve young children*, Michigan: High/Scope Press.

Pastor, C. (1998) 'Integration in Spain: a critical review', *European Journal of Special Needs Education*, vol 13, no 1.

Paterson, H. (1983) 'Incubus and ideology: The development of secondary schooling in Scotland 1900-1936', in W. Humes and H. Paterson (eds) *Scottish future and Scottish education 1800-1900*, Edinburgh: John Donald.

Paterson, L. (1991) 'Socio-economic status and educational attainment: A multi-dimensional and multi-level study', *Evaluation and Research in Education*, vol 3, no 5.

Paterson, L. (1992) 'Social origins of underachievement amongst school leavers', in H. Maguiness (ed) *Educational opportunity: The challenge of underachievement and social deprivation*, Paisley: Paisley College.

Paterson, L. (1997a) *Education and social disadvantage*, From a talk at the conference 'Poverty: The real barrier to lifelong learning?', organised by the Scottish Community Education Council and *The Times Educational Supplement Scotland*, Glasgow (9 April 1997, RSAMD).

Paterson, L. (1997b) 'Individual autonomy and comprehensive education', *British Educational Research Journal*, vol 3, no 23.

Paterson, L. (1997c) 'Student achievement and educational change in Scotland 1980–1995', *Scottish Educational Review*, vol 1, no 29, pp 10-19.

Paterson, L. (1997d) 'Trends in higher education participation in Scotland', *Higher Education Quarterly*, vol 1, no 51, pp 29-48.

Paterson, L. and Raffe, D. (1995) 'Staying on in full-time education in Scotland 1985–1991', *Oxford Review of Education*, vol 21, no 1, pp 3-23.

Pedroso, P. (1991) 'Política educativa e modelos de escolarização em Portugal: A democratização do acesso ao sistema educativo e os perfis de formação', mimeo, Lisbon: Instituto de Ciências Sociais da Universidade de Lisboa.

Pedroso, P. (1993) *A formação profissional inicial – da diversificação de iniciativas à produção de um novo enquadramento*, Lisbon: Instituto de Ciências Sociais da Universidade de Lisboa.

Pedroso, P. (1997) *Formação e desenvolvimento rural*, Oeiras: Celta.

Phillips, D.A.,Voran, M., Kisker, E., Howes, C. and Whitebook, M. (1994) 'Child care for children in poverty: Opportunity or inequity?', *Child Development*, no 65, pp 472-92.

Pijl, S. and Scheepstra, J.M. (1996) 'Being part of the group: The position of pupils with Down's syndrome in Dutch regular schools', *European Journal of Special Needs Education*, vol 11, no 3.

Pijl, Y. and Pijl, S. (1998) 'Are pupils in special education too "special" for regular education?', *International Review of Education*, vol 44, no 1, pp 5-20.

Pinto, J.M. (1991) 'Escolarização, relação com o trabalho e práticas sociais', in S.R. Sroer (ed) *Educação, ciências sociais e realidade portuguesa*, Porto: Afrontamento.

Pires, E.L. (1987) *Lei de Bases do Sistema Educativo. Apresentação e comentários*, Rio Tinto: Asa.

Planas, J. (1986) 'La formación profesional en España: Evolución y balance', *Educacion y Sociedad*, no 5, pp 71-112.

Plowden, Lady B. (1967) *Speech to a meeting of the Richmond-upon-Thames Association for the advancement of State education*, Confederation for the Advancement of State Education.

Powney, J., Glissov, P., Hall, S. and Karlen, W. (1995) *We are getting them ready for life: Provision for pre-fives in Scotland*, Scotland: Scottish Council for Research in Education,.

Prost, A. (1983) *Grandes orientations du groupe de travail national sur les seconds cycles*, Paris: Ministère de l'Education Nationale.

Pugh, G. (1998) *Children at risk of becoming socially excluded: An introduction to the 'problem'*, Paper presented at the Treasury Seminar on Social Exclusion, London: Coram Foundation.

Pugh, G. (1993) *30 years of change for children*, London: National Children's Bureau.

Quignard, J. (1972) 'La pedagogie differenciee', in P. Juif and L. Legrand (eds) (1980) *Textes de pédagogie pour l'école d'aujourd'hui. Les grands orientations de la pédagogie contemporaine*, Paris: F. Nathan.

Quoidbach, B. and Crahay, M. (1984) 'Sociocultural characteristics of children and curriculum realized in four preschool settings', *Scientia Paedagogica Experimentalis*, vol 1, no 21, pp 19-49.

Rademacker, H. (1996) *School social work*, Paper presented at the International Conference on Youth at Risk, Noordwijkerhout: Stichting Jeugdinformatie Nederland.

Rademacker, H. and Rodax, K. (1996) *Social inequality and education in Germany*, Paper presented at the International Conference on Youth at Risk, Noordwijkerhout: Stichting Jeugdinformatie Nederland.

Raffe, D. (1997) *Higher Still in European perspective*, Edinburgh: Centre for Educational Sociology, University of Edinburgh.

Raftery, A.E. and Hout, M. (1993) 'Maximally maintained inequality: Expansion, reform and opportunity in Irish education, 1921-75', *Sociology of Education*, no 66, pp 41-62.

Ranson, S. (1990) 'From 1944 to 1988: Education, citizenship and democracy', in M. Flude and M. Hammer (eds) *The Education Reform Act 1988: Its origins and implications*, Lewes: Falmer Press.

Reis, I.B. and Salgado, L. (1993) 'Reprodução social e práticas de avaliação escolar', in *Estruturas sociais e desenvolvimento*, Lisbon: Actas do 2° Congresso Português de Sociologia, Fragmentos, pp 381-405.

Ress, Ph. (ed) (1996) *Population and migration in the European Union*, London: John Wiley.

Reynolds, A.J., Mann, E., Miedel, W. and Smokowski, P. (1997) 'The state of early childhood intervention: Effectiveness, myths and realities, new directions', *Focus*, vol 1, no 19, pp 5-11.

Reynolds, A.J. and Wolfe, B. (1997) 'School achievement, early intervention and special education', *Focus*, vol 1, no 19, pp 18-21.

Reynolds, D. and Cuttance, P. (1992) *School effectiveness: Research, policy, and practice*, London: Cassell.

Riddel, W.C. (1992) 'Federal aid for the education of disadvantaged children', in P.Anthony and S.L.Jacobson (eds) *Helping at-risk students. What are the educational and financial costs?*, Newbury Park, California: Corwin Press, pp 12-37.

Riddell, S., Brown, S., and Duffield, J. (1994) 'Parental power and special educational needs: The case of specific learning difficulties', *British Educational Research Journal*, vol 3, no 20, pp 327-44.

Riddell, S., Dyer, S., and Thomson, G. (1990) 'Parents, professionals and social welfare models: The implementation of the Education (Scotland) Act 1981', *European Journal of Special Needs Education*, vol 2, no 5, pp 96-110.

Riddell, S., Stalker, K., Wilkinson, H., and Baron, S. (1997) *The meaning of the learning society for adults with learning difficulties. Report of phase one of the study* (October) Glasgow: University of Glasgow.

Rist, R.G. (1970) 'Student social class and teacher expectation: The self-fulfilling prophecy in ghetto education', *Harvard Educational Review*, no 40, pp 411-51.

Robertson, P. (1995) *Partnership for progress – The mid-term evaluation of the Home–School–Employment Partnership*, Strathclyde: Quality in Education Centre, University of Strathclyde.

Robinson, P. (1997) *Literacy, numeracy and economic performance*, London: Centre for Economic Performance, London School of Economics.

Roca Cortés, N. (1994) *Análisis crítico de una transformación de las prácticas de alfabetización y del trabajo en grupo inter-profesional*, Congreso Internacional sobre Nuevas Perspectivas Críticas en Educación, Libro de Comunicaciones, Barcelona: Edt. Fundación Bosch i Gimpera.

Roca Cortés, N. (1995) *Escritura y necesidades educativas especiales. Teoría y práctica de un enfoque constructivista*, Madrid: Edt. Fundación Infancia y Aprendizaje (First edition (1990) *Ensenyament – aprenentatge de l'escriptura en alumnes amb necessitats educatives especials*, Barcelona: ICE de la Universitat de Barcelona).

Roca Cortés, N. (1997) 'Grupos en Educación', in P. González (ed) *Psicología de los grupos, teoría y aplicación*, Madrid: Síntesis.

Roca Cortés, N. (1998) 'The notion of competence in disabled children: Changes in social and educational attributions', in P. Jaffe (ed) *Challenging mentalities: The future of children's rights / Défier les mentalités: Le futur des droits de l'enfant*, Ghent: Ghent University and Geneva University Pub., series on children's rights.

Roelandt, T., Martens, E., and Veenman, J. (1991) 'Ethnic minority children in Dutch education: Ethnic stratification, social class and migration', *Netherlands Journal of Social Sciences*, vol 2, no 27 pp 92-107.

Rogers, C. (1982) *A social psychology of schooling*, London: Routledge and Kegan Paul.

Roox, G. (1998) 'Houd moed, kinderen. De basisschool als zorgenkind', in *De Standaard Magazine*, 18 September, pp 4-8.

Rubovits, P. and Maehr, M. (1971) 'Pygmalion analyzed: Towards an explanation of the Rosenthal–Jacobson findings', *Journal of Personality and Social Psychology*, no 19, pp 197-203.

Ryan, P. (1997) *Towards prevention of early school leaving: An integrated approach*, Paper presented to Seminar on the Concept of Integration, May, Dublin.

Ryan, S. (1994) *Home-School-Community Liaison Scheme: Final Evaluation Report*, Dublin: Educational Research Centre.

Ryan, S. (1995) *The Home-School-Community Liaison Scheme - Summary Evaluation Report*, Dublin: Educational Research Centre.

Santos, M.O., Alçada, I. et al (1986) *Análise das condições de cumprimento da escolaridade obrigatória*, Lisbon: GGEP-ME.

Sastre, G. and Moreno, M. (1980) *Descubrimiento y construcción de los conocimientos*, Barcelona: Gedisa.

Scheerens, J. and Bosker, R.J. (1997) *The foundations of educational effectiveness*, Oxford: Pergamon Press.

Schwab, A. (1994) *The Koffiepot. Centre for work, knowledge, living and well-being in Laakkwartier-Noord*, The Hague.

Schwartz, J.B. (1985) 'Student financial aid and the college enrolment decision: The effect of public and private grants and interest subsidies', *Economics of Education Review*, vol 2, no 4, pp 129-44.

Scottish Office (1991) *The Parents' Charter in Scotland*, Edinburgh: Scottish Office.

Scottish Office (1993) *A parents' guide to special educational needs*, Edinburgh: Scottish Office.

Scottish Office (1994) *Higher Still – Opportunity for all*, Edinburgh: Scottish Office.

Scottish Office (1995a) *Programme for partnership*, Edinburgh: Scottish Office.

Scottish Office (1995b) *Provision of education for pupils with special educational needs*, Edinburgh: Scottish Office.

Scottish Office (1996) *School leavers survey – the 1994 leavers*, Edinburgh: SOIED.

Scottish Office (1996a) *Statistical Bulletin: Education Series*, (Edn/MI/1996/7) School meals and milk.

Scottish Office (1996b) *Education and training in Scotland – A national dossier*, Edinburgh: Scottish Office.

Scottish Office (1996c) *Examination results in Scottish schools 1994-1996*, Information for Parents Series, Edinburgh: Scottish Office.

Scottish Office (1996d) 'School meals and milk', *Statistical Bulletin, Education Series* (Edn/M1/1996/7).

Scottish Office (1997) *Attendance and absence in Scottish schools 1995-1996*, Information for Parents Series, Edinburgh: Scottish Office.

Scottish Office (1997) *Referral of children to reporters and children's hearings 1995*, Edinburgh: The Stationery Office.

Scottish Office (1997) 'Provision for pupils with special educational needs, 1995 and 1996', *Statistical Bulletin* (Edn/D2/1997/11).

Scottish Office (1997) 'Placing requests in Education Authority schools in Scotland 1985-86 to 1995-96', *Statistical Bulletin, Education Series* (B6/1997/2).

Scottish Office Education Department (1992) *Better information for parents in Scotland*, Edinburgh: Scottish Office.

Scottish Office Education Department (1994) *Effective provision for special educational needs*, Report by HM Inspectors of Schools, Edinburgh: Scottish Office.

Scottish Office Education and Industry Department (1995) 'School boards in Scottish schools: May 1994', *The Scottish Office Statistical Bulletin: Education Series*, Edinburgh: Scottish Office.

Scottish Office Education and Industry Department (1996) *Children and young persons with special educational needs: Assessment and recording*, Circular 4/96, Edinburgh: SOEID.

Scottish Office Education and Industry Department (1996) *The 1994 leavers*, Edinburgh: SOEID.

Scottish Office Education and Industry Department (1997) *Early intervention: Key issues*, Edinburgh: SOEID.

Scottish Office Education and Industry Department (1998) *Parents as partners: Enhancing the role of parents in school education*, Discussion Paper, Edinburgh: SOEID.

Sebba, J. and Ainscow, M. (1996) 'International developments in inclusive schooling: Mapping the issues', *Cambridge Journal of Education*, vol 26, no 1.

Sexton, J.J. and O'Connell, P. (1996) *Labour market studies: Ireland*, Luxembourg: Office for Official Publications of the European Communities.

Shavit, Y. (1984) 'Curriculum tracking and ethnicity', *American Sociological Review*, vol 2, no 49, pp 210-40.

Shavit, Y. and Blossfeld, H.P. (eds) (1993) *Persistent inequality: Changing educational attainment in thirteen countries*, Boulder: Westview Press.

Shield, B.J. (1986) 'A daily report experience', in C. Rogers (ed) *Freedom to learn*, Columbus: Merrill.

Silver, H. and Silver, P. (1991) *An educational war on poverty. American and British policy-making 1960-80*, New York and Melbourne: Cambridge University Press.

Simpson, M. and Ure, J. (1994) 'Studies in differentiation practices in primary and secondary schools', *Interchange*, no 30.

Simpson, M., Tuson, J., and Goulder, J. (1995) *Implementing 5-14 in secondary schools*, Edinburgh: SOEID.

Slavenburg, J.H. (1993) 'Voorschoolse stimuleringsprojecten', *Pedagogische Studiën,* vol 70, no 4, pp 309-15.

Slavin, R. (1990) *Cooperative learning. Theory, research and practice,* Englewood Cliffs, NJ: Prentice-Hall.

Slavin, R. and Madden, N. (1997) *Scaling up: Lessons learned in the dissemination of Success for All,* Baltimore, MD: Center for Research on the Education of Students Placed At Risk, (CRESPAR) (http:// scov.csos.jhu.edu/crespar/CReSPaR.html).

Smit, F., van Esch, W., and Walbert, H.J. (1993) *Parental involvement in education,* Njmegen: Netherlands: Institute for Applied Social Sciences.

Smith, C. (1996) *Developing parenting programmes,* London: National Bureau Enterprises Ltd.

Smith, P. (1991) *Ethnic minorities in Scotland,* Edinburgh: Scottish Office.

Smoorenburg, M.S.M. and van der Velden, R.K.W. (1995) *The labour market positions of types of education: Dimensions and stability,* Strasbourg: ESF Working Paper.

Smyth, E. (1998) *Do schools differ? Academic and personal development among pupils in the second-level sector,* Dublin: Economic and Social Research Institute.

Smyth, E. (1999) *School effectiveness,* Dublin: ESRI.

Smyth, E. and Hannan, D.F. (1995) *1985/86 School leavers: A follow-up study in 1992,* Dublin: ESRI Working Paper.

Smyth, E. and Surridge, P. (1996) *Educational differentiation and occupational allocation among school leavers in Ireland and Scotland, 1981-1991,* Strasbourg: ESF Working Paper.

Social Work Service Group (SWSG) (1997) *Scotland's children. The Children (Scotland) Act 1995 regulations and guidance,* Edinburgh: The Stationery Office.

Social Work Services Group (SWSG) (1993) *Scotland's children: Proposals for child care policy and law,* Cm 2286, Edinburgh: HMSO.

SOEID for Scottish office Education and Industry Department.

Solé, R. (1985) 'Ensenyar i arpendre a l'Escola Municipal Pau Vila. Seminari de Pedagogia Operatoria de la comarca del Garraf', Internal document, mimeo, Vilanova i la Geltrú (Garraf, Barcelona).

Sorenson, A.B. (1987) 'The organizational differentiation of students in schools as an opportunity structure', in M. Hallinan (ed) *The Social Organization of Schools,* New York: Plenum Press.

Souta, L. 'A educação multicultural', *Inovação*, vol IV, no 2-3, pp 45-52.

Stalker, K. (1995) 'The antinomies of choice in community care', in S. Baldwin and P. Barton (eds) *The International handbook of community care*, London: Routledge.

Stichting, D. Coens (1996) *Verslagboek 10 juar leerplichtverlenging*, Brussels: Stichting D. Coens.

Stinissen, J. (1992) 'De overgang van secundair naar hoger onderwijs: Effecten van veranderingen op de arbeidsmarkt, in gezinnen en in het onderwijssysteem', *Mens en Maatschappij*, no 2, pp 156-76.

Stoer, S.R. (1994) 'Construindo a escola democrática através do campo da recontextualização pedagógica', *Sociedade e Culturas*, no 1, Educação, pp 7-27.

Stoer, S.R. and Araújo, H.C. (1991) 'Educação e democracia num país semiperiférico' (no contexto europeu), in S.R. Stoer (ed) *Educação, ciências sociais e realidade portuguesa*, Porto: Afrontamento, pp 205-30.

Stoer, S.R. and Araújo, H.C. (1992) *Escola e aprendizagem para o trabalho num país da (semi)periferia europeia*, Lisbon: Escher.

Stoer, S., Stollerof, A., and Correia, J.A. (1990) 'O novo vocacionalismo na política educativa em portugal e a reconstrução da lógica da acumulação', *Revista Crítica de Ciências Sociais*, no 29, pp 11-53.

Stoer, S.R. (1986) *Educação e mudança social em Portugal. 1970-80*, uma década de transição, Porto: Afrontamento.

Storms, B. (1995) *Het Matteüseffect in de kinderopvang*, CSB-Berichten, Antwerp: Centre for Social Policy – UFSIA, September.

Stringfield, S., Billig, S.H., and Davis, A. (1991) 'Chapter 1 program improvement', *Educational Evaluation and Policy Analysis,* vol 4, no 13, pp 399-406.

Svendsen (1996) *Analysis of member state actions in favour of the Youth Start target group*, Copenhagen: Dell.

Task Force Human Resources Education Training Youth (EC) (1994) *Measures to combat failure at school: A challenge for the construction of Europe*, Luxembourg: Office for the official Publications of the European Communities.

Task Force Human Resources Education Training Youth (EC) (DG XXII) (1995) *The White Paper: Teaching and learning: Towards a learning society*, Luxembourg: Office for the official Publications of the European Communities.

Task Force on the Travelling Community (1995) *Report of the Task Force on the Travelling Community*, Dublin: Stationery Office.

Teberosky, A. and Cardoso, B. (1983) *Psicopedagogia de la llengua escrita*, Documents de classe, Institu Municipal d'Educació de Barcelona (IME).

Tesser, P. and Veenman, J. (1997) *Rapportage Minderheden 1997*, Rijswijk: SCP.

Tett, L. and Crowther, J. (forthcoming) *Families at a disadvantage: Class, culture and literacies*, Edinburgh: Heriot Watt University.

The Stationery Office (1998) *Meeting the childcare challenge: A childcare strategy for Scotland*, London: The Stationery Office.

Thomson, G.O.B. and Ward, K. (1994) *Patterns and pathways: Individuals with disabilities in transition to adulthood*, Edinburgh: Department of Education, University of Edinburgh.

Thomson, G.O.B., Riddell, S.I., and Dyer, S. (1990) 'The placements of pupils recorded as having special educational needs; an analysis of Scottish data 1986–1988', *Oxford Review of Education*, vol 2, no 16, pp 159-78.

Thomson, G.O.B., Stewart, M., and Ward, K.M. (1995) *Criteria for Opening Records of Needs*, Report to the Scottish Office Education Department, Edinburgh: Department of Education, University of Edinburgh.

Thys, L. and de Bleekere, T. (1993) 'Onderzoek naar schoolbeleving in Vlaanderen. Rapport 1: Spijbelgedrag', in *Caleidoscoop*.

Tisdall, E.K.M. (1997a) 'Constructing the "transitional problem" for young disabled people leaving school: Comparing policy and practice in Ontario and Scotland', *Compare*, vol 1, no 27, pp 75-90.

Tisdall, K. (1997b) *The Children (Scotland) Act 1995: Developing law and policy for Scotland's children*, Edinburgh: The Stationery Office.

Titmuss, R. (1968) *Commitment to welfare*, London: Unwin.

Tomlinson, S. (1982) *A sociology of special education*, London: Routledge and Keegan Paul.

Turner, E., Riddell, S., and Brown, S. (1995) *Gender equality in Scottish schools: The impact of recent educational reforms*, Glasgow: Equal Opportunities Commission.

Tussing, D. (1976) 'Labour force effects of 1967/68 changes in education policy in the Irish Republic', *Economic and Social Review*, no 7, pp 289-304.

Tussing, D. (1978) *Irish educational expenditure – past, present and future*, Dublin: ESRI.

Tyler, W. (1977) *The sociology of educational inequality*, London: Methuen.

Uit de Marge (1994) *De proef op de som. Over de relevantie van opleidings- en tewerkstellingsprojecten en schoolopbouwwerkprojecten voor maatschappelijk achtergestelde kinderen en jongeren*, Borgerhout: Uit de Marge.

UNESCO (1994) *The Salamanca Statement and Framework for Action on Special Needs Education*.

Van Assche, E. (1988) 'Een dagelijks lesuur lichamelijke opvoeding op school. Eenhaalbaar feit in Vlaanderen?', *Tijdschrift voor Lichamelijke Opvoeding*, no 4, pp 2-11.

Van Brusselem, B. and Nicaise, I. (1993) *Alle beetjeshelpen. Sociale doelmatigheid van de studietoelagen in het secundair onderwijs*, Leuven: HIVA.

Van Calster, L. (1991) *Children and youth at risk*, Paris: OECD/CERI.

Van De Velde, V., Denys, J., and Douterlungne, M. (1996a) 'De invloed van de leerplichtverlenging op de jongeren', in *Verslagboek 10 jaar leerplichtverlenging*, Brussels: Stichting Daniel Coens.

Van de Velde, V., van Brusselen, B., and Douterlungne, M. (1996b) *Gezin en school. Een onderzoek over het gezin als indicator voor schoolloopbaan in het secundair onderwijs*, Leuven: HIVA.

Van Erp, M. (1998) 'Verlengde schooldag maakt leerlingen socialer and leergieriger', *Didaktief and School*, no 5-6.

Van Eyken, M. (1988) 'Gezinsvariabelen als verklaring voor de relatie tussen sociaal stratum en het hebben van studieproblemen bij kinderen van het eerste leerjaar', *Tijdschrift voor Sociologie*, vol 9, no 4, pp 535-58.

Van Hooreweghe, B., van Regenmortel, T., and Nicaise, I. (1989) *Basisonderwijs: Gratis onderwijs? Een onderzoek naar de kosteloosheid van het kleuter – en lager onderwijs in Vlaanderen*, Leuven: HIVA.

Van Langen, A. and Portengen, R. (1998) *Decentralisatie van onderwijsachterstandenbeleid*, Nijmegen: ITS.

Van Rossum, T. and van Tilborg, L. (eds) (1996a) *Almanak Voortijdig Schoolverlaten '96*, Utrech: Sardes.

Van Tilborg, L. and van Rossum, T. (1996b) *Evaluation of regional action plans and impact reports*, Utrecht: Sardes.

Vanderstraeten, R. (1996-1997) 'De evolutie inzake onderwijsdeelname: naoorlogse tendensen en prognoses', *Tijdschrift voor Onderwijsrecht en – Beleid*, no 1, pp 21-29.

Vandevoort, L. (1997) *On going beyond access and quotas. Looking for strategies for minorities in higher education: The Flemish experience*, Paper presented at the 6th EAN Annual Convention, 25-28 June 1997, Cork.

Vanhoren, I., van de Velde, V., and Ramakers, J. (1995) *De evaluatie van het onderwijsbeleid voor migranten*, Leuven: Hoger Instituut voor de Arbeid.

Varela, J. (1991) *Arqueologia de la escuela*, Madrid: La Piqueta.

Veenman, J. (1996) 'Unemployment in the Netherlands – facts, causes, effects and policies', in *Youth Unemployment: International Conference on Youth at Risk*, Noordwijkerhout: Stichting Jeugdinformatie Nederland and Dutch Ministry.

Verhaeghe, J.P. (1994) *Zorgbreedte en zorgverbredingsbetioete in het ulaams basisonderwijs, Analyses op schoolniveau*, Brussels: VloR.

Verhaeghe, J.P., Vansieleghem, N., and van Keer, H. (1998) 'Tackling social exclusion through bridging the gap between school and family: From concept to action', Paper presented at the European Conference on Educational Research, Ljubljana.

Verhoeven, J.C. and Kochuyt, T. (1995) *Kansenongelijkheid in het onderwijs. Een biografisch onderzoek naar het schoolgaan in arbeiders – en kansarme gezinnen*, Brussels: Federale Diensten voor Wetenschappelijke, Technische en Culturele Aangelegenheden.

Vermeulen, H., Breemans, A., Mulder, L., and Tesser, P. (1987) *Onderzoek naar compensatieprogramma's in de Verenigde Staten en Groot-Brittanië*, Nijmegen: ITS.

Vettenburg, N. (1992) 'Sport in het beroepsonderwijs houdt kansen in', in P. de Knop and L. Walgrave (eds) *Sport als integratie van kansarme jongeren*, Brussels: Koning Boudewijnstichting.

Vettenburg, N. (1996) *Maatschappelÿke ontwikkelingen, motivatie en demotivatie van maatschappelÿk kuvetsbare beerlingen*, Leuven: Afd Jeugdcriminologie.

Vettenburg, N. and Thys, L. (1996) *Kansarmoede en onderwijs*, Brussels: Koning Boudewijnstichting.

Vieira, M.M. (1996) 'Ensino básico e secundário e trajectórias escolares: Uma breve incursão', *Revista de Educação*, vol V, no 2, pp 9-32.

Vincent, C. and Tomlinson, S. (1997) 'Home-school relations: The swarming of disciplinary mechanisms?', *British Educational Research Journal – Special Issue: Reflexive Accounts of Educational Reform*, vol 3, no 23, pp 361-79.

Vincent, C. (1994) *Professionals under pressure: The administration of special education in a changing context*, Paper presented to the British Educational Research Association Conference, September 1994, Oxford.

Vincent, C. (1996) *Parents' and teachers' power and participation*, London: Falmer Press.

Vlaams Centrum Woonwagenwerk (1997) *Tussen school en wagen. Onderwijs aan Voyageurs, Manoesjen en Roms*, Leuven: Vlaams Centrum Woonwagenwerk.

Vlaams Overleg Woonwagenwerk (1996) *Geïntegreerde opvang van kinderen van zigeuners en woonwagenbewoners in het basisonderwijs. Eindrapport van het project 1992-1996*, Leuven: Vlaams Overleg Woonwagenwerk.

Vlaamse Onderwijsraad (1998) *Denkkader inclusief onderwijs*, June 1998, Brussels: Voomse Onderwjsood.

Vliegen, M. (1975) 'Milieu-verschillen in schoolkeuze en schoolsuccess: Een statistische beschrijving', *Mens en Maatschappij*, no 50, pp 9-26.

Vollebergh, V. (1996) 'Racism and every day life of ethnic minority youth in ethnification of social conflicts', *International Conference on Youth at Risk*, Noordwijkerhout: Stichting Jeugdinformatie Nederland and Dutch Ministry.

Voncken, E. and Babeliowsky, M. (1994) *Over de grenzen van de school*, Amsterdam: SCO-KI.

Vos, M. and Nicaise, I. (1993) *Wolven in schapevacht... of zwarte schapen? Sociale doelmatigheid van het nieuwe inkomenscriterium in het stelsel van studietoelagen in het hoger onderwijs*, Leuven: HIVA.

Walford, G. (1995) 'Faith-based grant maintained schools: Selective international policy borrowing from the Netherlands', vol 10, no 3, pp 245-57.

Walker de Felix, Anderson, J.E. and Prentice, Baptiste H. (1992) 'Conclusion: Future directions for educating students at risk', in H.C. Waxman, J. Walker de Felix, J.E. Anderson and M. Prentice Baptiste (eds) *Students at risk in at-risk schools. Improving environments for learning*, Newbury Park, California: Corwin Press.

Ward, K., Riddell, S., Dyer, M., and Thomson, G. (1991) *The transition to adulthood of young people with recorded special educational needs*, Final Report to the Scottish Office Education Department, The Departments of Education of the University of Edinburgh and Stirling.

Weatherley, R. and Lipsky, S. (1977) 'Street-level bureaucrats and institutional innovation: Implementing special education reform', *Harvard Educational Review*, vol 2, no 47, pp 171-97.

Weikart, D. (1996) 'High-quality preschool programs found to improve adult status', *Childhood*, vol 1, no 3, pp 117-20.

Weiner, B. (1986) *An attributional theory of Motivation and Emotion*, New York: Springer-Verlag.

Westhoff, G. (ed) (1996) 'Careers and destinations: Young people at the second transition in youth unemployment', in *International Conference on Youth at Risk*, Noordwijkerhout: Stichting Jeugdinformatie Nederland and Dutch Ministry.

Westinghouse Learning Corporation (1969) *The impact of Head Start. An evaluation of the effects of Head Start on children's cognitive and effective development* (2 volumes), Athens/Ohio: Ohio University.

Widlake, P. (1986) *Reducing educational disadvantage*, Milton Keynes: Open University.

Williams, R. (1976) *Keywords, a vocabulary of culture and society*, London: Fontana.

Williams, R. (1989) *Resources of hope*, London: Verso.

Willis, P. (1977) *Learning to labour*, Hampshire: Gower.

Willms, D.J. (1986) 'Social class segregation and its relationship to pupils' examination results in Scotland', *American Sociological Review*, no 51.

Willms D.J. (1996) 'School choice and community segregation: Findings from Scotland', in A.C Kerckhoff (ed) *Generating social stratification: Toward a new research agenda*, pp 131-51.

Willms, D.J. (1997) *Parental choice and education policy*, Edinburgh: Centre for Educational Sociology (Briefing), Edinburgh University.

Wolfendale, S. (1989) *Parental involvement*, London: Cassell Educational Ltd.

Wolfendale, S. (ed) (1992) *Empowering parents and teachers*, London: Cassell Educational Ltd.

Wolff, M. and Stein, A. (1966) *Study I: Six months later. A comparison of children who had Head Start, summer 1965, with their classmates in kindergarten*, Washington, DC: Research and Evaluation Office, Office of Economic Opportunity.

Wortman, P.M. (1995) 'An exemplary evaluation of a program that worked', *Evaluation Practice*, vol 3, no 16, pp 257-65.

Wrésinski, J. (1987) 'Grandi pauvreté et précarité économique et sociale', *Journal Officiel de la République Française*, vol 6, p 104.

Wu, P. and Campbell, D.T. (1996) 'Extending latent variable LISREL analyses of the 1969 Westinghouse Head Start evaluation to blacks and full year whites', *Evaluation and Program Planning*, vol 3, no 19, pp 183-91.

Zigler, E., Muenchow, S. (1992) *Head Start: The inside story of America's most successful educational experiment*, New York: Harper Collins/Basic Books.

Zigler, E.F. (1995) 'Meeting the needs of children in poverty', *American Journal of Orthopsychiatry*, no 1, pp 6-9.

Appendix: Background information about poverty and education in the six countries covered by this study

Flanders

Figure A.1, taken from Eurydice Cedefop (1995), reflects the structure of the educational curriculum in Flanders. It is to be noted that the federal state (Belgium) is competent mainly for the legislation relating to compulsory education, which runs on a full-time basis from the age of 6 until 16, and on a part-time basis until the age of 18. The linguistic communities rule all other matters.

Compulsory education thus starts with primary school (from the age of 6 until 12), although participation in nursery school (age 3-6) is virtually generalised. During the spring of 1997, the Flemish Government proposed excluding children aged 2; this decision was heavily contested because of its possible negative consequences on equality of opportunities.

In secondary education, two 'types' (traditional and renewed) have coexisted for many years. Since the beginning of the 1990s, a 'unified structure' has been imposed, combining elements of both types. Secondary school now starts – at least theoretically – with a comprehensive cycle of two years. Then follows an 'orientation' cycle, also of two years, and a 'determination' cycle of two (sometimes three) years.

Compared with traditional secondary education, the philosophy behind the reform has been to postpone study orientation decisions until the age of 14 (start of the second cycle), whereas they were made at 12 in the previous period. In reality, the reform seems to have had a rather limited impact. Pupils who have had learning problems in primary school enter secondary education in so-called 'b classes', which are supposed to allow them to catch up with their fellows at a later stage.

However, Van de Velde et al (1996a) found that over 95% of starters in 'b' classes went on in a 'b-stream' where the second year is a preparation for vocational education. This vocational education is generally regarded as the 'weaker' stream. Within the 'a-stream', students are oriented to a 'general option' or a 'technical option' from the second year on.[1] Again,

Figure A.1: The structure of education in the Flemish community of Belgium

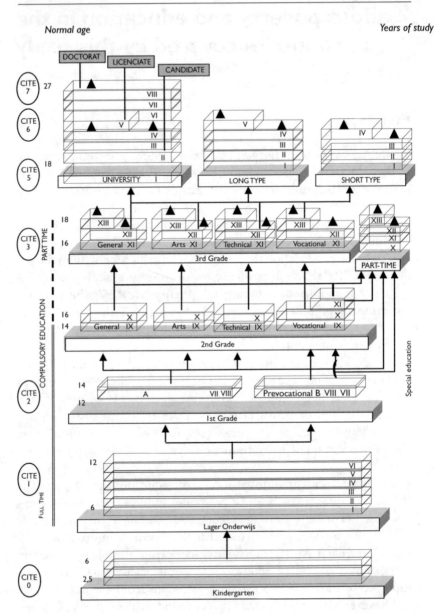

Table A.1: Selected indicators relating to social exclusion and education in Belgium

Country information	Education
Population 10,105,000 (1) Aged under 25 years: 31% (2)	**Participation rates** 16-18 age group: 88% in 1995 (5) 19-21 age group: 62% in 1995 (5)
Foreigners living in the country 9.1% in 1990 (3)	**Compulsory education (6)** Until 15-16 years full-time; until 18 years part-time
Unemployment rates (1) In 1995, General: 9.3% Aged under 25 years: 21.5%	**Repeating policies (6)** Possible every year. Maximum once each class unless exemption granted
Poverty % non-elderly families with incomes below 50% of the national median disposable income per consumption unit: 5.4% in 1985 (4) % inhabitants with incomes below 50% of the national median disposable income per consumption unit: 13% (8) Poverty incidence among children (below age 16): 15% in 1993(8)	**Children leaving school without any certificate (6)** Not available **Annual educational expenditure (% of GDP)** *Public*　　　　　*Public/Private Combined* Not available (2)　　Not available (2) **Public expenditure per pupil** In 1992, US $ (7) *Pre-School:* 2,350　　*Primary:* 2,910　　*Secondary:* 6,470　　*Tertiary:* 6,850

Sources: (1) Eurostat (1995); (2) European Commission (1995); (3) Ress (1996); (4) Förster (1994); (5) European Commission (1995); (6) European Commission (1995); (7) OECD (1995); (8) Eurostat (1997a)

all sorts of transitions are allowed for in theory, but according to Van de Velde et al (1996a), the transition from the technical option in the second year to general education in the next cycle is extremely rare (5%).

All options can yield certificates that give access to higher education. However, very few students enter tertiary education after graduating from vocational education.

From a poverty perspective, part-time vocational education (PTVE) deserves extra attention: PTVE is a provision where school-fatigued students from vocational or technical education can combine part-time school courses and part-time work from the age of 16[2] until the end of compulsory education (18). It was a response on the part of lawmakers to the possibility that not all young people will want to be enrolled in full-time education until their 18th birthday, and that some of them will prefer to leave school in favour of work and an income at an earlier point. In part-time education, the pupils can fulfil the requirements of compulsory education by enrolling in apprenticeship programmes for self-employment, job corps programmes (part-time non-formal education), or training in the part-time education system. The first system is part of a long-established tradition, but the other two have been specially created in response to the extension of the period of compulsory schooling.

Another innovation that has accompanied the extension of compulsory education is Renewed Secondary Vocational Education. This has involved pedagogical rather than structural reforms, in that the renewed curriculum yields the same certificates but contains elements such as thematic and project teaching, integration of theory and practice, the 'workshop class', modular organisation of the final year and so on, with the main aim being to increase pupil involvement.

Other measures that are relevant from the perspective of combating social exclusion are: Educational Priority Policy (until now mainly targeted at children from ethnic minorities), Extended Care (geared towards children with social and emotional problems in the transition phase from nursery to primary school), School Community Action (liaising between parents from disadvantaged backgrounds and schools), the student grant system at secondary and tertiary level, the (recently reformed) Centres for Pupil Guidance, and a series of pilot projects at the local or regional level.

Ireland

In Ireland, school attendance is compulsory from the age of 6 (see Figure A.2, taken from Eurydice). In practice, however, many children enter full-time education at the age of 4 or 5: 65% of 4-year-olds and almost all 5-year-olds are currently enrolled in primary schools (Department of Education, 1995).

Little systematic information is available on the participation of children in pre-school education, although the level of childcare and other pre-school provision is deemed to be low in Ireland compared with the rest of Europe (McKenna, 1988).

The vast majority of primary schools are state-aided denominational schools, established under diocesan patronage, but a minority (less than 2%) of pupils attend private primary schools which do not receive state funding. A similar proportion attend special schools targeted at those with physical and/or learning disabilities (Department of Education, 1996). While the majority of pupils attend co-educational schools, the single-sex sector is relatively large by European standards, with a quarter of primary pupils attending single-sex schools (Department of Education, 1996). The primary curriculum is formulated at a national level (by the National Council for Curriculum and Assessment), but no nationally standardised examinations exist for primary-level pupils.

Young people enter the second level of education at 12 or 13 years of age. Participation in full-time education is currently compulsory until the age of 15, but this is being increased to 16 years of age in the forthcoming academic year. Participation in secondary education is high, with an estimated 96% of 15-year-olds, 91% of 16-year-olds and 82% of 17-year-olds enrolled in full-time education (Department of Education, 1996).

There are three types of secondary-level institution: voluntary secondary, vocational, and community/comprehensive schools. All school types are publicly funded. Voluntary secondary schools are privately owned and controlled, mainly by religious orders, although they are subject to public regulation and inspection. Vocational schools are publicly owned and are administered by local education authorities. Voluntary secondary schools have traditionally been more academic in focus, in contrast to a greater practical and technical orientation in vocational schools. Community and comprehensive schools were established in an attempt to bridge the gap between the secondary and the vocational sectors by providing a broad curriculum catering for pupils of different backgrounds and ability levels.

Figure A.2: The structure of education in Ireland

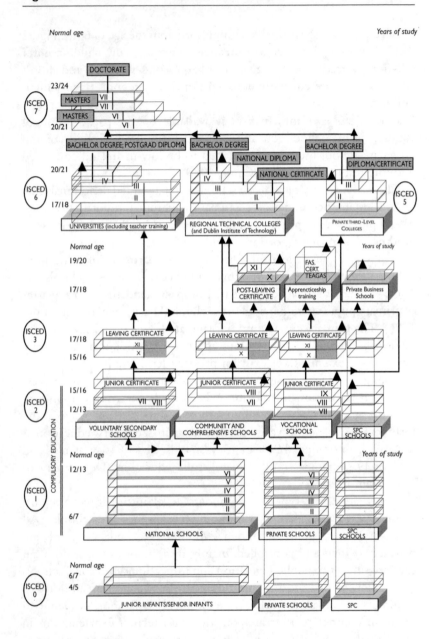

Table A.2: Selected indicators relating to social exclusion and education in Ireland

Country information

Population
3,536,000 (1)
Aged under 25 years: 43% (2)

Foreigners living in the country
Not available (3)

Unemployment rates (1)
In 1995, General: 12%
Aged under 25 years: 19.0%

Poverty
% non-elderly families with incomes below 50% of the national
median disposable income per consumption unit: 15.7 in 1987 (4)
% inhabitants with incomes below 50% of the national median
disposable income per consumption unit: 21% (8)
Poverty incidence among children (below age 16): 28% in 1993(8)

Education

Participation rates
16-18 age group: 86% in 1995 (5)
19-21 age group: 47% in 1995 (5)

Compulsory education (6)
Until 15 years full-time

Repeating policies (6)
Automatic promotion

Children leaving school without any certificate (6)
8% in 1989

Annual educational expenditure (% of GDP)

Public	Public/Private Combined
5.7% in 1992 (2)	5.7% in 1992 (2)

Public expenditure per pupil
In 1992, US $ (7)

Pre-School: 1,750	Primary: 1,770	Secondary: 2,770	Tertiary: 7,270

Sources: (1) Eurostat (1995); (2) European Commission (1995); (3) Ress (1996); (4) Förster (1994); (5) European Commission (1996b); (6)
European Commission (1995); (7) OECD (1995); (8) Eurostat (1997a)

Sixty per cent of secondary-level pupils are enrolled in voluntary secondary schools, with one quarter in vocational schools and 14% in community/comprehensive schools (Department of Education, 1996a). While there is a good deal of overlap between the sectors in the number and type of subjects taught at the secondary level, the sectors differ in their pupil composition, with a greater concentration of working-class and lower ability pupils in vocational schools (Hannan et al, 1996b).

In addition, the sectors differ in the gender mix of their pupils: 63% of voluntary secondary schools are single-sex, compared with only 2% of those in other sectors (Department of Education, 1996a). In spite of these differences within the secondary-level sector, the Irish system can be regarded as relatively undifferentiated in comparative context; while schools may vary to some extent in the subjects they provide, all school types draw from a unified national curriculum (Hannan et al, 1996a).

Pupils follow a three-year junior cycle programme, leading up to the national Junior Certificate examination. The curriculum and examination are nationally standardised (Hannan et al, 1996a), although schools and pupils have a degree of choice in the subjects chosen.

Pupils typically take eight or nine subjects for the Junior Certificate. Irish, English and mathematics are obligatory and can be taken at higher, ordinary or foundation levels, while other subjects can be taken at higher or ordinary levels. After taking the Junior Certificate exam, pupils may participate in a 'Transition Year' or they may proceed directly into the two-year senior cycle programme. The Transition Year programme is designed to expose pupils to a wider range of educational, cultural, social and development activities, along with providing a period of work experience. In 1994/95, over 21,000 pupils were participating in this programme (Department of Education, 1996b).

The two-year senior cycle programme leads to the Leaving Certificate. As with the Junior Certificate, curriculum and examinations are nationally standardised, though with some degree of school and pupil choice. Pupils typically take seven examination subjects. Irish and maths can be taken at higher, ordinary or foundation levels, while other subjects can be taken at higher or ordinary levels. In recent years, alternative senior cycle programmes such as the Leaving Certificate Vocational Programme and the Leaving Certificate Applied Programme have been introduced to prevent pupil dropout from upper secondary level, and to develop alternative modes of accreditation for pupils. In addition, a range of Post-Leaving Certificate (VPT2) courses designed to enhance vocational preparation among young people have been incorporated into the secondary-level system. These courses range from one to three years in duration and are available in a range of subject areas.

A 'points' system, whereby students are awarded 'points' on the basis of their Leaving Certificate grades, with allocation of places based on their subsequent ranking, determines entry to the third level. Demand, particularly in certain subject areas, currently exceeds the supply of third-level places. The third-level sector consists of universities, technological colleges (Dublin Institute of Technology, regional technical colleges), teacher training colleges, and private colleges. Courses are offered at the certificate (two years), diploma (three years) and degree (three to four years) levels. The third-level sector has expanded rapidly in recent years; the total number of full-time students at the third level increased from 66,000 in 1989/90 to 96,600 in 1994/95, an increase of 46% (Department of Education, 1996a). Since 1996, students are no longer required to pay fees for undergraduate courses at recognised third-level institutions.

The Netherlands

The formal structure of the Dutch educational system seems always to be on the move, partly due to political reasons, partly as a reaction to developments in society or – at least – problem definitions by significant actors in the system. Some of the motions in the educational system have to do with socially excluded children and youth.

This section will describe some of the main features of the Dutch educational system as it formally existed until just a few years ago and which, in most cases, still persists today. This section will also highlight the structural innovations in the system as these have recently occurred or will occur in the very near future (as far as they are relevant for socially excluded young people).

The Dutch educational system until 1996

In the Netherlands, full-time compulsory education now starts at the age of 5 and continues up to the end of the school year in which the student reaches the age of 16. It is followed by one year of part-time compulsory education for one or two days a week. Attending apprenticeship training or day-release courses for young people can satisfy the requirement for part-time formal education.

The Dutch education system comprises three main stages which are relevant to this study: primary education, general secondary education

Figure A.3: The structure of education in the Netherlands

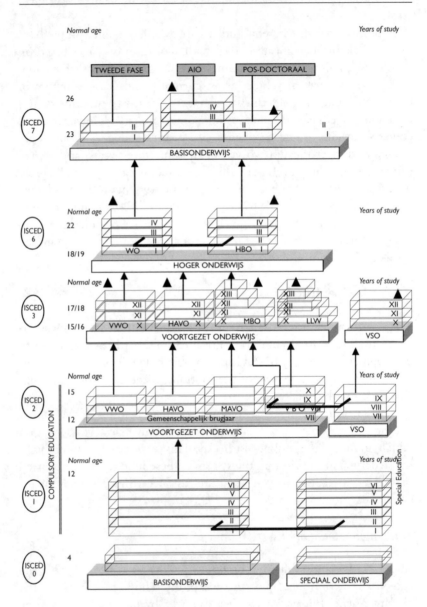

Table A.3: Selected indicators relating to social exclusion and education in the Netherlands

Country information	Education
Population 15,199,000 (1) Aged under 25 years: 33% (2)	**Participation rates** 16-18 age group: 90% in 1995 (5) 19-21 age group: 78% in 1995 (5)
Foreigners living in the country 4.6% in 1990 (3)	**Compulsory education (6)** Until 16 years full-time; until 18 years part-time
Unemployment rates (1) In 1995, General: 7.5% Aged under 25 years: 13.1%	**Repeating policies (6)** Possible every year
	Children leaving school without any certificate (6) 26% in 1986
Poverty % non-elderly families with incomes below 50% of the national median disposable income per consumption unit: 4.5% in 1987 (4) % inhabitants with incomes below 50% of the national median disposable income per consumption unit: 13% (8) Poverty incidence among children (below age 16): 16% in 1993(8)	**Annual educational expenditure (% of GDP)** *Public* *Public/Private Combined* 1.7% in 1992 (2) 5.0% in 1992 (2)
	Public expenditure per pupil In 1992, US $ (7) *Pre-School:* 2,230 *Primary:* 2,560 *Secondary:* 3,310 *Tertiary:* 8,720

Sources: (1) Eurostat (1995); (2) European Commission (1995); (3) Ress (1996); (4) Förster (1994); (5) European Commission (1996b); (6) European Commission (1995); (7) OECD (1995); (8) Eurostat (1997a)

and vocational education and training. Primary schools (the result of a merger of the former nursery schools and elementary schools) cater for children aged 4–12 years.

General secondary education is a two-track system. At the age of 12, a choice must be made between the academic track and the pre-vocational track. Within the academic track, there are three types of education, distinguished by level:

- VWO (*Voorbereidend Wetenschappelijk Onderwijs*/pre-university education). Courses last six years and prepare students both for university and for HBO (higher vocational education courses of study);
- HAVO (*Hoger Algemeen Voortgezet Onderwijs*/senior general secondary education). Courses last five years and prepare students for higher vocational education;
- MAVO (*Middelbaar Algemeen Voortgezet Onderwijs*/junior general secondary education). Courses last four years and prepare pupils for the MBO (senior secondary vocational education) or apprenticeship courses.

The pre-vocational track is called VBO (pre-vocational education). Courses last four years and prepare pupils for the different streams within MBO or for apprenticeship courses. It should be stressed that VBO is not by itself an initial vocational training qualification, although the courses do contain some vocationally oriented subjects. Within VBO, there is an individualised pathway called individual pre-vocational education which is designed for pupils with learning difficulties (IVBO).

It is common to refer to VBO, MAVO and the first four years of HAVO and VWO as the lower stage of general secondary education. The last (fifth) year of HAVO and the last two (fifth and sixth) years of VWO are usually called the upper stage of general secondary education.

At both the primary and secondary levels, there is a separate part of the system for children with disabilities and children with behavioural and/or learning difficulties; this is known as primary and secondary special education (SO and VSO). It will be clear that this part of the system, and especially its relationship with the other more mainstream parts, is extremely significant in relation to social exclusion, early school leaving, and so on. VSO does not in itself lead to a diploma; children in secondary special education have to take the ordinary school leaving examinations for the lower stage of general secondary education.

Secondary vocational education and training consists of two tracks: a school-based track and a dual track. In the Netherlands, the school-based track is usually called education while the dual track is called training, because of the dominance of the school in the former and of the firm in the latter.

In the Netherlands, the school-based track of vocational education/ training predominates quantitatively as well as in status. It is known as MBO (*Middelbaar Beroepsonderwijs* or senior secondary vocational education). MBO offers courses in relation to four broad sectors of the economy and contains several different streams:

- long MBO: four-year courses which are open to students with a VBO or MAVO certificate. At least one work experience placement is always part of the curriculum;
- short courses in MBO: two-year courses formerly known as KMBO (*kort middelbaar beroepsonderwijs*, or short MBO courses) which have no formal entry requirements but are meant to lead to qualifications at the same level as a primary apprenticeship. These courses were introduced in 1979, mainly as a compensation for the so-called 'gap in the mammoth', and also involve work experience placements. All short courses in MBO are modular in structure, consisting of 'units of certification'. For each successfully completed module, the student receives a certificate. A complete set of certificates can be exchanged for a full vocational qualification.
- Part-time MBO: the two- and four-year courses can also be taken in a part-time evening class mode, mostly attended by adults.

The apprenticeship system offers three levels of training courses, often given on a modular basis:

- Two- or three-year primary apprenticeship courses (depending on the sector of activity). These involve one day a week of theoretical study on courses provided in specific training institutions (*Beroeps-Begeleidend Onderwijs* – BBO or CBO colleges), and four days of practical work, mostly in firms. Courses usually last two years for students with a VBO or MAVO certificate, and sometimes last three years for those entering without any school leaving qualification. The lengths of the courses differ between the different sectors of industry. The qualification after completing the course is 'forthcoming craftsman/professional'.
- One- or two-year advanced apprenticeship courses, which enable the students to qualify as autonomous craftsmen/professionals.

- One-year courses in which students prepare themselves for self-employment or a particular specialisation.

Two specific pathways are closely connected with MBO and the apprenticeship system; both are directed at youth at risk and will therefore also be dealt with here. These are day-release courses for young people (*vormingswerk*) and 'guidance and bridging courses' (*oriëntatie en schakelen* – O&S).

The first type is not regarded as part of vocational education. Still, it is worth stressing the existence of day-release courses designed for young people who are still obliged to undertake part-time education (for one or two days a week) but are unable or unwilling to find an apprenticeship position. The guidance and bridging courses are provided for unqualified or poorly qualified prospective entrants to MBO or the apprenticeship system. Special guidance courses are available to help them choose a course, and bridging courses to bring them up to the level of MBO entry requirements.

Recent and ongoing reforms

As a response to problems of school failure and dropout, the Dutch authorities recently decided to introduce some structural reforms in (parts of) the educational system. We have already mentioned the merging of nursery schools and elementary schools into primary schools, simultaneous with lowering the age for compulsory education from six to five. Apart from organisation and administrative innovations (as regards a certain legal minimum of pupils for maintenance as a separate school, enlargements of schools, and more autonomy for school boards), no important structural innovations have taken place in the structure of primary education.

Especially over the last few years, plans have emerged for certain innovations in the structure of secondary phases of the system which may be of relevance to disadvantaged young people. Some of these (in particular, both the common core curriculum and the restructuring of secondary vocational education and training) have already been (partly) implemented. Other reforms in upper secondary education (such as streaming and profiling and the restructuring of VSO/MAVO/VBO) are on the way to being implemented, following their approval by parliament. All of these innovations will change the actual structure of the system - especially those parts that relate mostly to disadvantaged children and youth.

In this context, two of the most important measures have been the new common core curriculum in lower secondary education and the restructuring of VSO/MAVO/VBO.

First, although the introduction of the new organisational structure brought about by the 1968 Act had attenuated some of the problems of secondary education, this did not end the debate in the Netherlands on other more effective solutions (namely, the creation of unified, comprehensive lower secondary schools or, at least, a common curriculum for the early years of secondary education).

Following a long series of proposals in the 1970s and 1980s, the discussion finally culminated in 1992 with the adoption by parliament of an outline common core curriculum for the early years of general secondary education. The common core curriculum is normally meant to cover the first three years after primary education. It aims to raise educational standards, postpone the moment at which a career choice has to be made, and achieve greater equality between male and female pupils.

Second, some years ago (1994), an advisory committee proposed reforms in the structure of VBO and MAVO. This committee suggested that VBO and MAVO should no longer be divided into different levels (A to D), but rather into different routes: a general theoretical route; a vocational route; a combined theoretical/general and vocational route; an individualised route; and a route leading directly into the labour market ('Practical Education').

Despite the fact that the plea for a pathway leading directly into the labour market obviously conflicts with policies in favour of a minimum vocational qualification, the Dutch government did support the proposals of the committee, which will be implemented in the near future. There is one exception, however, and this pertains to the proposed separate individualised pathway. This is to be transformed into a 'supporting structure' for disadvantaged pupils in VBO, MAVO and VSO (special education), and will be aimed at ensuring that these pupils leave school with a regular qualification from one of the mainstream pathways. The Dutch parliament approved these proposals in 1997. The new curriculum track will be named VMBO (*Voorbereidend Middelbaar Beroepsonderwijs* or 'preparatory secondary vocational education').

Other changes are going to be made in the streaming and subject combinations, especially within general secondary education. To ease the process of transition into vocational education/training and the labour market, a diversification of study fields and subject combinations is currently being carried through in the last two years of general secondary education.

A third major reform in the Netherlands is the restructuring of secondary vocational education and training. In 1996, the Education and Vocational Training Act (WEB) became operative, which meant a fundamental restructuring of the whole VET system: MBO, apprenticeship and adult education. The aim is to develop an integrated and flexible system of training routes in which everyone can choose the pathway (short or long, dual or school-based) which best suits his/her needs and which provides the best preparation to meet the requirements of the labour market. Key concepts are accessibility and qualification for the labour market.

The two most characteristic pillars of the new structure are the national qualification structure and the newly formed, large, and relatively autonomous educational institutions called Regional Training Centres (ROCs). The national qualification structure, a countrywide uniform system of vocational qualifications, contains four levels of qualification that can in principle be regarded as end-levels within secondary vocational education and training.

A qualification in this national vocational qualifications system is obtainable through any of the courses in the 'VET course model', and all of these courses are awarded a status in accordance with the European Classification of Courses (CEDOC). A new level, which has explicitly been introduced, is the assistant level (EU level 1), particularly meant for young people who are unable or unwilling to reach level 2.

The Regional Training Centres are the outcomes of merging processes, whereby schools for MBO, BBO, or CBO and adult education are brought together within very large institutions. These more autonomous and integrated educational institutions should be able to respond effectively and in a flexible way to the heterogeneity of young people and of their abilities and wishes. This also means that they should offer opportunities for young (and adult) students to follow and transfer between all the various tracks that are offered by the Regional Training Centres.

Here it is most relevant to point out that, in the near future, both 'guidance and bridging courses' and day-release courses for young people within these institutions will, in essence, no longer be funded as such by government. Guidance, in principle, is perceived as a responsibility of secondary general education. Day-release courses for young people are perceived as a part of the 'supporting structure' (*voorbereidende en ondersteunende activiteiten* –VOA) for pupils from VMBO who experience difficulties in making the transition to (level 2 of) vocational education or training. It is to be expected that in the near future, big problems will occur with young people who will be excluded from general secondary education as well as from vocational education and training.

Apart from curricular innovations in the system, certain policy programmes that have been launched to combat the problems of disadvantage and exclusion in education should be mentioned; in particular, the Educational Priority Policy programme (OVB), 'Going to School Together' (WSNS – integrated education for pupils with special needs) and the 'Well-Prepared Start' (EGVS), all of which are discussed in various chapters of this book. At the same time, there is a shift of emphasis towards local approaches, with more responsibilities being devolved to municipalities and partnerships with all kinds of local actors.

Portugal

The present structure of the Portuguese education system is the result of a reform brought about by a new Education System Framework Law passed by Parliament in 1986. This law represents the consensus that has been achieved in Portuguese society after 20 years of fierce conflict as to the objectives and course of the Portuguese education system (on this subject see Stoer, 1986; Pires, 1987; Campos, 1989; Pedroso, 1991, 1993, 1997).

As a consequence of this law, a reform of the education system began which ended in a series of legislative initiatives and, in particular, a reform of the curriculum throughout the entire education system that has been in force since 1992.

The reform of the education system during the second half of the 1980s was designed to achieve five fundamental objectives (see Azevedo, 1994 and Campos in Pires, 1987):

1. the education of all Portuguese children, with the establishment of a basic, compulsory, universal and free education of nine years' duration, preceded by the raising of the attendance levels for pre-school education;
2. the reinforcement of basic technical education and the preparation of all youths with a view to helping them enter into working life by means of technical secondary education, vocational training and higher education;
3. the development of second-chance provisions for all those who leave school at an early stage;

Figure A.4: The structure of education in Portugal

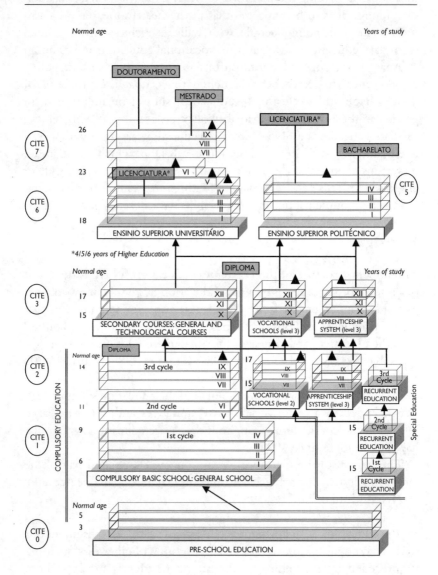

Table A.4: Selected indicators relating to social exclusion and education in Portugal

Country information	Education
Population 9,807,000 (1) Aged under 25 years: 35.5% (2)	**Participation rates** 16-18 age group: 76% in 1995 (5) 19-21 age group: 54% in 1995 (5)
Foreigners living in the country Not available (3)	**Compulsory education (6)** Until 15 years full-time or earlier if third cycle basic school is finished
Unemployment rates (1) In 1995, General: 7.1% Aged under 25 years: 16.0%	**Repeating policies (6)** Exceptional in primary level* Possible every year other levels
	Children leaving school without any certificate (6) 15% in 1991
Poverty % inhabitants with incomes below 50% of the national median disposable income per consumption unit: 26% (8) Poverty incidence among children (below age 16): 27% in 1993(8)	**Annual educational expenditure (% of GDP)** *Public* *Public/Private Combined* 5.2% in 1992 (2) Not available (2)
	Public expenditure per pupil In 1992, US $ (7) *Pre-School:* *Primary:* *Secondary:* 6,470 *Tertiary:*

Sources: (1) Eurostat (1995); (2) European Commission (1995); (3) Ress (1996); (4) Förster (1994); (5) European Commission (1996b); (6) European Commission (1995); (7) OECD (1995); (8) Eurostat (1997a)
* Since 1993–1994

4. the training of professionals and researchers at a very high standard by developing university education with a greater concern for quality;

5. the raising of the educational standards of the population in general by means of the intensification of basic education, using community education, the educational media and the new information technologies as means of support.

Since the education reform, the structure of the Portuguese school system has been as represented in Figure A.4 (adapted from Eurydice). It is composed of four main education types: pre-school education, the mainstream forms of school education, the special forms of school education, and out-of-school education.

For many years, pre-school education was a neglected segment of the education system. In 1990, the rate of enrolment in pre-school education was no more than 30% (see GEP, 1992). Pre-school education currently has a duration of three years and may be carried out in establishments belonging to the 'public network', for which the Ministry of Education is responsible, the 'social welfare network', which is composed of private welfare institutions supported by state funds from the Ministry of Labour and Solidarity, or the 'private network', which consists of profit-making establishments and cooperative entities without public funding.

In January 1997, the government introduced a programme for the expansion and consolidation of the pre-school education system, the primary objectives of which are the expansion of the public network, the guarantee of free pre-school education, and the establishment of new regulations governing the various pre-school education networks. Thus, with the combined effect of the expansion of the network and the growth in population, the government hopes to achieve a significant increase in the rate of attendance for pre-school education by the end of the decade.

In the so-called 'mainstream forms of school education', the basic/compulsory education system in Portugal is organised in three cycles, which were inherited from the previous system. The 1st cycle is taught using the single teacher method, whereas the 2nd and 3rd cycles are taught according to a subject-based system. In the 2nd cycle, the subjects are organised according to a group system, designed in such a way that one teacher deals with one group of subjects.

In many parts of the country, the 1st cycle and the 2nd and 3rd cycles are taught at different schools, although in new school buildings the concept of the integrated basic school is beginning to emerge under a form of school administration that groups into networks the different schools in a certain area which teach the basic education cycles.

The school network and the symbolic breaks between the cycles continue to be weak points as far as dropping out of school is concerned. In 1990, the enrolment rate in the 1st cycle was 99%, in the 2nd cycle it was 70%, and in the 3rd cycle only 55% (GEP, 1992).

In general, the schools of the 1st cycle are well distributed throughout the country, thus guaranteeing good accessibility to this level of education. For some years now, however, this sector has witnessed the closure of schools due to a lack of pupils.

The schools in the 2nd and, above all, the 3rd cycle are much less well distributed, hence creating problems of accessibility for pupils from more underprivileged groups. As far as the 2nd cycle is concerned, one of the ways of minimising accessibility problems is through the media-based basic education establishments. This solution consists of the use of educational support material on video, with monitors taking the place of the teacher.

Until the education reform came into force, the students received a diploma at the end of each of the study cycles that, together, now constitute basic education. This, too, was a factor that symbolically increased the potential to leave school without finishing this degree of education. With the new legislation, there is only one leaving certificate at the end of the period of compulsory education. This is the basic education diploma, which is awarded if the student completes the ninth grade successfully, or an attendance certificate in case the student fails to pass the final ninth year. The attendance certificate does not qualify for secondary education or for training programmes which demand the basic education diploma as a prerequisite.

The secondary education system has probably been the most controversial segment in the Portuguese education system structure. Since the early 1970s, the various political directions converged to create what was called the prolonged multivalent education model (see Pedroso, 1991, 1997), which removed career-oriented options from the curricula of regular secondary schools. The beginning of the 1980s saw the return, at first with an experimental character, of career-oriented options to secondary education (see Grácio, 1987; Pedroso, 1991).

With the reform of the education system, secondary education now consists of two types of course groups, both with a duration of three years and taught at multivalent schools: course groups of a general nature or, in the terminology of the Education System Framework Law, course groups "predominantly oriented towards higher education"; and the technological course groups, which are "predominantly oriented towards working life".

Both the general and the technical courses are organised into four study fields (sciences and nature, the arts, economic and social, and humanities). In each grouping there is one general subject and several technical subjects (out of a total of 11). Both tracks end with the awarding of the secondary education diploma. Students in the technical study fields are also awarded a level III professional qualification certificate.[3]

Finally, in the 'mainstream forms of school education' at the level of higher education, there are two types of routes; the university and the polytechnic. Universities award the '*Licenciatura*' degree and, at the post-graduate level, MBAs and PhD degrees. The Licenciatura degree courses have a variable duration of four to six years.

Together with the 'mainstream forms of education', the Education System Framework Law has created the 'special forms of school education', which presently consist of vocational training certified by both the school and the professional institute, recurrent education, and special education. These types of education are designed to create alternative opportunities for students with particular educational needs (in the case of special education), or to provide for a second-chance education (in the case of vocational training and recurrent education) for young people or adults who are already older than the official school-leaving age, and who wish to continue or recommence their education in a system offering a differentiated curricular organisation.

At present, there are two forms of vocational training with school and professional certification; these are the Vocational Schools and the Apprenticeship System. Both training models are based on the principle of alternating training, have different curricula to those in mainstream education and award diplomas equivalent to education and vocational certificates of levels I, II or III, depending on the courses.

The Vocational Schools, set up in 1989, have evolved in such a way that they have become very similar to technological secondary education. Although they can also offer level II courses for students who have completed the sixth year, their course offerings are concentrated on level III, which is designed for students who have completed the ninth year.

The Apprenticeship System, created in 1984 after a series of pilot tests, is an adaptation of the German dual system model. It focuses to a great extent on giving a second chance to students who did not complete basic education; it does this by means of level II courses, although it also offers level III courses.

Similar to vocational training courses, recurrent education is second-chance education, though its courses are organised only with a view to achieving school diplomas. The courses are organised, as a rule, in an after-working-hours timetable.

- The courses in the 1st cycle last 150 hours, with a curricular structure that covers essential knowledge of Portuguese, mathematics and the world today. They lead up to a certificate corresponding to the 1st cycle of basic education.
- The 2nd cycle courses last one school year and are organised according to subject. They end with the awarding of a certificate corresponding to the 2nd cycle.
- The 3rd cycle courses are based on the system of modular units and therefore do not have a fixed duration. The student completes the course when they complete all the modular units of all the subjects that make up the course. Upon completion of these units, the student is awarded the equivalent of the basic education diploma.

Special education is aimed at the rehabilitation and socioeducational integration of individuals with specific educational needs due to physical or mental handicaps. It comprises activities directed at the students and their families, as well as at teachers and the communities. Along with adapted curricula, it provides for extra technical and pedagogical support.

Finally, out-of-school education is a form of continuing education that is designed to create opportunities for personal development and improvement. The certificates awarded do not have academic equivalence and the activities may take on diverse forms; these include, in particular, reading, writing and basic education for adults; activities of retraining and professional improvement; the development of technological skills and technical knowledge; and sociocultural animation. The activities in out-of-school education may, however, be considered equivalent to activities in recurrent education, in order to promote mobility between this form of education and recurrent education.

Over recent years, a range of measures have been taken to cope with the specific needs of disadvantaged children: the Education for All Programme, directed to ensure (e)quality of treatment for minority groups; the introduction of educational animators; special pedagogical support in basic education; the '*Entreculturas*' programme; and the Priority Educational Territories (TEIP).

Nevertheless, Portugal still has to concentrate its efforts on the achievement of general compliance with the law on compulsory education. Early dropout continues to be a threat to the complete schooling of the younger generations. In view of the importance and gravity of this situation, specific programmes and projects continue to be drawn up, whose main objective is the development of conditions that will guarantee that pupils complete their compulsory education.

Spain

The first important reform of the Spanish education system in the post-war period took place in 1970, with the General Education Law or LGE (*Ley General de Educación*). The two most far-reaching measures in this reform were (i) the raising of the legal school leaving age from 12 to 14, which made school attendance compulsory for all children between the ages of 6 and 14 and gave this block of studies the name EGB (*Enseñanza General Básica*, Basic General Education); and (b) the division of the school curriculum into cycles: the 1st cycle (age 6-7), the 2nd cycle (age 8-11) and the 3rd cycle (age 12-14).

The concept of cycles, which has been maintained under the current reform, contained two important educational practices:

- the marking system was 'softened' by changing from percentages to graded categories (good/pass, very good, excellent and outstanding);
- assessments given after each year were replaced with an assessment for the whole cycle, which makes the education process for a school year at each level more flexible.

Under this system, a student could take one more year than is usual to cover each cycle, whether the student passed with good grades or not.

The first aspect of the cycle concept was put into practice straight away. The second, however, was not implemented in schools until the end of the 1980s.

The *Ley de Ordenación General del Sistema Educativo* (LOGSE, General Organisation of the Education System Act) has been in effect since 1990. It has introduced two important changes: raising the compulsory school leaving age, and altering the structure and content of the curriculum.

First, the school leaving age has been raised to 16. Thus, it covers the 14-16 age group, which was previously left in limbo, as students could leave school at 14 but were not able to start work until 16. However, it does not extend compulsory education for the younger age groups.

Figure A.5: The structure of education in Spain

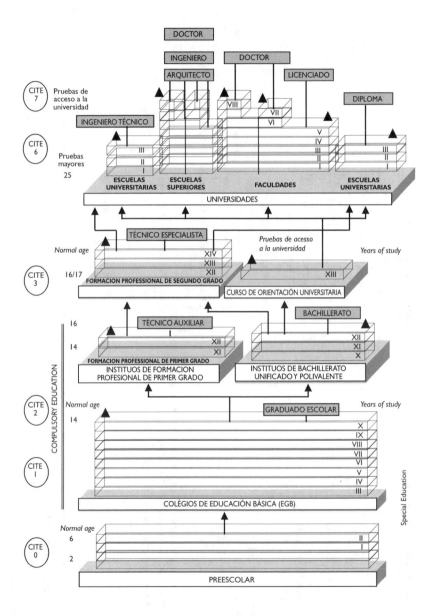

Table A.5: Selected indicators relating to social exclusion and education in Spain

Country information	Education
Population 38,749,000 (1) Aged under 25 years: 34.5% (2)	**Participation rates** 16-18 age group: 78% in 1995 (5) 19-21 age group: 55% in 1995 (5)
Foreigners living in the country Not available (3)	**Compulsory education (6)** Until 16 years full-time*
Unemployment rates (1) In 1995, General: 22.7% Aged under 25 years: 41.7%	**Repeating policies (6)** Possible every year other levels Possible every year in the lower secondary level (except for the first year) Possible every year in the upper secondary level
	Children leaving school without any certificate (6) 15% in 1991
Poverty % inhabitants with incomes below 50% of the national median disposable income per consumption unit: 20% (8) Poverty incidence among children (below age 16): 25% in 1993(8)	**Annual educational expenditure (% of GDP)** *Public* *Public/Private Combined* 5.2% in 1992 (2) Not available (2)
	Public expenditure per pupil In 1992, US $ (7) Pre-School: 2,100 Primary: 2,270 Secondary: 3,140 Tertiary: 3,770

Sources: (1) Eurostat (1995); (2) European Commission (1995); (3) Ress (1996); (4) Förster (1994); (5) European Commission (1996b); (6) European Commission (1995); (7) OECD (1995); (8) Eurostat (1997a)

* After the reform

Primary school education is still not legally enforced for children under 6, as compulsory education starts at the age of 6, even though most schools offer places for children from the age of 3, and the curriculum treats the 0–5 age groups as the pre-school cycle.

The LOGSE also requires that schools adapt their curricula to their social and anthropological environment, to take account of social and cultural diversity, to pay attention to the transmission of 'values' along with knowledge, and so on.

Thus far, the LOGSE educational reform has been implemented rather slowly and unequally across the country.

The opening up of the education system to new social groups, and the expansion of educational participation, is a recent process in Spain. In a short space of time, between 1982 and 1995, Spain has met three notable challenges:

- full basic/compulsory schooling (to the age of 14) was implemented in the early 1980s (1982);
- democratisation of secondary school, whether in the academic track or in vocational training, was accomplished in the late 1980s (1989), when a participation rate of 64% was reached among people between 16 and 17 years of age;
- full opening up of university education was achieved at the beginning of the 1990s: from 1991 to 1995, 20% of an entire generation took degrees, while 40% entered the first year of university.

During this short period of only 13 years, the average duration of school careers below the age of 18 rose from 11 years in 1982 to 12.2 years in 1994. If we compare this indicator with previous generations, the progress in schooling is highly significant.

The sharp rise in educational demand has been accompanied by significant investments in equipment, resources and teachers that have nearly tripled public expenditures in education in barely seven years. In 1985, a total of 6.3 billion ECU were spent, and 1992 saw 16.7 billion ECU invested in the sector. This continual growth in public expenditure can be explained by the political will to develop an entire public network of centres and to consolidate a broad grants policy.

As regards these student grants, the number of beneficiaries between 1982 and 1995 increased by 400%, rising from 162,269 beneficiaries to 816,251. If in 1985 the total amount represented 1.8% of the total of the national budget destined for education, in 1994 it represented 2.3%. If the horizon of comparison is widened to the period 1975–91, we observe how the basic priority in educational policy has consisted of improving available resources and increasing the services on offer in terms of the number of centres, in order to effectively implement the public right to education.

This set of indicators is clear evidence of the recent opening and democratisation of the post-obligatory stages, being the consolidation of a voluntaristic public policy in education, which was totally unknown in Spain since the time of the Second Republic (1931–39). The continual democratisation of access during the last decade and a half has, for the first time, allowed new generations to reach educational levels which, though not identical, are nonetheless more comparable with those of their European contemporaries.

Obviously, only the younger generations have benefited from the great investment in political education carried out in Spain during the past two decades, while other European countries implemented this in the 1960s. All of this took place under the impulse of welfare and equal opportunity policies that were previously unknown in Spain (until the mid-1980s). This fact should be borne in mind as a conditioner of the level of analysis and the limited knowledge in Spain regarding problems of educational inequality.

The educational expansion that took place in Spain is not consistent with the adverse conditions of the job market and youth transition. Job scarcity and rising unemployment restrain activity levels among the young, thus prolonging their schooling as a defence strategy. This may explain why three leading European countries in secondary and university education (Spain, Italy and Finland) are also the leading countries in unemployment among the young. At the same time, this sketch of the recent evolution helps to explain why more attention has been devoted to the general improvement of educational opportunities than to (social) equality of opportunities.

The theoretical debate around success and failure in school and their unequal social distribution was particularly lively at the end of the 1970s and throughout the 1980s in Spain. However, it was unaccompanied by wide-ranging empirical studies. For this reason, little information is available about the effective improvements brought about for disadvantaged groups. It is totally unknown whether greater democratisation in access to education has also meant greater success and a reduction in the dropout rate among the children of the most needy families. The fragmentary information available does not allow us to draw any sort of conclusions in this regard.

Nevertheless, we should note that there is a structural tendency in

Spain to generate a high overall failure rate and a high percentage of school leavers without qualifications or with very weak diplomas. The current educational reform seeks to bring the proportion of school leavers without any qualifications down from 46% to 25%. At the same time, it also aims at broadening out the numbers of those with intermediate qualifications and dissuading mass university access until the percentage of school leavers going on to higher education is down to 30%. Its success in achieving these goals cannot be assessed until the reform has been fully implemented in 2003.

Scotland[4]

Education in Scotland is governed by its own Scottish legislation, and the Secretary of State for Scotland is responsible to Westminster for the overall supervision and development of state education. The Scottish Office Education and Industry Department (SOEID) has direct responsibility for further and higher education. The Department has a close working relationship with the Scottish local authorities, which are responsible for the delivery of school and community education (including pre-school and compulsory education).

Compulsory schooling for children aged 5-16 in Scotland occurs within 'comprehensive' schools that children of all abilities attend.

Local authorities are under no obligation to provide early years services for all children although, since 1996, they must provide services for 'children in need'. Previously, all parents of 'pre-school' children (that is, 3½- to 4½-year-olds) received a 'nursery voucher', but this has been replaced since autumn 1998 with a pre-school place (through local authorities) for these children.

Primary schools follow a 5-14 curriculum, recently established on the basis of a recommendation by SOEID rather than by legislation or guidance. In primary schools, the curriculum covers language, mathematics, environmental studies, expressive arts, and religious, moral and social education. Progress is measured through the attainment of five levels; these levels are based on the expected performance of the majority of pupils at certain ages. Classes are of mixed ability.

For the first two years of compulsory secondary schooling (S1-2), students continue with a widened 5-14 curriculum. For the second two years (S3-4), the curriculum is designed around Standard Grade assessment, divided into eight modes: language and communication; mathematical studies; scientific studies and applications; social and environmental studies; technological activities and applications; creative

Figure A.6: Scotland's educational system

Age	Establishment		
18+	**Higher education institutions** • Degree level courses • Evening classes • Professional training	**Further education colleges** • Degree level courses (some FE colleges) • Profesional training (some FE colleges) • Non-advanced courses: vocational and general pre-employment off-the-job training evening classes • Vocational units leading to a SCOTVEC National Certificate or a General Scottish Vocational Qualification (GSVQ) • Advanced vocational awards: Higher National Certificate Higher National Diploma	
18 17	**Secondary schools (S5-S6)** • Higher grade • Certificate of Sixth Year Studies (S6 only) • Vocational units leading to a SCOTVEC National Certificate or a General Scottish Vocational Qualification (GSVQ)	**Further education colleges** As above and also: • link courses for school pupils)	**Youth training (skillseekers)** (which often involves off-the-job training at FE colleges)
16 15	**Secondary schools** • Standard Grade Curriculum: Foundation, General and Credit (S3-S4) • Vocational units leading to a SCOTVEC National Certificate or a General Scottish Vocational Qualification (GSVQ)		
14 13 12	• 5-14 curriculum (S1-S2)		
11 10 9 8 7 6 5	**Primary schools** • 5-14 curriculum		
4 3	**Nursery schools and classes** • Curriculum framework for children in pre-school year		

and aesthetic activities; physical education; and religious and moral education. Time is not allocated equally between the modes. Pupils are assessed against performance standards related to three levels of award: Foundation, General, and Credit. Students can also take vocational units, which can lead to vocational certification later on.

A pupil can stay on past age 16 in secondary school, although schools set entrance standards for certain courses and advise students to take

Table A.6: Selected indicators relating to social exclusion and education in the United Kingdom

Country information

Population
57,525,000 (1)
Aged under 25 years: 33% (2)

Foreigners living in the country
3.3 in 1990 (3)

Unemployment rates (1)
In 1995, General: 8.7%
Aged under 25 years: 15.5%

Poverty
% non-elderly families with incomes below 50% of the national
median disposable income per consumption unit: 12.4% in 1986 (4)

% inhabitants with incomes below 50% of the national median
disposable income per consumption unit: 22% (8)

Poverty incidence among children (below age 16): 32% in 1993(8)

Education

Participation rates
16-18 age group: 66% in 1995 (5)
19-21 age group: 28% in 1995 (5)

Compulsory education (6)
Until 16 years full-time

Repeating policies (6)
Automatic promotion

Children leaving school without any certificate (6)
8% in 1989

Annual educational expenditure (% of GDP)

Public	Public/Private Combined
4.1% in 1992 (2)	Not available (2)

Public expenditure per pupil
In 1992, US $ (7)

Pre-School: 1,860	Primary: 3,120	Secondary: 4,390	Tertiary: 15,060

Sources: (1) Eurostat (1995); (2) European Commission (1995); (3) Ress (1996); (4) Förster (1994); (5) European Commission (1996b); (6)
European Commission (1995); (7) OECD (1995); (8) Eurostat (1997a)

different routes. At this stage of schooling, there are three different types of courses: academically biased courses leading to the Scottish Certificate of Higher Education (Higher Grade); courses for those in S6 who have already achieved their Higher Grade, which can lead to the Certificate in Sixth-Year Studies; and vocationally biased units. In 1998, a new system of courses and qualifications was introduced called 'Higher Still'.

The framework of vocational qualifications has grown in recent years. Vocational units can be taken to gain Scottish Vocational Qualifications (SVQs). Particularly aimed at 16- to 19-year-olds and adult returners, within the SVQ framework is the General Scottish Vocational Qualification (GSVQ), which is designed to provide a broad training for employment and progression to higher education. Students can also gain a non-advanced certificate from such training, called the National Certificate by the Scottish Vocational Educational Council (SCOTVEC). At advanced levels, the awards are the Higher National Certificate and the Higher National Diploma.

Youth training (Skillseekers) guarantees a vocational training place, leading to a SCOTVEC qualification, to young people under 18. Local Enterprise Companies offer this training. Other training is available for young people over the age of 18. Students can go to FE colleges once they leave school at age 16. Admission requirements vary according to the courses of study. Non-advanced courses do not normally require formal qualifications. For higher education, the usual entry requirement is the Higher Grade (or other UK equivalents), but special access courses are designed to prepare adults for higher education. Many access courses guarantee a place in higher education if successfully completed.

Since the Act of Union, Scotland has retained its own education system, and this has been the source of much of its sense of national identity. A belief in meritocracy lies at the heart of Scottish educational values, although academics have tended to regard this belief in the essential impartiality of the educational system as something of a myth.

Some features of the organisation of the Scottish state school sector reflect the principles of equality of access, although these have tended to be undermined by the market-driven policies championed by the previous Conservative government. The comprehensive reorganisation of schools in Scotland, for example, was much more thoroughgoing than comprehensivisation in England, and there are currently no selective schools within the state sector north of the border. Social class differences in staying-on rates have narrowed, and girls are much more likely to stay on than boys (Paterson and Raffe, 1995).

Despite its meritocratic traditions, Scotland contains some of the poorest regions within the United Kingdom. The Scottish Declaration on Poverty (1996) delineated the extent of the problem of poverty within Scotland, as illustrated by the following statistics:

- 1 in 4 children in Scotland live in households dependent on Income Support;
- in 1994, 20% of children were eligible for free school meals; the figure for Glasgow is twice this;
- 38% of Scottish children under 16, and 42% of those under 5, are living in poverty.

A number of outcomes follow from these statistics. For example, children from affluent backgrounds are ten times more likely to get a degree than are children from deprived backgrounds.

Despite evidence of considerable poverty within the UK, the Conservative government, which was in power between 1979 and 1997, declared early war on notions of 'egalitarianism' which, during the late 1970s, were held responsible for Britain's economic decline. Poverty, the Conservative government argued, should be seen as an absolute, not a relative concept; therefore, since Britain was affluent by world standards, it did not make sense to talk about a problem of poverty. Rather than pursuing egalitarian solutions, the Conservative government decided that the way to achieve effectiveness, efficiency and value for money was through market mechanisms.

Within education, a range of policies were implemented to pursue these goals; some of these policies tended to centralise power, while others devolved power from the state and local authorities to individual parents and schools. Educational reforms in Scotland tended to take rather different forms from those south of the border. The major reforms introduced or planned during the lifetime of the previous government in Scotland are as follows:

- 5–14 curriculum and assessment programme;
- Higher Still curriculum programme;
- self-governing schools;
- parental choice of school;
- performance indicators and publication of school performance records;
- devolved school management.

Each of these measures had a particular impact on Scotland's comprehensive education system, sometimes furthering an equal access agenda, as happened in the context of curricular reforms, but at other times heightening social segregation, a product, for instance, of parental choice of school (Willms, 1997).

The Labour government, in line with other European countries, has not turned its back on the market, but early indications suggest that it intends to pursue a managed market or a mixed economy of service provision. One of the first acts of the Westminster government was to set up a Social Exclusion Unit, although schools have been told firmly that they are not to use poverty as an excuse for low standards. Given the continuing power of education to strongly influence future life chances and therefore to act as a crucible for wider social values, it is not surprising that it remains such a central political battleground.

In the Scottish case, this discussion is even more crucial because of the major presence of poverty in this region of the United Kingdom. However, because of the political and historical context, past educational research in Scotland, particularly at the national level, has tended not to focus on the effects of poverty and deprivation on children's educational attainment.

Nevertheless, free school meal entitlement[5] and parental education are currently being used as indices of disadvantage in the calculation of school attainment targets. This is part of the Scottish Office initiative 'Setting Targets: A Strategy To Raise Standards' currently being developed in conjunction with local education authorities to raise performance levels in schools throughout Scotland. The acknowledgement that school attainment targets should be linked to the school's socioeconomic profile marks a change in direction for the Scottish Office, no doubt prompted by the New Labour government.

Notes

[1] The main difference between technical and vocational education is that technical school includes more theoretical subjects, while vocational schools are focused on practice. Technical education has an 'intermediate' status between general and vocational education.

[2] Students who have a certificate of lower secondary education (fourth year) can enter PTVE earlier, at the age of 15.

[3] In Portugal, professional certificates obey the hierarchy of qualification levels adopted by the European Council of Ministers of 16 July, 1985.

[4] This section is largely based on SOEID 1996 and SOEID Internet information.

[5] This is a statutory entitlement for all children whose parents are unemployed and receiving Income Support or the income based Jobseekers Allowance.

Index

NOTE: Page numbers followed by *fig* indicate information is to be found in a figure, *tab* indicates information in a table and *n* indicates information in a note.

A

ability grouping *see* streaming systems

absenteeism 56-7, 59-60, 72, 292

Accelerated Schools Programme (ASP)(United States) 164, 175-6, 181, 319

active pedagogical methods 168-74, 180-1, 319

Adler, M. 205

adult education participation32-4

Advisory Council for Primary and Special Education (Netherlands) 236

Ainscow, M. 228, 237-8

alternating learning 291, 295, 299-305, 308, 309, 310, 323

alternative curricula 148, 149*tab*, 150*tab*, 151, 159, 162*n*, 319, 323
  as second-chance provision 293, 294-8, 308
  social implications 160, 161

Amadora Project (Portugal) 130, 142

Amaro, R. 217

Andersen, J. 5

'animators' (Portugal) 113, 142, 278, 286

apprenticeship systems 295, 297, 298, 300, 301, 304-5, 308, 310, 383-4, 392

art projects (Belgium) 214

Ashworth, K. 4

assessment practices 65-6
  see also performance measures; qualifications

Assistance to Schools in Designated Areas of Disadvantage (Ireland) 258, 266

Assistant Training scheme (Netherlands) 295

ATD-Fourth World 89, 225, 226

attendance rates *see* compulsory education; dropout rates; truancy

attribution theory 166

Autonomous Middle Schools (Belgium) 156

autonomy, pedagogy of 169

B

Back to School Clothing Allowance (Ireland) 82, 92

Ball, S. 204-5

Ballymun Initiative for Third-level Education (BITE) 85-6, 94

Barnardo's 139
Baron, S. 202
basic skills 98
Basin Street Project (Ireland) 276, 280, 286
Basque Plan (1982) 231
behavioural problems 167, 280
Belgium
  adult education 33*fig*
  compulsory education 53–4, 58–9, 61, 64, 66, 67, 71, 73, 196*n*
  curricular reforms 196*n*
  discriminatory practices 67
  dropout rates 58–9
  equal opportunities strategies 45–6*tab*, 58–9, 64–5, 71
  equal treatment strategies 41, 47–8*tab*
  grade retention 26
  literacy levels 30
  pre-school education 22, 126, 127, 128–9, 143
  socioeconomic background 28, 30, 32*tab*, 373*tab*
  special needs provision 222, 225
  teacher training 197*n*
  upper secondary participation 7, 8*fig*, 9, 25
  see also Flanders
Bernard van Leer Foundation 142
Blaug, M. 63
Bollens, J. 67, 266, 285
Booth, T. 237–8
Bowles, S. 19
Breaking the Cycle scheme (Ireland) 251*tab*, 256*tab*, 261, 266
Britain *see* United Kingdom

Bruto da Costa 83

C

Capitulaciones 92 (Spain) 142
care placement 20, 28, 225
careers advice 166, 280
Casa de los Niños, La (Spain) 139
categorical measures 42, 48*tab*
Centre for the Child and Society (CCS) 10
Centre d'Iniciatives i Recerques Europees a la Mediterrània (CIREM) 10
certification strategies 42, 47*tab*
  see also qualifications
Charlot, Bernard 65
child benefit 84, 85, 87, 88
child-centred approach 169
Child-Parent Centers (United States) 125
child poverty 5
Children (Scotland) Act (1995 & 1997) 59, 114, 117, 120
'children in need' services (England and Wales) 115
Children's Services Plans (Scotland) 114–15, 117
choice, parental *see* parental choice
Committee on Special Education (Spain) 231–2
communication between school and home *see* parent-school-community relationships
communicative perspective 176–9, 319
community environment 98–9
  community-based intervention programmes 140–3, 202

see also parent-school-
community relationships
Community of Learning Project
(Spain) 177-9, 181
compensatory education 143-4,
163-5, 180, 201, 274, 278, 286,
324
Compensatory Education
Actions/Programmes (Spain)
253*tab*, 256*tab*, 262
comprehensive curriculum
schools 155-9, 318-19, 320,
402, 404
compulsory education 40, 45*tab*,
53-74, 183, 196*n*, 317-18,
318-19
financial assistance strategies
78-83, 89-92, 95
see also curricula; school leaving
age; school starting age
Compulsory Education Act
(Netherlands, 1969) 57
constructivist pedagogy 169-74,
180-1, 319
consumer choice see parental
choice
continuing education
participation 32-4
continuing teacher training
190-3, 194-6, 197*n*, 323
core skills 98
'cost' of education 25, 34, 35*n*,
62, 76, 78-9
cost-benefit analysis of reform
strategies 325
Coves d'en Cimany school
(Spain) 170-2, 319
cross-national analysis 10
Crowther, J. 202, 210
cultural activities 103-5, 119,
278, 287

cultural interventions 86, 87,
95-6
cultural relativism 174
curricula
academic/vocational split 9,
18-19, 30, 31
equal outcomes strategies 41,
42, 47*tab*, 49*tab*
equal treatment strategies
147-62, 179-80, 196*n*, 318-20
reforms 64-5, 73, 147-62,
179-80, 384-7, 394
for teacher training courses
187-90, 195-6, 197*n*
see also alternative curriculum

D

Day, C. 2
daycare services 75-6, 77-8
De Buurt school (Belgium)
172-3, 319
De Graaf, P.M. 22-3
De Rank school (Belgium)
241-2, 319
De Wurpskes centre (Belgium)
141
De'Ath 201
democratisation in teaching
methods 183-4, 313
Demonstration Programme on
Educational Disadvantage
(Ireland) 110, 118, 252*tab*, 257
deprivation 4
differentiation 42, 49*tab*, 274, 287
see also pedagogy of diversity
disabled children
right to education 67, 227-8,
243-4
see also special educational
needs (SEN) provision

disadvantaged children:
  educational situation 3–6,
  15–35, 313–15, 371–405
discipline 273
discriminatory treatment 37–8,
  67
  see also equal treatment
  strategies
diversity, pedagogy of 159, 162*n*,
  164–5, 169, 180
Down's syndrome children 234,
  237
Dronkers, J. 16
dropout rates 22–6, 29, 34, 89,
  394
  strategies to prevent 40, 45*tab*,
  56–60, 72, 89, 91, 120, 291,
  292–3, 308
  see also school leavers; second-
  chance provision
Dyson, A. 225

E

early childhood education *see*
  pre-school education
early childhood intervention
  programmes 133–43, 179,
  208–10, 218–19, 255–6, 263,
  269, 277, 286, 316, 317
Early Intervention Programme
  (Scotland) 136–8, 253*tab*,
  255–6, 263, 269, 286, 316, 317
early school leaving 1, 22–6, 29,
  56–60, 151, 291–4
  see also dropout rates; school
  leavers
Early Start programme (Ireland)
  40–1, 133, 135–6, 208
Echols, F. 205

Economic and Social Council
  (France) 4
Economic and Social Research
  Institute (ESRI) 10
Education (Scotland) Act (1980)
  ]40 45*tab*, 67–8, 73, 203
education action zones (United
  Kingdom) 277
Education for All programme
  (Portugal) 40, 45*tab*, 60, 393
Education System Framework
  Law (Portugal, 1986) 387, 390,
  391–2
Education and Vocational
  Training Act
  (WEB)(Netherlands,) 71,
  311*n*
educational 'animators' (Portugal)
  113, 142, 278, 286
educational inequality 313–15
  causes of 15–19, 38
  strategies to combat 37–49
educational outcomes *see* equal
  outcomes strategies
educational participation
  adult education 32–4
  compulsory education 40,
  45*tab*, 53–74
  pre-school 22
  and social background 17–18,
  22–6, 155, 156
  upper secondary 7–9
Educational Policy for
  Disadvantaged Young People
  (Netherlands) 111
Educational Priority Areas
  251*tab*, 252*tab*, 256*tab*
educational priority policies
  (EPPs) 38–9, 42, 49*tab*, 249–71,
  322–3
  funding criteria 255–60

territorial approach 256–9, 266
Educational Priority Policy
(Belgium) 107, 109, 118, 250,
251*tab*, 256*tab*, 259, 261,
264–5, 271*n*, 281, 374
Educational Priority Policy
(OVB)(Netherlands) 252*tab*,
256*tab*, 259, 261–2, 266–8, 279,
282, 284, 287, 387
Educational Priority Territories
(TEIP)(Portugal) 252*tab*,
256*tab*, 262
Eimers, T. 291
El Margalló school (Spain)
240–1, 319
Employment-Oriented
Programme (Netherlands)
162*n*
equal opportunities strategies 38,
40–1, 45–6*tab*, 53–144, 314–15,
315–18
equal outcomes strategies 38–9,
42, 49*tab*, 249–313, 322–4
equal treatment strategies 38, 39,
41–2, 47–8*tab*, 147–245,
318–22
Erikson, R. 17
ESE (Escola Superior de
Educação)(Portugal) 186, 188,
196*n*
ethnicity
and educational outcomes 20,
23, 26, 67, 279
integrated services provision
101, 102, 105–6
multiculturalism in classroom
184–5
religious schools 206
European Commission
'social exclusion' as term 5

White Paper on Education and
Training 161
European Union 1–2, 3, 5
compulsory education 53, 54*fig*,
55–6, 60–3
Eurostat 61
Eurydice 53*fig*, 54–5, 60–1, 63–4
evaluation of research 324
Evans, J. 100
exchange programmes: costs of
79
exclusion from school 59, 67, 68
experiential education 169,
172–3
Experimental Compulsory
Secondary Schools (Spain)
156–8, 318–19
Extended Care policy (Belgium)
107, 109, 118, 138, 251*tab*,
255, 256*tab*, 257, 259, 261,
265–6, 284–5, 374
Extended School Day
experiment (Netherlands) 40,
104–5, 287, 315–16

F

failing schools 163–5, 217–18,
285
Family Clubs (Portugal) 216–17
family literacy programmes 202,
208–10
family size 20, 23–4, 27, 28
financial assistance strategies 40,
45*tab*, 75–96, 226, 316, 397–8
educational priority funding
38–9, 42, 49*tab*
see also educational priority
policies (EPPs)
Finland: costs of education 79

Flags and Banners project
(Belgium) 214
Flanders
adult education 33*fig*, 34
background information 371-4
compulsory education 58, 66,
371
costs of compulsory education
79
curricular reforms 149*tab*, 151,
152, 153, 155
drop-out rates 24-5, 58
educational priority policies
107, 109, 118, 250, 251*tab*,
256*tab*, 259, 261, 264-6, 271*n*,
281, 374
financial and material assistance
80, 84, 91-2, 93-4, 226
grade retention 26-7, 94
integrated services 101, 102,
103-4, 105-6, 107-9, 108*tab*,
116*tab*, 117, 118, 281-2
learning support 277-8, 279,
281-2, 284-5, 286, 287, 288*n*
literacy levels 30
parent-school-community
relationships 212-14, 219
pedagogical innovations 172-3,
319
pre-school education 76, 138,
140-1, 192-3, 371
second-chance provision 295,
300, 301-5, 310, 323
socioeconomic background 28,
30
special needs provision 225-6,
234-6, 239, 241-2, 319
teacher training 192-3
see also Belgium
Flecha, R. 165

Flemish Education Council
235-6
Flemish Fund for the Integration
of the Disadvantaged 103
flexible curricula 42, 147-8,
149*tab*, 150*tab*, 152, 153, 153-9, 161
Framework Programmes for
Research and Technological
Development (EU) 324
France: costs of education 78, 81,
82
free school meals
as material assistance 82, 83, 92
as measure of disadvantage 24,
31, 59, 82-3, 404
free school milk 77, 82
Fundación Encuentro 25-6
Funding for Regeneration
Strategies (Scotland) 253*tab*

G

Gamoran, A. 156
Ganzeboom, H.B.G. 22-3
geographical marginalisation 18
Germany
socioeconomic background
35*n*
upper secondary participation 7
Ghesquière, P. 235-6, 285
Gintis, H. 19
GOALS 2000: Educate America
Act 279
Goffinet 30, 225-6
Going to School Together Act
(Netherlands, 1994) 236-7,
282, 387
Goldthorpe, J.H. 314
Gordon, J. 65
governance of schools 200-1

grade retention 21, 26-7, 34, 94, 288*n*

grants 80, 82, 84-5, 87-9, 91-2, 93-4, 95, 374

'grassroots' initiatives 43
see also micro level policies

Grignon, C. 174

H

Hallett, C. 59-60

Hannan, D.F. 294

Harmon, C. 62

Head Start programme (United States) 124-5, 316, 317

health of disadvantaged children 20, 29, 226

healthcare 102-3

High/Scope Perry Pre-school Programme (United States) 125

higher education *see* third-level education

HMI (Her Majesty's Inspector of Schools, Scotland) 229, 231

Hoger Instituut voor de Arbeid (HIVA) 10

Holland *see* Netherlands

home-based intervention programmes 140, 143
literacy programmes 202, 208-10

home-environment 98-9

Home-School-Community Liaison (HSCL)(Ireland) 110, 116, 118, 210-12, 219

home-school-community relationships *see* parent-school-community relationships

Home-School-Employment Partnership (HSEP)(Scotland) 101, 117, 214-16, 219, 262-3, 268-9

homework clubs 102, 213, 278, 286

Household Panel survey 35*n*

Hout, M. 18

Hurell, P. 100

I

illiteracy *see* literacy levels

immigrant children 23, 25, 31, 102, 255, 278

inclusion of special needs pupils 42, 221, 226-44, 282, 319, 320

Inclusive Schools project (Portugal) 193

inequality *see* educational inequality; social inequality

initial teacher training 186-90, 194, 320-1

Innovative Project for Experiential Education (Belgium) 172-3

in-service teacher training 190-3, 194-6, 197*n*

Instituto de Estudos Económicos e Socias (IESE) 10

Instituut voor Toegepaste Sociale wetenschappen (ITS) 10

integrated curriculum option choice 152, 153

integrated services 40, 46*tab*, 58, 59-60, 66, 97-121, 142, 282, 315-16

integration contracts (Portugal) 81-2

integration of special needs pupils 42, 221, 226-44, 282, 319, 320 interagency cooperation *see* integrated services

intercultural nursery nurses (Belgium) 192–3

International Adult Literacy Survey 31–2

International Association for the Evaluation of Educational Achievement 159

International Education Association 30

Ireland 26, 32*tab*, 67
  adult education participation 33*fig*
  background information 375–9
  costs of compulsory education 78–9
  curricular reforms 149*tab*, 151, 153–4, 154–5, 156
  dropout rates 23–4, 59, 120
  educational outcomes and employment 21
  educational priority policies 251–2*tab*, 256*tab*, 261, 266
  equal opportunity strategies 40–1, 45–6*tab*, 59, 64–5, 315
  equal treatment strategies 41, 47–8*tab*
  financial and material assistance 76, 82, 84, 85–7, 88–9, 92, 94
  integrated services 101–2, 108*tab*, 110–11, 116, 118, 120, 210–12
  learning support 275–6, 279, 280, 281, 286
  literacy levels 30
  parent-school-community relationships 110, 116, 118, 206–7, 208, 210–12, 219
  pre-school education 22, 76, 126, 127*fig*, 132–3, 134–6, 138–9, 208, 375
  second-chance provision 294–5, 296, 305–7, 310
  socioeconomic background 22, 23–4, 31, 377*tab*
  special needs provision 223, 233–4, 240
  teacher training 188
  upper secondary participation 7, 8*fig*, 9, 23–4, 84

Italy: costs of education 79, 88

J

'job corps' (Belgium) 295

job skills 98

Jonsson, J.O. 17

Jungbluth 267

Junior Certificate Elementary Programme (JCEP)(Ireland) 294–5, 296, 378

K

Karsten, S. 206

Kellaghan, T. 258

Kennedy, M.M. 258

Kilkenny project (Ireland) 140

Kind en Gezin (Belgium) 128, 140–1

King Baudouin Foundation 40, 46*tab*, 101, 103–4, 105–6, 118, 212, 277–8, 286

KMBO courses (Netherlands) 297–8, 309–10, 311*n*, 323, 383

Koffiepot centre (Belgium) 141

Kolvin, I. 167

Kropp, D. 62–3

L

Labour government (United Kingdom) 229-30, 404
labour market 1, 21, 31, 62, 152, 289-311, 398
Lang, K. 62-3
language barriers/development 20-1, 23, 105-6, 140, 277-8, 279
large families 20, 23-4, 27, 28
league tables (United Kingdom) 59, 203, 217-18
learned helplessness 166
learning difficulties, children with 67, 68-9, 153
see also learning support; special educational needs (SEN) provision
learning duties/rights 53-74
Learning is Child's Play initiative (Scotland) 209
learning skills 280
learning support 273-88
Learning Support programme (Belgium) 278, 281, 282, 285, 286
Learning Support programme (Scotland) 282
Leaving Certificate Applied Programme (LCAP)(Ireland) 294-5, 296, 378-9
leaving school *see* school leavers
Leclerq, J.M. 168
Levin, H. 164, 175-6
Ley de Integracion Social del Minusvalido (Spain, 1982) 109
Ley de Ordenación General del Sistema Educativo (LOGSE)(Spain, 1990) 394, 396

Ley General de Educación (Spain, 1970) 394
life skills 98
Limerick Community-Based Educational Initiative (LCBEI) 85, 86, 94, 103
literacy skills 20, 30, 31-2, 34
home-based literacy programmes 202, 208-10
remedial work 279, 286
Litt, J. 152
loans for students 88-9, 93
Lothian Region HomeVisiting Scheme 140
Luxembourg: financial assistance 81

M

macro level policies 43, 45-9*tab*, 267
compulsory education 40, 45*tab*, 53-74
financial and material assistance 40, 45*tab*, 75-96
integrated services 106-15
learning support 281, 287
'magnet schools' (Belgium) 214, 219
management of schools 200-1
Margalló, El (Spain) 240-1, 319
material assistance 82-3, 92, 95
see also financial and material assistance
means-tested aid 77-8, 79-83, 84-7, 88, 95
media-based education 391
meso level policies 43, 45-9*tab*, 267, 281-3, 287
micro level policies 43, 45-9*tab*, 267, 271, 283-4, 287

financial and material assistance
85-7
integrated services 100-6
middle-class: educational
participation 17-18
migrant children 23, 25, 31, 102,
255, 278
minimum qualifications 28-9,
70-2, 73-4, 289, 291-2, 298-9,
300, 317
motivation of pupils 63, 273
multiculturalism 184-5, 192-3
Munn, P. 68
Murray, C. 59-60
Muslim schools (Netherlands)
206

N

National Child Development
Study (Scotland) 203
Netherlands 32*tab*
adult education participation
33*fig*
background information379-87
compulsory education 57-8,
71-2
costs of compulsory education
79
curricular reforms 149*tab*, 151,
153-4, 155, 162*n*
dropout rates 22, 23, 29, 57-8
educational outcomes and
employment 21
educational priority policies
252*tab*, 256*tab*, 259, 261-2,
266-8, 279
equal opportunities strategies
40, 45-6*tab*, 57-8, 71-2,
315-16

equal treatment strategies
47-8*tab*
financial and material assistance
76, 81, 83, 84, 88
grade retention 21, 26
integrated services 102, 104-5,
108*tab*, 111-13, 116*tab*, 118,
120, 315-16
learning support 273, 278, 279,
280, 281, 282-3, 284, 287,
288*n*
literacy levels 30
parent-school-community
relationships 206
pre-school education 76, 126,
127*fig*, 130-1, 140
second-chance provision 295,
296, 297-9, 309-10, 311*n*, 323
socioeconomic background 16,
22-3, 28, 31, 381*tab*
special needs provision 222,
236-8, 282, 283, 382
teacher training 192
upper secondary participation
7, 8*fig*, 9, 22-3, 84
New Labour (United Kingdom)
229-30
'new school' methods 168, 176
Nicaise, I. 25, 127, 166
non-means-tested aid 76-7, 78-9,
84, 90*tab*
numeracy skills 279, 286
nursery education *see* pre-school
education

O

OECD (Organisation for
Economic Cooperation and
Development) 55, 56, 97-8,
116-17

'open' activities 169, 182*n*
'overeducation' debate 289

P

parent-dependent grant systems
87-8
parent-school-community
relationships 38, 48*tab*, 98-9,
110, 199-220
parents as educators 101-2, 117,
119, 134, 201, 208-10
partnerships with parents 58,
201-2, 203, 215-16, 230,262-
3, 264*tab*, 268-9, 321-2
in pedagogical innovations 173,
208-17
pre-school education 134,
136-7, 208-10
social expectations 166-7
parental choice 203, 204-7,
217-18
and special needs provision 229,
231, 232-3, 234, 237
parental education
and educational outcomes 15,
17, 20, 22-3, 25, 255, 404
and literacy levels 30
and risk of poverty 31, 32*tab*
parental employment status 23,
24, 25, 28
Parents' Charter for Scotland 229
part-time compulsory education
53, 54, 64, 295, 374
part-time vocational education
(PTVE)(Belgium) 295, 300,
301-5, 310, 374, 404*n*
Partnership in Education Project
(Scotland) 253*tab*, 263, 269
partnerships with parents 58,
201-2, 203, 215-16, 230,
262-3, 264*tab*, 268-9, 321-2

Pastor 231, 232
Paterson, L. 155-6
pedagogical innovations 41,
47*tab*, 163, 167-81, 264*tab*, 319
Pedagogical Training School
(Belgium) 141
pedagogy of autonomy 169
pedagogy of compensation
143-4, 163-5
pedagogy of diversity 159, 162*n*,
164-5, 169, 180
pedagogy of self-management
169
'pedagogy of success' (Belgium)
66, 73
performance measures 26-7,
27-30, 135, 283-4
league tables (UK) 59, 203,
217-18
PETRA Programme 106, 162*n*
Pilton Early Intervention Project
(Scotland) 136-7, 209, 277,
286, 316
playgroups 130-1, 132
see also pre-school education
PMS centres (Belgium) 107, 109,
118, 278, 281-2, 285, 288*n*
policy levels 43-9
Portugal 5, 20, 32*tab*
background information
387-94
compulsory education 70, 74
costs of compulsory education
78
curricular reforms 150*tab*, 151,
152, 153, 162*n*
dropout rates 22, 26, 60, 89, 91,
394
educational priority policies
252*tab*, 256*tab*, 262, 271*n*

equal opportunities strategies
40, 45-6*tab*, 60, 74, 89, 91
equal treatment strategies 41,
47-8*tab*
financial and material assistance
76, 77, 78, 80-1, 81-2, 83, 89,
91, 92
geographical marginalisation 18
grade retention 27
integrated services 106, 108*tab*,
113, 116*tab*, 117, 118
learning support 276, 278, 281,
286
parent-school-community
relationships 216-17, 219
pre-school education 76, 77,
127, 129-30, 139, 142, 390
second-chance provision 295,
300, 310, 393
socioeconomic background 29-
30, 389*tab*
special needs provision 233,
393
teacher training 187-8, 192,
193, 196*n*, 197*n*, 320
upper secondary participation
7, 8*fig*, 9, 26
positive discrimination 38-9, 42,
249-50, 273, 322
post-compulsory education *see*
third level education; upper
secondary education
poverty 3-5, 6
educational implications 31-4,
218-19, 225-6, 371-405
Poverty and Primary Education
project (Belgium) 212-13
Practical Education scheme
(Netherlands) 295, 296
pre-school education

financial assistance strategies
75-8, 90*tab*, 95, 253*tab*, 255-6,
263, 399
integrated services 101, 316
participation levels 22, 126-33,
375, 390
programmes for disadvantaged
children 39, 54, 123-44,
192-3, 253*tab*, 255-6, 263, 316,
317
preventive measures 291, 292-3,
308
primary education 372, 375, 396,
399
curricular reforms 151, 279
equal opportunities strategies
40-1
financial and material assistance
78-83
grade retention 26-7
integrated services 101, 104-5
learning support 273-4, 276,
277, 278, 279, 280-1, 282-3,
284, 286
parent-school-community
relationships 212-213
and socioeconomic
background 29
special needs provision 241-2,
282
teacher training for 186-7, 193,
197*n*
Priority Education Territories
(PET)(Portugal) 113, 117, 118,
252*tab*, 256*tab*, 271*n*, 393
Priority Partnership Areas
(Ireland) 257
Priority Partnership Areas
(Scotland) 24, 136, 215, 219,
225, 244*n*, 253*tab*, 262-3, 268

Programme of Special Measures for Primary Schools (Ireland) 251*tab*

progressive pedagogical methods 168–74, 180–1, 182*n*

prolonged multivalent education model (Portugal) 391

Proyecto Avanzada project (Spain) 142

Proyecto Granada project (Spain) 141–2

Psychological, Medical and Social (PMS) guidance centres (Belgium) 107, 109, 118, 278, 281–2, 285, 288*n*

PTVE (Belgium) 295, 300, 301–5, 310, 374, 404*n*

Pugh, G. 201

pull-out model of remedial education 275, 276, 284, 286

'pupil guidance centres' (Belgium) 282, 288*n*, 374

pupil monitoring systems 287

Pygmalion effect 165–6

Q

qualifications 2, 378–9, 383, 384, 391–2, 402

  curriculum reforms 147, 386

  equal outcomes strategies 42, 47*tab*, 280, 289–311, 323–4

  integrated services improve 102

  minimum qualifications 28–9, 70–2, 73–4, 280, 289, 291–2, 298–9, 300, 317

  unqualified leavers 2, 65–6, 73, 110, 151, 289–311, 317–18, 399

R

Raftery, A.E. 18

Ramón Bajo school (Spain) 178–9, 319

rational choice model 17

reading promotion programme (Netherlands) 280

recreational opportunities 103

Regional Reporting and Coordination Function (RCF)(Netherlands) 57–8, 112, 120

Regional Training Centres (ROCs)(Netherlands) 386

religious schools 206

remedial education 42, 174–5, 180, 273, 274, 275–6, 281, 284, 286

  see also learning support; special educational needs (SEN) provision

Renewed Secondary Vocational Education (Belgium) 64–5, 374

'reorientation to education' measures 291*fig*, 293, 308

repetition of grades 21, 26–7, 34, 94, 288*n*

reproduction theory 19

research into educational reform 324–5

residential pupils (Portugal) 83

resource enhancement 275, 277–8, 286

Riddel, S. 258

'risk factors': disadvantaged children 3, 97

Robertson, P. 215–16

Robinson, P. 203

Roca Cortés, N. 173–4

Rutland Street project (Ireland)
133, 134–5, 208, 316

S

S. João de Deus School
(Portugal) 216–17, 219
'safety-net' provisions 291, 293
Salamanca Statement (UNESCO,
1994) 227–8, 235
Scandinavia: grants system 87, 88
Scheme of Assistance to Schools
in Designated Areas of
Disadvantage (Ireland) 251*tab*
School Community Action
(Belgium) 109, 118, 213–14,
219, 374
school environment 98–9, 283–4
see also parent-school-
community relationships
School-Environment Link
Project (Portugal) 106
school failure 163–5, 217–18, 285
school governance 200–1
school leavers
early school leaving 1, 22–6, 29,
56–60, 151, 291–4
equal outcomes strategies
289–311, 323–4
in labour market 1, 62, 289–90,
398
unqualified leavers 2, 65–6, 73,
110, 151, 289–311, 317–18,
399
school leaving age 40, 45*tab*,
53–4, 61, 62, 72, 375, 394
School Social Assistance scheme
(Portugal) 77, 80–1, 83
school starting age 53, 54, 72,
375
Scotland 26

background information
399–404
compulsory education 59–60,
64, 67–8, 73
curricular reforms 150*tab*, 151,
153–4, 155–6, 158, 162*n*
dropout rates 22, 59
educational inequality 19, 24,
35*n*
educational priority policies 24,
136, 215, 219, 225, 244*n*,
253*tab*, 255–6, 262–3, 268–9
equal opportunities strategies
45–6*tab*, 59–60, 70–1, 402
equal treatment strategies
47–8*tab*
financial and material assistance
76–7, 77–8, 82–3, 85, 92
integrated services 101, 108*tab*,
114–15, 116, 117, 118, 120
learning support 276, 277,
280–1, 282, 285, 286
literacy levels 30
parent-school-community
relationships 201, 205, 209,
214–16, 217–19
pre-school education 54, 76–7,
77–8, 131–2, 136, 140, 209,
255–6, 263, 269, 316, 399
second-chance provision
299–300, 310
socioeconomic background 24,
28, 30–1, 401*tab*, 403, 404
special needs provision 68–70,
223–4, 225, 229–31, 238–9,
244*n*, 283–4
see also United Kingdom
Scottish Declaration on Poverty
(1996) 403
Scottish Office 59, 68, 268, 284,
404

Scottish Office Education
Department (SOED) 229
Scottish Office Education and
Industry Department
(SOEID) 230, 399
Sebba, J. 228
second-chance provision 39, 42,
49*tab*, 289–311, 323, 393
secondary education 371, 375,
378, 382–7, 391–2, 399–400,
402
changing aims of 63–4
financial and material assistance
78–87
grade retention 27
integrated services 101
learning support 280–1, 283,
287, 288*n*
parent-school-community
projects 215–16
special needs provision 225
teacher training for 187–8
value of 62
see also curricular reforms;
dropout rates; upper
secondary education
segregated curriculum option
choice 152–3, 156
selective prevention measures
291*fig*, 292–3
self-fulfilling prophecy 165–6
self-image of pupils 166
self-management, pedagogy of
169
SEN *see* special educational
needs provision
Setúbal Teacher Training College
(Portugal) 193
Short Vocational Education *see*
KMBO

'sidetrack' certificates 42, 318,
320
'signalling' theory 63
single curriculum *see* unification
of curriculum
sixth-form education *see* upper
secondary education
Skillseekers programme
(Scotland) 70–1, 299–300, 310,
402
Smyth, E. 276
social exclusion
meaning of term 5, 6
young people at risk of 1–2,
313
see also disadvantaged children;
poverty
social expectations 163–82, 287
Social Guarantee programme
(Ireland) 305–6
Social Guarantee Programmes
(Spain) 40, 70, 301
Social Impulsion Fund
(Belgium) 103, 213
social inequality 1–2, 6
reproduced in schools 19, 314
social security 81–2
social services *see* integrated
services policies
social skills 280
socialisation 55
socioeconomic background
and choice of school 204–5,
217–18
and educational outcomes
15–16, 17, 20–35, 37, 403
and educational participation
17–18, 22–6, 155, 156
and parental participation 204
and social expectations 163–7,
174–9

and special needs 225–6
and streaming/tracking systems
19, 153
socioeconomic environment
liaison 106
Socrates Programme 11, 79
Spain 20, 32*tab*, 78
background information 394–9
curricular reforms 150*tab*, 151,
153–4, 156–8, 318–19, 394,
396
educational priority policies
253*tab*, 256*tab*, 262
equal opportunities strategies
40, 45–6*tab*, 60, 70
equal treatment strategies 41,
47–8*tab*, 318–19
financial and material assistance
76, 77, 80, 84–5, 88, 92–3,
397–8
geographical marginalisation 18
grade retention 26, 27
integrated services 108*tab*,
109–10, 116, 118, 142
parent-school-community
relationships 207
pedagogical innovations 170–2,
177–9, 319
pre-school education 76, 77,
126, 127*fig*, 130, 139, 141–2
second-chance provision 295,
296, 300–1, 305, 310
socioeconomic background
25–6, 29, 396*tab*
special needs provision 224,
231–3, 239–40, 240–1, 319
teacher training 188, 192, 196*n*,
197*n*
upper secondary participation
7, 8*fig*, 9, 25–6, 29, 84–5

Special Education Review
Committee (Ireland) 223, 234
special educational needs (SEN)
provision 68–70, 221–45,
283–4, 319, 375, 382, 393
in curriculum 151, 155, 160
integration of pupils 42, 221,
226–44, 282, 319, 320
and socioeconomic
background 30–1
teacher training 184
vocational training 71
see also learning support
Special and Integrated Education
Act (1986)(Belgium) 234–5
sports opportunities 103, 119
'starting qualifications' 29, 71,
289, 291–2, 298–9, 300
status quaestionis 10, 13–49
strategies for educational equality
6–9, 34–5, 37–49
see also equal opportunities
strategies; equal outcomes
strategies; equal treatment
strategies
Strathclyde Centre for Disability
Research (SCDR) 10
streaming systems 19, 34, 42, 151,
153, 156, 159, 371, 374
student grants 80, 84–5, 87–9,
91–2, 93–4, 95, 374
student loans 88–9, 93
Study Fees (Financial Assistance)
Act (Netherlands) 84
'study houses' (Netherlands) 280,
288*n*
Sure Start project (United
Kingdom) 142–3
Sustaining Effects Study (United
States) 284

Sweden: socioeconomic
  background 16, 18

T

teacher training 41, 47*tab*,
  183-97, 266, 320-1, 323
teachers: social expectations
  165-7, 287
technical education *see*
  vocational/technical
  education
temporary exclusion 59
Tesser, P. 299
Tett, L. 202, 210
third-level education
  financial assistance 85-9, 90*tab*,
    92-4
  integrated services 101-2
  participation 24, 26, 32-4, 379,
    396
Thomson, G.O.B. 69
time-on-task increases 275,
  277-8
TITLE I programme (United
  States) 275, 284
tracking systems *see* streaming
  systems
traditional teaching pedagogy
  167-8
training *see* teacher training
transition to work provisions
  291-2, 293, 294, 295, 299-305,
  308, 323
Transition Year Programme
  (Ireland) 378
'transitional pathways' 97-8,
  115-16, 386-7
travellers' children 25, 42, 67,
  133, 138-9, 255

Travelling Pre-schools (Spain)
  139
Trinity Access Project (TAP) 85,
  86-7
truancy 56, 57, 58, 72, 292
  see also dropout rates
'two-generation' intervention
  programmes 140-3

U

UN Convention on the Rights
  of the Child (1989) 227, 322
underperformance
  measures to combat 26-7,
    289-311
  and social background 27-30,
    34, 163
unemployment
  among school leavers 1, 289-90,
    398
  and social background 31, 33*fig*
UNESCO: Salamanca Statement
  227-8, 235
unification of curriculum 147,
  149*tab*, 150*tab*, 151, 152-3,
  154-5, 161, 184
United Kingdom 5, 32*tab*, 33*fig*
  compulsory education 61, 62
  educational inequality 18
  equal opportunities strategies
    62
  equal outcomes strategies 285
  learning support 275, 279
  literacy levels 30
  parent-school-community
    relationships 204-5
  pre-school education 126,
    127*fig*, 142-3
  special needs provision 226-7,
    228

upper secondary participation
7, 8*fig*, 9, 61, 62
see also Scotland
United States
learning support methods 275,
284, 285
pre-school education
programmes 124-6, 127-8,
316
upper secondary education 7-9,
22, 23, 25, 62, 155
financial and material assistance
84-7, 90*tab*, 92-4
integrated services 101-2
Urban Programme Funding
(Scotland) 253*tab*, 256*tab*, 262,
268

V

Van Calster, L. 25
Van Damme 30, 225-6
Van de Velde, V. 153, 371, 374
Veenman, J. 299
vocational guidance 166, 280
vocational skills 98
Vocational Training programme
(Spain) 301
vocational/technical education 9,
11*n*, 30, 31, 66, 382-7, 391-2,
402
alternating training 299-305
alternative curricula 295-8
curricular reforms 64-5, 151,
152, 153, 162*n*
dropout rates 22
equal outcomes strategies 42,
371, 374
minimum qualifications 28-9,
70, 73-4, 280, 298-9
timing of selection 18-19

voluntary secondary schools
(Ireland) 375

W

Walker, I. 62
Warnock Report (1978) 69,
223-4, 226-7, 229, 231
'watertight approach'
(Netherlands) 298-9
Well-prepared Start programme
(Netherlands) 40, 45*tab*, 71,
387
Wester Hailes Schools project
(Scotland) 137
Willms, D.J. 205
withdrawal model of remedial
education 275, 276, 284, 286
work experience 42, 302-5
working–class and educational
participation 17-18
workshop schools (Spain) 295,
296, 301, 310
Wresinski 4

Y

Youthreach Programme (Ireland)
110, 116, 118, 295, 305-7, 310